Manual on International Courts and Tribunals

Manual on International Courts and Tribunals

Editor

Philippe Sands
Professor of International Law, University of London,
School of Oriental and African Studies
Global Professor of Law, New York University Law School
Co-Director, Project on International Courts and Tribunals
Barrister, 3 Verulam Buildings, Gray's Inn

Assistant Editors

Ruth Mackenzie
Programme Director, FIELD
Assistant Director, Project on International Courts and Tribunals

Yuval Shany
Lecturer, School of Law of the Management College of Tel Aviv
Research Associate, Project on International Courts and Tribunals

Butterworths
London, Edinburgh, Dublin
1999

United Kingdom	Butterworths, a Division of Reed Elsevier (UK) Ltd, Halsbury House, 35 Chancery Lane, LONDON WC2A lEL and 4 Hill Street, EDINBURGH EH2 3JZ
Australia	Butterworths, SYDNEY, ADELAIDE, BRISBANE, CANBERRA, MELBOURNE and PERTH
Canada	Butterworths Canada Ltd, MARKHAM, Ontario
Hong Kong	Butterworths Asia (Hong Kong), HONG KONG
India	Butterworths India, NEW DELHI
Ireland	Butterworth (Ireland) Ltd, DUBLIN
Malaysia	Malayan Law Journal Sdn Bhd, KUALA LUMPUR
New Zealand	Butterworths of New Zealand Ltd, WELLINGTON and AUCKLAND
Singapore	Butterworths Asia, SINGAPORE
South Africa	Butterworths Publishers (Pty) Ltd, DURBAN
USA	Michie, Charlottesville, VIRGINIA

A CIP Catalogue record for this book is available from the British Library.

ISBN 0 406 92531 3

ISBN 0-406-92531-3

9 780406 925312

Typeset by B & J Whitcombe, Nr Diss, Norfolk, IP22 2LP
Printed by The Cromwell Press, Trowbridge, Wiltshire

Visit us at our website: http://www.butterworths.co.uk

Project on International Courts and Tribunals

The **Project on International Courts and Tribunals (PICT)** is a collaborative project between the Foundation for International Environmental Law and Development (FIELD), University of London and the Center on International Co-operation, New York University. PICT was established in 1997 to undertake a range of research and capacity-building activities in the field of international dispute settlement. It is an international project that includes scholars and practitioners from around the world as institutional partners and individual researchers, selected on the basis of their expertise in particular areas. The PICT Steering Committee guides activities under the project. The members of the Steering Committee, who participate in their personal capacity, are:

Georges Abi Saab (Graduate Institute of International Studies, Geneva).

Mahnoush H Arsanjani (United Nations, Office of Legal Affairs).

Laurence Boisson de Chazournes (University of Geneva, Faculty of Law).

Antonio A Cançado Trindade (University of Brasilia; Vice-President, Inter-American Court of Human Rights).

James Crawford SC (Whewell Professor of International Law, University of Cambridge; Director, Lauterpacht Research Centre for International Law; Member of the International Law Commission).

Pierre-Marie Dupuy (University of Paris II (Panthéon-Assas); Director, Institut des hautes études internationales).

Florentino Feliciano (Member, WTO Appellate Body).

Rita E Hauser (President, The Hauser Foundation; Chair, International Peace Academy).

Keith Highet (Partner, McDermott, Will & Emery).

Kamal Hossain (Senior Advocate, Supreme Court of Bangladesh; Commissioner, United Nations Compensation Commission).

Sir Robert Jennings (Former President of the International Court of Justice; LLD (Hons) Cantab; and DCL (Hons) Oxon; Manley Hudson Medal), PICT co-chair.

Maurice Kamto (University of Yaoundé II).

David Kennedy (Harvard Law School).

Hisashi Owada (Japan Permanent Representative to the UN; Professor, Global Law Faculty, NYU School of Law).

Monica Pinto (University of Buenos Aires).

Allan Rosas (Principal Legal Adviser, European Commission).

Mohammed Shahabuddeen (Vice-President, International Criminal Tribunal for the Former Yugoslavia), PICT co-chair.

Bruno Simma (University of Munich; Member of the International Law Commission).

Tullio Treves (Università degli Studi di Milano; Judge, International Tribunal for the Law of the Sea).

PICT is co-directed by Shepard Forman (Center on International Co-operation) and Philippe Sands (London University/FIELD and New York University), with the assistance of Cesare P R Romano (Center on International Co-operation) and Ruth Mackenzie (FIELD).

For further information on PICT see www.pict-pcti-org, or contact Louise Rands at FIELD, 46–47 Russell Square, London WC1B 4JP, UK (or by email on lr8@scas.ac.uk).

The Foundation for International Environmental Law and Development was established in 1989 to contribute to the progressive development of international law for the protection of the environment and the attainment of sustainable development, through research, teaching, training and the provision of legal advice. FIELD provides legal assistance to members of the international community, governmental and non-governmental, and is especially concerned with assisting, where possible on a pro bono basis, the economically disadvantaged. FIELD seeks to promote compliance with international legal obligations and to facilitate the access of disadvantaged sectors of the international community to dispute settlement processes.

The Center on International Co-operation was established in 1996 at New York University to conduct a program of policy research and development on the management and financing of the international public sector. CIC seeks to inform public debate on issues of multilateral commitment and responsibility by clarifying the legal, economic, political, and institutional foundations of effective multilateral action. CIC's current work focuses on four critical sectors: international law; humanitarian assistance; reconstruction aid; and reproductive health and population.

Foreword

by HE Judge Rosalyn Higgins

This manual emanates from the larger Project on International Courts and Tribunals – a judicial genome mapping. As a component part of that larger activity it has been decided to provide a manual which at once gives a general overview of the field as a whole and also specific details about the bodies that comprise it.

Nearly all of these bodies have come into existence since the end of the Second World War. The Permanent Court of Arbitration, it is true, has recently celebrated its centenary. Its role had ebbed and flowed during that hundred years and in recent times it has been adapting itself with vigour to the changed international climate. The Permanent Court of International Justice followed soon after, taking its seat also within the great Peace Palace in The Hague. It played an important judicial role in many matters, including in respect of the post World War I Minorities Treaties. It did not die, institutionally speaking, with the demise of the League; the International Court of Justice is its legal successor. The earlier case law of the Permanent Court continues to have relevance for the International Court today. What is different, however, is that the International Court was established as an integral part of the United Nations, a main organ of that body and its principal judicial organ.

As we look back at the turn of the century we see that three major phenomena occurred over the previous 50 years, each of which in turn has enormously changed the face of judicial and arbitral settlement. The first was the burgeoning of concern with human rights. The UN Charter itself provided some tentative first steps and the Universal Declaration of Human Rights sufficiently caught the moment later to be translated into treaty form in the two Covenants. Under the International Covenant on Civil and Political Rights a new quasi judicial body was born. The Universal Declaration had also, even more rapidly, led to detailed regional treaties with important judicial elements, in both Europe and South America. These sat side by side with the long-standing International Labour Organisation procedures, and were followed, to a certain extent, in Africa. In the meantime, particular subject matter areas succinctly articulated in the Covenants were later elaborated in more detail, sometimes with their own dispute settlement provisions.

While many of these bodies have the possibility for inter-state recourse, their phenomenal success lay rather in the opportunity they gave for individuals to bring claims against governments, often their own. In the last decade, the tables have been turned. With the introduction of the various International Criminal Tribunals there has begun to be an insistence upon the responsibility of individuals for acts which constitute major violations of international humanitarian law.

The second major phenomenon of the last half century has been the growth of regional instruments for co-operation and integration. This phenomenon has been seen in Europe – EFTA and the European Communities – in Africa, in Central and South America, and in the Americas more generally. These institutional arrangements have also generated a need for dispute settlement procedures. In Europe, in particular, a formidable body of law has emerged.

In the last decade the new models for the resolution of trade disputes have begun to take their place alongside earlier pioneering arrangements for international investment dispute resolution under the International Convention for the Settlement of Investment Disputes. Moreover, it has in recent years become apparent both that economic disputes must be resolved with speed and that, in our globalised world, states are no longer the only players. More flexible, open systems for norm-compliance and complaint procedures became necessary, and these have been pioneered by the great international and regional development banks.

We thus begin to see emerging certain de facto specialisation in international litigation and arbitration (with the International Court remaining as the great generalist jurisdiction for inter-state disputes, and always maintaining its special relationship with the UN).

But while the outlines of these developments are clear for all to see, many of these specialist bodies retain at the same time vestiges of a more general subject-matter competence. For example, points of general international law are still frequently contested within the World Trade Organisation dispute settlement system. Equally, environmental and trade matters may still be brought to the International Court. Moreover, disputes in real life rarely fall within neat subject-matter compartments. Treaty law, the law relating to expropriation of property, state responsibility, human rights, environmental law, sanctions, trading rules, are all often uncomfortably intermingled.

The practitioner of today is apt, perhaps, to be specialised in a particular field. But in reality he or she needs to know what is on offer globally by way of dispute settlement. It is essential both to see the larger picture, to realise that a matter whose centre of gravity appears to fall under tribunal X could in fact go to tribunal Y, with certain possible advantages. The skilled practitioner must be able to offer sophisticated advice on the appropriate forum, confident in his or her understanding of how various possible courts or tribunals operate.

The manual for the first time makes this a realistic possibility for the practitioner. As will be seen, a parallel system of information is provided for each body. Following an introductory section, detailed data is provided on how judges and arbitrators are chosen, on a variety of organisational matters, on jurisdiction and access, on procedure, on language, on financing and on the pursuit of proceedings. Whatever is special to that body alone is also recounted. While the information is deployed in succinct form, it is knowledgable, detailed and accurate, with appropriate citations to relevant sources.

This manual surely fills a real need and must find a place in the offices of embassies, ministries, legal advisers, officials of international organisations and practitioners in private practice. We live in a multifaceted world, but none of us can expect to be specialists in everything. The manual will ensure that at least we are aware of the full range of possibilities, and that we know how to use them.

Rosalyn Higgins

Contents

Contents

Table of international legislation

Europe

International legislation

Introduction and acknowledgments
by Philippe Sands

INTRODUCTION

A hundred years ago this summer – on 29 July 1899 – a select group of 28 states adopted a Convention for the Pacific Settlement of International Disputes. By this Convention they undertook 'to use their best efforts to ensure the pacific settlement of international differences' and to organise a Permanent Court of Arbitration.[1] Although the PCA was neither permanent nor a court, its creation constituted a landmark decision to establish the world's first standing body charged with adjudicating international disputes. In embryonic form it was the forerunner to the Permanent Court of International Justice and its successor, the International Court of Justice. The 1899 Convention marked a turning point in favour of international adjudication before standing bodies. In the intervening century an almost bewildering array of international courts, tribunals and other adjudicatory bodies have been established providing fora for the pursuit of international claims. The most recent is the International Criminal Court (ICC), the Statute for which was adopted at a widely-reported diplomatic conference in Rome last summer.[2] It joins a panoply of human rights committees, commissions and courts established to receive claims from states and individuals alleging violations of human rights norms; other mechanisms which have been put in place to allow foreign investors to bring arbitral claims against 'expropriating' states or permit aggrieved persons to challenge lending decisions of multi-lateral development banks; special arrangements to address disputes over trade matters and in respect of maritime issues; and courts within the context of regional economic and free trade arrangements to address a wide range of matters touching upon economic integration.

The transformation over the past two decades in particular has been a remarkable one. Alongside international organisations legislating standards there now exists an international 'judiciary' the powers of which seem to be ever more extensive and, consequentially, intrusive upon national sovereignty. It is a judiciary which increasingly relates to or impinges upon national proceedings and to which litigants can turn in their efforts to assert rights and enforce obligations. Indeed, in many countries international litigation – that is to say litigation before international courts – is frequently front page news. At the time of writing, 'banana wars' are being litigated before the WTO; by way of 'provisional measures' the United States is told by

1   UKTS 9 (1901), Cd 798, arts 1 and 20; see infra at p 23 et seq.
2   37 ILM 999 (1998).

the ICJ to refrain from carrying out sentences of execution; Yugoslavia brings ICJ proceedings against 10 NATO members challenging the legality of their acts in relation to Kosovo; Guinea is hauled up before the International Tribunal for the Law of the Sea to account for the imposition of customs duties in its exclusive economic zone; and the United Kingdom is told by the European Commission of Human Rights that a highly publicised domestic trial of two boys leading to their conviction for the murder of a two-year-old boy has violated the European Convention on Human Rights. National courts too are presented with issues raised by the existence of international bodies. This is evidenced in the most dramatic terms by the various proceedings before the House of Lords to consider whether Senator Pinochet should be extradited to Spain for acts carried out in Chile in the 1970s; these proceedings have raised most starkly the question of the proper relationship between national courts and the putative International Criminal Court, and the principle of 'complementarity' which is to govern their relations.

In short, there has been a sharp increase in the number of international adjudicatory bodies, and a greater willingness to resort to them.[3] Nevertheless, knowledge about the bodies – where they are, what they are, who sits on them, what they can do, how they relate to national proceedings – is limited even in well-informed legal circles. Many academics and practitioners in the field of international law are familiar with selected bodies, but few are informed about the range of international judicial and quasi-judicial bodies now available. And at the national level knowledge is opaque. In that sense, international courts – and practice – remains a somewhat exotic subject, and perhaps more marginal than they should be. The main purpose of this manual is to fill a gap by making information on these international bodies more easily available.

It is appropriate to note that the development of international adjudication may be seen to have occurred in four phases. Prior to the establishment of the PCA, international disputes were adjudicated almost exclusively between states alone and before ad hoc bodies often established to deal with a particular dispute, although there were some exceptions to that. The decision in 1899 to organise the PCA marked a turning point and an entry into a second phase, with the recognition of the need to establish a standing body. A third phase was initiated in the 1940s and 1950s with the establishment of the ICJ, the ECJ and the European Commission and Court of Human Rights. This phase lasted up to the early 1980s, and encompassed also the establishment of the International Centre for the Settlement of Investment Disputes. The fourth phase was decisively initiated by the creation of the International Tribunal for the Law of the Sea: this phase is characterised by compulsory jurisdiction and binding decision-making powers, as is now also reflected in the provisions of the WTO's Dispute Settlement Understanding (DSU). What is clear is that by the early 1980s there was already in place a growing number of international adjudicatory bodies with a permanent status. This reflected a movement away from the ad hoc arrangements which had dominated until the early years of this century,[4] and a trend towards 'judicialisation' and recourse to third party adjudication. Far from comprehensive in their coverage, these bodies nevertheless provided fora for

3 See E Lauterpacht *Aspects of the Administration of International Justice* (1991), especially at 9-22.
4 O Bowett *Law of International Institutions*, 4th edn (1982).

international litigation on general or specific matters, at the regional and global levels. Some had compulsory jurisdictions, others did not. At the global level the principal institutions were the PCA and the ICJ (established in 1945), both located in The Hague.[5] In the field of human rights, regional courts or commissions had been established for Europe, the Americas, and Africa, and the UN Human Rights Committee fulfilled a more limited (or less judicial) function at the global level.[6] In the international economic field, the Panel system of the General Agreement on Tariffs and Trade (GATT) was dealing with a growing number of cases and attracting increased support,[7] and the European Court of Justice in Luxembourg had established itself as an international tribunal with broad competence.[8] At various international organisations – the World Bank, the ILO, the UN, the OECD – administrative tribunals had been established to address employment disputes between the organisations and their employees.[9] And public and private arbitration mechanisms were available for the resolution of foreign investment disputes between states and non-state actors, respectively within the framework of the International Centre for the Settlement of Investment Disputes (ICSID)[10] and the International Chamber of Commerce,[11] as well as other arrangements, including ad hoc arbitration.[12] By the 1980s the network of institutions was already extensive, even if it was not comprehensive in terms of the jurisdiction it established, either in relation to the subject matters which could be addressed or the persons entitled to bring (or defend) claims. Nevertheless, the network reflected a growing willingness of states to accept the role of adjudication in international political relations. This trend is even more apparent if one takes into consideration the various ad hoc arrangements created to deal with particular situations (eg the Iran-US Claims Tribunal and the UN Compensation Commission).

Since the early 1980s several new international bodies have been created which present new opportunities for international litigation. Although the number may not seem significant in itself, it is if one considers it on a relative basis by reference to what pre-existed. The new developments have several features that distinguish them from the earlier arrangements, suggesting that

---

5 See Chapters 1 and 2.

6 See, for example, D McGoldrick *The Human Rights Committee: its role in the Development of the International Covenant on Civil and Political Rights* (1991) pp 44–61; Merrills *The Development of International Law by the European Court of Human Rights* (1993), pp 1–24; Davidson *The Inter-American Court of Human Rights* (1992), pp 28–60; and see Chapter 14, infra.

7 On the GATT panel system, see Hudec *The GATT Legal System and World Trade Diplomacy*, 2nd edn (1990).

8 See, for example, K P E Lasok *The European Court of Justice, Practice and Procedure*, 2nd edn (1994); and see Chapter 8, infra.

9 See, for example, C F Amerasinghe (ed) *Documents on International Administrative Tribunals* (1989).

10 Convention on the Settlement of Investment Disputes between States and Nationals of Other States, Washington, 18 March 1965, in force 14 October 1966. Reprinted in ICSID Basic Documents, ICSID/15; see Chapter 6, infra.

11 See, for example, W L Craig, W W Park, J Paulsson *International Chamber of Commerce Arbitration*, 3rd edn (1998).

12 States may also become involved in arbitration with international organisations. For example, the General Conditions used for loan documentation by the IBRD and IDA provide that disputes which have not been settled amicably are to be submitted to binding ad hoc arbitration. However, as yet these provisions have not been used. See M Augenblick and D A Ridgway 'Dispute Resolution in International Financial Institutions' (1993) 10 Journal of International Arbitration 73 at 74–5.

international litigation may be about to enter (or has already entered) a new phase. First, they reflect a trend in favour of compulsory jurisdiction for discrete areas of international law, such as the law of the sea and international trade law. Second, they point to the emergence of new types of 'non-contentious' proceedings designed to contribute towards greater compliance with specific treaty obligations and assist in the prevention or escalation of disputes, for example in the regime for the protection of the ozone layer.[13] Third, they reflect the growing role of individuals or groups of individuals, either as potential 'plaintiffs' or 'defendants', in cases involving states or international organisations. Examples of the latter include the Inspection Panels established by the World Bank and other multilateral development banks, and the International Criminal Tribunals for the former Yugoslavia and for Rwanda. And fourth, they present new opportunities for private lawyers to promote the interests of their clients – whether governmental or not – and become involved in international practice.

The trend towards compulsory jurisdiction

Recent developments suggest a trend towards the establishment within particular treaty regimes of dispute settlement arrangements having compulsory mandatory jurisdiction and binding decision-making powers. This is most evident in the arrangements established under the 1982 UN Convention on the Law of the Sea and the 1994 World Trade Organisation Dispute Settlement Understanding. It is also reflected in the non-compliance mechanism created in the ozone regime. Other recent developments reflecting this trend include the inspection panels established by the World Bank and some of the regional development banks, the International Criminal Tribunals for the former Yugoslavia and for Rwanda, and the International Criminal Court (the jurisdictional provisions of which appear to cause concern to certain states).

The emergence of compulsory non-contentious proceedings

In some new areas of international law states have been unwilling to introduce compulsory judicial or arbitral procedures, or even conciliation. The question of non-compliance with environmental agreements has received increased attention, and resulted in the creation of new approaches designed to enhance compliance with treaty obligations using non-contentious, non-judicial mechanisms. The non-compliance procedure established in 1990 under the 1987 Montreal Protocol on Substances that Deplete the Ozone Layer[14] is the first of its kind, and is being considered in the context of other environmental agreements.[15]

---

13 On this trend, see M Koskenniemi 'Breach of Treaty or Non-Compliance? Reflections on the Enforcement of the Montreal Protocol' (1992) 3 Yearbook of International Environmental Law 123; P Szell 'The Development of Multilateral Mechanisms for Monitoring Compliance' in W Lang (ed) *Sustainable Development and International Law* (1995).
14 16 September 1987, in force 1 January 1989, 26 ILM (1987) 154.
15 Provision is made for the development of non-compliance procedures under, for example, the 1992 UN Framework Convention on Climate Change (31 ILM (1992) 822), and the 1994 Protocol to the 1979 Convention on Long-range Transboundary Air Pollution on Further Reduction of Sulphur Emissions (33 ILM (1994) 1540).

The increasing role of non-state actors

A further factor that suggests that there will be an increase in international litigation: international adjudication is no longer a matter over which states have a monopoly, as more international courts, tribunals and other bodies are available to be used by individuals, associations and corporations, as well as international organisations. It is worth noting that the role of the private, non-state actor – whether as lawyer or litigant – is not without its controversial elements. A traditional approach to international law posits that it is a domain within which states have an exclusive competence, and that the system of international dispute settlement has a strong intergovernmental focus. The nature of the issues posed by the conflict between a traditional approach and more modern tendencies was recently highlighted in the context of the World Trade Organisation, when St Lucia (an intervening third party in the proceedings) sought to participate in Panel proceedings with the assistance of two lawyers from private law firms. Other WTO members objected, with the result that the private lawyers were prevented from participating by decision of the Panel. The same point was taken in the appeal proceedings to the Appellate Body, where there was a similar objection. The Appellate Body accepted that under customary international law states were generally entitled to choose whoever they wished to represent them. It found that there were no provisions in the Marrakech Agreement Establishing the World Trade Organisation (the 'WTO Agreement'), in the Dispute Settlement Understanding or in the Working Procedures that specified who could represent a government in making its representations in an oral hearing of the Appellate Body. It noted that –

'. . . representation by counsel of a government's own choice may well be a matter of particular significance – especially for developing-country Members – to enable them to participate fully in dispute settlement proceedings. Moreover, given the Appellate Body's mandate to review only issues of law or legal interpretation in panel reports, it is particularly important that governments be represented by qualified counsel in Appellate Body proceedings.'[16]

Subsequent WTO panels also have allowed private lawyers to participate in proceedings, marking a change in what seems to have been the last vestige of governmental monopoly in legal practice.

More international litigation

A further development is the almost universal increase in the number of cases being brought before the various international adjudicative bodies.[17] The ICJ is busier than it has ever been. ICSID has seen a significant increase in the number of cases being filed in the past four years. The volume of cases contributed to the establishment of a Court of First Instance at the ECJ. The WTO Dispute Settlement Understanding has, in just four years, received more cases than in the 45-year existence of the GATT. And there is no

16 WTO Appellate Body Report, European Communities – Regime for the Importation, Sale and Distribution of Bananas, WT/DS27/AB/R, 9 September 1997, at paras 11 and 12.
17 P Sands 'Enhancing Participation in International Litigation', 24 Commonwealth Law Bulletin 540 at 548–550.

indication that this trend is likely to change. The factors which contribute to international litigation – more rules, more actors, more bodies, the sense that international litigation is increasingly the norm rather than an exceptional act, changing perceptions about the function of international adjudication etc – appear to be well-established.

Policy issues

The increase in the number of international courts and tribunals raises a host of policy issues. The birth of many of these new bodies has not occurred in the context of a considered structure of the function of international adjudication. Little, if any, thought has been given to the relationship between the international bodies themselves, although this subject is now receiving increased attention. The subject of *litis pendens*, for example, has barely been considered in relation to these bodies. Appreciation of international decisions at the national level varies widely from jurisdiction to jurisdiction. In this regard, it is instructive to compare the approach of the US Supreme Court in the *Breard* case[18] with that of the Privy Council of the House of Lords in *Hilaire and Thomas*.[19] The appointment of international judges remains an ad hoc matter. And the whole question of a truly international bar – what characteristics do we expect our international lawyers to display – has received remarkably little consideration.

The great increase in the number of international courts and tribunals poses many issues, a factor which is reflected in a growing literature.[20] However, the literature has tended to focus on specific fora or on specific disputes, and is mostly concerned with procedural or substantive aspects. It is difficult to identify literature dealing with general trends in international litigation, and even a manual summarising the information on available international fora, which is comprehensive and easily accessible on the number and types of cases, as well as the participation of different categories of states, appears not to be available, although the internet is certainly making matters easier (it is now possible, for example, to obtain via the internet draft transcripts of oral arguments before the ICJ within a few hours of their having been delivered).

The manual

It is in the context of these developments and issues that the Project on International Courts and Tribunals has prepared this manual, inspired in part by the most useful *Handbook of the United Nations* published annually by the

18 *Breard v Greene* (1998) 118 S Ct 1352, 140 L Ed 2d 529.
19 Privy Council Appeal No 60 of 1998, *Thomas and Hilaire*, judgment of 27 January 1998, delivered on 17 March 1998.
20 For example: M W Janis (ed) *International Courts for the twenty-first Century* (1992); J G Merrills *International Dispute Settlement*, 3rd edn (1998); A Soons *International Arbitration: Past and Prospects* (1990); G Guillaume 'The Future of International Judicial Institutions' (1995) 44 ICLQ 848; T O Elias 'International Court of Justice: present trends and future prospects' in Elias (ed) *New Horizons in International Law* (1992); S Oda 'Dispute Settlement Prospects in the Law of the Sea' (1995) 44 ICLQ 863; L Sohn 'Settlement of Law of the Sea Disputes' (1995) 10(2) International Journal of Marine and Coastal Law 205; M M Ching 'Evaluating the Effectiveness of the GATT Dispute Settlement System for Developing Countries' (1992) 16(2) World Competition 81; P Kohona 'Dispute Resolution under the World Trade Organisation: an overview' (1994) 28 Journal of World Trade 23.

Government of New Zealand. This Introduction indicates the extent to which the number of fora available for international litigation has increased, particularly in recent years. Whether or not this reflects a 'genuine "renaissance" of international justice',[21] it points to conditions in which international litigation will proliferate. States, including developing countries and economies in transition, as well as other actors are likely to find themselves increasingly involved as litigants (whether as applicant/plaintiff, respondent/defendant, or intervenor) in disputes between states, between states and non-state actors, or in proceedings involving international organisations. Despite the general increase in international litigation it is also clear that a great many people, including journalists, practitioners and legal advisers, have little knowledge about many of these bodies: what are they? where are they? what are their powers? who sits on them? who may initiate proceedings before them? Surprisingly, no single text provides in a readily accessible format the answers to these basic questions. It is therefore the purpose of this manual to provide a reference guide to the principle international courts and tribunals which are now active.

In preparing the manual, the Project on International Courts and Tribunal was conscious of the need to provide a reliable source of basic information on the principal bodies – both global and regional. In deciding which bodies to include, and the degree of detail to enter into, we considered the activities of the bodies – past and present – and the amount of information a user might need to have. In deciding what material to include, it was considered appropriate to place oneself in the position of a potential user of the body, or someone who wanted to obtain the most basic information on the various bodies. In that regard, we have been especially conscious of the need to ensure that potential users who are most disadvantaged – developing states and non-state actors – are able to gain access to basic information. In relation to the principal bodies the manual therefore seeks to address the most commonly asked questions:

- What are the principal international courts and tribunals, where are they located, and how can they be contacted?
- What issues do they address?
- What rules and instruments govern their activities (constituent instrument, Statutes, Rules of Procedure, Regulations etc), and where can you find them?
- How are they organised and who are the judges?
- What is their contentious or advisory jurisdiction, in terms of persons, subject matter, and time?
- How do you institute proceedings, and what procedures govern their activities?
- Can they order provisional or interim measures (injunctions etc), and if so are they binding?
- How are written pleadings organised and oral arguments presented, and who is entitled to appear?
- Can you intervene as a third party?
- What powers do they have to take binding decisions and impose remedial measures?
- Are there any grounds of appeal?

21 See G Guillaume 'The future of international judicial institutions' (1995) 44 ICLQ 848.

- What are the likely costs of proceedings, and is financial assistance available?
- How can judgments or decisions be executed, including in the national courts?
- Where can more information be found, including reports of judgments, awards and decisions?

Each chapter is arranged with sub-headings to address these issues, together with footnote references to relevant instruments and a selected bibliography. The manual does not strive to be comprehensive. Certain bodies have not been addressed, either because they have fallen into desuetude, or they were established but in practice never become operational. Yet other bodies are on the verge of being established: by the time of the next edition there will surely be an individual complaints procedure in respect of the Convention on Elimination of Discrimination Against Women[22] and a mechanism for individual and group complaints alleging violations of the 1966 International Covenant on Economic, Social and Cultural Rights.[23] Nor is the manual intended to replace the specialist texts which provide the indispensable detail which the litigator is bound to rely upon, texts such as Guyomar's *Commentaire du Règlement de la Cour Internationale de Justice*,[24] Rosenne's *Law and Procedure of the ICJ*,[25] and Lasok's *Practice and procedure of the ECJ*.[26] Finally, we have not in this first edition sought to reflect the jurisprudence of each body, which is so important to a proper understanding of many of the procedural rules. We hope in future editions to integrate such references as appropriate. We welcome comments from readers on any errors which may have crept in (and for which responsibility is the Editor's alone) or suggestions as to other improvements which might be made in future editions.

ACKNOWLEDGMENTS

The manual is the result of an extensive team effort, involving many individuals with busy schedules. We have received constant guidance and support from the members of the PICT Steering Committee. In relation to the individual chapters, we have received significant support and assistance from the following individuals, for which we are extremely grateful:

Mr Eduardo Valencia Ospina, Registrar at the ICJ;

Ambassador Hans Jonkman and Ms Bette Shifman, formerly at the PCA;

Mr Gritakumar Chitty, Registrar, and Mr David Browne, at ITLOS;

Ms Christa Allott and Professor Lucius Caflisch, at OSCE Court of Conciliation and Arbitration;

Mr Jacob Werksman, in respect of the WTO Dispute Settlement System and the Implementation Committee under the Montreal Protocol on Substances that Deplete the Ozone Layer;

22 On 11 March 1999 the UN Commission on the Status of Women adopted a draft protocol introducing the right of complaint by individuals (or groups of individuals) to the Committee on the Elimination of Discrimination against Women: UN Doc E/CN 6/1999/WG/L 2 (10 March 1999).

23 See Draft Optional Protocol to the International Covenant on Economic, Social and Cultural Rights, UN Doc E/CN 4/1997/105 (1996).

24 Éditions A Pedone (1983).

25 Grotius (1986).

26 Supra, n 8.

Ms Margrete Stevens and Mr Antonio Parra, at ICSID;

M Fabien Gélinas, at the International Court of Arbitration of the ICC;

Mr Tom Kennedy, formerly at the ECJ;

Ms Diana Torrens, at the EFTA Court;

Ms Norma Allegra Cerrato, at the Central American Court of Justice;

Dr Manoush Arsanjani, at the United Nations in relation to the International Criminal Court;

Mr Jon Cina, at the International Criminal Tribunal for the former Yugoslavia;

Mr Gregory Townsend, at the International Criminal Tribunal for Rwanda;

Professor Laurence Boisson de Chazournes at the University of Geneva, in relation to the Inspection Panels of the World Bank, the Inter-American Development Bank and the Asian Development Bank;

Mr Marc Paquin and Mr David Markell, at the North American Commission for Environmental Co-operation;

Ms Leyla Kayacik-Tirmangil of the Council of Europe in relation to the European Social Charter;

Ms Veronica Gomez at the Inter-American Commission on Human Rights; and

Mr Maurice Sheridan of 3 Verulam Buildings in relation to the European Court of Justice.

In relation to the chapters on the human rights bodies, we are particularly grateful to Ms Natalia Schiffrin and her colleagues at INTERIGHTS, Anselm Chidi Odinkalu, Ibrahima Kane, Sara Hossain and Borislav Petranov, and also to Ms Kelli Loftman of the Centre for Justice and International Law and Mr Jeremy McBride of the University of Birmingham and Laura Cox QC, for having taken responsibility for final review.

We have also received great assistance from colleagues here at the Foundation for International Environmental Law and Development, one of the two project partners of PICT. Margaret Enstone and Louise Rands Silva have diligently contributed to the administrative and secretarial aspects with their usual huge commitment and attention to detail, with Margaret shepherding the final draft through the publication process with a remarkable thoroughness and patience, and Jacob Werksman and Erasmo Lara-Cabrera have similarly contributed to legal content. We have had input from a number of interns, including in particular Gabor Baranyai, Kristina Leggett, Tom Tadoc, Charlotte Salpan and Silvia Francescan. From the New York University side of our Project (the Center for International Co-operation), Cesare Romano has made numerous valuable suggestions which we have been pleased to incorporate, and Shepard Forman has provided his characteristic intellectual and strategic support, with the attendant enthusiasm which we have come to value so greatly. I would like to thank Judge Rosalyn Higgins for contributing the Foreword, and also for her support to this Project, which is all the more remarkable given the increasingly heavy and unpredictable case-load at the International Court. Finally, I would like to reserve my biggest thanks for the two colleagues with whom I have worked most closely: Ruth Mackenzie, my colleague at FIELD, who has added to her role as a Programme Director the meticulous preparation and review of each of the chapters, and who has been responsible for co-ordinating the preparation of the final drafts: and Yuval Shany, my doctoral student, who undertook the laborious task of preparing the first drafts where some of the institutions themselves were not able to do so. Over a remarkably short period of time he worked with enormous efficiency and diligence to produce a large number of first draft chapters (and in so doing, has hopefully also supported his own doctoral research!).

It is customary to conclude with a word of thanks for our publishers. In this case, thanks are especially due to Butterworths for their enthusiastic support of the Project. This includes undertaking to make available 500 copies of this manual at no charge in order that they can be distributed to lawyers and legal advisers in the developing world at no cost. It is, after all, important to recall that the roots of the Project on International Courts and Tribunals include a commitment to level the playing field and to ensure that the most disadvantaged international actors are able to participate as fully and effectively as possible in the international proceedings in which they will surely increasingly be involved. For making this Project possible we thank our funders, in particular the William & Flora Hewlett Foundation and The Ford Foundation. Finally, the materials in this volume seek to be up to date as at 1 June 1999. It is hoped that an accompanying volume setting out the basic documents for each court and tribunal will be published in Spring 2000.

Philippe Sands
47 Russell Square
London

1 June 1999

List of abbreviations

AB	WTO Appellate Body
AB Working Procedures	WTO Working Procedures for Appellate Review
ADB	Asian Development Bank
AJIL	American Journal of International Law
Am U J Int'l L & Pol	American University Journal of International Law and Politics
American HR Convention	American Convention on Human Rights
art	article
BISD	GATT Basic Instruments and Selected Documents
CACJ	Central American Court of Justice
CACJ Statute	Agreement on the Statute of the Central American Court of Justice
CAT	Convention against Torture and other Cruel, Inhuman or Degrading Treatment or Punishment
CAT Committee	Committee against Torture
CAT Rules	Rules of Procedure
CEC	Commission for Environmental Co-operation
CERD	1965 International Convention on the Elimination of All Forms of Racial Discrimination
CERD Committee	Committee on the Elimination of Racial Discrimination
CFI	Court of First Instance
CMLR	Common Market Law Reports
COMESA	Common Market for Eastern and Southern Africa
COMESA Treaty	Treaty establishing the Common Market for Eastern and Southern Africa
Council Res	Council Resolution
CPC	OSCE Conflict Prevention Centre
CSCE	Conference on Security and Co-operation in Europe
DSB	WTO Dispute Settlement Body
DSU	WTO Dispute Settlement Understanding
EC	European Community
EC Statute	Statute of the Court of Justice of the European Economic Community

List of abbreviations

EC Treaty	Treaty establishing the European Community
ECB	European Central Bank
ECJ	European Court of Justice
ECR	European Court Reports
ECSC	European Coal and Steel Community
EEA	European Economic Area
EEC	European Economic Community
EFTA	European Free Trade Association
EHR Convention	European Convention for the Protection of Human Rights and Fundamental Freedoms
EHRR	European Human Rights Reports
ETS	European Treaties
ETUC	European Trade Union Confederation
EU	European Union
Euratom	European Atomic Energy Community
Euratom Statute	Statute of the Court of Justice of the European Atomic Energy Community
Euratom Treaty	Treaty establishing the European Atomic Energy Community
GATS	General Agreement on Trade in Services
GATT	General Agreement on Tariffs and Trade
GEF	Global Environment Facility
HRC	Human Rights Committee
Hum Rts Q	Human Rights Quarterly
IAHR Commission	Inter-American Commission of Human Rights
IAHR Court	Inter-American Court of Human Rights
IBRD	International Bank for Reconstruction and Development
ICC	International Criminal Court
ICC	International Chamber of Commerce
ICC Court	International Court of Arbitration of the International Chamber of Commerce
ICCPR	International Covenant on Civil and Political Rights
ICJ	International Court of Justice
ICLQ	International and Comparative Law Quarterly
ICSID	International Center for Settlement of Investment Disputes
ICSID Additional Facility	ICSID Additional Facility for the Administration of Conciliation, Arbitration and Fact-Finding Procedures
ICSID Convention	1965 Convention on the Settlement of Investment Disputes between States and Nationals of Other States
ICTR	International Criminal Tribunal for Rwanda
ICTY	International Tribunal for the Prosecution of Persons Responsible for Serious Violations of International Humanitarian Law Committed in the Territory of the former Yugoslavia since 1991

IDA	International Development Association
IDB	Inter-American Development Bank
IGO	Inter-Governmental Organisation
ILM	International Legal Materials
ILO	International Labour Organisation
ILR	International Law Reports
Int'l Ct Arb Bulletin	ICC International Court of Arbitration Bulletin
IOE	International Organisation of Employers
ITLOS	International Tribunal for the Law of the Sea
Maastricht Treaty or EU Treaty	1992 Treaty on the European Union
MFMP	Multilateral Fund of the Montreal Protocol
Montreal Protocol	1987 Montreal Protocol on Substances that Deplete the Ozone Layer
MP-NCP	Montreal Protocol Non-Compliance Procedure
NAAEC	North American Agreement on Environmental Cooperation
NAFTA	North American Free Trade Agreement
New EC Treaty	Consolidated Version of the Treaty establishing the European Community
NGO	Non-Governmental Organisation
OAS	Organisation of American States
OAS Off Rec	Organisation of American States Official Record
OASTS	OAS Treaty Series
OAU	Organisation of African Unity
ODECA	Organisation of Central American States
OJ	Official Journal of the European Communities
OSCE	Organisation for Security and Co-operation in Europe
PCA	Permanent Court of Arbitration
PCIJ	Permanent Court of Justice
RIAA	UN Reports of International Arbitral Awards
SBDC	Sea-Bed Disputes Chamber of the Tribunal
SC Res	Security Council Resolution
SICA	Central American Integration System
TRIPS	Agreement on Trade-Related Aspects of Intellectual Property Rights
UN	United Nations
UN Doc	United Nations Document
UN GA Res	United Nations General Assembly Resolution
UNCIO	United Nations Conference on International Organisation
UNCITRAL	United Nations Commission on International Trade Law
UNCLOS	United Nations Convention on the Law of the Sea
UNDP	United Nations Development Programme
UNEP	United Nations Environment Programme

List of abbreviations

UNICE	Union of the Confederations of Industry and Employers of Europe
UNIDO	United Nations Industrial Development Organisation
UNTS	United Nations Treaty Series
WTO	World Trade Organisation
Y B Com Arb	Yearbook of Commercial Arbitration

General bodies

INTRODUCTION

This Part of the manual describes a diverse set of dispute settlement bodies. They have been grouped together here as they are either potentially available to all states and/or their subject-matter jurisdiction is potentially unlimited.

Thus, two of the bodies dealt with in this Part – the International Court of Justice and the Permanent Court of Arbitration – have potentially unlimited subject-matter jurisdiction relating to disputes involving any state. For its part, the International Tribunal for the Law of the Sea is potentially available to all states which are parties to the 1982 UN Convention on the Law of the Sea, in relation to disputes relating to that Convention, although in practice a great majority have opted in principle for recourse to other fora. The OSCE Court of Arbitration and Conciliation is available for the resolution of all types of disputes, but recourse to it is limited to states members of the OSCE.

As with the other bodies dealt with in this manual, the jurisdiction of the bodies addressed in this Part is based upon consent of the states concerned, expressed either ad hoc by way of a special agreement or *compromis*, or *ex ante*, by virtue of participation in a treaty or prior acceptance of jurisdiction by way of declaration.

The first tribunal addressed is the International Court of Justice (ICJ). Established in 1945 as the successor to the Permanent Court of International Justice, the ICJ is the principal judicial organ of the United Nations, and currently 187 States, including two non-members of the UN, are parties to its Statute. The court has considered cases involving an enormous range of subject-matters, including territorial disputes, maritime delimitation, use of force, transboundary watercourses, interpretation of treaties, consular protection and genocide. The principal limitation to the contentious jurisdiction of the ICJ is that it is limited to *states*. Thus the court is not empowered to hear disputes involving private parties or international organisations. In this respect at least, the jurisdiction *ratione personae* of many of the other disputes settlement bodies considered later in this manual is broader than that of the International Court.

In addition to its contentious jurisdiction, the court is also empowered to give advisory opinions on legal questions submitted to it by UN organs and authorised institutions.

After a period of relatively low use in the 1970s and 1980s, at the time of writing (July 1999) the ICJ is as busy as at any time in its history, with 22 contentious cases pending. It has recently re-examined its working methods in order to adapt to changing requirements, in particular its increased caseload and the budgetary constraints that it faces. In this regard, a key question which has arisen in the light of the proliferation of dispute settlement bodies reflected in this manual, is the relationship between the ICJ and the new courts and tribunals, such as ITLOS.

The second mechanism considered in this Part is the Permanent Court of Arbitration. Established under the 1899 and 1907 Hague Conventions for the Pacific Settlement of International Disputes, the PCA is potentially available for the resolution of disputes involving any subject matter. Unlike the ICJ, the Permanent Court of Arbitration is not a standing court, but an institution which maintains a roster of arbitrators nominated by Parties to the Hague Conventions. In addition to the procedures in the Hague Conventions, the PCA has adopted a range of Optional Rules for the arbitration for disputes. In contrast to the ICJ, the PCA is available for the resolution not only of disputes between states, but also has procedures for disputes between States and international organisations, states and private parties, and intergovernmental organisations and private parties. Nonetheless, the PCA has been little used in recent years, notwithstanding the efforts of the Bureau to build on its important early work. It has, however, provided facilities for inter-state arbitrations formally conducted outside its auspices. The PCA also offers a set of rules for the settlement of disputes by conciliation.

The International Tribunal for the Law of the Sea is a new body, established under the 1982 UN Convention on the Law of the Sea, but only operational since 1996. ITLOS is notable for at least two reasons: first, under UNCLOS it exercises compulsory jurisdiction in relation to certain types of dispute; and second, in accordance with the relevant provisions of UNCLOS, its jurisdiction *ratione personae* potentially extends beyond states, to include private parties (at least in the context of disputes over the seabed).

Part XV of UNCLOS provides that certain disputes arising under the Convention are subject to compulsory binding dispute settlement and, upon ratification of UNCLOS, Parties may select one or more of the dispute settlement mechanisms set out in Article 287. By February 1999, 13 Parties to UNCLOS have selected ITLOS in their declarations on the choice of dispute settlement procedure. In addition to exercising jurisdiction in these circumstances, ITLOS also has compulsory jurisdiction vis-à-vis Parties to UNCLOS in relation to certain specific causes of action enumerated in UNCLOS, notably prompt release of vessels.

ITLOS also comprises a Seabed Disputes Chamber to decide disputes under Part XI of UNCLOS. The Seabed Disputes Chamber has compulsory jurisdiction over certain types of disputes relating to activities in the seabed area. The personal jurisdiction of the Seabed Disputes Chamber extends beyond States Parties to UNCLOS, and includes the International Seabed Authority (established under UNCLOS) as well as private parties engaged in seabed activities.

At the time of writing, two cases have been submitted to ITLOS (although they arise out of the same facts and involve the same parties) and the Tribunal has issued one order for provisional measures. In addition to its contentious jurisdiction, ITLOS and the Seabed Disputes Chamber are also authorised to give advisory opinions in certain circumstances.

The Court of Conciliation and Arbitration of the Organisation for Security and Co-operation in Europe (OSCE) is also a new body, established under a 1992 Convention which entered into force in 1994. Unlike the other bodies dealt with in this Part it does not have potentially universal jurisdiction *ratione personae* but is limited to disputes between members of the OSCE. That said, in terms of subject matter its jurisdiction is potentially very wide. To date, no cases have been brought under the OSCE procedures. However, the establishment of the mechanism might be seen as representing the beginning of a move towards regional mechanisms for the settlement of disputes arising outside the economic sphere (which are dealt with in Part C).

CHAPTER 1
International Court of Justice

INTRODUCTORY

Name and seat of the body

1.1 The International Court of Justice (ICJ) is a permanent international court open to use by all states. It has its seat in The Hague, at the following address:

> The Peace Palace
> Carnegieplein 2
> 2517 KJ The Hague
> The Netherlands
>
> Tel: 31 70 302 23 23
> Fax: 31 70 364 99 28
> website: http://www.icj-cij.org

Introductory description

1.2 The ICJ is the principal judicial organ of the United Nations (UN) and its Statute forms an integral part of the UN Charter. It began its operation on 18 April 1946. The ICJ replaced the Permanent Court of International Justice (PCIJ), which had functioned since 1922 and which was dissolved after the Second World War. Although being a new institution, the powers and procedures of the ICJ were closely modelled on those of the PCIJ.

The court has two heads of jurisdiction. It may receive any legal dispute referred to it by states for settlement in accordance with international law and it may render advisory opinions on legal questions presented to it by the General Assembly and Security Council of the UN and other duly authorised UN organs and specialised agencies. All 185 members of the UN are parties to the Statute of the ICJ, and may bring cases to the court. Other states may join the statute of the court, on certain conditions (currently, there are two non-UN members that are parties to the court's statute – Nauru and Switzerland), or, subject to a distinct set of conditions, participate in cases before the court on an ad hoc basis, without joining the statute.

Since 1946 the court has delivered 67 judgments in contentious cases and 24 Advisory Opinions. As at June 1999, 19 contentious cases were pending before the ICJ.

INSTITUTIONAL ASPECTS

Governing texts

1.3   The two principal texts governing the structure, powers and work of the court are the UN Charter[1] and the Statute of the Court.[2] The Charter establishes the court and provides the general outlines of its powers; the Statute governs the composition and organisation of the court, its jurisdiction and the basic rules of procedure applicable to cases before it. Other relevant texts are the Rules of Court,[3] which provide detailed rules of procedure and the Resolution concerning the internal judicial practice of the court.[4]

1   The Charter of the United Nations, 26 June 1945, XV UNCIO 335 ('UN Charter').
2   Statute of the International Court of Justice, 26 June 1945, Annex to UN Charter, XV UNCIO 355.
3   Rules of Court, 1 July 1978, ICJ Acts and Documents concerning the Organisation of the Court, No 5 (1990), ('ICJ Rules').
4   Resolution concerning the internal judicial practice of the court, 12 April 1976, ICJ Acts and Documents concerning the Organisation of the Court, No 5 (1990). In 1998, the court re-examined its working methods and took various decisions in this respect, bearing in mind both the congested state of the General List of cases and the budgetary constraints it faces. A note outlining these measures will be transmitted to the Agents of the Parties in new cases at their first meeting with the Registrar.

Substantive law

1.4   The ICJ decides cases in accordance with international law. It applies international treaties to which the states before it are parties, international customary law and general principles of the law.[1] The court also uses, as subsidiary means for determining the law, judicial decisions and the writings of prominent international jurists. The parties may agree to authorise the court to decide a case on the basis of equitable considerations (*ex aequo et bono*).[2]

1   ICJ Statute, art 38(1).
2   Ibid, art 38(2). This, however, does not imply that the court may not apply equity in other cases, where international law calls for the application of such considerations. See eg *North Sea Continental Shelf* (FRG/Denmark; FRG/Netherlands) 1969 ICJ 4 at 48.

Organisation

Composition, appointment and disqualification

1.5   The court is composed of 15 independent judges, elected by the General Assembly and Security Council of the UN for a renewable term of nine years.[1] Judges must be persons of high moral character and they should possess qualifications for appointment to the highest judicial office in their own countries or be jurists of recognised competence in international law.[2] No two judges can have the nationality of the same state and the entire bench ought to represent the main forms of civilisation and the principal legal systems.[3] In practice, the court comprises judges from the five permanent members of the Security Council of the UN and from the different geographical regions of the world.[4] The court elects its President and Vice-President for a renewable period of three years (currently Judges Stephen M Schwebel and Christopher G Weeramantry, respectively).[5]

1   ICJ Statute, arts 3(1), 4(1), 13(1).
2   Ibid, art 2.

3   ICJ Statute, arts 3(1), 9; ICJ Rules, art 7(2).
4   The current composition of the court is:
      President: Stephen M Schwebel (United States of America), **Vice-President:** Christopher
      G Weeramantry (Sri Lanka), **Judges:** Shigeru Oda (Japan), Mohammed Bedjaoui
      (Algeria), Gilbert Guillaume (France), Raymond Ranjeva (Madagascar), Géza Herczegh
      (Hungary), Shi Jiuyong (China), Carl-August Fleischhauer (Germany), Abdul G Koroma
      (Sierra Leone), Vladlen S Vereshchetin (Russian Federation), Rosalyn Higgins (United
      Kingdom), Gonzalo Parra-Aranguren (Venezuela), Pieter H Kooijmans (Netherlands),
      Francisco Rezek (Brazil).
5   ICJ Statute, art 21(1).

AD HOC JUDGES

1.6   If a party to a case before the court does not have a judge of its
nationality on the bench, it may appoint an ad hoc judge to sit in the case.[1] Ad
hoc judges must meet the same service requirements as the permanent judges
and they participate in the deliberations of the court on terms of full equality
with the other judges.[2] An ad hoc judge may be of nationality other than that
of the appointing party, but should preferably be chosen from those persons
who were previously nominated as candidates to serve in the ICJ.[3] A party
that wishes to appoint an ad hoc judge should notify the court of its intention
as soon as possible and must provide the court with the name, nationality
and summary of biographical detail of its choice of an ad hoc judge not later
than two months before the date for submission of the Counter-Memorial.[4] If
both states parties are entitled to appoint ad hoc judges, one of the parties
may propose to the other that they both abstain from appointing them.[5]

1   ICJ Statute, art 31(2),(3).
2   Ibid, art 31(6).
3   Ibid, art 31(2),(3); ICJ Rules, art 35(1).
4   ICJ Rules, art 35(1).
5   Ibid, art 35(2).

DISQUALIFICATION OF JUDGES

1.7   A judge may not participate in a case in which he or she was previously
involved as a party representative, member of another dispute settlement
body, or in any other capacity.[1] The court will decide any doubts as to
whether past involvement in a dispute, or any other special reason, preclude
a judge from participation in a case.[2] A motion for disqualification will be
brought to the court by the President, acting on his or her own initiative or
upon the request of a party to the case (presented in confidentiality).[3] A party
to a case may file with the court an objection to the appointment of an ad hoc
judge by a party to the dispute (eg if an ad hoc judge does not meet the
service requirements).[4] Any objection must be presented within a time limit
fixed by the court (included in the notification on the appointment of the ad
hoc judge by the other party). The court will then decide on the objection, or
resolve any doubts of its own pertaining to the qualifications of the ad hoc
judge, after hearing the parties, if necessary.[5]

   In the event that a judge ceases to fulfil the conditions for service, as
required by the Statute, the other judges may decide, by way of consensus, to
remove him or her from office, after hearing the judge in question.[6] Such a
decision will be communicated to the Secretary-General of the UN, who will
declare the seat vacant.[7]

1   ICJ Statute, art 17(2).
2   Ibid, arts 17(3), 24.

3   ICJ Rules, art 34.
4   Ibid, art 35(3).
5   Ibid, art 35(4).
6   ICJ Statute, art 18; ICJ Rules, art 6.
7   ICJ Statute, art 18(3).

Plenary/chambers

1.8   The court can hear cases in plenary (the quorum is nine judges) or in chambers.[1] The Statute provides for the establishment of permanent and ad hoc chambers. As in cases before the plenary court, parties in cases brought before chambers are entitled to have judges of their nationality on the bench (either ICJ judges or, in their absence, ad hoc judges).[2] The procedure before chambers is generally similar to the procedure before the full court.[3]

1   ICJ Statute, arts 25, 26.
2   Ibid, art 31(4).
3   ICJ Rules, art 90. Specific procedures for written and oral pleadings for chamber proceedings are provided in art 92 of the Rules.

CHAMBER OF SUMMARY PROCEDURE

1.9   The court must annually form a Chamber of Summary Procedure.[1] The Chamber of Summary Procedure comprises five judges (three judges elected by the court and the President and Vice-President), who may be re-elected.[2] A request for referral of a case to a Summary Procedure Chamber is to be made in the document instituting proceedings, and the agreement of the other party to the case is required.[3] So far, no case has been brought before this chamber.

1   ICJ Statute, art 29.
2   Ibid, art 29; ICJ Rules, art 15(1),(2).
3   ICJ Rules, art 91(1).

CHAMBERS FOR PARTICULAR CATEGORIES OF CASES

1.10   The Statute authorises the court to form chambers for dealing with particular categories of cases (such as labour or transit and communication cases).[1] If the court decides to establish a permanent chamber, it will determine the category of cases to be referred to that chamber, the number of judges sitting in it and their term of office.[2] When electing judges for a permanent chamber, the court should take into consideration the particular knowledge, expertise or past experience of the candidates.[3] A case will be referred to a chamber for particular category of cases if the parties so agree (a request should be made at the initiation of proceedings).[4] So far, the ICJ has formed only one permanent chamber for a particular topic – the seven-member Chamber for Environmental Matters (created in July 1993). This chamber has not yet been utilised.

1   ICJ Statute, art 26(1).
2   ICJ Rules, art 16(1).
3   Ibid, art 16(2).
4   ICJ Statute, art 26(3); ICJ Rules, art 91(1).

AD HOC CHAMBERS

1.11   The ICJ may also hear cases in ad hoc chambers, formed to deal with particular cases.[1] Parties may request the court to form such a chamber at any time before the end of the written stage of the proceedings.[2] After ascertaining the views of the parties on the composition of the chamber, the court will elect an ad hoc chamber.[3] According to the Statute, the parties must approve only the number of judges sitting in the chamber. However, in all four cases that have taken place before a chamber to date, the selection of judges by the court conformed to the wishes of the parties.

1   ICJ Statute, art 26(2).
2   Ibid, art 26(3); ICJ Rules, art 17(1).
3   ICJ Statute, art 26(2); ICJ Rules, art 17(2)–(3).

Appellate structure

1.12   The ICJ has no appellate structure.

Scientific and technical experts

1.13   The parties to a case may introduce expert witnesses before the court.[1] The other party to the case may question the experts, under the control of the President; and the judges may also present questions to them.[2] The court may also arrange, on its own initiative, to seek information and to invite, if necessary, expert witnesses.[3] In addition, after hearing the parties the court can order that an enquiry or expert opinion be sought.[4] In this event, the court will determine the mandate of the experts, their number and method of appointment and the procedure they should follow. The parties will be then given an opportunity to comment upon the findings of the enquiry or on the expert opinion.[5]

The Statute and Rules also authorise the court to appoint assessors to sit on the bench (in full court or chamber cases) without voting rights.[6] The appointment of assessors (which is to be made by way of election by the court)[7] is intended to enable the court to enjoy the benefit of specialised knowledge of experts in a given area, which could be valuable in disputes of a highly technical nature. The need for appointment of assessors is to be decided by the court, acting on its own initiative, or upon a request made by a party not later than the end of the written proceedings.[8] No use has ever been made of the possibility to appoint assessors in the history of the ICJ (or the PCIJ).

1   ICJ Statute, art 43(5); ICJ Rules, art 63(1).
2   ICJ Statute, art 51; ICJ Rules, art 65.
3   ICJ Rules, art 62.
4   ICJ Statute, art 50; ICJ Rules, art 67(1).
5   ICJ Rules, art 67(2).
6   ICJ Statute, art 30(2); ICJ Rules, art 9(1), (4).
7   ICJ Rules, art 9(3).
8   Ibid, art 9(1).

Registry

1.14   The court appoints a Registrar and a Deputy Registrar (currently Eduardo Valencia-Ospina and Jean-Jacques Amaldes, respectively) for a renewable seven-year term.[1] The other members of the Registry are appointed by the court or by the Registrar (with the approval of the President).[2] The Registrar is responsible, inter alia, for the following functions: serving as the official channel of communications with the court; maintaining the archives of the court; preparing minutes of court meetings; providing translation and interpretation services; publishing decisions of the court and other publishable materials; supervising the administration of the court (including financial management); and assisting in maintaining relations between the ICJ and other UN bodies and agencies.[3]

The Registry operates under instructions and Staff Regulations, proposed by the Registrar, and approved by the court.[4] It is composed of a Department of Legal Matters, Department of Linguistic Matters and Department of Press and Information Matters; and also of the following Divisions: Financial; Computerisation; General Assistance; Archives, Indexing and Distribution; Shorthand, Typewriting and Reproduction; Documents-Library and Printing.

1 ICJ Statute, art 21(2); ICJ Rules, arts 22(1), 23.
2 ICJ Rules, art 25(1).
3 Ibid, art 26(1).
4 Ibid, art 28(3),(4).

Jurisdiction and access to the court

Ratione personae – parties

1.15 Only States may be parties to cases before the court.[1] The court is open to use by all states parties to its Statute[2] (ie the 185 UN members and Nauru and Switzerland)[3] or any other state that has deposited with the ICJ Registry a declaration that meets requirements laid down by the Security Council.[4] The exercise of jurisdiction by the court depends on consent being given by all parties to the case. Consent to the jurisdiction of the ICJ can be expressed in a number of ways.

1 ICJ Statute, art 34(1).
2 Ibid, art 35(1).
3 UN Charter, art 93. Accession of non-UN members to the Statute is subject to conditions. The conditions, which were set by the General Assembly and Security Council of the UN, are acceptance of the provisions of the Statute; undertaking to comply with the decisions of the International Court of Justice; and undertaking to make an annual contribution to the expenses of the court.
4 ICJ Statute, art 35(2). The conditions for participation of a state, which is not a party to the Statute, are, in essence, acceptance of the jurisdiction of the court and undertaking to comply in good faith with its decisions.

SPECIAL AGREEMENTS

1.16 The jurisdiction of the court encompasses all cases which the parties to a dispute refer to it.[1] Such cases normally come before the court by notification to the Registry of an agreement known as a special agreement (or *compromis*) concluded by the parties for the purpose of presenting a case to the ICJ. In practice, the court has also been willing to infer ad hoc consent to its jurisdiction from the conduct of the parties to the dispute (eg if they appear before the court and do not challenge its jurisdiction).[2]

1 ICJ Statute, art 36(1). So far, 14 cases have been brought to the court on the basis of special agreements.
2 See eg *Corfu Channel (UK v Albania)* 1948 ICJ 15.

PROVISIONS IN TREATIES AND CONVENTIONS

1.17 The jurisdiction of the court also comprises all matters specially provided for in treaties and conventions in force.[1] These include compromissory clauses referring to the ICJ disputes concerning the interpretation or application of the treaty in question,[2] or general dispute settlement treaties providing for submission of all disputes, or some categories of disputes, once they arise, to the jurisdiction of the ICJ.[3] The Statute explicitly states that the ICJ will also have jurisdiction based on treaties and conventions in force, which refer disputes between the contracting parties to the PCIJ (or other tribunals established by the League of Nations).[4]

1   ICJ Statute, art 36(1).
2   See eg Genocide Convention, 9 December 1948, art 9, 78 UNTS 278.
3   See eg American Treaty on Pacific Settlement, Bogota, 30 April 1948, art XXXI, 449 UNTS 83.
4   ICJ Statute, art 37.

DECLARATIONS UNDER THE OPTIONAL CLAUSE

1.18   A state may submit to the Secretary-General of the UN a declaration under art 36(2) of the Statute, recognising ipso facto the compulsory jurisdiction of the ICJ (referred to as declaration under the optional clause).[1] Such declaration may be relied upon by any other state that has also made a declaration under art 36(2). Declarations may be made unconditionally or on conditions (eg for a certain time, or excluding certain categories of disputes).[2] Old declarations accepting the compulsory jurisdiction of the PCIJ, which are still in force, are deemed as declarations of acceptance of the ICJ's jurisdiction.[3] At present there are 62 optional clause declarations in force; however, many of them contain conditions and limitations on the acceptance of the jurisdiction of the court. The ICJ has held in the past that in cases brought on the basis of art 36(2), in accordance with the condition of reciprocity provided for in that Article, jurisdiction is conferred upon the court only to the extent to which the applicant's and respondent's Declarations coincide in conferring it.[4]

1   ICJ Statute, art 36(2),(4).
2   Ibid, art 36(3).
3   Ibid, art 36(5).
4   *Certain Norwegian Loans (France v Norway)* 1957 ICJ 9 at 23–24.

Ratione materiae

1.19   Parties may refer to the court any legal dispute arising between them. However, the instrument constituting the basis for jurisdiction may restrict the subject matter competence of the ICJ. In cases brought in pursuance of declarations under the optional clause the court may deal (subject to conditions and limitations found in the declarations) with all legal disputes concerning: (i) the interpretation of a treaty; (ii) any question of international law; (iii) the existence of any fact which, if established, would constitute a breach of an international obligation; (iv) the nature or extent of the reparation to be made for the breach of an international obligation.[1]

1   ICJ Statute, art 36(2).

Ratione temporis

1.20   In general, there are no time limits for reference of disputes to the ICJ. Nonetheless, such restrictions may be found in the instruments constituting the basis of jurisdiction.

Advisory jurisdiction

1.21 By virtue of art 65 of the Statute, the court may give an advisory opinion on any legal question at the request of a body authorised to request such an opinion under the UN Charter.[1] The UN Charter authorises the General Assembly and the Security Council to refer any legal question to the ICJ, and permits other UN organs and specialised agencies, authorised by the General Assembly, to present requests for advisory opinions on legal questions arising within the scope of their activities.[2]

A request for an advisory opinion is to be presented to the ICJ by the Secretary-General of the UN, or the chief administrative officer of the specialised agency making the request.[3] The request should be made in written form and include an exact statement of the question on which the opinion is sought and any relevant documents likely to throw light on the question. The Registrar will notify all states of the request, and will invite states and international organisations that in the view of the court are likely to provide it with relevant information to submit written statements within fixed time limits.[4] These states and international organisations will also be given the opportunity to comment upon the written submissions of each other, in accordance with time limits and procedure determined by the court.[5] The court may also decide to hold oral hearings on the request in which the states and international organisations concerned will be able to make oral statements.[6]

The procedure of advisory proceedings generally conforms to the rules of procedure applicable in contentious cases.[7] In urgent cases, upon request of the body that referred the case to the court, or on the court's own motion, the procedure will be accelerated.[8] In the event that the ICJ finds that the request for advisory opinion relates to a legal dispute pending between two or more states, it will enable these states to appoint ad hoc judges.[9]

The decision of the court is in the form of an advisory opinion containing the following information:
(a) date of delivery;
(b) names of participating judges;
(c) summary of the proceedings;
(d) statement of the facts;
(e) reasons in points of law;
(f) reply to the question put before the court;
(g) number and names of the judges of the majority; and
(h) statement as to which text is authoritative.[10]

Any judge may append to the opinion his or her separate or dissenting opinion.[11] The opinion is to be made public.[12]

1 ICJ Statute, art 65(1).
2 UN Charter, art 96. The following organs and agencies are at present authorised to request advisory opinions:
    General Assembly; Security Council; Economic and Social Council; Trusteeship Council; Interim Committee of the General Assembly; International Labour Organisation; Food and Agriculture Organisation of the United Nations; United Nations Educational, Scientific and Cultural Organisation; World Health Organisation; International Bank for Reconstruction and Development; International Finance Corporation; International Development Association; International Monetary Fund; International Civil Aviation Organisation; International Telecommunications Union; International Fund for Agricultural Development; World Meteorological Organisation; International Maritime Organisation; World Intellectual Property Organisation; United Nations Industrial Development Organisation; International Atomic Energy Agency.

General bodies

3 ICJ Statute, art 65(2); ICJ Rules, art 104.
4 ICJ Statute, art 66(1),(2).
5 Ibid, art 66(4). ICJ Rules, art 105.
6 ICJ Statute, art 66(2); ICJ Rules, art 105(2)(b).
7 ICJ Statute, art 68; ICJ Rules, art 102(2).
8 ICJ Rules, art 103.
9 Ibid, art 102(3).
10 Ibid, art 107(2).
11 Ibid, art 107(3).
12 ICJ Statute, art 67; ICJ Rules, art 107(1).

PROCEDURAL ASPECTS

Languages

1.22 The two official languages of the ICJ are English and French.[1] The parties may agree that the proceedings will be conducted in only one of the official languages, otherwise, either of the two languages can be used.[2] Normally, all oral presentations made in one official language will be interpreted into the other.[3] The court may authorise a party to use another language in its submissions; however, that party must provide for translation or interpretation into one of the official languages.[4]

1 ICJ Statute, art 39(1).
2 Ibid, art 39(1),(2); ICJ Rules, art 51(1).
3 ICJ Rules, art 70(1).
4 ICJ Statute, art 39(3); ICJ Rules, arts 51(2),(3), 70(2), 71(2).

Instituting proceedings

1.23 Cases may be initiated before the ICJ either by way of unilateral application or notification of a special agreement referring a case to the court.[1]

1 ICJ Statute, art 40(1).

Application

1.24 An application should be made in writing and filed with the Registrar. It should include the following information:
(a) the party making the application;
(b) the state against which the claim is brought;
(c) the subject of the dispute;
(d) the legal grounds upon which the jurisdiction of the court is based;
(e) the precise nature of claim – including a succinct statement of facts and legal grounds; and
(f) the name of agent for applicant.[1]

1 ICJ Statute, art 40(1); ICJ Rules, arts 38(1),(2), 40(2). In cases brought by a state not party to the Statute (either by way of application or notification), a declaration conforming to the condition set by the Security Council in accordance with Article 35(2) of the Statute must also be appended (if not already submitted to the court): ICJ Rules, art 41.

Notification

1.25 A notification can be made by all of the parties to the special agreement or by one or more of them. It will be accompanied by a copy of the special agreement, and will indicate the names of the parties and the subject matter of the dispute (unless it is apparent from the agreement).[1]

As soon as a case is initiated, the Registrar will forward the application or notification to the other parties to the case.[2] Additional copies will be sent to the UN Secretary-General, and to all states parties to the Statute.[3]

After the initiation of proceedings, the President will summon the agents of the parties to meet him, as soon as possible, in order to ascertain the views of the parties on questions of procedure.[4]

1   ICJ Rules, art 39.
2   ICJ Statute, art 40(2); ICJ Rules, arts 38(4), 39(1).
3   ICJ Statute, art 40(3); ICJ Rules, art 42.
4   ICJ Rules, art 31.

Financial assistance

1.26   States that wish to present a case to the court by special agreement, but that need financial assistance to enable them to do so, may apply for assistance from the Secretary-General's Trust Fund to Assist States in the Settlement of Disputes through the International Court of Justice, established on 1 November 1989.[1]

1   28 ILM 1589 (1989).

Provisional measures

1.27   The ICJ may indicate provisional measures where such measures are necessary to preserve the respective rights of the parties.[1] A party can bring a request for such measures to a case at any time during the proceedings. The request is to be made in writing and should specify the measures requested and the anticipated consequences in the event that they are not granted.[2] The court can also raise on its own initiative the question of whether it should indicate provisional measures.[3] Until the decision on whether to indicate provisional measures has been taken, the President may call on the parties to act in a way which would not frustrate possible measures that the ICJ may indicate.[4]

A request for provisional measures will be treated as a matter of urgency and will have priority over all other cases.[5] The parties are to be given the opportunity of participating in oral proceedings and may submit to the court their observations.[6] The measures indicated by the court may be different from those requested, and any of its decisions on provisional measures may be reviewed at a later date, if a change in the situation is demonstrated.[7] The court may also request information on the implementation of the provisional measures.[8]

However, the question of whether the implementation of provisional measures indicated by the court falls under the provisions of article 94 of the Charter concerning the implementation of the court's decision has not been answered definitely. On some occasions in the past such provisional measures have been ignored by parties to a case.[9]

1   ICJ Statute, art 41(1). Provisional measures have been requested so far in 32 cases.
2   ICJ Rules, art 73.
3   Ibid, art 75(1). See *Case Concerning the Vienna Convention on Consular Relations (Germany v United States of America)*, Order on Request for the Indication of Provisional Measures, 3 March 1999.
4   ICJ Rules, art 74(4).

5   ICJ Rules, art 74(1),(2).
6   Ibid, art 74(3).
7   Ibid, arts 75(2),(3), 76.
8   Ibid, art 78.
9   See eg *United States Diplomatic and Consular Staff in Tehran (United States v Iran)* 1979 ICJ 7 (provisional measures); *Vienna Convention on Consular Relations (Paraguay v US)*, Order of Provisional Measures, 9 April 1998, <http://www.icj-cij.org/idocket/ipaus/ipausframe.htm>.

Preliminary objections

1.28   A party which objects to the jurisdiction of the court, the admissibility of the application or to any other issue of a preliminary nature may file a preliminary objection with the Registry before the expiration of the time limit fixed for the submission of the Counter-Memorial (see para 1.30 below).[1] The objection must set out the arguments of fact and the law upon which it is based, indicate evidence relevant to the objection that the objecting party intends to present and include copies of supporting documents.[2]

Upon the filing of a preliminary objection the proceedings are suspended and the court fixes a time limit for the other party to submit its written observations and submissions on the matter.[3] All other proceedings on the motion are normally oral.[4] After hearing the parties, the court renders its decision on the objection in the form of a judgment. The judgment may uphold or reject the objection, or defer the decision by joining jurisdictional issues to the merits stage.[5]

1   ICJ Rules, art 79(1). Preliminary objections have been filed in 25 cases so far, while questions of jurisdiction or admissibility have also been brought forward in some 13 other cases.
2   ICJ Rules, art 79(2),(5).
3   Ibid, art 79(3).
4   Ibid, art 79(4).
5   Ibid, art 79(7). The parties may also agree that any preliminary objection will be decided together with the decision on the merits: art 79(8).

PROCEEDINGS

1.29   Proceedings before the ICJ are divided into two parts – written and oral.[1]

1   ICJ Statute, art 43(1).

Written proceedings

1.30   Written proceedings open with the filing of a Memorial on behalf of the applicant and the subsequent filing of a Counter-Memorial by the respondent.[1] In cases brought by way of Special Agreement, the parties may agree on the number and order of written pleadings. However, in the absence of such agreement, they will each file a Memorial and Counter-Memorial within the same time limits.[2] In all cases the court may authorise the submission of an applicant's Reply and a respondent's Rejoinder, if it finds such pleadings to be necessary (upon request of a party, or acting *proprio motu*), or if the parties so agree.[3] After the closing of the written proceedings, no documents may be submitted to the court, except with the consent of the other party, or the authorisation of the court (in which case, the other party will be able to comment upon it and present additional supporting documents).[4]

In 1998, in a re-examination of its working methods, the court offered guidance to parties who come before it to the effect that in cases submitted to it by mutual consent it would permit written pleadings to be filed consecutively by parties, and not simultaneously as provided in principle by the rules of the court. This type of procedure may moderate the number of exchanges of written pleadings. The court also urged parties to disputes to ensure that the content of Memorials is clear and that annexes are selectively provided.[5]

A Memorial is to include a statement of the relevant facts and law and the submissions of the party.[6] A Counter-Memorial will contain admission or denial of the facts stated in the Memorial, any additional facts, observations on the applicant's statement of law, a statement of law in answer thereto and the respondent's submissions.[7] The Reply and Rejoinder should focus on points that still divide the parties (and not contain mere repetition of contentions submitted already).[8] Relevant supporting documents must be attached to the pleadings.[9] The written pleadings must be filed at the Registry, and must be presented in a number of copies required by the Registry (including a copy for the other party).[10] Time limits for filing of all submissions are determined by the court, after ascertaining the views of the parties.[11] Any agreement between the parties on the schedule of the case will normally be given effect, unless it results in unjustified delay.[12]

The respondent party may present a Counter-Claim, provided that it is directly connected to the subject matter of the original claim and falls under the jurisdiction of the ICJ.[13] A Counter-Claim must be included in the Counter-Memorial, and it will constitute part of the submissions of the respondent state.[14] The applicant may challenge the admissibility of the Counter-Claim before the court, which shall decide on the matter, after hearing the parties.[15]

1 ICJ Statute, art 43(2); ICJ Rules, art 45(1).
2 ICJ Rules, art 46.
3 ICJ Statute, art 43(2); ICJ Rules, arts 45(2), 46(2).
4 ICJ Rules, art 56.
5 ICJ Press Communiqué 98/14, 16 April 1998.
6 ICJ Rules, art 49(1).
7 Ibid, art 49(2).
8 Ibid, art 49(3).
9 Ibid, art 50(1).
10 ICJ Statute, art 43(4); ICJ Rules, art 52(1).
11 ICJ Statute, art 43(3); ICJ Rules, art 44(1).
12 ICJ Rules, art 44(2).
13 Ibid, art 80(1).
14 Ibid, art 80(2).
15 Ibid, art 80(3).

Oral arguments

1.31 After the end of the written stage of the proceedings, the court is to fix dates for holding of oral hearings.[1] It will also determine, after ascertaining the views of the parties, the order of the oral proceedings (including whether evidence or arguments will be presented first), method of handling of evidence (including examination of witnesses) and number of representatives to be heard on behalf of each party.[2]

The oral statements of the parties are to be as succinct as possible, within the limits of what is necessary for adequate presentation of each party's case. The statements must focus on issues which still divide the parties (and should not be a mere repetition of the written submissions).[3] The court may indicate points or issues on which it would like the parties to elaborate or refrain from arguing (since they have already been sufficiently argued).[4] The court may also put questions and ask for explanations from the representatives of the parties (including a call for production of evidence necessary to elucidate matters at issue).[5] At the conclusion of the last statement made by each of the parties, a representative of that party will read the final submission of the party, a copy of which is to be filed with the court and communicated to the other party.[6]

During oral hearings the parties may call witnesses and experts on their behalf to testify before the court.[7] A list of prospective witnesses must be communicated to the Registrar in sufficient time before the opening of the oral stage of the proceedings.[8] Witnesses not on the list can be summoned only if the other party does not object or with the authorisation of the court. The court may also summon, on its own initiative, witnesses and experts to testify in the proceedings.[9] The parties (under the control of the President) and the judges may question the witnesses and experts.[10] A verbatim record of the oral proceedings will be prepared by the ICJ Registry and provided to the judges and the parties (relevant parts will also be shown to the witnesses and experts).[11]

Oral hearings before the ICJ are public, unless the court decides otherwise, or unless the parties demand, at any time, that some or all sessions will be closed to the public.[12]

1 ICJ Statute, art 48; ICJ Rules, art 54(1).
2 ICJ Rules, art 58.
3 Ibid, art 60(1).
4 Ibid, art 61(1).
5 Ibid, arts 61(2)–(4), 62(1). If the court receives answers or evidence after the end of oral proceedings, it will communicate the submission to the other party, and may reopen the proceedings, if necessary: art 72.
6 ICJ Rules, art 60(2).
7 ICJ Statute, art 43(5); ICJ Rules, art 63(1).
8 ICJ Rules, art 57.
9 Ibid, art 62(2).
10 ICJ Statute, art 51; ICJ Rules, art 65.
11 ICJ Rules, art 71.
12 ICJ Statute, art 46; ICJ Rules, art 59.

Third party intervention

1.32   A third state that has an interest of a legal nature, which may be affected by the decision in a case, may request to intervene in proceedings before the ICJ.[1] In addition, in disputes relating to the interpretation of a convention to which states other than the states litigating before the court are parties, those third states have the right to intervene in the proceedings.[2]

A request for intervention due to a legal interest (referred to as intervention under article 62 of the ICJ Statute) must be filed with the Registry as soon as possible, and not later than at the end of the written stage of the proceedings (except in extraordinary circumstances).[3] The application should specify the following details:
(a) the interest of a legal nature that might be affected by the decision in the case;
(b) the precise object of the intervention;
(c) any basis of jurisdiction between the intervening state and the parties to the case; and

(d) list and copies of supporting documents.[4]

A state that wishes to intervene in cases concerning interpretation of a treaty (referred to as intervention under article 63 of the ICJ Statute), must file a declaration to this effect with the Registry – whether it has received a notification from the Registry indicating that the construction of a treaty to which it is party is at issue, or not.[5] The declaration should also be submitted as soon as possible, and not later than on the date of closure of the written proceedings (unless there are exceptional circumstances). It must include the following information:

(1) the basis on which the declaring state considers itself to be a party to the relevant convention

(2) the particular provisions of the convention the construction of which it considers to be in question;

(3) the construction of those provisions which the intervening party contends; and

(4) list and copies of supporting documents.[6]

The Registrar will communicate copies of article 62 applications or article 63 declarations to the parties to the case, which will be invited to provide written observations on the request within time-limits fixed by the court (or President).[7] Additional copies are sent to the Secretary-General of the UN and to the states parties to the Statute and, in article 63 cases, to the convention at issue.[8]

The court will then decide, as a matter of priority, whether to accept the application for intervention or whether a declaration of intent to intervene is admissible. In the event that an objection is filed, the court will decide the motion only after hearing the intervening state and any party to the case that objects to the intervention.[9] If a request to intervene is granted, copies of pleadings and documents will be made available to the intervening party, and it will be entitled to participate in the written and oral pleadings.[10] So far, the court has received requests for intervention on several occasions, but intervention has been permitted in two cases only.[11]

1 ICJ Statute, art 62.
2 Ibid, art 63.
3 ICJ Rules, art 81(1).
4 Ibid, art 81(2),(3).
5 ICJ Statute, art 63; ICJ Rules, art 82(1),(3).
6 ICJ Rules, art 82(2).
7 Ibid, art 83(1).
8 ICJ Rules, art 83(2).
9 ICJ Statute, art 62(2); ICJ Rules, art 84.
10 ICJ Rules, arts 85, 86.
11 *Haya de la Torre Case* 1951 ICJ 77i. *Land, Island and Maritime Frontier Dispute (El Salvador/Honduras)* 1990 ICJ 92. Requests for intervention have been made in six cases under art 62 of the Statute, and in three art 63 cases.

Multiple proceedings

1.33 The Statute of the ICJ clearly envisages multi-party proceedings. For instance, it specifies that in the event that several parties to a case are of the same legal interest they will appoint one ad hoc judge only.[1] The ICJ may also direct that proceedings in two or more cases be formally joined or litigated together without formal joinder.[2]

1 ICJ Statute, art 31(5); ICJ Rules, art 36.
2 ICJ Rules, art 47.

Amicus curiae briefs

1.34 In contentious proceedings, any international organisation (ie *inter-governmental* organisation) may file on its own initiative a Memorial with the Registry in relation to any case before the ICJ. The Memorial is to be submitted before the closing of the written pleadings and is to include any information relevant to the case.[1] The court may ask the organisation for further information – in writing or orally.[2] The parties will then be given the opportunity to comment (orally or in writing) on the information presented by the international organisation.

In addition, the court may, acting *proprio motu*, or upon the request of a party, ask for information from an international organisation, even if the latter did not submit a Memorial.[3] In the event that the constituent instrument of an international organisation, or an international convention adopted under its auspices, is at issue, the court must notify the concerned international organisation accordingly. The organisation may then submit its observations within fixed time limits, and may be invited to participate in the oral hearings.[4]

In relation to advisory proceedings, the court's statute provides for the participation of international organisations considered likely to be able to furnish information on the question at hand.[5]

1 ICJ Statute, art 34(2); ICJ Rules, art 69(2),(4).
2 ICJ Statute, art 34(2); ICJ Rules, art 69(2).
3 ICJ Rules, art 69(1).
4 ICJ Statute, art 34(3); ICJ Rules, art 69(3).
5 ICJ Statute, art 66(2).

Representation of parties

1.35 Parties to disputes before the court are to be represented by agents who must have an address for service at the seat of the court. Parties may have the assistance of counsel or advocates before the court.[1]

1 ICJ Statute, art 42; ICJ Rules, art 40.

Decision

1.36 The final decision of the ICJ in the dispute will be in the form of a judgment. The judgment will contain the following details:
(a) date on which it is read;
(b) names of judges participating in it;
(c) names of parties;
(d) names of representatives of the parties (ie agents, counsel, and advocates);
(e) summary of the proceedings;
(f) submissions of parties;
(g) statement of the facts;
(h) legal reasons for the decision;
(i) operative provisions of the judgment;
(j) decisions, if any, in regard to costs;
(k) number and names of judges constituting the majority; and
(l) statement as to the text of the judgment which is authoritative.[1]
All questions before the ICJ are decided by a majority of the judges.[2] Any

judge may append to the judgment his or her separate or dissenting opinions.[3] The judgment is read in public and it becomes binding on the parties on the day of the reading.[4]

1 ICJ Statute, art 56; ICJ Rules, art 95(1).
2 ICJ Statute, art 55. If the votes are even, the President will cast a decisive vote.
3 Ibid, art 57, ICJ Rules, art 95(2).
4 ICJ Statute, art 58; ICJ Rules, art 94(2).

Interpretation and revision of judgment

1.37 In the event that a dispute arises between the parties as to the meaning or scope of the judgment, they may request the ICJ to interpret it.[1] The request can be made by way of unilateral application or joint notification of a special agreement between the parties referring to the court a question for interpretation. In any case, the request must specify the precise points in dispute between the parties.[2] If the request was made through an application, the court will enable the other party to file its observations within a fixed time limit.[3] In all cases the ICJ may request the parties to provide additional written or oral explanations.[4]

An application for revision of a judgment can be made only on the basis of discovery of a new fact of such a nature as to be a decisive factor in the outcome of the case. This fact must have been unknown to the court and to the party requesting a revision when the judgment was rendered, and the ignorance of the party must not have been due to negligence.[5] An application for revision must be filed within six months from the date of discovery of the new fact, and in no case after ten years from the date of judgment.[6] The application will include all particulars necessary to show that the conditions for revision have been met, and should be supported by relevant documents.[7] The other party will be given the opportunity to submit written observations on the admissibility of the application within a time limit fixed by the court.[8] The court then decides on the admissibility of the application, after providing the parties additional opportunity of presenting their views, if necessary.[9] If the court finds the application admissible, it will fix time limits for proceedings on the merits of the application (after ascertaining the views of the parties, if necessary).[10]

The decision of the court in both motions for interpretation and revision is made in the form of a judgment.[11] In cases relating to judgments rendered by a chamber of the ICJ, the request for interpretation or revision will be dealt with by the same chamber.[12]

1 ICJ Statute, art 60; ICJ Rules, art 98(1). So far, an application for interpretation was made in two cases; in another case an application was made for interpretation and revision.
2 ICJ Rules, art 98(2).
3 Ibid, art 98(3).
4 Ibid, art 98(4).
5 ICJ Statute, art 61(1).
6 Ibid, art 61(4),(5).
7 ICJ Rules, art 99(1).
8 Ibid, art 99(2).
9 ICJ Statute, art 61(2).
10 ICJ Rules, art 99(4).
11 Ibid, art 100(2).
12 Ibid, art 100(1).

Appeal

1.38   The judgments of the court are final and binding and are not subject to appeal.[1]

1   ICJ Statute, art 60.

Costs

1.39   The expenses of the ICJ are borne by the states parties to the Statute.[1] In the event that a state not party to the ICJ Statute (that does not contribute to the budget of the court) appears before the court, the court will fix the amount it must pay towards the expenses of the court.[2] Each of the parties to any case before the court bears its own expenses, unless the court decides otherwise.[3]

1   ICJ Statute, art 33. That Article provides that the UN will bear the expenses of the court. Non-UN members that are parties to the court's Statute have been also required to pay their share of the court's expenses.
2   ICJ Statute, art 35(3).
3   Ibid, art 64; ICJ Rules, art 97.

Execution of decision, recognition and enforcement

1.40   The judgments of the court are final and binding, and must be complied with.[1] In the event that a party to a case fails to perform the obligations incumbent upon it under a judgment, the other party may have recourse to the Security Council, which may adopt recommendations or binding decisions pertaining to the enforcement of judgment.[2] To date, the Security Council's judgment-enforcement powers have never been used.

1   UN Charter, art 94(1).
2   Ibid, art 94(2).

REFERENCE

Sources of previous case law, including case reports

Judgments and orders of court are published in a series titled 'Reports of Judgments, Advisory Opinions and Orders' (in short, ICJ Reports). Since 1949 an ICJ Reports volume is published each year (before that, a biannual volume covered 1947–48). Recent decisions of the court can also be accessed at the court's website. It is now the practice of the Registry to make judgments available on the court's website as soon as they have been handed down.

Selected bibliography

Official publications

ICJ Yearbooks published annually.

Summaries of Judgments, Advisory Opinions and Orders of the International Court of Justice, 1948–1991, United Nations, New York (1992) (ST/LEG/SER. F/1); Idem, 1992–1996, United Nations, New York (1998) (ST/LEG/SER. F/1/ Add 1). (Also available in other official languages of the United Nations.)

Books

G Abi-Saab *Les exceptions préliminaires dans la procédure de la Cour Internationale: étude de notions fondamentales de procédure et des moyens de leur mise en oeuvre*, Paris (1967).

A Bloed and P van Dijk (eds) *Forty years International Court of Justice : Jurisdiction, Equity and Equality* (1988).

D Bowett and others *The International Court of Justice: Process, Practice and Procedure* (1997).

Lori F Damrosch (ed) *The International Court of Justice at a Crossroads* (1987).

Pierre Michel Eisemann, Vincent Coussirat-Coustere and Paul Hur *Petit manuel de la jurisprudence de la Cour Internationale de Justice*, 4th edn, Paris (1984).

T O Elias *The United Nations Charter and the World Court* (1989).

A Eyffinger *The ICJ 1946–1996* The Hague (1996).

Gerald Fitzmaurice *The Law and Procedure of the International Court of Justice*, 2 Vols (1986).

Geneviève Guyomar *Commentaire du Règlement de la Cour Internationale de Justice adopté le 14 Avril 1978 – Interprétation et pratique* (1983).

Vaughan Lowe and Malgosia Fitzmaurice (eds) *The International Court of Justice as a World Court, Fifty Years of the International Court of Justice* 3 at 13 (1996).

A S Muller, D Raic and J M Thuronsky (eds) *The World Court at the Turn of the Century* (1997).

Connie Peck and Roy S Lee (eds) *Increasing the Effectiveness of the International Court of Justice, Proceedings of the ICJ/UNIITAR Colloquium to celebrate the 50th anniversary of the court* (1997).

Shabtai Rosenne *Intervention in the International Court of Justice* (1993).

Shabtai Rosenne *The Law and Practice of the International Court of Justice, 1920–1996*, 3rd edn, in 4 volumes (1997).

Shabtai Rosenne *The World Court : What it is and How it Works*, 5th edn (1995).

Stephen M Schwebel *Justice in international law: selected writings* (1994).

Renata Szafarz *The compulsory jurisdiction of the International Court of Justice* (1994).

H W A Thirlway *The Law and Procedure of the International Court of Justice* (1996).

Articles

Robert Ago 'Binding Advisory Opinions of the International Court of Justice' (1995) 85 American Journal of International Law 439.

Jonathan I Charney 'Compromissory Clauses and the Jurisdiction of the International Court of Justice' (1987) 81 American Journal of International Law 855.

General bodies

Christine Chinkin 'Third Party Intervention Before the International Court of Justice' (1986) 80 American Journal of International Law 495.

Keith Highet 'The Peace Palace Heats Up: The World Court in Business Again?' (1991) 85 American Journal of International Law 646 at 654.

Robert Y Jennings 'The International Court of Justice after Fifty Years' (1995) 89 American Journal of International Law 493.

Eduardo Jimenez de Arechaga 'The Amendments to the Rules of Procedure of the International Court of Justice' (1973) 67 American Journal of International Law 1 at 2.

Abdul G Koroma 'International Justice in Relation to the International Court of Justice' in Kalliopi Koufa (ed) *International Justice* – XXVI Thesaurus Acroasium 421 (1997).

Stephen Schwebel 'Ad Hoc Chambers of the International Court of Justice' (1987) 81 American Journal of International Law 831.

Stephen Schwebel 'Reflections on the Role of the International Court of Justice' (1985) 61 Washington Law Review 1061, reprinted in *Justice in International Law* 3, (1994).

ANNEX

States recognising the compulsory jurisdiction of the court (with or without reservations)

Australia, Austria, Barbados, Belgium, Botswana, Bulgaria, Cambodia, Cameroon, Canada, Colombia, Costa Rica, Cyprus, Democratic Republic of Congo, Denmark, Dominican Republic, Egypt, El Salvador, Estonia, Finland, Gambia, Georgia, Greece, Guinea, Guinea-Bissau, Haiti, Honduras, Hungary, India, Japan, Kenya, Liberia, Liechtenstein, Luxembourg, Madagascar, Malawi, Malta, Mauritius, Mexico, Nauru, Netherlands, New Zealand, Nicaragua, Nigeria, Norway, Pakistan, Panama, Philippines, Poland, Portugal, Senegal, Somalia, Spain, Sudan, Suriname, Swaziland, Sweden, Switzerland, Togo, Uganda, United Kingdom, Uruguay, Yugoslavia.

CHAPTER 2

Permanent Court of Arbitration

INTRODUCTORY

Name and seat of the body

2.1 The Permanent Court of Arbitration (PCA) is located in the Peace Palace, The Hague, The Netherlands. The postal address of the Secretary-General of the International Bureau of the PCA is:

> Permanent Court of Arbitration
> Peace Palace
> Carnegieplein 2
> 2517 KJ The Hague
> The Netherlands
>
> Tel: 31 70 302 4165/302 4242
> Fax: 31 70 302 4167
> email: pca@euronet.nl
> website: http://www.euronet.nl/users/pca

Although the headquarters of the PCA are located in The Hague, arbitrations held under its auspices may take place outside The Hague – in any other location agreed upon by the parties.

Introductory description

2.2 The PCA, the first global institution for international adjudication, was established by the 1899 Hague Conference which adopted the Convention for the Pacific Settlement of International Disputes, subsequently replaced by the 1907 Hague Convention of the same title.[1] The two Hague Conventions have been ratified by 88 states (some have ratified only one of the Conventions – see Annex to this chapter). Chapter II of Part IV of the 1899 Convention established the PCA as an optional mechanism for peaceful settlement of disputes. Thus, while under no direct obligation to do so, any two states could agree to refer any dispute between them to the PCA for arbitration.

It has been noted elsewhere that the Permanent Court of Arbitration is a misnomer: since it is not a real court, it cannot be a permanent court. Rather the PCA is a permanent secretariat which maintains a readily available roster of potential arbitrators, named in advance by all state parties to the Hague Convention. Whenever a dispute is referred to the PCA, the parties to the dispute, with the assistance of the PCA International Bureau (the secretariat), establish an ad hoc arbitral tribunal – drawn from the PCA list of arbitrators or from persons outside this list.

The administration of the PCA is assigned to two standing bodies – the Administrative Council and the International Bureau. The Administrative Council comprises diplomatic representatives accredited to the Netherlands of the state parties to the Hague Conventions. The Council provides general guidance to the work of the PCA, supervises its administration and expenditure, and promulgates rules of procedure and other regulations.[2] The International Bureau serves as the operative secretariat of the PCA. It maintains the permanent roster of potential arbitrators; receives communications directed to the PCA (including requests for arbitration); and provides ongoing administrative services to the arbitral tribunals, including the provision of the facilities of the PCA building.[3] If the parties so wish, the Bureau acts as registry to a tribunal.

Thirty-three arbitration cases have been submitted to the PCA since its establishment (the first case was presented in 1902), the great majority in its early years. In addition, the services of the PCA have been provided, on occasion, for the conduct of fact-finding and conciliation proceedings. Furthermore, in a number of arbitrations, although not conducted under the auspices of the PCA, the technical facilities of the PCA were used. The most notable of these arbitration procedures is the Iran-US Claims tribunal, which has been operating with the support of the PCA since 1981. Another recent inter-state arbitration (Eritrea/Yemen Case) took place, not under the PCA, but with its assistance.

Nonetheless, in an attempt to increase its caseload, the Administrative Council has in recent years adopted several sets of rules designed to open up the PCA to arbitrations involving international actors other than states – ie international organisations and private parties. In addition, the PCA offers conciliation and fact-finding services to parties to international disputes.[4]

1 Convention for the Pacific Settlement of International Disputes, 29 July 1899, The Hague Conventions and Declarations of 1899 and 1907, p 41 (Scott, 2d edn, 1915) ('1899 Hague Convention'); Convention for the Pacific Settlement of International Disputes, 18 October 1907 ('1907 Hague Convention').
2 1899 Hague Convention, art 28; 1907 Hague Convention, art 49.
3 1899 Hague Convention, arts 22–23, 26; 1907 Hague Convention, arts 43, 44, 46, 47.
4 Permanent Court of Arbitration Optional Conciliation Rules (1996) ('Conciliation Rules').

INSTITUTIONAL ASPECTS
Governing texts
Procedural law

2.3   The principal texts governing the activities of the PCA are the 1899/1907 Hague Conventions for the Pacific Settlement of International Disputes. The Conventions (of which the 1907 Convention is the more detailed) regulate the institutional structure of the PCA; the composition of the list of arbitrators; the composition of ad hoc tribunals; financial aspects of PCA operations; and the basic rules of procedure applicable to PCA good offices and mediation, inquiry and arbitration proceedings (although the parties may choose not to apply them).[1]

In addition, different sets of Rules of Procedure will be applicable upon the choice of the parties, as alternatives to the rules of procedure found in the Hague Conventions. The Arbitration Rules are:

- Optional Rules for Arbitrating Disputes between Two States (1992);[2]
- Optional Rules for Arbitrating Disputes between Two Parties of which only One is a State (1993);[3]
- Optional Rules for Arbitration involving International Organisations and States (1996)[4] (encompassing, inter alia, arbitration between two international organisations);
- Optional Rules for Arbitration between International Organisations and Private Parties (1996).[5]

The other rules are:

- Optional Conciliation Rules (1996); and
- Optional Rules for Fact-finding Commissions of Inquiry (1997).

The four sets of Optional Arbitration Rules are modelled on the UNCITRAL Arbitration Rules and are drafted in a similar manner, including a number of identical articles. Parties to a dispute may agree in writing to modify certain provisions of the PCA Optional Rules.[6]

If parties to an inter-state dispute agree to arbitrate before the PCA, but fail to select an appropriate set of PCA Optional Rules, or an alternative set of rules (eg UNCITRAL Arbitration and Conciliation Rules), the proceedings will be governed by the rules of arbitration set out in the 1899/1907 Hague Conventions.

Finally, the functioning of the two administrative organs of the PCA – the Permanent Administrative Council and the International Bureau – is governed by an additional set of rules.[7]

1 1899 Hague Convention, arts 20, 30; 1907 Hague Convention, arts 41, 51.
2 Permanent Court of Arbitration Optional Rules for Arbitrating Disputes between Two States (entry into force 20 October 1992) ('Inter-State Rules').
3 Permanent Court of Arbitration Optional Rules for Arbitrating Disputes between Two Parties of which only One is a State (entry into force 6 July 1993) ('State/Non-State Rules').
4 Permanent Court of Arbitration Optional Rules for Arbitration involving International Organisations and States (entry into force 1 July 1996) ('IGO/State Rules').
5 Permanent Court of Arbitration Optional Rules for Arbitration between International Organisations and Private Parties (entry into force 1 July 1996) ('IGO/Private Parties Rules').
6 Inter-State Rules, art 1(1); State/Non-State Rules, art 1(1); IGO/State Rules, art 1(1); IGO/Private Parties Rules, art 1(1).
7 Rules of Procedure of the Administrative Council, 19 September 1900, reprinted in *Permanent Court of Arbitration – Convention and Rules of Procedure* 22 (1993); Rules concerning the Organisation and Internal Working of the International Bureau of the Permanent Court of Arbitration, 8 December 1900, id at 25.

Substantive law

2.4 An arbitral tribunal established under the PCA system is generally expected to apply the substantive law agreed upon by the parties. In the absence of an agreement, the tribunal will apply either the applicable rules of general international law or another body of law prescribed by choice of law rules.[1] In cases involving international organisations, the tribunal is directed to take due account of the rules of the organisation concerned and to the law of international organisations; and in cases involving private parties, the tribunal is directed to pay attention to the terms of the contracts or agreements in question and take into account the relevant trade usage. Finally, with the agreement of the parties, the tribunal may also apply equity (ie *ex aequo et bono*).

1 Inter-State Rules, art 33; State/Non-State Rules, art 33; IGO/State Rules, art 33; IGO/Private Parties Rules, art 33. The two Hague Conventions make a more ambiguous reference to settlement 'on the basis of respect for law': 1899 Hague Convention, art 15; 1907 Hague Convention, art 37.

Organisation

Composition, appointment and disqualification

LIST OF ARBITRATORS

2.5 Each Party to the 1899 or 1907 Hague Conventions is entitled to nominate up to four persons of established competence in international law and high moral reputation, who have agreed to serve as PCA arbitrators, to a roster maintained by the International Bureau.[1] Two or more states may select the same persons to the list of arbitrators. The International Bureau transmits the list, as amended from time to time, to the states parties.

The current panel includes over 265 international jurists. The selected individuals (referred to as members of the PCA) serve for a renewable six-year period.

1 1899 Hague Convention, art 23; 1907 Hague Convention, art 44.

COMPOSITION OF THE ARBITRAL TRIBUNAL

2.6 According to the Optional Rules, if the parties to a dispute fail to agree on the number of arbitrators (ie sole arbitrator, three or five arbitrators), the tribunal shall be composed of three arbitrators.[1] In the case of a three-member tribunal, each party to the dispute is to appoint one arbitrator and the two appointed arbitrators are to agree upon the identity of the third arbitrator. In the absence of agreement on the third arbitrator, or upon failure on the part of one of the parties to appoint an arbitrator, the third arbitrator will be appointed by an appointing authority agreed upon by the parties. In the absence of such agreement, the appointing authority will be designated by the Secretary-General of the PCA (head of the International Bureau).[2]

If the parties agree to arbitrate their dispute before a sole arbitrator, they are free to agree on the identity of that arbitrator or, alternatively, to jointly designate an appointing authority. If no agreement is reached, the Secretary-General of the PCA shall designate an appointing authority, which shall appoint the sole arbitrator in consultation with the parties.[3]

If the parties agree on a five-member tribunal, each party shall nominate one arbitrator, and the two nominated arbitrators shall select the remaining three. If no agreement is reached, or if a party fails to appoint an arbitrator, the same procedures for completing the composition of the tribunal applicable to a three-member tribunal shall be resorted to.[4]

In contrast with the Hague Conventions, the Optional Rules specifically permit the selection of arbitrators who are not members of the PCA, that is to say, not listed on the permanent roster of arbitrators.[5]

In proceedings governed by the Hague Conventions rather than by the Optional Rules, the procedure of appointment is different. First, all appointed arbitrators must be members of the PCA. Furthermore, in the absence of agreement of the parties on the size and composition of the panel of arbitrators, the tribunal shall normally include five arbitrators. Each party should select two arbitrators (under the 1907 Convention, only one of the two selected arbitrators can be a national of the appointing state, or its designated member to the PCA list of arbitrators). The Umpire is then selected by the four appointed arbitrators or, in the alternative, by an agreed-upon third party.[6] If no agreement is reached in this manner, the Conventions provide for delegation of appointment power to two party-appointed third states. Under a unique approach, the 1907 Convention provides, as a last resort, that the Umpire be selected by a draw by lot from a shortlist of four members of the PCA prepared by the two designated third parties (excluding citizens or nominees to the PCA of either party to the dispute).[7]

Under the 1907 Hague Convention, the parties may agree to arbitrate their dispute in an expedited summary procedure. In that case, the tribunal shall normally include three arbitrators (appointed in a manner similar to the method of appointment of a five-member panel).[8]

1   Inter-State Rules, art 5; State/Non-State Rules, art 5; IGO/State Rules, art 5; IGO/Private Parties Rules, art 5.
2   Inter-State Rules, art 7; State/Non-State Rules, art 7; IGO/State Rules, art 7; IGO/Private Parties Rules, art 7.
3   Inter-State Rules, art 6; State/Non-State Rules, art 6; IGO/State Rules, art 6; IGO/Private Parties Rules, art 6. All of the rules provide for a consultation mechanism based upon the circulation of a list of potential arbitrators between the parties for objections, and designation of an arbitrator not objected to by any of the parties; or if no such arbitrator exists – designation of an arbitrator at the appointing authority's discretion (preferably, in cases involving states, not a national of any of the states parties to the dispute).
4   Inter-State Rules, art 7; IGO/State Rules, art 7. The two other sets of Optional Rules do not provide in any case for a five-member arbitral tribunal.
5   Inter-State Rules, art 8(3); State/Non-State Rules, art 8(3); IGO/State Rules, art 8(3); IGO/Private Parties Rules, art 8(3).
6   1899 Hague Convention, art 24; 1907 Hague Convention, art 45.
7   Unlike the Optional Rules, no stipulation is made in either of the Hague Conventions to resolve a situation in which one of the parties refuses to appoint its two designated arbitrators.
8   1907 Hague Convention, arts 86, 87. The main difference between the two procedures is that in case of disagreement among the two selected arbitrators as to the identity of the third one, the arbitrators themselves (and not the designated third parties) compose the shortlist of four arbitrators to draw from. The involvement of a third party is not sought under this procedure.

CHALLENGE PROCEDURES

2.7   Under the various Optional Rules, a party may institute a challenge directed against the appointment or continued service of an arbitrator, if it becomes aware of circumstances which raise justifiable doubt as to the impartiality or independence of that arbitrator.[1] If the other party agrees to the challenge, or the arbitrator withdraws from office, a new arbitrator will be appointed (in a manner similar to that in which the retiring arbitrator was appointed).[2] Otherwise, the challenge is to be presented before the tribunal's appointing authority (which might be designated exclusively for the purpose of challenge procedures). The authority shall decide on the merits of the motion.[3]

1   Inter-State Rules, art 10; State/Non-State Rules, art 10; IGO/State Rules, art 10; IGO/Private Parties Rules, art 10.
2   Inter-State Rules, art 11; State/Non-State Rules, art 11; IGO/State Rules, art 11; IGO/Private Parties Rules, art 11. The procedure for replacement of an arbitrator is prescribed by art 13 of each set of Rules.
3   Inter-State Rules, art 12; State/Non-State Rules, art 12; IGO/State Rules, art 12; IGO/Private Parties Rules, art 12.

General bodies

Plenary/chambers

2.8   Arbitration tribunals established under the PCA system sit in plenary. If for some reason one of the arbitrators in a three or five-member tribunal fails to participate in the proceedings, he or she will normally be replaced.[1] However, the truncated tribunal may decide to continue and hear the dispute notwithstanding the arbitrator's failure to attend its meetings.[2]

1   1899 Hague Convention, art 35; 1907 Hague Convention, art 59; Inter-State Rules, art 13(1),(2); State/Non-State Rules, art 13(1),(2); IGO/State Rules, art 13(1),(2); IGO/Private Parties Rules, art 13(1),(2). Under art 14 to all Optional Rules, the tribunal may decree that the hearing shall be repeated in the event of replacement of an arbitrator.
2   Inter-State Rules, art 13(3); State/Non-State Rules, art 13(3); IGO/State Rules, art 13(3); IGO/Private Parties Rules, art 13(3). The parties may agree to restrict or expropriate the discretion of the tribunal on the matter.

Appellate structure

2.9   There is no right of appeal over PCA arbitral awards. The awards are final and binding.[1]

1   1899 Hague Convention, art 54; 1907 Hague Convention, art 81; Inter-State Rules, art 32(2); State/Non-State Rules, art 32(2); IGO/State Rules, art 32(2); IGO/Private Parties Rules, art 32(2).

Scientific and technical experts

2.10   Under the Optional Rules, an arbitral tribunal may appoint an expert (or several experts) and instruct them to prepare a written report on specified issues. The parties must provide the expert (or experts) with any document or goods requested; and may submit additional information they wish the expert to consider. The parties shall have the opportunity to review the expert's report and the documents he or she relied on, and comment upon them in writing to the tribunal. The parties also have the right to question the expert and introduce their own expert witnesses.[1]

1   Inter-State Rules, art 27; State/Non-State Rules, art 27; IGO/State Rules, art 27; IGO/Private Parties Rules, art 27.

Registry

2.11   The PCA International Bureau, headed by the Secretary-General (currently Mr Tjaco T van den Hout), provides the arbitral tribunal with all administrative services, including registry and secretarial services, and constitutes a channel of communication between the parties and the tribunal.[1] In addition, the International Bureau files documents from all PCA cases in its archives. Under the Optional Rules the International Bureau is expected to assume most of its administrative functions vis-à-vis the proceedings only upon the written request of the parties (and it may refuse requests to provide its administrative services for arbitrations conducted outside The Hague).[2]

1   1899 Hague Convention, art 22; 1907 Hague Convention, art 43.
2   Inter-State Rules, art 1(2); State/Non-State Rules, art 1(4); IGO/State Rules, art 1(3); IGO/Private Parties Rules, art 1(4).

Jurisdiction and access to the PCA

Ratione personae

2.12　The original jurisdiction of the PCA under the 1899/1907 Conventions was limited to inter-state disputes.[1] Furthermore, exercise of this jurisdiction depends upon an agreement (normally, in writing) between the parties to refer a dispute to PCA arbitration. Such agreement can be made ad hoc, or in a compromissory clause found in a valid treaty.

The various Optional Rules expanded the scope of jurisdiction of the PCA and, at present, the following parties may agree to bring a case before the PCA, in accordance with the relevant Optional Rules:

- any two states (the use of the PCA is not limited to states parties to the Hague Conventions);[2]
- a state and an international organisation (ie an intergovernmental organisation);
- two international organisations;
- a state and a private party; and
- an international organisation and a private party.

The agreement to refer a dispute to the PCA may be made by way of a separate agreement or through an arbitration clause in a contract or other legal instrument. It should be noted that under the Optional Rules, an arbitration clause shall be considered independent of the other terms of the documents in which it is contained, for the purposes of establishing jurisdiction. Thus invalidity of the contract, agreement or instrument shall not ipso facto deprive the arbitral tribunal of jurisdiction.[3]

Finally, under the two sets of Optional Rules providing for the involvement of a private party, consent to the application of the rules constitutes a waiver of sovereign immunity from jurisdiction on the part of the state or international organisation concerned.[4]

1　1899 Hague Convention, arts 15, 21; 1907 Hague Convention, arts 37, 42.
2　1899 Hague Convention, art 26; 1907 Hague Convention, art 47.
3　Inter-State Rules, art 21(2); State/Non-State Rules, art 21(2); IGO/State Rules, art 21(2); IGO/Private Parties Rules, art 21(2).
4　State/Non-State Rules, art 1(2), IGO/Private Parties Rules, art 1(2).

Ratione materiae

2.13　The potential subject-matter jurisdiction of the PCA is unlimited.[1] However, in each case the scope of jurisdiction of the arbitral tribunal is determined subject to the wording of the applicable arbitration clause (or the *compromis*).

1　1899 Hague Convention, art 21; 1907 Hague Convention, art 42.

Ratione temporis

2.14　The various rules of procedure do not place any temporal limits upon the referral of disputes to PCA arbitration. However, such restrictions may be indicated in the instrument concluded by the parties (ie arbitration clause or *compromis*), which establishes jurisdiction.

Advisory jurisdiction

2.15 PCA arbitral tribunals have only contentious jurisdiction, and arbitral awards are final and binding.[1] The PCA also renders conciliatory services, under its Rules of Conciliation and fact-finding services under the 1907 Hague Convention. These are addressed separately in para 2.31 below.

1 1899 Hague Convention, art 54; 1907 Hague Convention, art 81; Inter-State Rules, art 32(2); State/Non-State Rules, art 32(2); IGO/State Rules, art 32(2); IGO/Private Parties Rules, art 32(2).

PROCEDURAL ASPECTS

Languages

2.16 The language (or languages) of any proceedings will be agreed upon by the parties. In the absence of such agreement it will be determined by the tribunal.[1] Under the Optional Rules, the tribunal may require that the parties translate documents submitted to the tribunal into the language (or languages) of the proceedings.

1 1899 Hague Convention, art 38; 1907 Hague Convention, art 61; Inter-State Rules, art 17; State/Non-State Rules, art 17; IGO/State Rules, art 17; IGO/Private Parties Rules, art 17.

Instituting proceedings

2.17 Under all Optional Rules, the party initiating arbitration (ie the claimant) is to serve the other party (ie the respondent) with a notice of arbitration.

The notice of arbitration is to contain the following information:
(a) a demand that the dispute be referred to arbitration;
(b) names and addresses of the parties;
(c) reference to an arbitration clause or arbitration agreement;
(d) reference to the treaty, agreement, contract or other legal instrument (eg constituent instrument or decision of an international organisation) out of which, or in relation to which the dispute arose;
(e) general nature of the case and indication of the amount involved;
(f) relief or remedy sought; and
(g) proposal as to the number of arbitrators.[1]
Under the procedures envisaged by the Hague Conventions, no formal notice of arbitration is required. Thus the parties can move at any time to establish a tribunal and draft a *compromis*.[2] Only when the tribunal is constituted and the *compromis* agreed upon should the International Bureau be notified.[3]

1 Inter-State Rules, art 3; State/Non-State Rules, art 3; IGO/State Rules, art 3; IGO/Private Parties Rules, art 3.
2 1899 Hague Convention, art 24; 1907 Hague Convention, art 45.
3 1899 Hague Convention, art 24; 1907 Hague Convention, art 46. Under the 1899 Convention, the parties should notify the International Bureau that the tribunal has been created (even if no *compromis* has been negotiated). Under the 1907 Hague Convention, if no agreement on the contents of the *compromis* is reached, the parties may authorise the tribunal to settle a *compromis*. Furthermore, under those rules, in cases brought on the basis of a general arbitration agreement (ie an agreement which refers all future inter-state disputes or certain categories of such disputes to arbitration), or a contractual debt claim presented on behalf of a national of the claimant, the tribunal is competent to draft a *compromis* acting on a request made by one party only: 1907 Hague Convention, art 53.

Financial assistance

2.18 In 1995, the Secretary-General of the PCA established a Financial Assistance Fund for the Settlement of International Disputes, with the approval of the Administrative Council. The Fund comprises voluntary financial contributions made by states, international organisations, NGOs and natural or legal persons. Only states (or state-controlled entities) are eligible to receive financial support, provided that they meet the following requirements:

(a) participation in either the 1899 or 1907 Hague Conventions;

(b) they have concluded an agreement to refer a dispute (or disputes) to settlement before the PCA;

(c) they are listed on the Development Assistance Committee List of Aid recipients (as prepared by the OECD).

A request for financial assistance in order to facilitate recourse to PCA arbitration, conciliation and fact-finding is to be submitted by the requesting state to the Secretary-General. The request should include:

(a) a copy of the dispute settlement agreement (in the case of a general agreement, a brief description of the dispute);

(b) an estimate of costs for which financial assistance is sought; and

(c) an undertaking to submit an audited statement of account on the expenditure made with the received funds.

The Fund is administered by the International Bureau, with the supervision of a Board of Trustees, which must approve every request for assistance (the Board of Trustees is to be appointed by the Secretary-General, with the approval of the Administrative Council). In addition, the Secretary-General periodically reports to the Administrative Council on the activities of the Fund.

Provisional measures

2.19 Under the Optional Rules, the tribunal may order interim measures of protection, in the form of an interim award, at the request of a party, if such measures are viewed by the tribunal as necessary to preserve the respective rights of the parties or the subject-matter of the dispute. These measures may include, in commercial disputes, the deposit of goods with third parties or the sale of perishable goods. The tribunal is also entitled to require from the requesting party security for the costs associated with these measures. It is further provided in the Optional Rules that the parties are free to agree to restrict the power of the tribunal to issue interim awards; and may seek interim protection in alternative venues as well.[1]

The 1899/1907 Hague Conventions do not expressly provide for a similar authority to issue interim measures of protection.

1 Inter-State Rules, art 26; State/Non-State Rules, art 26; IGO/State Rules, art 26; IGO/Private Parties Rules, art 26.

Preliminary proceedings/objections

2.20 The various sets of Optional Rules provide for a preliminary procedure to establish the arbitral tribunal's jurisdiction. A plea alleging lack of competence of the tribunal must be raised in the written pleadings, at the statement or defence stage (or in the reply to a counter-claim). The tribunal should normally rule on the plea concerning its jurisdiction as a preliminary matter. However, it may also defer its decision to the final award, by joining jurisdictional issues to the merits.[1]

In addition, challenge proceedings against an arbitrator, made in pursuance of the Optional Rules, must be initiated within 30 days from the appointment of the challenged arbitrator, or within 30 days from the date the circumstances constituting the basis for the challenge became known to the challenging party.[2]

The Hague Conventions do not provide for a preliminary procedure.

1 Inter-State Rules, art 21; State/Non-State Rules, art 21; IGO/State Rules, art 21; IGO/Private Parties Rules, art 21.
2 Inter-State Rules, art 11(1); State/Non-State Rules, art 11(1); IGO/State Rules, art 11(1); IGO/Private Parties Rules, art 11(1).

Written pleadings

2.21   After the notice of arbitration, and once the tribunal has been constituted and has directed the order of proceedings, the written stage of the proceedings (conducted in pursuance with the Optional Rules), opens with the statement of claim submitted by the claimant to the respondent, the arbitrators and the International Bureau. The statement of claim should include the following information:
(a) names and addresses of the parties;
(b) statement of facts supporting the claim;
(c) the points at issue; and
(d) relief or remedy sought.
The claimant should attach to the statement of claim all relevant documents, including those supporting the jurisdictional basis of the PCA tribunal. In addition, the claimant may indicate further documents or evidence it intends to submit in the future.[1]

In reply, the respondent will submit to the other party and the tribunal a statement of defence which shall address particulars (b)–(d) of the statement of claim, together with supporting documents, and make reference to additional documents or evidence it intends to submit.[2]

The respondent may also include in its statement of defence (or, if the tribunal allows it, in a subsequent statement) a counter-claim arising out of the same treaty, agreement, contract or other legal instrument, or a claim for set-off, which relies upon a claim arising from the said instrument. The counter-claim or set-off claim statement should meet the procedural requirements applicable to an ordinary statement of claim.[3]

The parties may amend or supplement their written submissions at any time, unless the tribunal considers those amendments as inappropriate given the delay in their introduction, the prejudice they cause to the other party, or any other circumstances. In no case can the claim be amended in a manner that exceeds the jurisdiction of the tribunal.[4]

Finally, the tribunal is authorised to decide whether additional submissions in writing are required.[5]

The Hague Conventions provide for a less detailed procedure. However, their rules also call for submission of written pleadings in the form of communication of cases, replies and counter-cases, with all relevant documents attached. Pleadings must be submitted to the tribunal, and a certified copy made for the other party.[6]

Under the Optional Rules and the Hague Conventions, the timetable for submission of pleadings will be determined by the tribunal (except under the 1907 Hague Convention which calls upon the parties to introduce a timetable for submissions in the *compromis*).[7] However, under the Optional Rules, such periods should not normally exceed 90 days (45 days in cases involving a state and a non-state actor) for each submission.[8]

1   Inter-State Rules, art 18; State/Non-State Rules, art 18; IGO/State Rules, art 18; IGO/Private Parties Rules, art 18.
2   Inter-State Rules, art 19(2); State/Non-State Rules, art 19(2); IGO/State Rules, art 19(2); IGO/Private Parties Rules, art 19(2).
3   Inter-State Rules, art 19(3)–(4); State/Non-State Rules, art 19(3)–(4); IGO/State Rules, art 19(3)–(4); IGO/Private Parties Rules, art 19(3)–(4).
4   Inter-State Rules, art 20; State/Non-State Rules, art 20; IGO/State Rules, art 20; IGO/Private Parties Rules, art 20.
5   Inter-State Rules, art 22; State/Non-State Rules, art 22; IGO/State Rules, art 22; IGO/Private Parties Rules, art 22.
6   1899 Hague Convention, arts 39–40; 1907 Hague Convention, arts 63–64.
7   1899 Hague Convention, art 49; 1907 Hague convention, art 63; Inter-State Rules, arts 18(1), 19(1), 22; State/Non-State Rules, arts 18(1), 19(1), 22; IGO/State Rules, arts 18(1), 19(1), 22; IGO/Private Parties Rules, arts 18(1), 19(1), 22.
8   Inter-State Rules, art 23; State/Non-State Rules, art 23; IGO/State Rules, art 23; IGO/Private Parties Rules, art 23.

Oral arguments

2.22   The parties are entitled, under the Optional Rules, to request oral hearings and the presentation of evidence by witnesses (including expert witnesses). In the absence of such a request, the tribunal will decide whether to hold oral hearings, or conduct the proceedings solely on the basis of written submissions, documents and other material.[1] If witnesses are to be heard, each party is to communicate to the tribunal and the other party the names and addresses of the witnesses it intends to introduce, at least 30 days in advance.[2]

Under the Hague Conventions, proceedings include oral discussions. The parties are entitled to present orally to the tribunal all arguments relevant to the defence of their case; and the tribunal may put questions to them on their presentation.[3] However, if the parties choose to conduct the proceedings in summary procedure there will normally be no oral hearings.[4]

Under the Hague Convention and the Optional Rules, oral hearings are conducted in camera unless the parties agree otherwise.[5] However, under the Hague Conventions, agreement of the parties will not be sufficient to make the proceedings public and an additional decision of the tribunal is required.

1   Inter-State Rules, art 15(2); State/Non-State Rules, art 15(2); IGO/State Rules, art 15(2); IGO/Private Parties Rules, art 15(2).
2   Inter-State Rules, art 25(2); State/Non-State Rules, art 25(2); IGO/State Rules, art 25(2); IGO/Private Parties Rules, art 25(2).
3   1899 Hague Convention, arts 45, 47; 1907 Hague convention, arts 70, 72.
4   1907 Hague Convention, art 90.
5   Inter-State Rules, art 25(4); State/Non-State Rules, art 25(4); IGO/State Rules, art 25(4); IGO/Private Parties Rules, art 25(4). 1899 Hague Convention, art 41; 1907 Hague Convention, art 66.

Third-party intervention

2.23   While generally third-party intervention in PCA proceedings are not permissible, there is no reason why a dispute between more than two parties could not be referred to the PCA, with the agreement of all parties. The various Optional Rules contain guidelines for their adaptation to multi-party proceedings.[1] Special agreement will be necessary, including on the method of appointment of arbitrators and costs. The Secretary-General of the International Bureau has expressed his willingness to render assistance to the parties to a multi-party dispute in the adaptation of the Optional Rules to the dispute.

An exception to the general rule precluding third-party intervention may be found in the two Hague Conventions. In disputes involving the interpretation of treaties to which other states are parties, the parties to the dispute are to notify those other states, which will have the right to intervene in the proceedings. In this case, the award shall be considered equally binding for them.[2] The Conventions do not specify rules of procedure to regulate such intervention.

1 *Guidelines for adapting the Permanent Court of Arbitration Rules to Disputes arising under Multilateral Agreements and Multiparty Contracts.*
2 1899 Hague Convention, art 56; 1907 Hague Convention, art 84.

Amicus curiae

2.24 There is no provision in the Hague Convention or the Optional Rules governing the issue of amicus curiae briefs. Given the nature of PCA arbitration (involving party control over the course of the procedure), it seems unlikely that a tribunal would accept third-party amicus curiae briefs, unless the parties to a case so agree.

Representation of parties

2.25 In relation to arbitration, under the 1907 Hague Convention, the parties are entitled to appoint special agents to attend the tribunal to act as intermediaries between themselves and the tribunal, and may retain counsel or advocates.[1] The Inter-State Arbitration rules provide that parties shall appoint an agent and may also be assisted by persons of their choice.[2] A similar provision is contained in the State/Non-State Rules, the IGO/State Rules and the IGO/Private Party Rules.[3]

1 1899 Hague Convention, art 37; 1907 Hague Convention, art 62.
2 Inter-State Rules, art 4.
3 State/Non-State Rules, art 4; IGO/State Rules, art 4; IGO/Private Parties Rules, art 4.

Decision

2.26 The final decision of the tribunal is in the form of a written award decided by the majority of arbitrators.[1] The award will state the reasons for the decision, unless the parties agreed that no reasons are to be provided.[2] Under the Optional Rules, the award will not be made public (unless the parties agree to publicise it) whereas under the Hague Conventions it will normally be publicised.[3] The award is final and binding upon the parties and is to be executed without delay.[4]

The Optional Rules allow parties to a dispute that reached a settlement agreement before the end of the proceedings to request the tribunal to record their agreement in the form of an arbitral award on agreed terms.[5]

1 1899 Hague Convention, art 52; 1907 Hague Convention, art 78; Inter-State Rules, art 31; State/Non-State Rules, art 31; IGO/State Rules, art 31; IGO/Private Parties Rules, art 31.

2 1899 Hague Convention, art 52; 1907 Hague Convention, art 79; Inter-State Rules, art 32(3); State/Non-State Rules, art 32(3); IGO/State Rules, art 32(3); IGO/Private Parties Rules, art 32(3).
3 1899 Hague Convention, art 53; 1907 Hague Convention, art 80; Inter-State Rules, art 32(5); State/Non-State Rules, art 32(5); IGO/State Rules, art 32(5); IGO/Private Parties Rules, art 32(5).
4 1899 Hague Convention, arts 54; 1907 Hague Convention, art 81; Inter-State Rules, art 32(2); State/Non-State Rules, art 32(2); IGO/State Rules, art 32(2); IGO/Private Parties Rules, art 32(2).
5 Inter-State Rules, art 34(1); State/Non-State Rules, art 34(1); IGO/State Rules, art 34(1); IGO/Private Parties Rules, art 34(1).

Interpretation and revision of award

2.27 Under the Optional Rules, either party may approach the tribunal after the award has been issued and ask for interpretation of the award, correction of errors in computation, clerical or typographical errors, or request an additional award on claims presented during the proceedings but omitted from the award. Requests for interpretation or correction are to be presented within 60 days from the day the award was received by the parties (30 days in state/non-state cases); a request for an additional award should be presented within 60 days. The rules provide that the tribunal should reply to requests for interpretation within 45 days from the receipt of the request and to requests for additional award within 60 days.[1] The tribunal is authorised to correct errors in the award, of the type mentioned above, on its own initiative – if acting within 30 days from the date of communication of the award.

Under the 1907 Hague Convention, the parties may normally submit any question related to the interpretation and the execution of the award to the original tribunal.[2] In addition, under both Hague Conventions, if the parties agree on the *compromis* to this effect, the tribunal may re-examine the award in light of the discovery of a new fact calculated to have a decisive influence on the award, which was unknown during the proceeding to the tribunal and to the party requesting revision. The period of time in which requests for revision can be made should be fixed in the *compromis*.[3]

1 Inter-State Rules, arts 35–37; State/Non-State Rules, arts 35–37; IGO/State Rules, arts 35–37; IGO/Private Parties Rules, arts 35–37.
2 1907 Hague Convention, art 82.
3 1899 Hague Convention, art 55; 1907 Hague Convention, art 83.

Appeals

2.28 There is no right of appeal in respect of awards rendered by tribunals established under the PCA system.

Costs

2.29 The costs of PCA arbitration include the fees and expenses of the arbitrators, which are to be determined by the tribunal, normally in consultation with the appointing authority. They will also include the costs of expert advice, and other assistance provided to the tribunal; fees and expenses of the appointing authority; and the expenses of the Secretary-General and the International Bureau. Additionally, parties to the proceedings will incur their own costs in respect of legal representation and assistance.

Normally, under the Optional Rules and the Hague Conventions, each party incurs its own costs of arbitration (ie all of its legal expenses and an equal share of the other costs of arbitration).[1] However, under the Optional Rules, the tribunal may apportion the costs between the parties in any other reasonable manner warranted by the circumstances. Exceptions to this rule are found under the Optional Rules for Arbitrating Disputes between Two Parties of which only one is a State, and the Optional Rules for Arbitration between IGOs and Private Parties, which provide that the unsuccessful party should normally incur all costs.[2] However, here again, the tribunal may decide to apportion costs in a different manner.

Under the various Optional Rules the tribunal may request the parties to deposit funds in advance during the proceedings; and it may require additional deposits at a later stage of the proceedings.[3]

1   1899 Hague Convention, art 57; 1907 Hague Convention, art 85; Inter-State Rules, arts 38–40; State/Non-State Rules, arts 38–40; IGO/State Rules, arts 38–40; IGO/Private Parties Rules, arts 38–40.
2   State/Non-State Rules, art 40(1); IGO/Private Parties Rules, art 40(1).
3   Inter-State Rules, art 41; State/Non-State Rules, art 41; IGO/State Rules, art 41; IGO/Private Parties Rules, art 41.

Execution of decision, recognition and enforcement

2.30   PCA Optional Rules governing proceedings involving states and/or international organisations do not provide for any mechanism of enforcement. The Optional Rules do, however, state that the parties undertake to carry out the award without delay.[1]

In cases involving private parties that are governed by the Optional Rules on Arbitration between States and Non-States or between International Organisations and Private Parties, the tribunal is expected to file or register its award in accordance with the municipal arbitration laws of the country in which the arbitration took place. Such registration is intended to facilitate recognition and enforcement of the award in municipal courts.[2]

In cases involving private parties on one hand, and entities that enjoy sovereign immunity on the other hand, the implied agreement to waiver of immunity which is stated in the Optional Rules for Arbitrating Disputes between Two Parties of which only One is a State and for Arbitration between International Organisations and Private Parties, does not apply to the enforcement procedures, and a separate explicit waiver should be sought.[3]

1   Inter-State Rules, art 32(2); State/Non-State Rules, art 32(2); IGO/State Rules, art 32(2); IGO/Private Parties Rules, art 32(2).
2   State/Non-State Rules, art 32(7); IGO/Private Parties Rules, art 32(7).
3   State/Non-State Rules, art 1(2); IGO/Private Parties Rules, art 1(2).

Conciliation and fact-finding under the PCA

2.31   In addition to arbitration the PCA also offers conciliation services, under its Rules of Conciliation, and fact-finding services under the 1907 Hague Convention.

The Rules of Conciliation, modelled after the UNCITRAL Conciliation Rules, are designed to apply in disputes in which at least one of the parties is a state, state entity or enterprise or an international organisation.[1] Conciliation takes place before a panel of one, two or three conciliators selected with the agreement of the parties. In the absence of such agreement, the conciliators will be appointed in a manner similar to the appointment of arbitrators under the various Optional Rules.[2] The conciliator (or conciliators) is to attempt to reach an amicable settlement of the dispute and conducts proceedings towards this aim, in any manner he or she considers appropriate, taking into account the wishes of the parties.[3] At any stage of the proceedings, the conciliator may propose a settlement and assist the parties in drawing up an agreement.[4] The International Bureau shall render the conciliation proceedings any administrative support required by the parties or the conciliator (with consent of the parties).[5]

Under the 1907 Hague Convention, the International Bureau of the PCA may also provide administrative assistance to the work of Commissions of Inquiry.[6] Such proceedings may be initiated by any two states which are in dispute over points of fact.[7] A Commission of Inquiry is constituted in a manner similar to that of PCA arbitration tribunals.[8] The Commission is then authorised to conduct an investigation of the facts in dispute and issue a report, which the parties may adopt or reject.[9] Alternatively, parties to factual disputes (including non-parties to the Hague Conventions) may agree to apply the 1997 Optional Rules for Fact-finding Commissions of Inquiry.[10] These Rules do not merely intend to supplement the non-mandatory provisions of the 1907 Convention, but form a self-contained procedural framework.

1 International Bureau of the Permanent Court of Arbitration, Introduction, *PCA Optional Rules of Conciliation* xi (1996).
2 Conciliation Rules, arts 3, 4.
3 Ibid, art 7.
4 Ibid, arts 7(4), 13.
5 Ibid, art 8.
6 1907 Hague Convention, art 15.
7 Ibid, art 9.
8 Ibid, art 12.
9 Ibid, art 35.
10 Permanent Court of Arbitration Optional Rules for Fact-Finding Commission of Inquiry (entry into force 15 December 1997).

REFERENCE

Sources of previous case law, including case reports

In most cases the parties have not objected to publication of awards. The primary source of PCA case law is The Hague Court Reports Series (James B Scott (ed), Oxford University Press, 1916–1932), where most early PCA awards are published. In addition, PCA arbitration cases are published in commercial publications such as International Law Reports (ILR) and the UN Reports of International Arbitral Awards (RIAA).

Selected bibliography

James Brown Scott (ed) *The Reports to the Hague Conventions of 1899 and 1907* (1917) (containing the *travaux préparatoires* of the Conventions).

William E Butler 'The Hague Permanent Court of Arbitration' in Mark W Janis (ed) *International Courts for the Twenty-First Century* 43–53 (1992).

Manley O Hudson *International tribunals: past and future* 67 (1944).

General bodies

Manley O Hudson 'The Permanent Court of Arbitration' (1933) 27 AJIL 440.

Bette E Shifman 'The Revitalisation of the Permanent Court of Arbitration' (1995) 23 International Journal of Legal Information 284.

Hans Jurgen Schlochaur 'The Permanent Court of Arbitration' (1981) 1 Encyclopedia of Public International Law 157, Rudolf Benhardt (ed).

A M Stuyt *Survey of International Arbitrations 1794-1970* (1972).

Annual Reports of the PCA (can be ordered from the International Bureau of the PCA).

Permanent Court of Arbitration – Basic Documents. Conventions, Rules, Model Clauses and Guidelines.

The Permanent Court of Arbitration: International Arbitration and Dispute Resolution. Summaries of Awards, Settlement Agreements and Reports.

ANNEX

List of states parties to the 1899/1907 Conventions (as at 15 March 1999)

Argentina,* Australia, Austria, Belarus, Belgium, Bolivia, Brazil, Bulgaria,* Burkina Faso, Cambodia, Cameroon, Canada, Chile, China, Colombia, Croatia,* Cuba, Cyprus,† Czech Republic,† Denmark, Dominican Republic, Ecuador,* Egypt,† El Salvador, Eritrea,* Fiji,* Finland,† France, Germany, Greece,* Guatemala, Guyana,† Haiti, Honduras, Hungary, Iceland, India,* Iran,* Iraq, Israel,† Italy,* Japan, Jordan,† Kyrgyzstan, Laos, Lebanon, Libya,† Liechtenstein,† Luxembourg, Malta,† Mauritius,* Mexico, Netherlands, New Zealand,* Nicaragua, Nigeria,† Norway, Pakistan,* Panama, Paraguay, Peru,* Poland,† Portugal, Romania, Russia, Senegal, Singapore,† Slovak Republic,† Slovenia,* South Africa, Spain, Sri Lanka,* Sudan,† Suriname,† Swaziland,† Sweden, Switzerland, Thailand, Turkey,* Uganda,† Ukraine, United Kingdom, United States, Uruguay,* Venezuela,* Yugoslavia, Zaire, Zimbabwe.*

* Party only to the 1899 Hague Convention.
† Party only to the 1907 Hague Convention.

CHAPTER 3

International Tribunal for the Law of the Sea

INTRODUCTORY

Name and seat of the body

3.1 The International Tribunal for the Law of the Sea (ITLOS or 'the tribunal') is a permanent court intended to adjudicate disputes in accordance with the United Nations Convention on the Law of the Sea (UNCLOS).[1] It has its seat in the Free and Hanseatic City of Hamburg in the Federal Republic of Germany. The temporary premises of ITLOS are:

> International Tribunal for the Law of the Sea
> Wexstrasse 4, 20355
> Hamburg, Germany.

> Tel: 49 (40) 35607-0
> Fax: 49 (40) 35607-245
> email: itlos@itlos.hamburg.de
> website: http://www.un.org/Depts/los/

At the end of 1999 the Tribunal will move to its permanent premises situated in Hamburg at Nienstedten. The new postal address will be 380 Elbchausee, 22609 Hamburg, Germany.

1 United Nations Convention on the Law of the Sea, 10 December 1982, art 284, UN Doc A/CONF 62/122 (1982), 21 ILM 1261 (1982) ('UNCLOS').

Introductory description

3.2 ITLOS is an independent international judicial body, established by the 1982 United Nations Convention on the Law of the Sea. It forms an integral part of the regime established under Part XV of UNCLOS for the peaceful settlement of disputes concerning the interpretation or application of the Convention and other agreements related to its purposes. The tribunal is governed by its Statute (Annex VI of the Convention), Part XV and relevant provisions in Part XI section 5 of the Convention. The tribunal is open to states parties and, in specific circumstances, to other states, international organisations and entities other than states, including private persons and corporations.

Disputes arising under UNCLOS between states parties are subject to binding third-party settlement (with the exception of some categories of disputes). The states parties may select, upon ratification of UNCLOS or at any time thereafter, one or more dispute settlement mechanisms from a menu of four procedures enumerated in art 287 of UNCLOS – the 'choice of procedure' clause. The four alternatives are – ITLOS, the International Court of Justice, arbitration (under Annex VII of UNCLOS), or special arbitration (under Annex VIII of the Convention). In the event that two states have accepted the same procedure, it will apply in disputes between them. In the absence of agreement over the adjudication forum, the disputes may only be submitted to arbitration.

Additionally, ITLOS enjoys mandatory jurisdiction over all 130 states parties to UNCLOS in some specific causes of actions (disputes relating to activities in the sea-bed area; prompt release of detained vessels and crews; and requests for provisional measures, even when the dispute is submitted to arbitration, in certain circumstances), and may receive cases on the basis of international agreements other than UNCLOS.

The tribunal was established on 1 August 1996. The 21 judges of the tribunal took the oath of office on 18 October 1996. The first application instituting a case before ITLOS was received on 13 November 1997, seeking the prompt release of a vessel (the M/V *Saiga*) and its crew under art 292 of UNCLOS. The judgment of the tribunal was delivered on 4 December 1997.[1]

On 13 January 1998, the tribunal received a second case concerning a request for the prescription of provisional measures. On 11 March 1998 the tribunal gave its first order on provisional measures in that case.

The parties submitted the case on the merits involving a range of issues relating to coastal state rights and jurisdiction and to the freedoms of navigation. The judgment on the merits was delivered on 1 July 1999.[2]

1 *The M/V 'Saiga' (St Vincent and the Grenadines v Guinea)* judgment of 4 December 1997, available at <http://www.un.org/Depts/los/judg_1.htm>.
2 *The M/V 'Saiga' (No 2) (St Vincent and the Grenadines v Guinea)* judgment of 1 July 1999, available at <http://www.un.org/Depts/los/judg_t.htm>.

INSTITUTIONAL ASPECTS

Provisions of the Convention and other legal instruments governing the functions of the tribunal

3.3 The provisions of the legal instruments that govern the functions of ITLOS are:

(a) section 2 of Part XV of UNCLOS, which provides for the submission of disputes to compulsory procedures under Part XV upon the request of any party;

(b) section 5 of Part XI of UNCLOS, relating to disputes concerning the international seabed area and advisory opinions requested by the International Seabed Authority heard by the Seabed Disputes Chamber of the Tribunal (SBDC);

(c) Statute of the Tribunal,[1] contained in Annex VI to UNCLOS, which regulates the organisation of ITLOS, its competence and procedure and the SBDC (ITLOS Statute);

(d) Rules of the Tribunal,[2] which provide detailed rules of procedure (Rules of the Tribunal);

(e) Guidelines concerning the Preparation and Presentation of Cases before the Tribunal,[3] which provides potential parties with practical information concerning the preparation and presentation of their cases; and

(f) Resolution on the internal judicial practice of the Tribunal,[4] which outlines the procedures by which the tribunal deliberates and drafts its judgments.

ITLOS is to decide the cases before it in accordance with the substantive provisions of UNCLOS and other rules of international law not incompatible with the Convention.[5] If the parties agree, the tribunal can decide a case *ex aequo et bono*.[6] The SBDC, as well as applying the Convention and rules of international law, shall apply the rules, regulations and procedures of the International Seabed Authority and the terms of contracts concerning activities in the area in matters relating to those contracts.[7]

1   UNCLOS, Annex VI – Statute of the International Tribunal for the Law of the Sea, ('ITLOS Statute').
2   Rules of the Tribunal, Doc ITLOS/8 ('ITLOS Rules').
3   Guidelines concerning the preparation and presentation of cases before the Tribunal, Doc ITLOS/9.
4   Resolution on the Internal Judicial Practice of the Tribunal, Doc ITLOS/10.
5   UNCLOS, art 293(1); ITLOS Statute, art 23.
6   UNCLOS, art 293(2).
7   ITLOS Statute, art 38.

Organisation

Composition, appointment and qualifications

3.4   The tribunal is composed of 21 independent judges, elected by the states parties to UNCLOS from among persons enjoying the highest reputation for fairness and integrity and of recognised competence in the field of the law of the sea.[1] The representation of the principal legal systems of the world and equitable geographical distribution is to be assured, and no two judges may be nationals of the same State.[2] Judges will normally be elected for a nine-year term and may be re-elected; however, the terms of 14 judges elected at the first round election are shorter, in order to allow for staggered replacement of judges.[3] The tribunal elects a President (currently Judge Thomas A Mensah) and a Vice-President (currently Judge Rüdiger Wolfrum) for a three-year term.[4]

Every party to a dispute before ITLOS (or an ITLOS Chamber) is entitled to have a judge of its nationality on the bench. If there is no such judge, the concerned party may appoint a judge ad hoc (not necessarily of its nationality).[5] Judges ad hoc will participate in a case on equal footing to the other judges.[6]

No judge may participate in a case in which he or she was previously involved as a lawyer, member of another dispute settlement body, or in any other capacity.[7] The President may bring doubts pertaining to the previous involvement of a judge before the tribunal, which shall decide the issue by a majority of the other judges.[8] The President may act in this manner on his or her own initiative or following information communicated to him or her by a party to the case, in confidentiality.

Furthermore, if a judge ceases to fulfil the conditions for service, as required by the ITLOS Statute, the other judges may decide unanimously to remove him or her from office.[9]

1   ITLOS Statute, art 2(1). The current composition of the tribunal is:
      Joseph Akl (Lebanon), David Heywood Anderson (UK), Hugo Caminos (Argentina), Gudmundur Eiriksson (Iceland), Paul Bamela Engo (Cameroon), Anatoly Lazarevich Kolodkin (Russian Federation), Edward Arthur Laing (Belize), Vincente Marotta Rangel

(Brazil), Mohamed Mouldi Marsit (Tunisia), Thomas A Mensah (Ghana), Tafsir Malick Ndiaye (Senegal), L Dolliver M Nelson (Grenada), Choon-Ho Park (Korea), P Chandrasekhara Rao (India), Tullio Treves (Italy), Budislav Vukas (Croatia), Joseph Sinde Warioba (Tanzania) Rüdiger Wolfrum (Germany), Soji Yamamoto (Japan), Alexander Yankov (Bulgaria) and Lihai Zhao (China). On 24 May 1999 José Luis Jesus (Cape Verde) was elected to replace Judge Warioba.

2   ITLOS Statute, arts 2(2), 3(1).
3   ITLOS Statute, arts 4(4), 5(1). Seven of the first 21 judges will serve a three-year term, another seven judges a six-year term, and only seven judges will serve a full nine-year term.
4   ITLOS Statute art 12(1).
5   Ibid, art 17; ITLOS Rules, art 19(1).
6   ITLOS Rules, art 8(1).
7   ITLOS Statute, art 8(1).
8   Ibid, art 8(4); ITLOS Rules, art 18.
9   ITLOS Statute, art 9; ITLOS Rules, art 7.

Plenary/chambers

3.5 ITLOS normally hears cases in plenary (a quorum of 11 judges is required).[1] However, the tribunal may form special chambers, composed of three or more judges, for dealing with particular categories of disputes.[2] To date the tribunal has established a Chamber for Fisheries Disputes and a Chamber for Marine Environment Disputes. Furthermore, ITLOS annually forms a five-member chamber (including ex officio ITLOS President and Vice-President), which may hear and determine disputes by summary procedure ('Summary Procedure Chamber').[3]

The Seabed Disputes Chamber of the tribunal has exclusive and compulsory jurisdiction over disputes with respect to activities in the sea-bed area (in pursuance of Part XI of UNCLOS).[4] Its jurisdiction, powers and functions are provided in section 5 of Part XI of UNCLOS, section 4 of the ITLOS Statute and section B of Part II of the Rules of Tribunal. The SBDC consists of 11 judges, elected by the body of judges of ITLOS, who serve for three years and are eligible for re-election.[5] Their composition also reflects the principal legal systems and equitable geographical distribution. The members of the SBDC elect their President (currently Judge Joseph Akl).

At the request of all parties to any case, a special ad hoc chamber of ITLOS can be formed to deal with that particular dispute. The tribunal, with the approval of the parties, will determine the composition of such ad hoc chamber.[6] Such a request is to be submitted to the tribunal within two months from the date of initiation of proceedings. In addition, any party to an inter-state dispute before the SBDC may request the establishment of a three-judge ad hoc chamber of the SBDC.[7] The composition of the chamber is to be determined by the SBDC with the agreement of the parties. However, if they fail to agree, each party will nominate an SBDC judge and the third judge will be agreed upon or nominated by the President of the SBDC. In no case can an ad hoc SBDC chamber member be a national of one of the parties to the dispute (or be in its service). The request for an ad hoc SBDC chamber should be made within three months from the date of initiation of proceedings.[8]

1   ITLOS Statute, art 13(1),(3).
2   Ibid, art 15(1); ITLOS Rules, art 29. As far as possible, special chambers should be composed of judges having special expertise in the subject matter entrusted to the chamber.
3   ITLOS Statute, art 15(3); ITLOS Rules, art 28.
4   UNCLOS, art 186; ITLOS Statute, art 14.
5   ITLOS Statute, art 35; ITLOS Rules, art 23.

6   ITLOS Statute, art 15(2); ITLOS Rules, art 30.
7   UNCLOS, art 188(1)(b); ITLOS Statute, art 36.
8   ITLOS Rules, art 27(1).

Appellate structure

3.6   ITLOS has no appellate structure.

Scientific and technical experts

3.7   The tribunal may on its own initiative, or in accordance with a request made by a party to a case, select, in consultation with the parties, two or more scientific or technical experts.[1] The experts are to be chosen, preferably, from a list of experts maintained, in accordance with provision of Annex VIII to UNCLOS, by a variety of international organisations.[2] Experts should be independent and enjoy the highest reputation for fairness, competence and integrity.[3] A request by a party for appointment of experts is to be presented not later than at the closure of written proceedings, but in appropriate cases the tribunal may receive subsequent requests (in any case, before the end of the oral proceedings).[4] Once appointed, the experts will sit on the bench during the proceedings, but will not be able to vote. The same provision will apply mutatis mutandis to any chamber of ITLOS.[5]

In addition, if ITLOS considers it necessary, it can, after hearing the parties, arrange for an inquiry or an expert opinion.[6] In such case, the tribunal will issue an order defining the subject of inquiry or opinion; the number and method of appointment of suitable persons; and the procedure to be followed. The report or opinion will be communicated to the parties and they will be given the opportunity to comment upon it.[7]

The parties may also present expert testimony before the tribunal as part of the oral proceedings.[8] The parties, under the control of the President, and the judges may question expert witnesses.[9]

1   UNCLOS, art 289; ITLOS Rules, art 15.
2   UNCLOS, Annex VIII, art 2.
3   ITLOS Rules, art 15(3).
4   Ibid, art 15(1).
5   Ibid, art 15(4).
6   Ibid, art 82(1).
7   Ibid, art 82(2).
8   Ibid, art 78.
9   Ibid, art 80.

Registry

3.8   The tribunal elects its Registrar and Deputy Registrar for a renewable term of seven years from among candidates nominated by the judges (the current Registrar and Deputy Registrar are, respectively, Mr Gritakumar E Chitty and Mr Philippe Gautier).[1] The rest of the staff of the Registry is appointed by the tribunal on proposals submitted by the Registrar, or by the Registrar with the approval of the President.[2]

The Registrar is the chief executive officer of the tribunal. He or she is in charge of the Registry, which serves as the secretariat for the tribunal. In this capacity, the Registrar, inter alia, is the channel for all communications with parties; provides the range of substantive and procedural legal services;

executes budgetary, financial and treasury functions; records all relevant documents; arranges translation and interpretation services; and is responsible for the administration and financial management of ITLOS.[3]

1 ITLOS Statute, art 12(2); ITLOS Rules, arts 32(1), 33.
2 ITLOS Rules, art 35(1).
3 Ibid, art 36.

Jurisdiction and access to the tribunal

Ratione personae

3.9 The jurisdiction *ratione personae* of ITLOS encompasses the states parties to UNCLOS and other states and entities other than states in certain cases.[1] Any two states parties may ad hoc, or through general or special declarations of acceptance, to be made at any time under the 'choice of procedure' clause, submit any dispute concerning the interpretation or application of UNCLOS to ITLOS.[2]

In addition, ITLOS enjoys compulsory jurisdiction over all states parties to UNCLOS with respect to certain matters. In cases involving requests for prompt release of vessels and crews, ITLOS will exercise jurisdiction over any two states parties or entities authorised by a state party, if the parties to the dispute fail to agree upon an alternative forum and one of the parties submits the dispute to the tribunal.[3] An application for prompt release of a vessel can be made by the flag state of the detained vessel, or on its behalf. Upon the submission of a dispute, the SBDC, except in specific circumstances, exercises compulsory jurisdiction over sea-bed area related disputes between all states parties to UNCLOS.

ITLOS is also open to state and non-state entities, which are parties to agreements, other than UNCLOS (but related to the purposes of that Convention), which confer jurisdiction on the tribunal.[4] An agreement can explicitly provide for settlement of disputes arising under it before ITLOS;[5] or, if the agreement in question precedes UNCLOS, ITLOS will have jurisdiction in disputes over its interpretation or application, upon the consent of all parties to that agreement.[6]

1 ITLOS Statute, art 20(1).
2 UNCLOS, art 287(1),(4).
3 Ibid, art 292(1).
4 UNCLOS, art 288(2); ITLOS Statute, arts 20(2) and 21.
5 For example, UN Agreement for the Implementation of the Provisions of the UN Convention on the Law of the Sea of 10 December 1982 Relating to the Conservation and Management of Strad-dling Fish Stocks and Highly Migratory Fish Stocks, 1995, art 30, 5 December 1995, UN Doc A/CONF 164/37, reprinted in 34 ILM 1542 (1995); Agreement to Promote Compliance with International Conservation Measures by Vessels on the High Seas, 1993, art 9, 33 ILM 968 (1994).
6 ITLOS Statute, art 22.

SBDC

3.10 The jurisdiction ratione personae of the SBDC includes:
(a) disputes between states parties to UNCLOS;
(b) disputes between a state party and the International Sea-Bed Authority established to administer the sea-bed area;
(c) disputes between parties to a contract governing activities in the sea-bed area (states parties, the Authority, state enterprises, or natural or juridical persons sponsored by a state party);

(d) disputes between the Authority and prospective contractors (which are state enterprises or natural or juridical persons sponsored by a state party).[1] It should be noted that each party to a contractual dispute over the interpretation or application of a contract or plan of works may request that the dispute be referred to commercial arbitration.[2] However, such arbitral tribunal must refer to SBDC for a ruling on any question of interpretation of Part XI of UNCLOS (regulating the sea-bed area) and the Annexes relating to it.

1   UNCLOS, art 187.
2   Ibid, art 188(2).

Ratione materiae

3.11   The jurisdiction *ratione materiae* of ITLOS includes any dispute concerning the interpretation and application of UNCLOS which is submitted to it in accordance with the Convention.[1]

Although certain categories of disputes may be excluded from compulsory dispute settlement (and consequently from the jurisdiction of ITLOS),[2] such disputes may be submitted to ITLOS through the agreement of the parties to the dispute.[3] Furthermore, some of the disputes exempted from binding third-party settlement may be submitted to mandatory conciliation.[4]

As indicated above, ITLOS has compulsory jurisdiction over all states parties to UNCLOS in certain cases. Firstly, the tribunal has compulsory jurisdiction in certain circumstances with respect to the prompt release of a vessel and its crew. Where a vessel flying the flag of a state party has been detained by another state party and it is alleged that the detaining state has not complied with the provisions of UNCLOS for the prompt release of the vessel or its crew upon the posting of a reasonable bond or other financial security, the question of release from detention may be submitted to any court or tribunal agreed upon by the parties or, failing such agreement within 10 days from the time of detention, to a court or tribunal accepted by the detaining state under art 287 or to ITLOS.[5]

Secondly, the tribunal has compulsory jurisdiction in certain cases where a party wishes to request provisional measures. Pending the constitution of an arbitral tribunal to which a dispute is being submitted in accordance with UNCLOS, any court or tribunal agreed upon by the parties or, failing such agreement within two weeks from the date of the request for provisional measures, ITLOS may deal with the request for provisional measures.[6]

Moreover, ITLOS can exercise jurisdiction over disputes concerning the interpretation and application of international agreements, other than UNCLOS, which confer jurisdiction on ITLOS, if such agreements relate to the purposes of UNCLOS.[7]

1   UNCLOS, art 288(1); ITLOS Statute, art 21.
2   These include certain disputes over the exercise of sovereign rights or jurisdiction by coastal states, marine scientific research and fisheries disputes. In addition, states parties may exclude disputes over marine delimitation, military and law enforcement activities and Security Council measures from compulsory dispute settlement, by way of submitting a declaration to this effect.
3   UNCLOS, art 299.
4   Ibid, arts 297(2),(3), 298(1)(a). The procedure for compulsory conciliation is set out in UNCLOS, Annex V, section 2.
5   UNCLOS, art 292(1).
6   Ibid, art 290(5). Similar authorities were granted to the SBDC.
7   Ibid, art 288(2); ITLOS Statute, art 21.

SBDC

3.12 The SBDC has exclusive jurisdiction, which can be instituted by any party, over the following disputes pertaining to activities in the seabed area:

(1) inter-state disputes over the interpretation or application of Part XI of UNCLOS and related Annexes, subject to the possibility of the parties to a dispute submitting a dispute to a special chamber of ITLOS;[1]

(2) disputes between a state party and the Authority over acts or omissions of either party which are allegedly in contravention of Part XI of UNCLOS, related Annexes, or rules, regulations or procedures adopted by the Authority;[2]

(3) disputes between a state party and the Authority over acts of the Authority which are allegedly in excess of jurisdiction, or misuse of power;[3]

(4) disputes between parties to a contract over the interpretation or application of a contract or a plan of work, subject to the possibility of a dispute being submitted to commercial arbitration;[4]

(5) contractual disputes over acts or omissions of a party to a contract relating to activities in the sea-bed area and directed to the other party or directly affecting its legitimate interests;[5]

(6) disputes between the Authority and a prospective contractor over refusal of a contract or a legal issue arising during negotiation of the contract;[6]

(7) disputes over the liability of the Authority vis-à-vis the other party to a contract for any damage arising out of wrongful acts in the exercise of its powers and functions.[7]

1 UNCLOS, arts 187(a) and 188(1)(a).
2 Ibid, art 187(b)(i).
3 Ibid, art 187(b)(ii), 189.
4 Ibid, arts 187(c)(i) and 188(2).
5 Ibid, art 187(c)(ii).
6 Ibid, art 187(d).
7 Ibid, art 187(e); Annex III, art 22.

Ratione temporis

3.13 In general, there are no time limits for reference of disputes to ITLOS or the SBDC. There are, however, some temporal restrictions in relation to requests for prompt release of vessels and crews and provisional measures. A request for prompt release can be submitted by the flag state of the detained vessel to ITLOS only if the parties failed to agree on an alternative forum within ten days from the date of detention.[1] A request for provisional measures pending the constitution of an arbitral tribunal may be submitted to ITLOS only if the parties failed to agree on an alternative forum within two weeks from the date on which the requesting party notified the other party of the request.[2]

1 UNCLOS, art 292(1).
2 Ibid, art 290(5); ITLOS Rules, art 89(2).

Advisory jurisdiction

3.14 Under UNCLOS, the SBDC is authorised to render advisory opinions at the request of the Assembly or Council of the International Seabed Authority on legal questions arising within the scope of their activities.[1]

Opinions will be given as a matter of urgency.[2] All states parties to UNCLOS and international organisations who are likely to furnish information will be notified of the request and given time to prepare and submit a statement.[3] The chamber may hold oral proceedings and invite states and international organisations to participate in them. At the end of the proceedings the SBDC issues an opinion which will contain the following information:

(a) date of delivery of opinion;
(b) names of judges participating in the proceedings;
(c) question on which opinion was requested;
(d) summary of proceedings;
(e) statement of facts;
(f) reasons of law on which the opinion is based;
(g) reply to the question before the chamber;
(h) names of judges in majority and minority;
(i) statement as to the text of the opinion which is authoritative.[4]

Separate or dissenting opinions may be attached to the opinion of the chamber.

ITLOS may render advisory opinions on a legal question if an international agreement related to the purposes of UNCLOS specifically provides for the submission to ITLOS of such an opinion.[5] The procedure governing such a request for advisory opinion will be in accordance with the said agreement and the rules of procedure on SBDC advisory proceedings.[6]

1 UNCLOS, arts 159(10), 191.
2 Ibid, art 191; ITLOS Rules, art 132.
3 ITLOS Rules, art 133.
4 Ibid, art 135.
5 Ibid, art 138(1).
6 Ibid, art 138(2),(3).

PROCEDURAL ASPECTS

Languages

3.15 The official languages of ITLOS are English and French.[1] All pleadings ought to be submitted in one or both of the official languages.[2] A party may plead or introduce evidence in a non-official language, but in the case of written submissions or documents it must produce a certified translation into an official language, and in the case of oral pleadings and testimony it must make arrangements for interpretation.[3]

1 ITLOS Rules, art 43.
2 Ibid, art 64(1).
3 Ibid, arts 64(2),(3), 85.

Instituting proceedings

3.16 Disputes are submitted to the tribunal either by written application or by notification of a special agreement, addressed to the Registrar.[1] An application will indicate the following information:

(a) the identity of the claiming party;
(b) the identity of the party against which the claim is brought;
(c) the subject of the dispute;
(d) the legal grounds upon which the jurisdiction of the tribunal is based;
(e) the precise nature of the claim;

(f)   a brief statement of the facts and grounds on which the claim is based.[2]
If proceedings are initiated by way of special agreements, one or both of the parties will notify the Registrar accordingly and append to the notification a certified copy of the special agreement.[3] The notification must indicate the precise subject of the dispute and identify the parties to it, unless such information is apparent from the agreement. The Registrar is required to notify all states parties whenever proceedings are instituted.[4]

1   ITLOS Statute, art 24(1).
2   ITLOS Rules, art 54(1),(2).
3   Ibid, art 55.
4   ITLOS Statute, art 24(3).

SBDC cases involving non-state entities

3.17   In cases before the SBDC involving disputes which are not exclusively between states parties or between states parties and the International Seabed Authority, the application must also include details pertaining to the permanent residence, address or registered office of any natural or legal person; the identity of the state sponsoring the non-state party; address for service at the seat of the tribunal; the subject of the dispute and the legal grounds on which jurisdiction is said to be based; the precise nature of the claim, together with a statement of the facts and the legal grounds on which the claim is based; the decision or measure sought; and the evidence on which the application is founded.[1]

The Registrar then transmits a certified copy of the application to the respondent and transmits a copy of the application to the state sponsoring the activities of the non-state entity.[2] That state may join proceedings in cases involving natural and juridical persons of its own initiative or, following a request by the other state to the dispute, appear in the proceedings on behalf of that person.[3]

The respondent should lodge a defence within two months from the date of service of the application. A statement of defence must include the following information:

(a)   name of respondent (where respondent is a natural or juridical person, the permanent residence or address or registered office address);
(b)   address for service at seat of tribunal;
(c)   matter at issue between the parties and the facts and legal grounds on which the defence is based;
(d)   decision or measure sought by the respondent;
(e)   evidence on which defence is founded.[4]

Where proceedings are brought before the SBDC by notification of a special agreement, the notification should indicate the parties and any sponsoring state; the subject of the dispute; the precise nature of the claims of the parties; facts and legal arguments on which the claims are founded; decisions or measures sought by the parties; and the evidence on which the claims are founded.[5]

1   ITLOS Rules, art 117.
2   Ibid, arts 54(4), 118(1).
3   UNCLOS, art 190; ITLOS Rules, art 119. According to UNCLOS, a state may join proceedings involving a natural or juridical person sponsored by it. In cases where a private party is the claimant and a state a respondent, that state may require the sponsoring state to appear in the proceedings on behalf of the sponsored person. Failing such appearance, the

respondent state may arrange to be represented by a juridical person of its own nationality.
4   ITLOS Rules, art 118.
5   Ibid, art 120.

Financial assistance

3.18   At present, there is no mechanism for providing financial assistance for prospective parties to ITLOS cases.

Preliminary proceedings/objections

Preliminary proceedings

3.19   In disputes over issues which are exempt under article 297 of UNCLOS from the compulsory jurisdiction of ITLOS (or other alternative binding dispute settlement procedures),[1] ITLOS may decide by way of preliminary proceedings to take no further action in the case.[2] For this to occur, the tribunal must determine, acting either on a request by a party, or *proprio motu* (within two months from the initiation of proceedings),[3] that the claim on hand constitutes an abuse of legal process or is prima facie unfounded. A request by a party for preliminary dismissal is to be presented within a time limit fixed by the President.[4] The respondent is notified, upon service of the application to initiate proceedings, of the date until which it is entitled to request preliminary proceedings. The request must be made in writing and allege the two following grounds for dismissal:
(1) the application is made in respect to an article 297 dispute;
(2) the claim is an abuse of legal process or prima facie unfounded.[5]
Upon the receipt of such a request, or acting on its own initiative, ITLOS (or the President) will fix a time period (not exceeding 60 days) for the parties to lodge written observations and submissions.[6] Further proceedings, in which the tribunal may request parties to present their legal and factual arguments and introduce evidence, will normally be oral.[7] At the end of the preliminary proceedings, throughout which the proceedings on the merits will be suspended, ITLOS will issue a judgment.[8]
It should be noted that institution of preliminary proceedings does not affect the right of any party to a dispute to raise preliminary objections.[9]

1   See supra, para 3.11.
2   UNCLOS, art 294; ITLOS Rules, art 96(1).
3   ITLOS Rules, art 96(3).
4   Ibid, art 96(2).
5   Ibid, art 96(4).
6   Ibid, art 96(5).
7   Ibid, art 96(6),(7).
8   Ibid, art 96(5),(8).
9   UNCLOS, art 294(3).

Preliminary objections

3.20   Preliminary objections to the jurisdiction of the tribunal or to the admissibility of the application, or other objections of a preliminary nature, are to be made in writing within 90 days from the date of institution of proceedings.[1] The request should set out the facts and legal arguments on which it is based and include the submissions of the requesting party.[2] Upon receipt of a preliminary objection, the proceedings on the merits shall be suspended and the tribunal (or President) will fix a time limit (not exceeding 60 days) for the other party to present its observations and submissions on the request.[3] The requesting party may be allocated additional time (not exceeding 60 days) to reply. Further proceedings, in which the tribunal may request parties to present their legal and factual arguments and introduce evidence, will normally be oral.[4] The tribunal will give its decision in the form of a judgment, by which it shall uphold the objection or reject it or declare that it does not possess an exclusively preliminary character.[5] The parties may agree that an objection be heard and determined in the merits stage.[6]

1 ITLOS Rules, art 97(1).
2 Ibid, art 97(2).
3 Ibid, art 97(3).
4 Ibid, art 97(4),(5).
5 Ibid, art 97(6).
6 Ibid, art 97(7).

Provisional measures

3.21 ITLOS and its SBDC have the power to prescribe provisional measures in order to preserve the respective rights of the parties to a case or prevent serious harm to the marine environment pending the final outcome of the claim.[1] The tribunal (or chamber) must, however, be satisfied that it has prima facie jurisdiction over the dispute and that the measures requested are appropriate under the circumstances. As indicated above, ITLOS and the SBDC may in certain circumstances also have jurisdiction to issue provisional measures in cases that are to be referred to arbitration, pending the constitution of an arbitral tribunal.[2] In such cases, the ITLOS must also be satisfied that the arbitral tribunal which will be constituted shall have prima facie jurisdiction over the dispute and that the urgency of the situation justifies an order at this stage.[3]

A request for provisional measures in a case adjudicated before ITLOS or SBDC can be submitted at any time during the course of the proceedings.[4] Requests for provisional measures, pending the constitution of an arbitral tribunal for the merits of the case, can be presented to ITLOS (or SBDC) if the parties fail to agree within two weeks from the date of the request for provisional measures to submit the request to another court or tribunal.[5] However, the parties may agree to present such a request to ITLOS (or SBDC) before or after the said two-week period.

The request for provisional measures is to be made in writing and indicate:
(a) the measures requested;
(b) the reasons for the request;
(c) the possible consequences for the preservation of the respective rights of the parties or the prevention of serious harm to the marine environment, if the request will not be granted.[6]

Requests made pending the constitution of an arbitral tribunal, must also specify:
(d) legal grounds for jurisdiction of the arbitral tribunal which is to be constituted;
(e) the urgency of the situation.[7]

Proceedings on the request for preliminary measures will take precedence over all other procedures before the tribunal (with the possible exception of requests for prompt release of vessels and crews),[8] and hearings will be set for the earliest possible date before the tribunal, SBDC or Chamber for Summary Procedure.[9]

The tribunal may accept or reject the request, or prescribe measures different in whole or in part from those requested.[10] Rejection of a request for provisional measures will not prevent the party which made it from making a new request in the same case based on new facts.[11] Furthermore, a party can also request the modification or revocation of provisional measures.[12] The parties to a dispute must comply promptly with any provisional measures prescribed by ITLOS or one of its chambers.[13]

1 UNCLOS, art 290(1); ITLOS Statute, art 25(1); ITLOS Rules, art 89(1).
2 UNCLOS, art 290(5).
3 UNCLOS, art 290(5); ITLOS Rules, art 89(4).
4 ITLOS Rules, art 89(1).
5 UNCLOS, art 290(5); ITLOS Rules, art 89(2).
6 ITLOS Rules, art 89(3).
7 Ibid, art 89(4).
8 Ibid, arts 90(1), 112(1). Article 112(1) states that if the tribunal has to deal with both an application for the release of a vessel or crew and a request for the prescription of provisional measures, it shall take the necessary measures to ensure that both the application and the request are dealt with without delay.
9 ITLOS Rules, arts 90(2), 91, 115.
10 Ibid, art 89(5).
11 Ibid, art 92.
12 UNCLOS, art 290(2),(3); ITLOS Rules, art 93.
13 UNCLOS, art 290(6).

Prompt release of vessels and crews

3.22 Where the authorities of a state party to UNCLOS have detained a vessel flying the flag of another state party, and it is alleged that the detaining state has not complied with the provisions of UNCLOS for the prompt release of the vessel and crew upon the posting of a reasonable bond or other financial security, the question of release from detention may be submitted to ITLOS.[1] The application for prompt release can only be made to it by way of agreement of the parties, or if within 10 days from the date of detention the parties have failed to agree on an alternative venue.[2] An application for release can be made only by, or on behalf of, the flag-state of the vessel.[3]

The application is to include the following information:
(1) statement of facts on which the application is based, including:
    (a) time and place of detention of the vessel and the present location of the vessel and crew (if known);
    (b) relevant information on the vessel and crew including, where appropriate, name, flag, port or place of registration of vessel, tonnage, cargo capacity, data relevant to the determination of its value, the name and address of the vessel owner and operator and particulars of the crew;
    (c) amount, nature and terms of bond or other financial security imposed by the detaining state and the extent to which these conditions have been met;
    (d) further information relevant to the determination of the amount of a reasonable bond or other financial security and to any other issue in the proceedings;
(2) statement of legal grounds on which the application is based;
(3) supporting documents.[4]
An application submitted on behalf of a state must also include an

authorisation from the flag state, and certification that a copy of the application has been delivered to that state.[5]

The application will be forwarded by the Registrar to the detaining state, which is entitled to submit a statement in reply (with supporting documents) not later than 24 hours before the date set for hearings.[6] Although the tribunal is entitled to request supplementary statements, the rest of the proceedings are to be, as a rule, oral.[7] The application is to be heard before the plenary tribunal or, upon request of the parties, before the Chamber of Summary Procedure.[8]

Upon receiving an application for prompt release, the tribunal will deal without delay with the question of release exclusively (without prejudice to other aspects of the dispute).[9] It will give priority to applications for release of vessels or crews over all other proceedings before the tribunal (with the possible exception of requests for provisional measures), and hearings will be set for the earliest date possible (in no case more than 10 days after the application was filed).[10] Normally, each party will be given one day of hearings to present its evidence and arguments.

ITLOS shall issue its decision on the application in the form of a judgment, not later than ten days from the last day of hearings.[11] If the tribunal finds that the allegation made by the applicant that the detaining state has not complied with a provision of UNCLOS for the prompt release of the vessel or the crew upon the posting of a reasonable bond or other financial security is well founded, it shall determine the amount, nature and form of the bond or financial security to be posted for the release of the vessel or the crew.[12] Upon the posting of the bond or other financial security determined by the tribunal, the authorities of the detaining State are to comply promptly with the decision of ITLOS and release the vessel and/or its crew.[13]

1 UNCLOS, art 292(1).
2 Ibid.
3 Ibid, art 292(2); ITLOS Rules, art 110(1).
4 ITLOS Rules, art 111.
5 Ibid, art 110(2),(3). The authorisation should contain information on the competent authorising state authority; the name and address of the person authorised; the office designated to receive notice of an application and the most expedient method of delivery of notices thereto; and any further clarifications, modifications or withdrawal of authorisation.
6 ITLOS Rules, art 111(4).
7 Ibid, art 111(5),(6).
8 Ibid, art 112(2).
9 UNCLOS, art 292(3).
10 ITLOS Rules, art 112(1),(3).
11 Ibid, art 112(4).
12 Ibid, art 113(2).
13 UNCLOS, art 292(4).

PROCEEDINGS

3.23 The proceedings consist of two parts – written and oral proceedings. The procedure in contentious cases before ITLOS and the SBDC is, subject to the provisions of UNCLOS, ITLOS Statute and ITLOS Rules relating specifically to the SBDC, generally similar.[1]

1 ITLOS Rules, art 115.

Written proceedings

3.24 In a case begun by means of an application, the pleadings will consist
of a Memorial by the applicant and a Counter-Memorial by the respondent.[1]
The Memorial is to contain a statement of the relevant facts, a statement of
law and the submissions of the applicant.[2] A Counter-Memorial is to contain
an admission or denial of the facts stated in the memorial; any additional
facts, if necessary; observations concerning the statement of law in the
memorial; a statement of law in answer thereto; and the submissions of the
respondent.[3] The parties must append to their submissions supporting
documents.[4] All submissions must be filed in a number of copies required by
the registrar; however, further copies may be requested at a later date.[5] A
certified copy of every written submission and any document annexed
thereto is to be communicated by the Registrar to the other party.[6]

The tribunal may authorise or direct the parties to file a reply (on behalf of
the applicant) and a rejoinder (on behalf of the respondent), if the parties
agree to such procedure, or if the tribunal decides that such additional
submissions are necessary. The tribunal can reach this conclusion on the basis
of a request by one of the parties, or on its own initiative.[7] No further
documents may be submitted to the tribunal after the closure of the written
proceedings, except with the consent of the other party or by authorisation of
the tribunal.[8]

The number and order of filing of pleadings and the time limits for every
submission are to be determined by the tribunal, after the President has
ascertained the view of the parties.[9] In any case, the time limit for each stage
of pleading will not exceed six months unless extended by the tribunal (but
only on account of adequate justifications held valid by the tribunal).[10]

In cases brought to ITLOS on the basis of a special agreement between
the parties to the dispute, the number and order of the pleadings are to be
governed by the provisions of the agreement, unless the tribunal, after
ascertaining the views of the parties, decides otherwise.[11] If the terms for
filing written submissions were not agreed upon, both parties shall file a
Memorial and Counter-Memorial within the same time limit and replies
and rejoinder will not be admissible, unless the tribunal finds them
necessary.[12]

A respondent party may present a Counter-Claim, provided that it is
directly connected to the principal claim and falls under the jurisdiction of the
tribunal.[13] It should be presented in the Counter-Memorial, as part of the
submissions of the respondent.[14]

1 ITLOS Rules, art 60(1).
2 Ibid, art 62(1).
3 Ibid, art 62(2).
4 Ibid, arts 44(2), 63.
5 Ibid, art 65(1).
6 Ibid, art 66.
7 Ibid, art 60(2).
8 Ibid, art 71(1),(2).
9 ITLOS Statute, art 27; ITLOS Rules, art 59(1).
10 ITLOS Rules, art 59.
11 Ibid, art 61(1).
12 Ibid, art 61(2),(3).
13 Ibid, art 98(1).
14 Ibid, art 98(2).

Request for ruling presented to the SBDC by a commercial arbitral tribunal

3.25 Where a question of interpretation of Part XI of UNCLOS or the Annexes related thereto arises before a commercial arbitration tribunal established in pursuance of article 188(2) of UNCLOS, the question will be referred for ruling by the SBDC. In this case, upon receipt of the question the President will fix time limits (not exceeding three months) for the parties to the proceedings and the states parties to submit written observations on the question.[1]

1 ITLOS Rules, art 123. In addition, each of the parties may request oral hearings, provided that the request is presented within one month from the expiration of the time period fixed for presentation of written submissions: ibid, art 123(3).

Oral arguments

3.26 After the closure of the written proceedings and the initial deliberations (exchange of views of ITLOS judges over the written proceedings), the tribunal fixes a date for the opening of the oral proceedings (within six months of the closure of the written proceedings).[1] The date of the oral hearings will be determined with regard to the need to proceed without undue delay, the urgency of the case, the workload of the tribunal and the views expressed by the parties.[2] The tribunal also determines, after ascertaining the views of the parties, the order in which the parties will be heard; the number of representatives to be heard on behalf of each party; the method of introducing evidence and examination of witnesses and experts; and whether arguments are to be made before or after introduction of evidence.[3]

The oral statements of the parties are to be as succinct as possible, within the limits necessary for adequate presentation of the contentions, and should focus on issues which are still in dispute between the parties after the written pleadings.[4] During the proceedings, the tribunal can indicate any points or issues that it would like the parties to address, or that it considers have been sufficiently argued already.[5] In addition, the tribunal may put questions and ask for explanations from the representatives of the parties;[6] and it may call upon the parties to produce evidence or explanations necessary for the elucidation of any aspect of the matters in issue.[7] The tribunal can also seek on its own initiative other information for this purpose, and arrange for the attendance of witnesses or experts.[8]

During the oral proceedings, the parties may call any witnesses or experts, provided that they appeared on a list communicated to the Registrar in good time before the start of the oral hearings.[9] Further witnesses or experts can also be called only with the consent of the other party, or if the tribunal so authorises. Witnesses and experts can be examined by the representatives of the parties, under the control of the President, and can also be subject to questioning by the judges.[10]

At the conclusion of the last statement made by each of the parties, a representative of that party will read the final submission of the party. A copy of this text must be filed with the tribunal and transmitted to the other party.[11]

Hearings are to be public unless the tribunal decides otherwise or the parties demand that the public be not admitted.[12]

1 ITLOS Rules, arts 68, 69(1).
2 Ibid, art 69(2).

3 Ibid, art 73.
4 Ibid, art 75(1).
5 Ibid, art 76(1).
6 Ibid, art 76(2).
7 Ibid, art 77(1).
8 Ibid, art 77.
9 Ibid, arts 72, 78(1). The list should include the name, nationality, description and place of
   residence of each witness or expert and the points on which their evidence will be directed.
10 ITLOS Rules, art 80.
11 Ibid, art 75(2).
12 ITLOS Statute, art 26(2); ITLOS Rules, art 74.

Third-party intervention

3.27   Under article 31 of the ITLOS Statute, a state party may submit a request
to the tribunal to intervene in a case, if it considers that it has an interest of a
legal nature, which may be affected by the decision of the tribunal in the
dispute.[1] There is no requirement for an intervening state to have accepted the
jurisdiction of ITLOS under the 'choice of procedure' clause (article 287 of
UNCLOS).[2]

An application for permission to intervene shall be filed within 30 days of
the Counter-Memorial being made available in accordance with ITLOS Rules
to the intervening state (following a request on that state's behalf to receive a
copy of that document).[3] In exceptional circumstances subsequent
applications may also be admitted. The application to intervene must state
the following information:

(1)   name and address of an agent;
(2)   details of the case to which the application relates;
(3)   the interest of a legal nature which the state party applying to intervene
      considers may be affected by the tribunal's decision;
(4)   the precise object of the intervention;
(5)   supporting documents and a list of those documents.[4]

An additional basis for intervention is found under article 32 of the ITLOS
Statute in relation to cases that raise a general question of treaty interpretation or application. States parties to UNCLOS or parties to any other
international agreement which confers jurisdiction on ITLOS may join
proceedings in which the interpretation and application of the instrument to
which they are parties is adjudicated, and be bound by the interpretation
given to it by ITLOS.[5] The Registrar notifies all states parties to UNCLOS, or
all parties to any other agreement, of any proceedings in which a question of
the interpretation or application of the relevant instrument has arisen.[6] Any
party wishing to intervene is to file a declaration to that effect within 30 days
from the date of the Counter-Memorial becoming available to it (although,
again, in exceptional circumstances a time extension may be allowed).[7] The
declaration must state the following information:

(1)   name and address of an agent;
(2)   details of the case to which the declaration relates;
(3)   the particular provisions of UNCLOS or another international agreement
      the interpretation or application of which the declaring party considers to
      be in question;
(4)   the interpretation or application of those provisions for which the
      declaring party contends;
(5)   supporting documents and a list of those documents.[8]

Certified copies of application or declaration of intent to intervene (under either article 31 or 32 of the ITLOS Statute) are to be communicated to the parties to the case and they will be invited to furnish their written observations on the request within a time-limit fixed by the tribunal (or President).[9] The tribunal then decides whether the request to intervene should be granted (or declared admissible).[10] However, if within the time limit fixed by the tribunal an objection is filed to the attempted intervention, the tribunal will hear the party seeking to intervene and the parties to the case before deciding.[11]

If the request to intervene is granted, the intervening party will receive copies of pleadings and documents and will be entitled to participate in the written and oral pleadings.[12]

1 ITLOS Statute, art 31(1).
2 ITLOS Rules, art 99(3).
3 Ibid, arts 67(1), 99(1).
4 Ibid, art 99(2),(4).
5 ITLOS Statute, art 32.
6 Ibid, art 32(1),(2).
7 ITLOS Rules, arts 67(1), 100(1).
8 Ibid, art 100(2).
9 Ibid, art 101(1).
10 Ibid, art 102(1).
11 Ibid, art 102(2).
12 Ibid, arts 103, 104.

Multiple proceedings

3.28 The Statute of ITLOS also envisages disputes between more than two parties. Thus, for example, where several parties share the same legal interest, they will be considered as a single party for the purpose of appointment of an ad hoc judge.[1] Furthermore, even in cases filed separately, the tribunal may order the joining of proceedings.[2]

1 ITLOS Statute, art 17(5).
2 ITLOS Rules, art 47.

Amicus curiae briefs

3.29 Any international organisation (ie intergovernmental organisation) which is not a party to a case before the tribunal may submit a memorial to the Registry with information relevant to the case before ITLOS, before the end of written pleadings.[1] The tribunal may also, on its own initiative, request information or further clarifications on information already supplied by the international organisation, by way of written and/or oral submissions. ITLOS will invite an international organisation to submit written observations and/or participate in oral proceedings in all cases where the construction of the organisation's constituent instrument, or an international convention adopted under its auspices, is in question before the tribunal.

1 ITLOS Rules, art 84.

Representation of parties

3.30 Parties to disputes before ITLOS are to be represented by agents and may have the assistance of counsel or advocates before the tribunal.[1]

1 ITLOS Rules, art 53.

Decision

3.31   The final decision of ITLOS on the dispute before it will be in the form of a judgment. The judgment will contain the following details:
(a)   date on which it is read;
(b)   names of judges participating in it;
(c)   names of parties;
(d)   names of representatives of the parties (ie agents, counsel, and advocates);
(e)   names of experts appointed under art 289 of UNCLOS;
(f)   summary of the proceedings;
(g)   submissions of parties;
(h)   statement of the facts;
(i)   reasons of law on which the decision is based;
(j)   operative provisions of the judgment;
(k)   decision on costs;
(l)   the number and names of the judges constituting the majority and those constituting the minority, on each operative provision;
(m) statement as to the text of the judgment which is authoritative.[1]
All questions are decided by a majority of the judges,[2] and separate or dissenting opinions may be appended to the judgment.[3] The judgment shall be read at a public sitting of the tribunal and becomes binding on the parties on the day of the reading.[4]

The decision of the tribunal is final and is to be complied with by all the parties to the dispute. However, it has binding force only between the parties to the case and with respect to the dispute to which it relates.[5]

1   ITLOS Statute, art 30(1),(2); ITLOS Rules, art 125(1).
2   ITLOS Statute, art 29(1).
3   Ibid, art 30(3), ITLOS Rules, art 125(2).
4   ITLOS Rules, art 124(2).
5   UNCLOS, art 296; ITLOS Statute, art 33(1),(2).

Interpretation and revision of judgment

3.32   In the event of dispute as to the meaning or scope of a judgment, any party to the case may make a request for its interpretation.[1] The request may be submitted by a unilateral application, or through agreement of the parties. In any case, the precise point (or points) in dispute should be indicated.[2] In cases brought by application, the tribunal will allow the other party to file its observations within a time limit fixed by the tribunal (or President).[3] In all cases, ITLOS may request the parties to present further written or oral explanations.[4]

A request for revision of a judgment can be made only when it is based upon the discovery of a fact of such a nature as to be a decisive factor, which was unknown to the tribunal and to the party requesting a revision when the judgment was given; and provided that such ignorance was not due to negligence.[5] The request is to be presented within six months from the discovery of the new fact, and in no case after ten years from the date of judgment. It will include all particulars necessary to show that conditions for revision have been met, and will have attached to it supporting documents.[6] The tribunal will fix a time limit for the other party to submit observations on the admissibility of the request; and may afford the parties additional opportunity to present their views on the question of admissibility.[7] If the tribunal finds that the request is admissible, it will fix time limits for such further proceedings on the merits of the application as, after ascertaining the views of the parties, it considers necessary.[8]

The decision on the request for interpretation or revision will be given in the form of a judgment, normally by the chamber or plenary tribunal which rendered the original judgment.[9]

1 ITLOS Statute, art 33(3); ITLOS Rules, art 126(1).
2 ITLOS Rules, art 126(2).
3 Ibid, art 126(3).
4 Ibid, art 126(4).
5 Ibid, art 127(1).
6 Ibid, art 128(1).
7 Ibid, art 128(2),(3).
8 Ibid, art 128(5).
9 Ibid, art 129.

Appeal

3.33 The decision of the tribunal is final and not subject to appeal.[1]

1 UNCLOS, art 296(1); ITLOS Statute, art 33(1).

Costs

3.34 The expenses of the tribunal are borne by the states parties to UNCLOS and by the International Sea-Bed Authority.[1] However, when an entity other than a state party or the International Seabed Authority is a party to a case submitted to the tribunal, the tribunal will fix the amount which that party is to contribute towards the expenses of the tribunal.[2]

As to the legal costs and other expenses of the parties, each party will bear its own costs, unless otherwise decided by the tribunal.[3]

1 ITLOS Statute, art 19(1).
2 Ibid, art 19(2).
3 Ibid, art 34.

Execution of decision, recognition and enforcement

3.35 Judgments of ITLOS are binding upon the parties and must be complied with.[1] However, the Convention and other instruments do not explicitly provide for an enforcement mechanism. On the other hand, decisions of the SBDC are to be enforceable in the territories of the states parties in the same manner as judgments or orders of the highest court of that state party.[2]

1 UNCLOS, art 296(1); ITLOS Statute, art 33(1).
2 ITLOS Statute, art 39.

REFERENCE

Sources of previous case law, including case reports

Copies of the judgments and orders of the tribunal can be obtained from the United Nations website and from the Registry. Arrangements for the publication of the case law of the tribunal are being made at present.

Selected bibliography

Official publications

Basic Texts/Textes de base: *International Tribunal for the Law of the Sea* Kluwer (1998).

The Law of the Sea: Official Texts of the United Nations Convention on the Law of the Sea of 10 December 1982 and of the Agreement relating to the Implementation of Part XI of the United Nations Convention on the Law of the Sea of 10 December 1982 (United Nations, New York, 1997).

Report of the Preparatory Commission under Paragraph 10 of Resolution I Containing Recommendations for Submission to the Meeting of States Parties to be Convened in Accordance with Annex VI, art 4, of the Convention Regarding Practical Arrangements for the Establishment of the International Tribunal for the Law of the Sea, Volumes I to IV (United Nations, document LOS/PCN/152, 1995).

Press releases of the Tribunal, available on the web site and from the Registry.

Books

A O Adede *The System for Settlement of Disputes under the UNCLOS* (1987).

John Graham Merrills *International Dispute Settlement* 170, 3rd edn (1998).

Myron H Nordquist (ed) *United Nations Convention on the Law of the Sea, 1982: a Commentary* (1995).

Articles

Joseph Akl 'The Sea-Bed Disputes Chamber of the International Tribunal for the Law of the Sea' (1997) 37 Indian Journal of International Law 435.

David H Anderson 'Investigation, Detention and Release of Foreign Vessels and Crews under the UN Convention on the Law of the Sea' (1996) 11 International Journal for Marine and Coastal Law 165.

Alan E Boyle 'Settlement of Disputes relating to the Law of the Sea and the Environment in Kalliopi Koufa (ed) *International Justice* – XXVI Thesaurus Acroasium 295 (1997).

Gudmundur Eiriksson 'The Role of the International Tribunal for the Law of the Sea in the Peaceful Settlement of Disputes' (1997) 37 Indian Journal of International Law 347.

Rainer Lagoni 'The Prompt Release of Vessels and Crews before the International Tribunal for the Law of the Sea' (1996) 11 International Journal for Marine and Coastal Law 147.

Edward A Laing 'Automation of an International Judicial Organ: A Preliminary Analysis' (1997) 37 Indian Journal of International Law 452.

Jersey Makarczyk 'Contribution to the Problem of the Settlement of Disputes Concerning the Exploitation of Seabed Resources' in Reno-Jean Dupuy (ed) *The Settlement of Disputes on the New Natural Resources* 53 at 56–57 (1983).

General bodies

Thomas A Mensah 'The Place of the International Tribunal for the Law of the Sea in the International System for the Peaceful Settlement of Disputes' (1997) 37 Indian Journal of International Law 466.

Thomas A Mensah 'United Nations Activities – Law of the Sea – The International Tribunal and the Protection and Preservation of the Marine Environment' (1998) 28 Environmental Policy and Law 216.

L D M Nelson 'The International Tribunal for the Law of the Sea: Some Issues' (1997) 37 Indian Journal of International Law 388.

John E Noyes 'The Third Party Dispute Settlement Provisions of the 1982 United Nations Convention on the Law of the Sea: Implications for States Parties and for Nonparties' in Myron H Nordquist and John Norton Moore (eds) *Entry into force of the Law of the Sea Convention* 213 (1995).

Shigeru Oda 'Dispute Settlement Prospects in the Law of the Sea' (1995) 44 ICLQ 863.

Bernard H Oxman 'International Decisions – The M/V "Saiga" – First judgment by International Tribunal for the Law of the Sea, applying new procedure for prompt release on bond of detained vessel and crew' (1998) 92 American Journal of International Law 273.

Bernhard H Oxman 'Observations on Vessels Release under the United Nations Convention on the Law of the Sea' (1996) 11 International Journal for Marine and Coastal Law 201.

Shabtai Rosenne 'Establishing the International Tribunal for the Law of the Sea' (1995) 89 American Journal of International Law 806.

Louis B Sohn 'The Importance of the Peaceful Settlement of Disputes Provisions of the United Nations Convention on the Law of the Sea' in Myron H Nordquist and John Norton Moore (eds) *Entry into force of the Law of the Sea Convention* 265 (1995).

Tullio Treves 'The Jurisdiction of the International Tribunal for the Law of the Sea' (1997) 37 Indian Journal of International Law 396.

Budislav Vukas 'The International Tribunal for the Law of the Sea: Some Features of the New International Judicial Institution' (1997) 37 Indian Journal of International Law 372.

Rüdiger Wolfrum 'Provision al Measures of the International Tribunal for the Law of the Sea' (1997) 37 Indian Journal of International Law 420.

Alexander Yankov 'The International Tribunal for the Law of the Sea: Its Place within the Dispute Settlement System of the UN Law of the Sea Convention' (1997) 37 Indian Journal of International Law 356.

ANNEX

Quick reference list of parties to the Convention (130)

Algeria, Angola, Antigua and Barbuda, Argentina,* Australia, Austria,* Bahamas, Bahrain, Barbados, Belgium,* Belize, Benin, Bolivia, Bosnia and Herzegovina, Botswana, Brazil, Brunei Darussalam, Bulgaria, Cameroon,

Cape Verde,* Chile,* China, Comoros, Cook Islands, Costa Rica, Côte d'Ivoire, Croatia, Cuba, Cyprus, Czech Republic, Democratic Republic of the Congo, Djibouti, Dominica, Egypt, Equatorial Guinea, European Community, Fiji, Finland,* France, Gabon, Gambia, Georgia, Germany,* Ghana, Greece,* Grenada, Guatemala, Guinea, Guinea-Bissau, Guyana, Haiti, Honduras, Iceland, India, Indonesia, Iraq, Ireland, Italy,* Jamaica, Japan, Jordan, Kenya, Kuwait, Lao People's Democratic Republic, Lebanon, the former Yugoslav Republic of Macedonia, Malaysia, Mali, Malta, Marshall Islands, Mauritania, Mauritius, Mexico, Micronesia (Federated States of), Monaco, Mongolia, Mozambique, Myanmar, Namibia, Nauru, Nepal, Netherlands, New Zealand, Nigeria, Norway, Oman,* Pakistan, Palau, Panama, Papua New Guinea, Paraguay, Philippines, Poland, Portugal,* Republic of Korea, Romania, Russian Federation, Saint Kitts and Nevis, Saint Lucia, Saint Vincent and the Grenadines, Samoa, Sao Tome and Principe, Saudi Arabia, Senegal, Seychelles, Sierra Leone, Singapore, Slovakia, Slovenia, Solomon Islands, Somalia, South Africa, Spain, Sri Lanka, Sudan, Suriname, Sweden, Togo, Tonga, Trinidad and Tobago, Tunisia, Uganda, United Kingdom of Great Britain and Northern Ireland, United Republic of Tanzania,* Uruguay,* Viet Nam, Yemen, Yugoslavia, Zambia, Zimbabwe.

* Parties that have accepted the compulsory jurisdiction of ITLOS under the 'Choice of Procedure' clause.

CHAPTER 4

Court of Conciliation and Arbitration within the Organisation for Security and Co-operation in Europe (OSCE)

GENERAL INFORMATION

4.1   The Organisation for Security and Co-operation in Europe (OSCE)[1] was established in 1995 as a permanent institutional framework for political co-operation between 55 states in Europe and North America. It replaced the Conference on Security and Co-operation in Europe (CSCE), which consisted primarily of periodic meetings of high-level state representatives that had been taking place since 1973. The principal organs of the OSCE are the Council of Ministers for Foreign Affairs, the Committee of Senior Officials, the Parliamentary Assembly, the biennial Review Conference (or Summit) and a permanent Secretariat.

An important task assumed by the CSCE/OSCE has been the promotion of peaceful resolution of inter-state disputes.[2] In this context, in 1992 the CSCE Council of Ministers adopted the Convention on Conciliation and Arbitration within the CSCE ('the Convention'),[3] which established the Court of Conciliation and Arbitration ('the court').[4] The Convention entered into force in 1994 and has been ratified by 27 OSCE member states.

The court is not a standing judicial body, but rather a permanent roster of conciliators and arbitrators appointed by the states parties to the Convention. Every state appoints two conciliators and one arbitrator (and, in addition, one alternate arbitrator) to serve as members of the court for renewable periods of six years.[5] Five of the members of the court are elected by the plenary court to serve on the court's Bureau, which has certain supervisory powers on the conduct of conciliation and arbitration proceedings.[6] Proceedings before the court are governed by the Convention and the Rules of the Court.[7] According to the latter, the official languages of the court are English, French, German, Italian, Russian and Spanish.[8] The administrative needs of the court are fulfilled by the Registry.

1   Although this body has been included in the section of the manual on 'General bodies' it should be noted that participation in the Convention establishing the Court on Conciliation and Arbitration (see below) is limited to OSCE member states.
2   Final Act of the Conference on Security and Co-operation in Europe, 1 August 1975, principle V (1975) 14 ILM 1292.
3   Convention on Conciliation and Arbitration within the CSCE/OSCE, 15 December 1992, (1993) 32 ILM 557 ('Convention on Conciliation and Arbitration').
4   Convention on Conciliation and Arbitration, art 1.
5   Ibid, arts 3, 4. All appointees must be nationals of OSCE states and at least one of the conciliators must be a national of the appointing state. The members of the court must have recognised competence in international law (or international relations – in the cases of conciliators) or in the settlement of disputes.
6   Convention on Conciliation and Arbitration, art 7. The Bureau comprises the court's President, Vice-President and three members of the court.

7 Rules of the Court of Conciliation and Arbitration within the OSCE, 1 February 1997 ('Rules of Court').
8 Rules of Court, art 3.

CONCILIATION

4.2 Any dispute that arises between the states parties to the Convention, which the parties are unable to settle by way of negotiation within a reasonable period of time, may be referred to the court for conciliation by any party, acting unilaterally, or by agreement between all parties to the dispute.[1] Conciliation may also be initiated by way of agreement between states parties to the Convention and other OSCE participating states not parties to it.[2]

Each party to a case is to appoint one conciliator, normally from the court's list,[3] and the Bureau will appoint three additional conciliators after consultation with the parties.[4] The conciliation commission will determine its own procedure after consultation with the parties and with the approval of the Bureau.[5] Proceedings before the commission will generally be confidential.

The conciliation proceedings aim at assisting the parties in finding a settlement in accordance with international law and their OSCE commitments.[6] If the commission fails to facilitate an agreement, it will prepare a report containing a statement of facts and proposals for the settlement of the dispute.[7] The parties are expected to notify the commission, within 30 days from the issuance of the report, whether they accept the proposed settlement.[8] They may also agree in advance to accept the proposals of the commission as binding.[9] In any case, the commission will notify the OSCE Council (through the Committee of Senior Officials) of the outcome of the case, and will forward its report to it.[10]

1 Convention on Conciliation and Arbitration, art 18; Rules of Court, art 15(1).
2 Convention on Conciliation and Arbitration, art 20(2); Rules of Court, art 15(2).
3 If a party to the case is an OSCE member state, which is party to the dispute but not party to the Convention, it may appoint any qualified national of an OSCE state to serve as conciliator (including non-members of the court).
4 Convention on Conciliation and Arbitration, art 21(5); Rules of Court, art 16.
5 Convention on Conciliation and Arbitration, art 23(1); Rules of Court, art 19.
6 Convention on Conciliation and Arbitration, art 24.
7 Ibid, art 25(1),(2); Rules of Court, art 21(1),(2).
8 Convention on Conciliation and Arbitration, art 25(3); Rules of Court, art 21(3).
9 Rules of Court, art 21(3).
10 Convention on Conciliation and Arbitration, art 25(1),(5).

ARBITRATION

4.3 Arbitration before the court may be initiated by an agreement between any two or more OSCE participating states (at least one of which must be a party to the Convention).[1] In addition, states parties to the Convention may accept, by way of a declaration based on an optional clause of the Convention, the compulsory jurisdiction of the court over all disputes or over all disputes except those relating to certain specified matters (such as territorial and national defence issues).[2] A declaration thus made under the optional clause may be relied upon by other states that have made a similar declaration. However, unilateral applications for arbitration based on optional clause declarations may only be submitted after the case has been first submitted to conciliation, and not before 30 days have passed from the date of transmission of the conciliation commission's report to the OSCE Council.[3] So far, only four states have made declarations accepting the compulsory arbitral jurisdiction of the court.

The arbitral tribunal which will be constituted to adjudicate a given dispute shall include the arbitrators appointed to the court by the parties to the dispute (or, other nationals of OSCE states in the case of states which are not parties to the Convention) and one or more members of the court appointed by the Bureau.[4] Each arbitral tribunal thus constituted shall adopt its rules of procedure after consulting with the parties and seeking the approval of the Bureau.[5] In any event, the proceedings are to consist of written and oral hearings and will normally be held in camera.[6] At its conclusion, the tribunal will render a reasoned award, which will be final and binding upon the parties. The award is to decide the dispute in accordance with international law,[7] but the parties may authorise the arbitral tribunal to decide *ex aequo et bono*.[8] Awards will be published by the Registrar.[9]

To date, no cases have been referred to the court for either conciliation or arbitration.

1 Convention on Conciliation and Arbitration, art 26(1); Rules of Court, art 23(1).
2 Convention on Conciliation and Arbitration, art 26(2). The issues that can be excluded from the compulsory jurisdiction of the court are disputes concerning the territorial integrity of states, national defence, sovereignty over land territory or competing claims of jurisdiction over other areas.
3 Convention on Conciliation and Arbitration, art 26(3).
4 Ibid, art 28; Rules of Court, art 24.
5 Rules of Court, art 27(1).
6 Convention on Conciliation and Arbitration, art 29(1),(6); Rules of Court, art 27(6).
7 Convention on Conciliation and Arbitration, arts 30, 31(1),(3); Rules of Court, art 34.
8 Convention on Conciliation and Arbitration, art 30; Rules of Court, art 22.
9 Convention on Conciliation and Arbitration, art 32.

THE VALLETTA PROCEDURE

4.4 Independently of the court, the CSCE in 1991 established a distinct procedure for providing assistance to participating states in settling disputes which may arise between them ('the Valletta Procedure').[1] Unlike the Convention, the Valletta Procedure is applicable ipso facto to all of the 55 participating states of the OSCE. Although this procedure can in principle apply to any dispute between OSCE participating states, a state may object to its invocation in certain specified classes of disputes (disputes over territory, jurisdiction over other areas, national defence).[2]

In the event of a dispute arising between OSCE participating states, any of them may bring the matter before the Committee of Senior Officials.[3] If no negotiated settlement is reached within a reasonable period of time, each party may request the establishment of an OSCE Dispute Settlement Mechanism.[4] The Mechanism shall be composed of one or more persons, not being nationals or residents of the parties to the dispute, selected by the latter through agreement, normally from a permanent roster of candidates maintained by the OSCE Conflict Prevention Centre ('CPC') (each OSCE state may nominate up to four persons to the roster). If the parties are unable to agree on the composition of the Mechanism, the Director of the Secretariat of the CPC will appoint seven members of the roster to serve on the Mechanism.

Each of the parties may reject up to three of the Director's nominees, so that, in the end, the dispute may go before a single person.[5]

The Mechanism is designed to assist the parties in identifying a suitable dispute settlement procedure and may issue its comments or advice in this regard.[6] It is to conduct proceedings in an informal and flexible manner, according to methods of work devised by it.[7] If no agreement on the merits of the dispute or on a dispute settlement procedure emerges, any party may notify the Mechanism, the other party and the Committee of Senior Officials accordingly.[8] Any party may then request the Mechanism, within three months of the date of notification of failure to reach a settlement or agreement on procedure, to provide general or specific comments or advice on the substance of the dispute.[9] The parties may also agree that the Mechanism will serve as a fact-finding or expert commission or accept the reports of the Mechanism as binding upon them.[10]

As an alternative to the Mechanism, the parties to a dispute may agree to refer the case to conciliation, outside both the Valletta Procedure and the 1992 Convention. In that case, a conciliation commission will be established from the Valletta register.[11] The Council of Ministers or the Committee of Senior Officials may also direct the parties to establish a commission, even without their consent. This power may be exercised by the Council and the Committee whenever the parties to the dispute have been unable to settle it within a reasonable period of time,[12] with the exception of disputes over territory, jurisdiction over other areas, or national defence.[13] The commission will conduct its proceedings in accordance with the Provisions for a CSCE/OSCE Conciliation Commission, adopted by the CSCE/OSCE Council, and rules of procedure to be decided by the commission after consulting with the parties.[14] The administrative needs of the commission will be taken care of by the Director of the Conflict Prevention Centre of the OSCE.[15]

The commission shall facilitate an amicable settlement of the case and may recommend possible terms for its settlement, which the parties may accept or reject within time limits fixed by the commission.[16] Furthermore, the parties may agree, ad hoc or by a general declaration filed with the OSCE Secretariat, to accept the recommendations of the commission as binding, on condition that the other party to the dispute has made a similar pledge.[17]

To date, the Valletta Procedure and the conciliation procedures have not been utilised.

1 Provisions for a CSCE Procedure for Peaceful Settlement of Disputes, Report of Valletta, 8 February 1991, (1991) 30 ILM 390 ('Valletta Procedure').
2 Valletta Procedure, sec XII.
3 Ibid, sec II.
4 Ibid, sec IV.
5 Ibid, sec V.
6 Ibid, sec VII–VIII.
7 Ibid, sec VI(1).
8 Ibid, sec IX.
9 Ibid, sec XI.
10 Ibid, sec XIII.
11 Provisions for a CSCE/OSCE Conciliation Commission, 15 December 1992, sec V, CSCE/3-C/Dec.1, Annex III, 32 ILM 568 ('Provisions for Conciliation'). Each party to the dispute is to appoint one conciliator, and the third conciliator is elected by agreement, or appointed by the Secretary-General of the PCA.
12 Provisions for Directed Conciliation, 15 December 1992, para 1, CSCE/3-C/Dec.1, Annex IV, 32 ILM 570, E ('Provisions for Directed Conciliation').

General bodies

13 Provisions for Directed Conciliation, para 5(c).
14 Provisions for Conciliation, sec VI(1).
15 Provisions for Conciliation, sec XVII.
16 Ibid, sec IX–XI.
17 Ibid, sec XIV.

CONTACT INFORMATION

4.5 The Secretariat of the OSCE Court of Conciliation and Arbitration is located at:

> OSCE Court of Conciliation and Arbitration
> Villa Rive-Belle
> 266 Route de Lausanne
> 1292 Chambesy, Geneva
> Switzerland
>
> Tel: 41 22 758 00 25
> Fax: 41 22 758 25 10
> website: http://www.osceprag.cz/inst/court/

The Secretariat of the OSCE is located at:

> OSCE
> Kärntnerring 5–7, 4th floor
> 1010 Vienna
> Austria
>
> Tel: 43 1 514 36 0
> Fax: 43 1 514 36 96
> email: webmaster@osceprag.cz
> website: http://www.osceprag.cz/inst/secret/

REFERENCE

Annual Reports from 1993 to 1998 can be found on the OSCE web-site.

Selected bibliography

Official publications

Decisions are published annually by OSCE and a Handbook (1996) is also available from OSCE.

Articles

O Racic 'Conciliation and arbitration: from the Hague Conventions to the Convention on Conciliation and Arbitration within the OSCE' (1996) Yugoslavenska Revija za meunarodno Pravo.

R Szafarz 'OSCE procedures for peaceful settlement of international disputes' Polish Yearbook of International Law (1995–1996).

ANNEX

List of OSCE member states

Albania, Andorra, Armenia, Austria, Azerbaïjan, Belarus, Belgium, Bosnia and Herzegovina, Bulgaria, Canada, Croatia, Cyprus, Czech Republic, Denmark, Estonia, Finland, France, Georgia, Germany, Greece, Holy See, Hungary, Iceland, Ireland, Italy, Kazakstan, Kyrgyzstan, Latvia, Liechtenstein, Lithuania, Luxembourg, former Yugoslav Republic of Macedonia, Malta, Moldova, Monaco, Netherlands, Norway, Poland, Portugal, Romania, Russia, San Marino, Slovakia, Slovenia, Spain, Sweden, Switzerland, Tajikistan, Turkey, Turkmenistan, Ukraine, United Kingdom, United States of America, Uzbekistan, Yugoslavia.[1]

1   Suspended from participation since 8 July 1992.

List of states parties to the Convention on Conciliation and Arbitration

Albania, Germany, Austria, Cyprus, Croatia, Denmark,* Finland,* France, Greece,* Hungary, Italy, Latvia, Liechtenstein, Lithuania, former Yugoslav Republic of Macedonia, Moldova, Monaco, Norway, Poland, Romania, San Marino, Slovenia, Sweden,* Switzerland, Tajikistan, Ukraine, Uzbekistan.

*   States that have made declarations accepting the compulsory arbitral jurisdiction of the court.

Trade, commercial and investment protection dispute settlement bodies and rules

INTRODUCTION

This Part of the manual is concerned with three procedures for the settlement of disputes arising out of international trade rules and international commercial and investment activities. Special arrangements within regional bodies for the resolution of these types of disputes are dealt with in the following Part.

The first mechanism to be addressed is the Dispute Settlement System of the World Trade Organisation (WTO). The WTO System provides for the settlement of disputes between states, arising out of their obligations under the international trade rules contained in the WTO agreements, including the General Agreement on Tariffs and Trade (GATT) 1994. The system was adopted as part of the conclusions of the Uruguay Round in 1993, and represents a move towards more formal dispute settlement than the panel system which had previously existed within the international trade regime.

A significant innovation in the 1994 Dispute Settlement Understanding was the establishment of a formal appeal system with the WTO, through the establishment of a standing Appellate Body. In addition, the new system provides that reports of the disputes settlement panels and Appellate Body will be adopted (and hence legally binding) unless there is a consensus *against* adoption. Previously, consensus was required *for* the adoption of a dispute settlement panel report, so that a losing party could effectively block adoption of the report.

The new system has seen a significant increase in the number of disputes submitted for settlement. The coverage of the system is increasing, as 134 states and the European Union are now WTO Members, and a number of other states are in the process of becoming members. Since its establishment in 1994, there have been nearly 170 cases initiated under the WTO dispute settlement procedure, and some 26 of these have been the subject of appeal. There is, therefore, a growing body of WTO panel and Appellate Body jurisprudence. While it is beyond the present scope of this manual to go into detail into the content of Appellate Body decisions, it should be noted that beyond the substantive issues with which it has been faced, the Appellate Body has made a number of rulings of procedural importance, ranging from the right of private lawyers to attend proceedings of the Appellate Body to the right of non-state actors to file amicus curiae briefs.

Despite its sophistication, and the implications of its decisions for the private sector and civil society, the WTO remains a forum solely for the resolution of disputes between WTO Members, ie states and customs territories such as the

European Union, arising out of their rights and obligations under the WTO agreements. The WTO does not provide for the settlement of disputes between states and private individuals, nor does it provide an effective opportunity for participation or intervention in dispute settlement by non-members of the WTO, such as private companies, individuals or non-governmental organisations.[1]

By way of contrast to the WTO, the International Centre for the Settlement of Investment Disputes (ICSID), established by the 1965 Convention on the Settlement of Investment Disputes (ICSID Convention), provides direct recourse to arbitration for private investors involved in disputes with foreign states parties to the ICSID Convention arising out of investment agreements. ICSID, which is part of the World Bank Group, is part of a process aimed at depoliticising investment disputes between states and foreign investors. In order to utilise ICSID procedures, generally speaking one party to the dispute must be a state party to the ICSID Convention and the other must be a private individual from another state party. Parties to a dispute must consent to submission of the dispute to ICSID arbitration. States may give such consent either ad hoc, by way of a *compromis*, or in advance, eg through a clause in a bilateral investment treaty, in a foreign investment law or in an investment agreement with the investor in question. In addition to its regular procedures, ICSID provides an Additional Facility, which allows for the resolution of disputes in which the parties do not fulfil normal ICSID requirements. The Additional Facility is available, inter alia, for the resolution of disputes under the investment provisions of the North American Free Trade Agreement (see Chapter 13) and the 1994 Energy Charter Treaty.

The third mechanism addressed in this Part, the International Court of Arbitration of the International Chamber of Commerce (ICC) provides another direct mechanism for the settlement of disputes between states and private entities in relation to commercial and investment disputes. Unlike the WTO and ICSID arrangements the ICC approach is not based upon intergovernmental agreement, but rather is a private system of international adjudication (in which governments nevertheless frequently are parties). The jurisdiction of the ICC Court of Arbitration depends upon the prior or ad hoc agreement of the parties to the dispute. Since its establishment in 1923 it has dealt with more then 10,000 cases. In 1998 alone, 466 new requests for arbitration were filed.

Although they vary in their procedures, parties and subject-matter, the mechanisms in this Part illustrate a growing tendency towards providing direct legal, rule-based mechanisms for the resolution of disputes arising in the fields of international trade and investment. By providing access to private parties, as well as states, ICSID and the ICC Court of Arbitration facilitate the avoidance of recourse to diplomatic protection (and hence interstate disputes) where investment-related disputes arise involving states and private investors. It is notable that all three of these mechanisms have seen a significant increase in their case-load in recent years.

---

1   See para 5.24.

CHAPTER 5

Dispute Settlement System of the World Trade Organisation

INTRODUCTORY

Name and seat of the body

5.1   The 1994 Agreement Establishing the WTO includes an Annex on dispute settlement referred to as the 'Understanding on Rules and Procedures Governing the Settlement of Disputes'. The Dispute Settlement Understanding (DSU) of the World Trade Organisation (WTO) is intended to prevent and resolve disputes arising under the WTO Charter and related instruments. The system established under the DSU comprises a Dispute Settlement Body (DSB), ad hoc panels and a standing Appellate Body (hereinafter AB). The bodies are located in Geneva, Switzerland. The contact details are:

> World Trade Organisation
> Centre William Rappard
> 154 rue de Lausanne
> CH1211 Genève 21
> Switzerland
>
> Tel: 41 22 739 51 11
> Fax: 41 22 731 42 06
> website: http://www.wto.org/

Introductory description

5.2   The WTO is an international organisation invested with powers and functions designed to promote and regulate international trade at the global level. It was established in 1995 as a new international organisation to replace the less structured system of the General Agreement on Tariffs and Trade (hereinafter GATT), which had provided, since 1948, a negotiating framework for several rounds of multilateral trade agreements. By June 1999, 135 states or 'separate customs territories' (including the European Communities) were WTO Members.

The DSB is a political body comprising representatives from all members of the WTO.[1] It is charged with administering the dispute settlement process: it supervises the process of consultations between disputing members; establishes adjudicative panels on request of a party to a dispute; adopts panel or Appellate Body recommendations relating to the resolution of the dispute; maintains surveillance over the implementation of the recommendation; and may authorise trade sanctions in the face of non-compliance with adopted panel or Appellate Body recommendations.

In the event of a dispute between members of the WTO over their respective obligations under the WTO Agreement, a party may request the other to enter into consultations and should notify the DSB of this request.[2] If such consultations fail, each party may propose that other dispute settlement procedures (good offices, conciliation or mediation) be employed between the parties, with the possible assistance of the Director-General (head of the WTO Secretariat).[3] Alternatively, it may request the DSB to establish an ad hoc panel.[4] Panels conduct hearings on the dispute referred to them, and issue a report on the merits of the case. The recommendations of a panel are binding only after they have been adopted by the DSB (however, adoption is automatic, unless there is a consensus against *adoption* in the DSB).[5]

The panel report may be appealed, on legal grounds, before a standing seven-member Appellate Body. The appeal is heard before a three-member division of the Appellate Body, which may uphold, modify or reverse the legal findings of the panel. The report of the Appellate Body is then to be adopted by the DSB and granted binding force, unless the DSB decides otherwise by consensus.

Since the WTO was established on 1 January 1995, 175 requests for consultation have been initiated before the DSB, involving 134 distinct disputes.[6] This compares to 196 cases brought before the parallel GATT procedures in its 45 years of existence. Of these 175 WTO requests, 44 were presented by developing states. In 21 cases in relation to which a panel was established, the DSB has adopted a panel or subsequent Appellate Body report: five more reports are pending adoption; 18 cases are pending before panels at present and some three more cases are on appeal before the Appellate Body. In some of the other cases, no motion to establish a panel has yet been filed. It should be emphasised that the WTO system of dispute resolution encourages settlement agreements, even after the initiation of legal proceedings. Hence, in 37 of the 134 disputes brought before the DSB, a settlement was reached and the cases were discontinued.

The DSU specifically preserves the right of the parties to a dispute to agree to resolve their differences by way of arbitration within the WTO as an alternative means of dispute settlement.[7]

1 In fact, the DSB is the alter ego of the General Council of the WTO. Agreement Establishing the World Trade Organisation, 15 April 1994, art IV(3), (1994) 33 ILM 1263 ('WTO Agreement').
2 Understanding on Rules and Procedures Governing the Settlement of Disputes, art 4 (Annex 2 to the Agreement Establishing the World Trade Organisation) ('DSU').
3 DSU, art 5.
4 Ibid, arts 4(7), 5(4).
5 Definition of consensus, WTO Charter Article IX.1 note 1.
6 As at 19 April 1999. For up-to-date information see the Overview of the State of Play of WTO disputes on the WTO web-site at http://www/wto.org/wto/dispute/bulletin.htm.
7 DSU, art 25.

INSTITUTIONAL ASPECTS

Governing texts

5.3 The procedures of the WTO dispute settlement system are governed by the following texts:

- Articles III–IV, Agreement Establishing the World Trade Organisation, 1994 (establishing the DSB and vesting it with dispute resolution powers) ('WTO Agreement');[1]

- Understanding on Rules and Procedures Governing the Settlement of Disputes (Annex 2 to the WTO Agreement) (outlining the procedure of the WTO dispute settlement system) ('DSU');
- Working Procedures (Appendix 3 to the DSU) (specifying the procedure for Panel proceedings) ('Panel Working Procedures');
- Working Procedures for Appellate Review (as amended on 28 February 1997) (specifying the procedure of the Appellate Body) ('Appellate Body Working Procedures');[2]
- Rules of Conduct for the Understanding on Rules and Procedures Governing the Settlement of Disputes (adopted on 11 December 1996) (addressing the need to preserve the integrity, impartiality and confidentiality of the various persons involved in the dispute settlement mechanism – including panel and Appellate Body members, experts and Secretariat staff) ('Rules of Conduct').[3]

In addition, where WTO disputes involve questions governed by specific trade agreements that provide for special or additional rules of procedure, these special or additional rules will prevail.[4]

1 Agreement Establishing the World Trade Organisation, 15 April 1994, art IV(3), (1994) 33 ILM 1263 ('WTO Agreement').
2 Working Procedures for Appellate Review (as amended), WTO Doc WT/AB/WP/3, 28 February 1997 ('AB Working Procedures').
3 Rules of Conduct for the Understanding on Rules and Procedures Governing the Settlement of Disputes, WTO Doc WT/DSB/RC/1, 11 December 1996, ('Rules of Conduct').
4 DSU, art 1(2). The list of specific or additional rules of procedure is enumerated in Appendix 2 to the DSU.

Substantive law

5.4   The substantive law to be applied by the panel or Appellate Body is to be found in the agreements listed in Appendix 1 of the DSU (the 'covered agreements'), including the WTO Agreement, Multilateral Trade Agreements and Plurilateral Trade Agreements.

Article 3(2) of the DSU provides that the dispute settlement system of the WTO is a central element in providing security and predictability to the multilateral trading system. It goes on to state that the members recognise that the dispute settlement system serves to preserve the rights and obligations of members under the covered agreements and to clarify the existing provisions of those agreements in accordance with customary rules of interpretation of international law. Finally, art 3(2) provides that the recommendations and rulings of the DSB cannot add to or diminish the rights and obligations provided in the covered agreements.[1]

In its first case the Appellate Body confirmed that the trade rules are not to be read in clinical isolation from public international law.[2]

1 DSU, art 3(2); WTO Charter, art IX.2.
2 Case AB-1996-1, US – Standards for Reformulated and Conventional Gasoline, Report of the Appellate Body, 29 April 1996, at p 18, WTO Doc WT/DS2/9.

Organisation

Composition, appointment and disqualification of a panel

5.5   Panels are normally composed of three persons, although the parties to a dispute can request the enlargement of a panel so as to include five persons.[1] The Secretariat of the WTO proposes the nomination of panel members, normally on the basis of a roster of prospective panel members maintained by the Secretariat, which is composed of names put forward by the members and approved by the DSB. The parties are expected to agree to this composition, unless they have compelling reasons for objecting.[2] No national of the disputing parties may serve as a panel member, unless the parties agree otherwise.[3]

If the parties cannot agree on the composition of the panel within 20 days from the date of the DSB's decision to establish a panel, any party may request the Director-General (head of the WTO Secretariat) to appoint a panel, after consulting with the parties and with the Chairmen of the DSB and of the relevant WTO Council.[4]

1 DSU, art 8(5). However, the request must be made within ten days from the establishment of the panel.
2 DSU, art 8(6).
3 Ibid, art 8(3).
4 Ibid, art 8(7).

DISQUALIFICATION OF A PANEL MEMBER

5.6 If a party to the dispute possesses information indicating a breach of the obligations of independence, impartiality or confidentiality on the part of a panel member, or has knowledge of direct or indirect conflicts of interest which may impair the integrity, impartiality or confidentiality of the dispute settlement process, it must submit this information promptly to the Chairman of the DSB.[1] The Chairman then transmits the information to the concerned panellists, and subsequently to all other parties. If the panellist does not withdraw, the Chair of the DSB may, after consulting with other WTO officials, the parties and the concerned panellist, revoke the appointment of the panellist.[2]

1 Rules of Conduct, r VIII.
2 Ibid, r VIII(6)–(8).

Plenary/chambers

5.7 As noted above, panels comprise three (or exceptionally five) persons. The Appellate Body, on the other hand, hears cases in divisions of three members.[1]

1 DSU, art 17(1).

Appellate structure[1]

5.8 The Appellate Body serves as a permanent forum for appeals over *legal* findings of the ad hoc panels. The AB is composed of seven members elected by the DSB for a once-renewable four-year period. The members of the AB are all independent experts with recognised authority in international trade law and their composition should be representative of the membership in the WTO. The AB sits in divisions of three persons selected for each case on the basis of rotation.[2] The AB is headed by a Chairman, elected by the members of the AB for a one-year term. In addition, each division is headed by a Presiding Member.[3] The original members of the AB took their oath of office on 3 December 1995.[4]

Although the AB hears appeals in divisions of three members, the Working Procedures for Appellate Review contain provisions for collegiality. AB members are to convene on a regular basis to discuss matters of policy, practice and procedure, and all AB members are to receive all documents filed in any appeal. To ensure consistency and coherence in decision-making, the division responsible for deciding each appeal is to exchange views with other AB members before finalising the appellate report for circulation to WTO Members.[5]

Disqualification of an AB member is executed in a similar manner to that of a panel member. However, the request should be presented not to the Chair of the DSB, but to the AB itself, which decides whether to accept or reject the request.[6]

1 See also paras 5.27 and 5.28, below dealing with revision of a judgment and appeals.
2 DSU, art 17.
3 AB Working Procedures, rr 5, 7.
4 The composition of the Appellate Body is: James Bacchus (US); Christopher Beeby (New Zealand); Claus-Dieter Ehlermann (Germany); Said El-Naggar (Egypt); Florentino Feliciano (Philippines); Julio Lacarte Muro – Chairman (Uruguay); and Mitsuo Matsushita (Japan).
5 AB Working Procedures, r 4. See also r 11, paras 2 and 3.
6 Rules of Conduct, r VIII(14)–(17); AB Working Procedures, r 10(5).

Scientific and technical experts

5.9 A WTO panel may seek information and technical advice from any individual or body it deems appropriate, provided that the member state with jurisdiction over that person or body has been previously notified.[1] In addition, the panel may appoint an expert review group, composed of independent professional experts, and instruct it to prepare an advisory report.[2] The rules governing the establishment and operation of an expert review group are set out in a separate Appendix to the DSU.[3]

1 DSU, art 13(1).
2 Ibid, art 13(2).
3 Ibid, Appendix 4.

Registry

5.10 All administrative services are provided to the panels by the WTO Secretariat.[1] Thus, all written submissions to the panels are served through the Secretariat.[2] In addition, the Secretariat provides panels with assistance on the legal, historical and procedural aspects of each case. These services are normally provided by the Legal Affairs Division, but may also involve other specialised divisions. The Secretariat also caters for the logistical needs of the DSB and the Appellate Body. The Appellate Body is assisted by its own Secretariat, which provides administrative and legal support.

When involved in panel or AB-related activities, staff of the WTO and AB Secretariats are subject to rules of conduct similar to those applicable to panel and AB members.[3]

1 DSU, art 27.
2 Ibid, art 12(6). A similar rule applies in regard to submissions to the AB: AB Working Procedures, art 18.
3 Rules of Conduct, r IV(1).

Jurisdiction and access to the system

Jurisdiction of panels

RATIONE PERSONAE

5.11 The compulsory jurisdiction of the WTO panel system encompasses all members of the WTO, which include at present 135 states or separate customs territories. Non-members (including private entities, individuals and non-contracting states) do not have a right of standing before the WTO dispute settlement body. Any state or separate custom territory possessing full autonomy in the conduct of its external commercial relations and over other matters covered by the WTO agreements, can seek to join the WTO,[1] and will thereby subject itself to the compulsory jurisdiction of the dispute settlement system. The AB has decided that members do not have to show a 'legal interest' in order to prosecute a particular claim.[2]

1 WTO Agreement, art XII.
2 AB Report, EC Bananas III, paras 132–138.

RATIONE MATERIAE

5.12 The subject-matter jurisdiction of the WTO dispute settlement mechanism includes all disputes between members arising under the so-called 'covered agreements', ie the WTO Agreement, the multilateral agreements on trade in goods (including the GATT 1994), the General Agreement on Trade in Services (GATS),[1] the Agreement on Trade-Related Aspects of Intellectual Property Rights (TRIPS)[2] and the DSU, as enumerated in Appendix I to the DSU.[3]

The substantive conditions for initiation of proceedings are governed by Article XXIII of the GATT 1994 or corresponding provisions of the other Agreements. A WTO member may present under Article XXIII of the GATT 1994 a claim, based on evidence that:
(1) a benefit accruing to it under a relevant agreement to which it is a party has been nullified or impaired,[4] or
(2) that the attainment of the object of that agreement is being impeded.
In either case, it must be demonstrated that the unwarranted result was caused by an act or omission on the part of the respondent member constituting one of the following:
(a) failure to meet obligations under the relevant agreement;
(b) application of a measure incompatible with the relevant agreement; or
(c) any other situation.[5]
In cases where there is an infringement of the obligations assumed under a covered agreement, the action is considered prima facie to constitute a case of nullification or impairment. This means that there is normally a presumption that a breach of the rules has an adverse effect on other members parties to that covered agreement, and in such cases it shall be up to the member against whom the complaint has been made to rebut the charge.[6]

1 WTO Agreement, Annex 1B.
2 Ibid, Annex 1C.
3 DSU, Appendix 1. The other side-agreements enumerated are the Agreement on Trade in Goods, Agreement on Trade in Civil Aircraft, Agreement on Government Procurement, International Dairy Arrangement, Arrangement on Bovine Meat. The applicability of the Understanding to all these agreements (except the Agreement on Trade in Goods) is dependent upon a decision taken by the signatory parties to each agreement.

4   DSU, art 3.3. In practice, all WTO/GATT complaints, to date, purported nullification or impairment of benefits.
5   It should be noted that with regard to intellectual property related disputes the dispute settlement system shall have, until the year 2000, jurisdiction over violation claims only (ie failure to meet obligations): Agreement on Trade-Related Aspects of Intellectual Property Rights, art 64, (Annex 1C to the WTO Agreement).
6   DSU, art 3(8).

RATIONE TEMPORIS

5.13   The WTO dispute settlement mechanism only has jurisdiction over proceedings initiated at the DSB after the entry into force of the WTO Agreement (1 January 1995).[1] Disputes addressed by the former GATT system are excluded from the scope of the WTO system.

Any Party to a dispute may seek the establishment of a panel only after the expiration of a period of 60 days from the day it has submitted a request for consultation to the other party, if consultations fail to resolve the dispute.[2] However, the parties may agree to submit the request for a panel before the expiration of 60 days, or to extend that period in order to engage in good offices, conciliation or mediation.[3]

In urgent cases the establishment of a panel may be sought within 20 days.[4]

1   DSU, art 3(11).
2   Ibid, art 4(3). The parties must enter into consultations within 30 days; and consultations should be concluded within another 30 days: ibid, art 4(7).
3   DSU, art 5.
4   Ibid, art 4(8). The parties must enter into consultations within 10 days; and consultations should be concluded within 20 days.

Advisory jurisdiction

5.14   The panels only have contentious jurisdiction and cannot issue advisory opinions.

As to the nature of the contentious jurisdiction, panels only have recommendatory powers. Their reports are non-binding until adopted by the DSB. However, under the DSU the DSB must adopt panel reports (or Appellate Body reports, in case of an appeal), unless it decides by consensus not to adopt the report.[1] Such a consensus will be difficult to achieve, since the agreement of the parties to the dispute in question will be needed. In practical terms, panel reports will result in corresponding recommendations and rulings of the DSB binding upon the parties to the dispute subject to any appeal. Nevertheless, adopted panel reports are part of the GATT acquis and are often considered by subsequent panels, creating legitimate expectations amongst members.[2]

Finally, it may be noted that only the Ministerial Conference has the authority to render authoritative interpretations of the WTO and related agreements of general application.[3]

1   DSU, art 16(3),(4).
2   AB Report, Japan – Taxes on Alcoholic Beverages, p 14.
3   WTO Agreement, art IX(2).

Appellate jurisdiction

5.15   The Appellate Body may hear an appeal of panel reports on points of law submitted by a party to panel proceedings (as opposed to a third party, or any other member of the WTO).[1] The appeal must be limited to issues of law covered by the panel's report and legal interpretations developed by the panel.[2] The AB has, however, looked into legal issues which the panel did not address in its report.[3]

The submission of an appeal must precede the decision of the DSB to adopt the report. That decision must be taken within 60 days from the date of circulation of the panel report to the WTO members, but not before 20 days have passed.[4] If within that period no notice of appeal has been presented to the DSB, it will be expected to adopt the report.

1 DSU, art 17(4).
2 Ibid, art 17(6).
3 See, for example: Canada – Certain Measures Concerning Periodicals WT/DS31/AB/R, 30 June 1997; United States – Import Prohibition of Certain Shrimp and Shrimp Products, WT/DS58/AB/R, 12 October 1998.
4 DSU, art 16(1),(4).

PROCEDURAL ASPECTS

Languages

5.16 The official languages of the WTO are English, French and Spanish. The parties may use any of the three languages in the proceedings. To date, most proceedings have been conducted in English only.

Instituting proceedings

5.17 A request for panel establishment is to be presented before the DSB, after the expiration of 60 days from the date on which a request for consultations was presented to the other party to the dispute (20 days in urgent cases).[1] The DSB must establish a panel at its first or a following meeting after the date on which the request has been presented, unless it decides by way of consensus not to establish a panel.[2] Upon the establishment of a panel, the DSB vests it with terms of reference (which are normally standard terms).[3]

Under art 6 of the DSU, the request for establishment of a panel should contain the following information:
(a) whether consultations were held;
(b) the specific measure at issue;
(c) brief summary of legal arguments necessary to present the problem clearly; and
(d) whether non-standard terms of reference are suggested and, if so, what terms are proposed.

1 DSU, arts 4(7),(8), 5(4).
2 Ibid, art 6(1).
3 Ibid, art 7.

Financial assistance

5.18 Although participation in WTO dispute settlement proceedings is free, parties to a case bear their own costs. In cases involving developing countries, the Secretariat will provide, upon request, technical and legal assistance to the developing country (or countries) party to the proceedings. Such assistance may include providing the services of a legal expert from the WTO technical co-operation services.[1] In addition, the Secretariat is obliged to conduct training seminars on the WTO dispute settlement system intended for experts from interested members.[2]

1   DSU, art 27(2).
2   Ibid, art 27(3).

Provisional measures

5.19   The panel and AB do not have authority to issue provisional measures. However, when an urgent situation presents itself, the DSU provides for a shorter period of consultations (20 days instead of 60 days),[1] and for accelerated procedures.[2] The panel is instructed in urgent cases, including cases pertaining to perishable goods, to aim and complete its work within three months from the date of its constitution (instead of the six months allowed in normal cases).[3]

1   DSU, art 4(8).
2   Ibid, art 4(9).
3   Ibid, art 12(8).

Preliminary proceedings/objections

5.20   The DSU and other relevant instruments do not expressly provide for a separate procedural stage for the raising of preliminary objections. However, it is the practice of panels to permit the raising of preliminary objections (eg inadequate specificity of the request for establishment of a panel, lack of legal standing, right of representation by private legal counsel) at the beginning of the proceedings.[1]

The only preliminary procedure enumerated in the relevant WTO dispute settlement instruments is the disqualification procedure described in the Rules of Conduct. According to those rules, information concerning a member of the panel, AB, or the Secretariat, or an expert providing information to a dispute settlement body, must be presented in confidentiality, at the earliest possible time before the relevant body (the Chair of the DSB, Director-General of the WTO or the AB).[2] The procedure for dealing with the allegations must be concluded within fifteen working days from the date in which the said information was received.[3]

1   See eg EC – Regime for the Importation, Sale and Distribution of Bananas, Complaint by Ecuador, Report of Panel, WTO Doc WT/DS26/R/ECU, 22 May 1997, pp 3–15.
2   Rules of Conduct, r VIII(1).
3   Ibid, r VIII(4).

Written pleadings

5.21   Written submissions to the panel are presented in accordance with the timetable set by the panel, subject to the requirement that the overall proceedings should not as a rule exceed nine months from the date the panel was established.[1] According to the proposed timetable, set out in the Working Procedures (Appendix 3 to the DSU), the complaining party is expected to deposit its submission within three to six weeks after the establishment of the panel, and the respondent has two to three more weeks in order to respond. While, in principle, the complaining party submits its submission first, the panel may decide, after consulting with the parties, that the initial submissions of both parties will be made simultaneously.[2] The initial submissions should include a presentation of the facts of the case and the elaboration of the relevant legal arguments.[3]

After the first session (which is normally held one to two weeks after the receipt of the respondent's submission), the parties should submit written rebuttals, which are to be generally presented simultaneously within two to three weeks of the first session.[4] The panel may also request the parties, at any time, to submit explanations in writing to specific questions.[5]

Each written document submitted by one of the parties to the panel, shall also be made available to the other party (or parties) to the dispute. In cases involving developing country members the panel is to ensure that the country has sufficient time to prepare its arguments, subject to the rule that proceedings are expected to be completed within a maximum period of nine months.[6]

1   DSU, art 20.
2   Ibid, art 12(6).
3   Ibid, Appendix 3, r 4.
4   DSU, art 12(6); Panel Working Procedures, r 12(b).
5   Panel Working Procedures, r 8.
6   DSU, art 12(10).

Oral arguments

5.22   The complaining member is invited to present its case orally at the first meeting of the panel (usually within one to two weeks from the receipt of the response of the party complained against), and the member complained against will be invited at the same session to present its views.[1] In the next meeting (usually within one to two weeks from the receipt of rebuttals) the responding party shall first make an oral rebuttal, and the complaining party shall take the floor immediately thereafter.[2] The panel may address questions to the parties for oral explanation during any meeting.[3]

Written transcripts of all oral arguments must be made available to the panel and the other party (or parties). However, the conduct of WTO dispute settlement proceedings is confidential.[4]

1   Panel Working Procedures, r 5.
2   Ibid, r 7.
3   Ibid, r 8.
4   DSU, arts 4(6), 14, 17(10).

Third-party intervention

5.23   Any member having a substantial interest in a case pending before the panel has the right to join the proceedings as a third-party intervenor, after serving a notification to that effect to the DSB.[1] The panel shall invite third parties to attend a special meeting (or meetings) dedicated to the presentation of third parties' views.[2] In addition, third parties may make written submissions to the panel (which are to be circulated among the parties to the dispute) and are entitled to receive a copy of the first submissions of the original parties to the case.

In addition, any member (including a third party) who meets the required jurisdictional conditions may initiate separate proceedings pertaining to the same dispute.[3] The DSB will refer this new case, if possible, to the original panel. In this event, the proceedings will be conducted in a manner which will guarantee to the greatest extent possible that the rights that the parties would have had if separate proceedings had taken place would not be impaired. If one of the complaining parties in a consolidated case requests so, the panel shall issue separate reports.[4]

1   DSU, art 10(2).
2   Panel Working Procedures, r 6.
3   DSU, art 10(4).
4   Ibid, art 9.

Amicus curiae

5.24   There is no specific indication in the instruments governing the procedure of the WTO system that amicus curiae briefs submitted by non-members (ie non-WTO members, international organisations, NGOs, or natural or legal persons) are admissible. However, pursuant to Article 13 of the DSU, each panel has the right to seek information and technical advice from any individual or body or relevant source which it deems appropriate. In a recent case, where amicus briefs were sent to the panel by non-governmental organisations, the panel declined to take them into consideration, but permitted the parties to the dispute to incorporate them into their own submissions if they so wished. The AB stated that a panel has the discretionary authority to accept or reject information and advice submitted to it, whether requested by a panel or not. Furthermore, it was said that the panel acted within the scope of its authority under Articles 12 and 13 of the DSU in allowing any party to the dispute to attach the briefs by non-governmental organisations, or any portion thereof, to its own submissions.[1]

1   DSU, art 13 and US-Import Prohibition of Certain Shrimp and Shrimp Products, Appellate Body Report, WTO Doc WT/DS58/AB/R, 12 October 1998, paras 99–110.

Representation of the parties

5.25   The DSU does not explicitly address the issue of representation of the parties before WTO panels and the Appellate Body.

In a recent WTO proceeding an objection was raised as to the presence of private counsel in panel proceedings. This issue was subsequently raised before the Appellate Body in the same case. The AB noted that it found –

> '. . . nothing in the Marrakesh Agreement establishing the WTO . . . the DSU or the Working Procedures, nor in customary international law or the prevailing practice of international tribunals, which prevents a WTO Member from determining the composition of its delegation in Appellate Body proceedings.'

The AB ruled that it is for a WTO member to decide who should represent it as members of its delegation in an oral hearing of the Appellate Body.[1] In practice, private counsel do now appear in panel proceedings.

1   For example, WTO Appellate Body Report *European Communities – Regime for the Importation, Sale and Distribution of Bananas*, WT/DS27/AB/R, 9 September 1997, at paras 11 and 12.

Decision

5.26   The final decision of the panel is in the form of a report comprising a descriptive part, including the facts of the case and the arguments of the parties, and the panel's finding and conclusions. Where a panel concludes that a measure taken by a member is inconsistent with a covered agreement, it shall recommend that the member concerned bring the measure into conformity with that agreement.[1]

The report is to be adopted by the DSB in 20–60 days from the date it was circulated to the members of the WTO,[2] unless the DSB decides by way of consensus not to adopt the report or if an appeal is lodged to the Appellate Body.

Upon its adoption the report becomes binding on the parties. The parties are expected to comply promptly with the recommendation of the panel, and the DSB shall supervise the implementation of the report. The losing party must inform the DSB within 30 days from the date of adoption of the report on its intentions as to compliance with the recommendation, or indicate a reasonable period for implementation (which should generally not exceed 15 months).[3] If an agreement on the period for implementation cannot be reached within 45 days, arbitration for the determination of the implementation period may be requested. The arbitrator shall give his award within 90 days of the adoption of the report by the DSB.[4]

Upon failure to bring a measure into compliance within a reasonable period, the non-implementing party must enter into negotiations with the complaining party (or parties), with a view to agreeing upon acceptable compensation. If no agreement is reached within 20 days, the complaining party may seek the authorisation of the DSB for suspension of concessions or other obligations applicable vis-à-vis the non-complying member, until compliance is restored.[5] Disputes on the level of suspension may go to arbitration.[6] The DSB grants authorisation for suspension of concessions by reverse consensus.

1   DSU, art 19(1).
2   Ibid, art 16(1),(4).
3   Ibid, art 21(3)(c).
4   Ibid, art 21(3)(c).
5   Ibid, art 22(2),(8). If a dispute arises regarding the disproportionality of the authorised trade sanctions, the case will be referred to arbitration, preferably before the original panel: ibid, art 22(6),(7).
6   Ibid, art 22(6).

Revision of report

5.27   The DSU introduces a 'built in' procedure for revision. Before a panel report is issued, the parties receive the descriptive parts of the report for written comments (generally two to four weeks after the rebuttal session).[71] The parties are normally expected to submit their comments within two weeks.[2]

In addition, the panel circulates between the parties an interim report before the conclusion of the final version. The interim report is generally issued within two to four weeks after the receipt of the parties' comments on the descriptive part of the report. Each party may submit (generally within a week from the date of receipt of the interim report) a written request for the panel to review precise aspects of the interim report and may also request a special review meeting for presentation of oral arguments.[3] The final report shall include a discussion of the arguments made at the interim review stage.[4]

1   DSU, art 15(1). Panel Working Procedures, r 12(e).
2   Panel Working Procedures, r 12(f).
3   DSU, art 15(2).
4   Ibid, art 15(3).

Appeals

5.28 Appeals against legal conclusions of panel reports may be lodged with the AB by any of the parties to the dispute (not including third parties).[1] There is no provision barring the prevailing party from appealing a panel report if it objects to certain aspects thereof.

Notice of appeal is to be submitted at the same time to the Appellate Body and the DSB.[2] The notice of appeal must include the following information:

(a) title of panel report under appeal;
(b) name of appealing party;
(c) necessary details for future service of documents; and
(d) brief statement of the nature of the appeal, including allegation of legal errors in the report.[3]

The complete submission of the appellant is to be presented to the AB within ten days after the deposition of the notice of appeal. The full submission should include the precise statement of grounds of appeal, legal basis of arguments and description of the decision or ruling sought.[4] Other appellants to submissions are due within 15 days.[5] Any party to the dispute who wishes to respond may file an appellee's submission (to be lodged within 25 days after the filing of the notice of appeal). The responding submission should include a statement of the grounds for opposing the appeal (pertaining to each ground of the appeal and each allegation of legal error), legal basis for arguments and description of the decision or ruling sought.[6]

Oral hearings will be conducted, as a rule, within 30 days from the filing of the notice of appeal.[7] As is the case for panels, the AB may request the parties at any time to submit answers to questions.[8] The AB is expected to issue an Appellate Report within 60 days and in any case not later than 90 days from the filing of the notice of appeal.[9]

AB reports (and the panel reports as adopted, modified or reversed) are to be adopted by the DSB within 30 days from their circulation to the parties, unless the DSB decides by way of consensus not to adopt the report.

1 DSU, art 17(4),(6).
2 AB Working Procedures, r 20.
3 Ibid, r 20(2).
4 Ibid, r 21.
5 Ibid, r 23.
6 Ibid, r 22.
7 Ibid, r 27.
8 Ibid, r 28(1).
9 DSU, art 17(5).

Costs

5.29 The costs of the WTO dispute settlement system are borne by the WTO. However, parties to a case must meet their own expenses.

Implementation of decision, recognition and enforcement

5.30 The surveillance of implementation of panel or AB reports is assigned to the DSB, which monitors the compliance of the losing party with the recommendations of the report.[1] If a party fails to bring the measure at issue into conformity with the relevant agreements immediately or within a reasonable period of time, the concerned party is to initiate negotiations with the complaining party for payment of mutually acceptable compensation. If no such agreement is reached, the latter party may seek the authorisation of the DSB to impose temporary trade sanctions against the recalcitrant party, until compliance is restored.[2]

There is no provision in any of the WTO instruments as to the enforcement of panel or AB reports in municipal courts.

1 DSU, art 21.
2 Ibid, art 22(2),(6) and (8). See also: European Communities – Regime for the Importation, Sale and Distribution of Bananas. Recourse to Arbitration by the European Communities under art 22(6) of the DSU, Decision by the Arbitrators, WTO Doc WT/DS27/ARB, 9 April 1999.

REFERENCE

Sources of previous case law, including case reports

Adopted GATT panel reports are found in *GATT Basic Instruments and Selected Documents* Series (BISD). WTO panel and AB reports can be found on the WTO website and in a commercial publication titled *The International Trade Law Reports* (Cameron May, London, 1996).

Selected bibliography

Books

James Cameron & Karen Campbell (eds) *Dispute Resolution in the World Trade Organisation* (1998).

Robert Hudec *Enforcing International Trade Law: The Evolution of the Modern GATT Legal System* (1993).

John H Jackson *The World Trading System: Law and Policy of International Economic Relations* 107, 2nd edn (1997).

Pierre Pescatore (ed) *Handbook of WTO/GATT Dispute Settlement* (1997).

Pierre Pescatore, William J Davey, Andreas F Lowenfeld (eds) *Handbook of GATT Dispute Settlement* (1991).

Ernst-Ulrich Petersmann (ed) *International Trade Law and the GATT/WTO Dispute Settlement System* (1997).

Ernst-Ulrich Petersmann *The GATT/WTO Dispute Settlement System: International Law, Organisations and Dispute Settlement* Kluwer Law International (1997).

Frank Warren Swacker, Kenneth Robert Redden, Larry B Wenger, and Marion Fountain McCurdy (eds) *World Trade Without Barriers: The World Trade Organisation (WTO) and Dispute Resolution* (1995) (includes pocket parts).

Articles

Grant D Aldonas 'The World Trade Organisation: Revolution in International Dispute Settlement' (1995) 50 Dispute Resolution Journal 73.

Judith H Bello 'The WTO Dispute Settlement Understanding: Less is More' (1996) 90 American Journal of International Law 416.

Judith H Bello and Alan F Holmer 'Dispute resolution in the New World Trade Organisation: Concerns and Net Benefits', US Trade Law and Policy Series No 24 (1994) 28 International Lawyer 1095.

John Jackson 'The Legal Meaning of a GATT Dispute Settlement Report: Some Reflections' in N Blokker and S Muller (eds) *Towards More Effective Supervision by International Organisations* 149–164 (1994).

A P Lowenfeld 'Remedies along with rights: institutional reform in the new GATT' (1994) 88 American Journal of International Law 447.

Ernst-Ulrich Petersmann 'The GATT/WTO Dispute Settlement System and the GATT Case Law on Trade-related Environmental Measures' in Kalliopi Koufa (ed) (1997) *International Justice* XXVI Thesaurus Acroasium 475.

Ernst-Ulrich Petersmann 'The Dispute Settlement System of the World Trade Organisation and the Evolution of the GATT Dispute Settlement System since 1948' (1994) 31 Common Market Law Review 1157.

ANNEX

List of parties to the WTO[1]

Antigua and Barbuda, Angola, Argentina, Australia, Austria, Bahrain, Bangladesh, Barbados, Belgium, Belize, Benin, Bolivia, Botswana, Brazil, Brunei Darussalam, Bulgaria, Burkina Faso, Burundi, Cameroon, Canada, Central African Republic, Chad, Chile, Colombia, Congo, Costa Rica, Côte d'Ivoire, Cuba, Cyprus, Czech Republic, Democratic Republic of the Congo, Denmark, Djibouti, Dominica, Dominican Republic, Ecuador, Egypt, El Salvador, Estonia, European Communities, Fiji, Finland, France, Gabon, Gambia, Germany, Ghana, Greece, Grenada, Guatemala, Guinea Bissau, Guinea, Guyana, Haiti, Honduras, Hong Kong (China), Hungary, Iceland, India, Indonesia, Ireland, Israel, Italy, Jamaica, Japan, Kenya, Korea, Kuwait, Kyrgyz Republic, Latvia, Lesotho, Liechtenstein, Luxembourg, Macau, Madagascar, Malawi, Malaysia, Maldives, Mali, Malta, Mauritania, Mauritius, Mexico, Mongolia, Morocco, Mozambique, Myanmar, Namibia, Netherlands (and the Netherlands Antilles), New Zealand, Nicaragua, Niger, Nigeria, Norway, Pakistan, Panama, Papua New Guinea, Paraguay, Peru, Philippines, Poland, Portugal, Qatar, Romania, Rwanda, Saint Kitts and Nevis, Saint Lucia, Saint Vincent & the Grenadines, Senegal, Sierra Leone, Singapore, Slovak Republic, Slovenia, Solomon Islands, South Africa, Spain, Sri Lanka, Suriname, Swaziland, Sweden, Switzerland, Tanzania, Thailand, Togo, Trinidad and Tobago, Tunisia, Turkey, Uganda, United Arab Emirates, United Kingdom, United States, Uruguay, Venezuela, Zambia, Zimbabwe.

1   There are 134 members as at 10 February 1999.

CHAPTER 6

International Centre for Settlement of Investment Disputes (ICSID)

INTRODUCTORY

Name and seat of the body

6.1 The International Centre for Settlement of Investment Disputes (ICSID or 'the Centre') was established in 1966 to provide facilities for the conciliation and arbitration of investment disputes between states and nationals of other states. The seat of the Centre is at the principal office of the World Bank. The contact details are as follows:

> ICSID
> 1818 H Street, NW
> Washington, DC 20433
> USA
>
> Tel: 202 458-1534
> Fax: 202 522-2615 or 202 522-2027
> website: http://www.worldbank.org/icsid

ICSID is one of the five international organisations that make up the World Bank Group. As in the case of the other organisations in the group, the Centre was established by a multilateral treaty, the 1965 Convention on the Settlement of Investment Disputes between States and Nationals of Other States.[1] As of 1 March 1999, 131 countries had signed and ratified the ICSID Convention to become Contracting States.[2]

Under art 62 of the Convention, ICSID arbitration proceedings are held at the seat of the Centre unless the parties agree otherwise. Article 63(a) of the Convention provides for the conclusion by ICSID of special arrangements with other appropriate institutions for the holding of proceedings at the seat of those institutions if the parties so agree. As of 1 March 1999, special arrangements had been made with six other institutions.[3] Article 63(b) of the Convention provides that proceedings may be held at other places agreed by the parties, and approved by the tribunal, after consultation with the Secretary-General of ICSID.

1 Convention for the Settlement of Investment Disputes between States and Nationals of Other States, 18 March 1965, 575 UNTS 159, reprinted in ICSID Doc 15, ICSID Basic Documents (January 1985). For the legislative history, see *ICSID, Convention on the Settlement of Investment Disputes between States and Nationals of Other States, Analysis of Documents Concerning the Origin and the Formulation of the Convention* (1970).
2 For an up-to-date listing of ICSID contracting states, see *List of ICSID Contracting States and Other Signatories of the Convention* published by the Centre, available on the ICSID website.

3 The institutions with which such arrangements have been concluded are the Permanent Court of Arbitration at The Hague, the Regional Arbitration Centres of the Asian-African Legal Consultative Committee at Cairo and Kuala Lumpur, the Australian Centre for International Commercial Arbitration at Melbourne, the Australian Commercial Disputes Centre at Sydney and the Singapore International Arbitration Centre.

Introductory description

6.2 Under the Convention, ICSID provides facilities for conciliation and arbitration of investment disputes between contracting states and individuals and companies that qualify as nationals of other contracting states.[1] ICSID does not itself conciliate or arbitrate such disputes. This is the task of conciliation commissions and arbitral tribunals which are constituted for each dispute, normally through appointments by the parties.

The organisational structure of ICSID consists of an Administrative Council and a Secretariat. The Council is the Centre's governing body and is composed of one representative of each contracting state.[2] The President of the World Bank serves as non-voting Chairman of the Council.[3] Pursuant to the Convention, the Administrative Council has adopted the Centre's Administrative and Financial Regulations, the Rules of Procedure for the Institution of Conciliation and Arbitration Proceedings, the Rules of Procedure for Conciliation Proceedings, and the Rules of Procedure for Arbitration Proceedings. The Council has also approved the administrative arrangements concluded between the World Bank and ICSID.[4] Recurrent responsibilities of the Council include the approval of ICSID's Annual Report and administrative budget.[5] Finally, the Council is charged with the election of the Secretary-General of ICSID, under whose direction the Secretariat's day-to-day work is carried out.[6]

Besides providing facilities for conciliation and arbitration under the ICSID Convention, the Centre has, since 1978, had a set of Additional Facility Rules under which the ICSID Secretariat is authorised to administer certain proceedings between states and nationals of other states that fall outside the scope of the Convention. These include conciliation and arbitration proceedings for the settlement of investment disputes where one of the parties is not a contracting state or a national of such a state, as well as conciliation and arbitration proceedings for the settlement of disputes that do not arise out of an investment, provided that the underlying transaction is not an 'ordinary commercial' one and at least one of the parties is a contracting state or a national of a contracting state. Fact-finding proceedings may also be conducted under the Additional Facility Rules, whenever any state and foreign national wish to institute an inquiry to examine and report on facts.[7]

Another activity of ICSID in regard to the settlement of disputes has consisted in the Secretary-General of ICSID undertaking to act as the appointing authority of arbitrators for ad hoc (ie non-institutional) arbitrations. This has mostly been done in the context of agreements providing for arbitration under the 1976 Arbitration Rules of the United Nations Commission on International Trade Law, or UNCITRAL, which are specially designed for ad hoc proceedings.

As of 1 March 1999, 59 disputes had been brought under the Convention, including five under the ICSID Additional Facility. The disputes involved 42 different governments. Twenty-five cases were pending as of 1 March 1999.

Most of the disputes that have been brought to ICSID have been arbitration cases.

1   See Convention, art 25(1).
2   Ibid, art 4(1).
3   Ibid, art 5.
4   Ibid, art 6(1)(a)–(d).
5   Ibid, art 6(1)(f),(g).
6   Ibid, art 10(1).
7   See Rules Governing the Additional Facility for the Administration of Proceedings by the Secretariat of the International Centre for Settlement of Investment Disputes, r 2 ('Additional Facility Rules').

INSTITUTIONAL ASPECTS

Governing texts

Procedural law

6.3   The ICSID Convention provides the institutional and procedural framework for the settlement, through conciliation and arbitration, of investment disputes between governments and foreign investors and determines the scope of the jurisdiction of the Centre. Detailed rules of procedure for the institution and conduct of proceedings,[1] as well as the above-mentioned financial and administrative regulations under which the ICSID Administrative Council and the Secretariat operate, have been adopted pursuant to the Convention. Under the ICSID Convention, the parties are given considerable freedom to decide the procedural framework for the conduct of proceedings. In general, these rules apply only in the absence of agreement of the parties to the contrary. If any question of procedure arises which is not covered by the Convention, the rules of procedure for conciliation or arbitration proceedings, or any rules agreed by the parties, the tribunal shall decide the question.

Pursuant to the Rules Governing the Additional Facility, separate sets of procedural rules apply to proceedings brought under the Additional Facility.[2] The latter set of rules is generally similar to the rules of procedures governing ordinary ICSID proceedings.

The operations of the Administrative Council and the Secretariat are governed by ICSID Administrative and Financial Regulations 1984.[3]

1   See Rules of Procedure for the Institution of Conciliation and Arbitration Proceedings ('Institution Rules'); Rules of Procedure for Arbitration Proceedings ('Arbitration Rules'); and Rules of Procedure for Conciliation Proceedings ('Conciliation Rules'). ICSID proceedings will be governed by the rules of procedure in force at the time at which consent to ICSID jurisdiction was granted, unless the parties agree otherwise.
2   Additional Facility Rules, Sch C: Arbitration (Additional Facility) Rules ('Arbitration (Additional Facility) Rules'); Additional Facility Rules, Sch B: Conciliation (Additional Facility) Rules ('Conciliation (Additional Facility) Rules'). In arbitration conducted under the Additional Facility, the parties may agree to apply other sets of procedural rules only to the extent that they are consistent with the Additional Facility Rules: Arbitration (Additional Facility) Rules, art 29(2).
3   Administrative and Financial Regulations 1984, ICSID Basic Documents 33 (1985), 1 ICSID Reports 35 (1993) ('Administrative Regulations').

Substantive law

6.4   Under article 42 of the Convention, an ICSID tribunal must decide a dispute in accordance with such rules of law as may be agreed by the parties.

88

In the absence of such agreement, the tribunal will apply the law of the contracting state party to the dispute (including its rules on the conflicts of laws) and such rules of international law as may be applicable. Similar choice of law principles also applies in arbitrations conducted under the auspices of the Additional Facility.[1] The tribunal may, if the parties so agree, decide a dispute *ex aequo et bono*.

1 Arbitration (Additional Facility) Rules, art 55.

Organisation

Composition, appointment and disqualification

PANELS OF CONCILIATORS AND OF ARBITRATORS

6.5 ICSID maintains a Panel of Conciliators and a Panel of Arbitrators.[1] These are rosters, each consisting of up to four persons designated by each contracting state and up to ten persons designated by the Administrative Council Chairman, all for renewable six-year terms. Members of conciliation commissions and arbitral tribunals may be appointed from outside the panels, except in the case of the appointments by the Chairman of the Administrative Council. As of 1 March 1999, 424 designations had been made to the Panels of Conciliators and of Arbitrators.

1 Convention, art 13.

COMPOSITION OF CONCILIATION COMMISSIONS AND ARBITRAL TRIBUNALS

6.6 As shown above, the Centre is not in any way a court but simply an administrative body under whose auspices conciliation commissions and arbitral tribunals may be established and proceedings conducted. A conciliation commission or arbitral tribunal will generally consist of one conciliator or arbitrator appointed by each of the disputing parties and a third, presiding, conciliator or arbitrator appointed by agreement of the parties. The provisions of the Convention give the parties considerable latitude but ensure at the same time that the absence of agreement between the parties will not prevent the constitution of a conciliation commission or arbitral tribunal. If the commission or tribunal cannot be constituted within a certain time limit, either party may require the Chairman of the Administrative Council to make the necessary appointment or appointments.[1] In practice, the Chairman performs this appointing authority function on the recommendation of the Secretary-General. In conciliation proceedings the only requirement is that the commission have one or any uneven number of conciliators.[2] In the case of arbitration proceedings there is the further requirement that the majority of the members of the tribunal must be of a nationality other than the state which is a party to the dispute and of the state whose national is the other party to the dispute. The parties may however depart from this rule if each member of the tribunal (or the sole arbitrator) has been appointed by agreement of the parties.[3] Appointment procedures under the Additional Facility Rules are generally similar to those applicable in ordinary ICSID cases.[4]

ICSID conciliators have the duty of clarifying the issues in dispute between the parties and endeavouring to bring about agreement between them on mutually acceptable terms. The conciliators may recommend terms of settlement to the parties, who must give any such recommendation their most serious consideration.[5] If the parties nevertheless fail to reach an agreement, the conciliators must close the proceeding with a report noting the failure.[6]

In contrast, the ICSID Convention provides that the award of the arbitrators shall be binding on the parties.[7]

1 Convention, art 37(2)(b) and Arbitration Rules, r 3(1).
2 Convention, art 29(2)(b).
3 Convention, art 39.
4 Arbitration (Additional Facility) Rules, arts 6–11. In contrast to ordinary ICSID proceedings, where chairpersons for arbitration tribunals, who are picked by the Chairman of the Administrative Council, can come only from the Panel of Arbitrators, there is no such limitation in cases conducted under the Additional Facility auspices.
5 Ibid, art 34(1).
6 Ibid, art 34(2).
7 Ibid, art 53(1).

CHALLENGE PROCEDURES

6.7 A party may propose to a tribunal the disqualification of any of its members on account of any fact indicating a manifest lack of the qualities of integrity, competence and independence required by the Convention for members of the Panels of Conciliators and of Arbitrators.[1] A proposal to disqualify an arbitrator must be made promptly, and in any event before the proceeding is declared closed. Unless the proposal relates to a majority of the members of the tribunal, the other members must promptly consider and vote on the proposal in the absence of the arbitrator concerned. If those members are equally divided, they will notify the Chairman of the Administrative Council of the proposal, of any explanation furnished by the arbitrator concerned and of their failure to reach a decision. The Chairman will then decide the matter within 30 days after he has received the proposal. While the proposal for disqualification is pending, the arbitral proceedings are suspended.[2]

1 Convention, art 57.
2 Arbitration Rules, r 9.

Plenary/chambers

6.8 Unless the parties agree otherwise, the presence of a majority of the tribunal is required at its sittings. In practice, parties often agree that the full tribunal shall be present at its sittings.[1]

1 Arbitration Rules, r 14(2).

Appellate structure

6.9 Arbitral awards rendered under the ICSID Convention 'shall be binding on the parties and shall not be subject to appeal or to any other remedy except those provided for in this Convention'.[1] The exclusion of appeal is absolute. Four remedies are provided in the Convention. These are: rectification or supplementation, interpretation, revision and annulment. A request for rectification or supplementation of the award will be submitted to the tribunal that rendered the award. If possible, a request for interpretation and revision of an award will also be submitted to the tribunal that rendered the award. If this is not possible, a new tribunal will be constituted.[2] An application to annul an award will be referred to a three member ad hoc committee appointed by the Chairman of the Administrative Council. The committee members must be drawn from the Panel of Arbitrators. None of them may be a member of the tribunal that rendered the award, or have the same nationality of any such member. Nor may an ad hoc committee member have the nationality of the state party to the dispute, of the state whose national is a party to the dispute or have been designated to the Panel of Arbitrators by either of those states. An ad hoc committee member may moreover not have acted as a conciliator in the same dispute. The ad hoc committee has authority to annul the whole award or a part thereof.[3] There is no comparable annulment procedure under the Additional Facility Rules.

1   See Convention, art 53(4).
2   Ibid, arts 50 and 51.
3   Ibid, art 52.

Scientific and technical experts

6.10   The tribunal may call upon the parties to produce experts, and the parties may present oral testimony of expert witnesses before the tribunal. The tribunal may also admit evidence given by an expert in a written deposition. In addition, the tribunal may, with the consent of both parties, arrange for the examination of an expert otherwise than before the tribunal itself. In that case the parties may participate in the examination.[1]

1   Arbitration Rules, r 36. See also Arbitration (Additional Facility) Rules, arts 42, 43. Under these provisions the tribunal may also appoint one or more experts to prepare a report and testify before it.

Registry

6.11   The role of the Secretariat is principally defined in the Administrative and Financial Regulations. These Regulations require the Secretariat to maintain case registers;[1] to serve as the channel of written communications between the parties and the arbitrators;[2] to administer the finances of the direct costs of the proceeding;[3] to make arrangements for hearings and other meetings of ICSID tribunals;[4] to provide 'other assistance' as requested;[5] and to perform depositary functions.[6] The Secretariat is headed by a Secretary-General elected by the Council for a period of six years.[7] The ICSID Secretariat also provides for the administrative needs of the Additional Facility.[8]

The existence, current status and final disposition of the case are matters of public record in ICSID proceedings. Under the Administrative and Financial Regulations, the Secretary-General is required to maintain a register for each request for arbitration. The Secretary-General must enter into the register all significant data concerning the institution, conduct and disposition of the case. The particular data concerning the method of constitution and membership of the arbitral tribunal must be entered, and in regard to any award, data concerning any request for any of the Convention's post-award remedies of rectification or supplementation, interpretation, revision and annulment, and any stay of enforcement of the award. The Administrative and Financial Regulations provide that the registers shall be open for inspection by any person. In addition, register entries for pending cases are published in the Annual Report of the Centre and in its semi-annual newsletter, *News from ICSID*.[9]

1   Administrative Regulations, reg 23.
2   Ibid, reg 25.

3   Ibid, reg 14.
4   Ibid, reg 26.
5   Ibid, reg 25(c).
6   Ibid, reg 28.
7   Convention, art 10(1).
8   Rules Governing the Additional Facility for the Administration of Proceedings by the ICSID Secretariat, 1978, Sch A: Administrative and Financial Rules (Additional Facility).
9   Administrative Regulations, reg 23.

Jurisdiction and access

6.12   The principal provision regarding the jurisdiction of the Centre is article 25(1) of the ICSID Convention:

'The jurisdiction of the Centre shall extend to any legal dispute arising directly out of an investment, between a Contracting State (or any constituent sub-division or agency of a Contracting State designated to the Centre by that state) and a national of another Contracting State, which the parties to the dispute consent in writing to submit to the Centre. When the parties have given their consent, no party may withdraw its consent unilaterally.'

Thus, while consent has often been referred to as the 'cornerstone of the jurisdiction of the Centre,'[1] the further requirements relating to the nature of the dispute and the parties thereto must also be met.

1   See 1965 Report of the Executive Directors of the World Bank, para 23.

Ratione personae

6.13   Article 25(1) requires that one of the parties must be a contracting state and the other party must be a 'national of another Contracting State'. The facilities of the Centre are therefore not available for disputes between non-state parties or for disputes between states; they are available only for disputes between non-state parties on the one hand and state parties on the other hand. The non-state party must be a 'national of another Contracting State'. This term covers both natural and juridical persons. Under article 25(2) of the Convention, a natural person is precluded from access to the Centre, if the person, in addition to being a national of another contracting state, is also a national of the state party to the dispute. In contrast, a juridical person that is a national of the state party to the dispute may be a party to an ICSID proceeding if it and the state party to the dispute have agreed to treat the juridical person as a national of another contracting state because of foreign control.[1]

The Rules Governing the Additional Facility have expanded the application of ICSID's facilities so as to include parties that do not meet the jurisdictional requirements of the ICSID Convention. Under those rules, a state (or a constituent division or agency thereof) and a national of another state may agree to utilise the Additional Facility, even if one of the relevant states (ie the state party to the dispute or the state of nationality of the private party) is not a party to the ICSID Convention.[2] However, prior to the initiation of proceedings, the agreement of the parties to accept the jurisdiction of the Additional Facility must be approved by the Secretary-General. The Secretary-General will grant approval only if satisfied that (a) one of the relevant states is not party to the Convention; and (b) the parties have agreed to accept the jurisdiction of ICSID arbitration (in lieu of Additional Facility arbitration) in case the jurisdictional requirements under the Convention will be met before the initiation of proceedings.[3] As a practical matter, parties submit their Additional Facility arbitration agreements (or draft agreements) to the approval of the Secretary-General as early as possible, or agree upon alternative dispute settlement mechanisms, in case the Secretary-General withholds approval of the agreement.

1 See Broches 'The Convention on the Settlement of Investment Disputes between States and Nationals of Other States', in *Selected Essays* (1965) at 201.
2 Additional Facility Rules, art 4(3).
3 Ibid, art 4(4).

Ratione materiae

6.14 The Convention requires that the dispute must be a 'legal dispute arising directly out of an investment'. The Convention does not define the term 'legal dispute' or 'investment'. In their 1965 Report on the ICSID Convention, the Executive Directors of the World Bank stated, in connection with the former term, 'that while conflicts of rights are within the jurisdiction of the Centre, mere conflicts of interests are not.' The Report said further that 'the dispute must concern the existence or scope of a legal right or obligation, or the nature or extent of the reparation to be made for breach of a legal obligation'. Although a number of definitions of 'investment' were considered at the time of the negotiation of the Convention, none was agreed upon 'given the essential requirement of consent by the parties'.

As is the case in other forms of international arbitration, there can be no recourse to arbitration under the ICSID Convention unless the parties have agreed to this in writing. Once both parties have consented, neither may revoke its consent unilaterally. The consent may be given in regard to an existing dispute or with respect to a defined class of future disputes. The consent of the parties need not be given in a single instrument. In the above-mentioned 1965 Report, the Executive Directors suggested that 'a host State might in its investment promotion legislation offer to submit disputes arising out of certain classes of investments to the jurisdiction of the Centre, and the investor might give his consent by accepting the offer in writing'.[1]

Some 30 countries have adopted this approach in their investment legislation setting forth general consents to submit disputes with foreign investors to ICSID arbitration. In the 1990s such general consents have also widely been incorporated by states in their bilateral investment treaties. These treaties (which now number some 1,300) generally provide investors that qualify as a national of the other state broad guarantees against unfair and discriminatory treatment, expropriation and currency transfer restrictions. In provisions comparable to those in the investment laws just referred to, nearly one thousand such treaties also set forth the consent of each state party to submit to arbitration under the ICSID Convention disputes arising out of investments made in its territory by the investors of the other state party. This type of general consent has also been included in the investment provisions of several multilateral treaties: the North American Free Trade Agreement (NAFTA); the Cartagena Free Trade Agreement; the Colonia Investment Protocol of the Common Market of the Southern Cone (Mercosur); and the Energy Charter Treaty.

Upon ratification of the Convention states may exclude certain classes of investment disputes from the jurisdiction of the Centre.[2] To date, only a few states have availed themselves of this opportunity.

The parties to a case may refer to the Additional Facility a dispute that does not arise directly from an investment, subject to the prior approval of the Secretary-General, before initiation of proceedings. The Secretary-General shall approve an arbitration agreement only if he or she is satisfied that the underlying transaction has features which distinguish it from an ordinary commercial transaction.[3] However, if the Secretary-General believes that an arbitral tribunal might consider the dispute to be an investment dispute, he or she may require the parties to refer the case first to ordinary ICSID proceedings (provided that personal jurisdiction requirements have been met).[4]

1 See Broches 'The Convention on the Settlement of Investment Disputes between States and Nationals of Other States', in *Selected Essays* (1965), at 207.
2 Convention, art 25(4).
3 Additional Facility Rules, art 4(3).
4 Ibid, art 4(4).

Ratione temporis

6.15 The ICSID Convention and the Additional Facility Rules do not provide time limits for the submission of disputes to ICSID. This question is governed by the parties' consent, which may be given in respect of an existing dispute, or in respect of a defined class of future disputes.

It may be noted that under the ICSID Convention, a contracting state may require the exhaustion of local administrative or judicial remedies as a condition for its consent to arbitration under the Convention.[1] Furthermore, bilateral investment treaties generally stipulate that the parties to an investor-state dispute shall attempt to settle the dispute amicably, often for a period of six months, before invoking the dispute settlement mechanisms provided in the treaty.

1 Convention, art 26.

Advisory jurisdiction

6.16 The Convention does not provide for the rendition by ICSID tribunals of advisory opinions. It may, however, be recalled that cases may be brought for non-binding conciliation under the Convention or Additional Facility Rules or for fact-finding under the Additional Facility Rules.

PROCEDURAL ASPECTS

Languages

6.17 The Centre has three official languages: English, French and Spanish.[1] The parties to a proceeding are free to agree to the use of one or two of these languages in the proceeding. The parties may agree on a language that is not an official language of the Centre, provided the tribunal, after consultation with the Secretary-General, gives its approval. If two procedural languages are selected by the parties, any instruments may be filed in either language and either language may be used at the hearings, provided that the necessary arrangements are made for translation and interpretation.[2]

1   Arbitration Rules, r 22(1).
2   Ibid, r 22(2). See also Arbitration (Additional Facility) Rules, art 30.

Instituting proceedings

6.18   The Convention sets forth procedures for the registration of requests for conciliation or arbitration, requiring the claimant, or both parties, to provide information concerning the issues in dispute, the identity of the parties and their consent to the jurisdiction of the Centre.[1] Under the Convention, the Secretary-General is required to register the request, unless he finds, on the basis of the information contained in the request, that the dispute is manifestly outside the jurisdiction of the Centre.[2] The registration procedure serves the purpose of screening requests and is not a procedure to determine jurisdiction. As emphasised in the Report on the Convention of the World Bank's Executive Directors, 'registration of a request by the Secretary-General does not, of course, preclude a Commission or Tribunal from finding that the dispute is outside the jurisdiction of the Centre'.[3] Detailed provisions on the institution of proceedings are contained in the Institution Rules. These provide that the request shall be drawn up in an official language of the Centre, and shall be dated and signed by the requesting party. The Institution Rules stipulate that the request shall:

'(a)   designate precisely each party to the dispute and state the address of each;

(b)   state, if one of the parties is a constituent subdivision or agency of a contracting state, that it has been designated to the Centre by that state pursuant to Article 25(1) of the Convention;

(c)   indicate the date of consent and the instruments in which it is recorded, including, if one party is a constituent subdivision or agency of a contracting state, similar data on the approval of such consent by that state unless it had notified the Centre that no such approval is required;

(d)   indicate with respect to the party that is a national of a contracting state:

  (i)   its nationality on the date of consent; and

  (ii)   if the party is a natural person:

    (A)   his nationality on the date of the request; and

    (B)   that he did not have the nationality of the contracting state party to the dispute either on the date of consent or on the date of the request; or

  (iii)   if the party is a juridical person which on the date of consent had the nationality of the contracting state party to the dispute, the agreement of the parties that it should be treated as a national of another contracting state for the purposes of the Convention; and

(e)   contain information concerning the issues in dispute indicating that there is, between the parties, a legal dispute arising directly out of an investment.'[4]

The request must be submitted in the form of a signed original accompanied by five copies, and a non-refundable lodging fee of US$1,000. Where a request is registered by the Secretary-General, the parties are on the same day notified of the registration and invited to proceed to constitute a tribunal. A proceeding under the Convention is deemed to have been instituted on the date of the registration of the request.[5] Under the Additional Facility arbitration rules the complaining party should submit a 'notice of arbitration' drafted in similar form to a request for arbitration under the ICSID Rules.[6]

1 Convention, art 36.
2 Institution Rules, at r 6.
3 1965 Report of the Executive Directors of the World Bank, para 38.
4 Institution Rules, r 2.
5 Ibid, r 7.
6 Arbitration (Additional Facility) Rules, arts 3, 4.

Financial assistance

6.19 Since the inception of ICSID, the World Bank has met the Centre's administrative budget in full. As a result, ICSID's administrative charges have been limited to reimbursement of its out-of-pocket expenditures for the proceeding in question (for communications charges, interpretation services and the like). In addition, parties to ICSID proceedings stand to benefit from the infrastructure of the World Bank Group for the proceeding (for meeting rooms, for example). Such support of the Bank can represent substantial savings for parties to ICSID proceedings. Nevertheless ICSID does not offer any special programme of financial assistance to the parties to a case before it.

Preliminary proceedings/objections

6.20 The Convention provides that any objection by a party to a dispute that the dispute is not within the jurisdiction of the Centre, or for other reasons is not within the competence of the tribunal, shall be considered by the tribunal which determines whether to deal with the objection as a preliminary question or to join it to the merits.[1] Under the Arbitration Rules, a jurisdictional objection shall be made as early as possible and in any event no later than the expiration of the time limit for the filing of the counter-memorial.[2] Upon the filing of jurisdictional objections, the proceeding on the merits is suspended and the president of the tribunal fixes time limits within which the parties may file observations on the objections.[3]

The tribunal decides whether or not there shall be a hearing on the objections to jurisdiction. The Arbitration Rules further provide that if the tribunal upholds jurisdiction or joins the objections to the merits, it shall fix time limits for the further procedures.[4] If the tribunal declines jurisdiction it shall render an award to that effect.[5] It may be added that the tribunal may at any stage of the proceeding, on its own initiative, consider whether the dispute before it is within the jurisdiction of the Centre and its own competence.[6]

1 Convention, art 41(2). See also Arbitration (Additional Facility) Rules, art 46.
2 Arbitration Rules, r 41(1).
3 Ibid, r 41(2).
4 Ibid, r 41(4).
5 Ibid, r 41(5).
6 Ibid, r 41(2).

Provisional measures

6.21 At any time during a proceeding a party may request that provisional measures for the preservation of its rights be recommended by the tribunal. A request for provisional measures shall specify the right to be preserved, and the circumstances that require such measures. The tribunal may also recommend provisional measures on its own initiative or recommend measures other than those specified in a request. The tribunal may only recommend provisional measures, or modify or revoke its recommendations, after giving each party an opportunity of presenting its observations. Parties to ICSID Convention arbitration proceedings may request judicial or other authorities to order provisional measures, but only if the agreement recording their consent to arbitration so stipulates.[1]

1   Convention, art 47; Arbitration Rules, r 39. See also Arbitration (Additional Facility) Rules, art 47.

Written pleadings

6.22 An arbitration proceeding under the ICSID Convention (or the Additional Facility) generally comprises two distinct phases: a written procedure followed by an oral one.[1] In addition to the request for arbitration, the written procedure normally consists of a memorial by the requesting party, a counter-memorial by the other party, a reply by the requesting party, and a rejoinder by the other party. The Arbitration Rules provide that a memorial shall contain a statement of the relevant facts, a statement of law and the submissions. A counter-memorial, reply or rejoinder shall contain an admission or denial of the facts stated in the last previous pleading; any additional facts, if necessary; observations concerning the statement of law in the last previous pleading; a statement of law in answer thereto; and the submissions. All written pleadings are filed within time limits fixed by the tribunal.[2] Instruments and documents are introduced into ICSID proceedings by filing them with the Secretary-General. Instruments are generally filed in the form of a signed original accompanied by five copies. The Secretary-General arranges for appropriate distribution of the copies while retaining the original in the archives of the Centre.[3]

1   Arbitration Rules, r 29; Arbitration (Additional Facility) Rules, art 36.
2   Ibid, r 31; Arbitration (Additional Facility) Rules, art 38.
3   Administrative Regulations, reg 24(2).

Oral arguments

6.23 The oral procedure consists of the hearing by the tribunal of parties and their representatives and of any witnesses and experts.[1] A proceeding may have separate written and oral procedures in regard to such matters as a request for provisional measures and objections to jurisdiction, as well as in regard to the merits of the dispute. The tribunal shall determine, with the consent of the parties, which persons (except the parties, their testifying witnesses and officers of the tribunal) may attend oral hearings.[2]

Since 1984, the Arbitration Rules have provided for the possibility of holding a pre-hearing conference between the tribunal and the parties. Such hearing may be held at the request of the Secretary-General or at the discretion of the president of the tribunal to arrange for an exchange of information and the stipulation of uncontested facts in order to expedite the proceeding. A pre-hearing conference may also take place at the request of the parties to consider issues in dispute with a view to reaching an amicable settlement.[3]

The Additional Facility Arbitration Rules pertaining to oral hearings are generally similar to those governing ordinary ICSID proceedings.[4]

1   Arbitration Rules, r 32.
2   Arbitration Rules, r 32(2). See also Arbitration (Additional Facility) Rules, art 39(2).
3   Ibid, r 21.
4   Arbitration (Additional Facility) Rules, arts 29, 39–43.

Third-party intervention

6.24   There may be third-party interventions in ICSID or ICSID Additional Facility proceedings if the parties to the proceeding so agree.

Amicus curiae

6.25   The ICSID Convention and the ICSID Additional Facility Rules do not provide for the submission of amicus curiae briefs. Such briefs may of course be submitted as expert opinions by the parties.

Representation of the parties

6.26   Parties to ICSID Convention proceedings may appear in person or be represented by any other person of their choice.[1] Although legal representation is, therefore, not a requirement, parties to ICSID proceedings have generally retained counsel.

1   Arbitration Rules, r 18.

Decision

6.27   The final decision of a tribunal is rendered in the form of an award. Under the Convention the arbitral tribunal shall decide questions by a majority of the votes of its members. The award shall be in writing and signed by the members of the tribunal who voted for it and shall deal with every question submitted to the tribunal, and state the reasons on which it is based.[1]

The award must be drawn up and signed within 60 days after the closure of the proceeding. This period may be extended by the tribunal for a further 30 days if it would otherwise be unable to draw up the award.[2]

The Arbitration Rules require that the award contain:

'(a)   a precise designation of each party;
 (b)   a statement that the tribunal was established under the Convention, and a description of the method of its constitution;
 (c)   the name of each member of the tribunal, and an identification of the appointing authority of each;
 (d)   the names of the agents, counsel and advocates of the parties;
 (e)   the dates and place of the sittings of the tribunal;
 (f)   a summary of the proceeding;

(g) a statement of the facts as found by the tribunal;

(h) the submissions of the parties;

(i) the decision of the tribunal on every question submitted to it, together with the reasons upon which the decision is based; and

(j) any decision of the tribunal regarding the cost of the proceeding.'[3]

If parties to an arbitration proceeding agree to settle their dispute before the award is rendered, they may request the tribunal to record the settlement in the form of its award.[4] Once issued, the award is final and binding upon the parties.[5] The award will be published by ICSID only with the consent of the parties.[6]

1 Convention, art 48.
2 Arbitration Rules, r 46.
3 Ibid, r 47. See also Arbitration (Additional Facility) Rules, art 53. However, the Additional Facility Rules require only that particular (i) be specified.
4 Ibid, r 43(1). See also Arbitration (Additional Facility) Rules, art 53(4).
5 Convention, art 53. See also Arbitration (Additional Facility) Rules, art 53(4).
6 Convention, art 48(5). Arbitration Rules, r 48(4). There is no equivalent provision under the Arbitration (Additional Facility) Rules.

Rectification or supplementation, revision and interpretation of awards

6.28 On the request of a party made within 45 days of the rendition of an award, the tribunal may, after notice to the other party, decide any question which it had omitted to decide in the award.[1] The tribunal shall also rectify any clerical, arithmetical or similar error in the award. The tribunal's decision shall become part of the award. If a dispute arises between the parties in regard to the meaning or scope of an award, either party may request an interpretation. As noted above, a request for interpretation of an award will, if possible, be submitted to the same tribunal that rendered the award.[2]

Either party may also request revision of the award on the ground of discovery of some fact of such a nature as decisively to affect the award, provided that when the award was rendered that fact was unknown to the tribunal and to the requesting party. It is a further requirement that the requesting party's ignorance was not due to negligence.[3]

If it considers that the circumstances so require it, the tribunal may stay the enforcement of its award following the submission of a request for interpretation or revision. Under ICSID Additional Facility Rules only requests for an additional decision, correction of errors and interpretation are possible; no provisions exist for a request for revision.[4]

1 Convention, art 49. Arbitration Rules, r 49.
2 Convention, art 50. Arbitration Rules, r 50.
3 Convention, art 51. Arbitration Rules, r 50.
4 Arbitration (Additional Facility) Rules, arts 56–58.

Appeals/annulment

6.29 The ICSID arbitration procedure is governed exclusively by the Convention and neither the procedure nor the awards rendered under the Convention can be challenged in national courts of contracting states. It has already been noted above that an ICSID arbitral award is binding on the parties, and that such awards can only be the subject of remedies provided for in the Convention. In addition to the above mentioned remedies of rectification or supplementation and interpretation and revision, a party may apply for the annulment of an award.[1] Under the Convention, such annulment is available on five limited grounds: that the arbitral tribunal was not properly constituted; that it manifestly exceeded its powers; that one of its members was corrupt; that there was a serious departure from a fundamental rule of procedure; and that the award failed to state the reasons on which it was based. As mentioned earlier, a request for annulment is referred to a three-member ad hoc committee appointed by the Chairman of the Administrative Council from the ICSID Panel of Arbitrators. Such a committee has the authority to annul the award in whole or in part on any of the stated grounds. Proceedings before the Committee shall be conducted in accordance with the procedures applicable in ordinary arbitration proceedings.[2] To date, annulment has been requested in six cases; in three of them the award has been annulled in part or in full.

The ICSID Additional Facility Rules do not allow for annulment procedures.

1 Convention, art 52.
2 Arbitration Rules, r 53.

Costs

6.30 The costs of ICSID proceedings include:
1. the parties' expenses, including in particular counsel fees;
2. fees and expenses of commission or tribunal members; and
3. out-of-pocket expenses of the Centre.
Aside from counsel fees, which in most proceedings constitute the largest expenditure, the fees of the arbitrators and conciliators, their travel and other expenses, as well as the Centre's out-of-pocket expenses, are met from funds that the parties are requested to advance to ICSID at intervals of three to six months.

In the case of conciliation proceedings the fees and expenses of members of the commission as well as the charges for the use of the facilities of the Centre, are borne equally by the parties. Each party bears any other expenses it incurs in connection with the conciliation proceeding. In contrast, in the case of arbitration proceedings, the tribunal will, unless the parties agree otherwise, assess the expenses incurred by the parties in connection with the proceeding, the fees and expenses of the tribunal members, and the expenses of the Centre, and decide how and by whom those expenditures shall be paid. The tribunal's decision on the apportionment of costs will form part of the award.[1]

1 Convention, art 61; Administrative Regulations, regs 14–16. See also Arbitration (Additional Facility) Rules, art 59; Administrative Rules (Additional Facility), arts 5–7.

Execution of decision, recognition and enforcement

6.31 Recourse to conciliation and arbitration under the ICSID Convention is entirely voluntary. No contracting state or national of such a state is obliged to resort to such conciliation or arbitration without having consented to do so. However, once the parties have consented, they are bound to carry out their undertaking and, in the case of arbitration, to abide by the award. Moreover, all contracting states, whether or not parties to the dispute, are required to recognise awards rendered pursuant to the Convention as binding and to enforce the pecuniary obligations imposed thereby, as if it were the final judgment of a court in that state.[1]

1 Convention, art 54(1). There is no similar provision on recognition and enforcement under the Additional Facility Rules.

REFERENCE

Sources of previous case law, including case reports

Most ICSID awards have been published in publications such as *ICSID Reports, International Legal Materials, International Law Reports* and *Yearbook Commercial Arbitration*. Where the parties have given their consent for ICSID to publish the award, such awards have been published in the *ICSID Review – Foreign Investment Law Journal*. Citations for published decisions and awards are published in the *ICSID Bibliography*. In addition to references to decisions rendered in ICSID proceedings, including several national court decisions relating to ICSID, the *ICSID Bibliography* contains references to numerous other articles and books dealing with ICSID and the ICSID Convention.

Selected bibliography

The *ICSID Bibliography* is posted on the ICSID web-site (http://www.worldbank.org/icsid).

ICSID Annual Reports.

Books

Moshe Hirsch *The Arbitration Mechanism of the International Center for Settlement of Investment Disputes* (1993).

Wolfgang Peter *Arbitration and Renegotiation of International Investment Agreements* (1995).

Stephen J Toope *Mixed International Arbitration* (1990).

Articles

Amerasinghe 'Jurisdiction Ratione Personae under the Convention on the Settlement of Investment Disputes between States and Nationals of Other States' (1974) 227 British Yearbook of International Law.

Aron Broches 'The Convention on the Settlement of Investment Disputes between States and Nationals of Other States' (1972) 136 Hague Recueil 331.

A Giardina 'The International Center for Settlement of Investment Disputes between States and Nationals of Other States' in P Sarcevic (ed) *Essays on International Commercial Arbitration* (1989).

Kenneth S Jacob 'Reinvigorating ICSID with a New Mission and with Renewed Respect for Party Autonomy' (1992) 33 Virginia Journal of International Law 123.

Carolyn B Lamm 'Jurisdiction of the International Center for Settlement of Investment Disputes' 6 ICSID Review – Foreign Investment Law Journal.

Carolyn B Lamm and Abby Cohen Smutney 'The International Center for Settlement of Investment Disputes: Responses to Problems and Changing Requirements' (November 1997), 12 Mealey's International Arbitration Report 20.

David A Lopina 'The International Center for Settlement of Investment Disputes: Investment Arbitration for the 1990s' (1988) 4 Ohio State Journal on Dispute Resolution 107.

Moore 'International Arbitration between States and Foreign Investors – The World Bank Convention' (1966) 18 Stan LR 1359.

A Parra 'Provisions on the Settlement of Investment Disputes' (1997) 12 ICSID Review – Foreign Investment Law Journal 297.

William Rand, Robert H Hornick and Paul Friedland 'ICSID's Emerging Jurisprudence: The Scope of ICSID's Jurisdiction' (1986) 19 New York University Journal of International Law and Politics 33.

Michael Reisman 'The Breakdown of the Control Mechanism in ICSID Arbitration' (1989) Duke Law Journal 739.

Ibrahim F I Shihata 'The Settlement of Disputes regarding Foreign Investment: The Role of the World Bank with particular reference to ICSID and MIGA' (1986) 1 American University of International Law and Policy 97.

Christoph Schreuer 'Decisions Ex Aequo et Bono Under the ICSID Convention' (1996) 11 ICSID Review – Foreign Investment Law Journal 37.

Tupman 'Case Studies in the Jurisdiction of the International Center for Settlement of Investment Disputes' (1986) 35 ICLQ 813 at 837–8.

– 'Commentary on the ICSID Convention' Articles 25 (cont), 26 and 27 (1997) 12 ICSID Review – Foreign Investment Law Journal 59.

– 'Commentary on the ICSID Convention', Articles 41, 42, 43 and 44 (1997) 12 ICSID Review – Foreign Investment Law Journal 365.

– 'Commentary on the ICSID Convention' Articles 45, 46, 47, 48 and 49 (1998) 13 ICSID Review – Foreign Investment Law Journal 150.

– 'The Interpretation of ICSID Arbitration Agreements' in K Wellens (ed) *International Law: Theory and Practice*, 719–35 (1998).

ANNEX

Parties to the ICSID Convention (as at 1 March 1999)

The 146 states listed below have signed the Convention on the Settlement of Investment Disputes Between States and Nationals of Other States on the dates indicated. The names of the 131 states that have deposited their instruments of ratification are in bold, and the dates of such deposit and of the attainment of the status of Contracting State by the entry into force of the Convention for each of them are also indicated.

State	Signature	Deposit of Ratification	Entry into force of Convention
Afghanistan	30 Sep 1966	25 June 1968	25 July 1968
Albania	15 Oct 1991	15 Oct 1991	14 Nov 1991
Algeria	17 Apr 1995	21 Feb 1996	22 Mar 1996
Argentina	21 May 1991	19 Oct 1994	18 Nov 1994
Armenia	16 Sep 1992	16 Sep 1992	16 Oct 1992
Australia	24 Mar 1975	2 May 1991	1 June 1991
Austria	17 May 1966	25 May 1971	24 June 1971
Azerbaïjan	18 Sep 1992	18 Sep 1992	18 Oct 1992
Bahamas	19 Oct 1995	19 Oct 1995	18 Nov 1995
Bahrain	22 Sep 1995	14 Feb 1996	15 Mar 1996
Bangladesh	20 Nov 1979	27 Mar 1980	26 Apr 1980
Barbados	13 May 1981	1 Nov 1983	1 Dec 1983
Belarus	10 July 1992	10 July 1992	9 Aug 1992
Belgium	15 Dec 1965	27 Aug 1970	26 Sep 1970
Belize	19 Dec 1986		
Benin	10 Sep 1965	6 Sep 1966	14 Oct 1966
Bolivia	3 May 1991	23 June 1995	23 July 1995
Bosnia and Herzegovina	25 Apr 1997	14 May 1997	13 June 1997
Botswana	15 Jan 1970	15 Jan 1970	14 Feb 1970
Burkina Faso	16 Sep 1965	29 Aug 1966	14 Oct 1966
Burundi	17 Feb 1967	5 Nov 1969	5 Dec 1969
Cambodia	5 Nov 1993		
Cameroon	23 Sep 1965	3 Jan 1967	2 Feb 1967
Central African Republic	26 Aug 1965	23 Feb 1966	14 Oct 1966
Chad	12 May 1966	29 Aug 1966	14 Oct 1966
Chile	25 Jan 1991	24 Sep 1991	24 Oct 1991
China	9 Feb 1990	7 Jan 1993	6 Feb 1993
Colombia	18 May 1993	15 July 1997	14 Aug 1997
Comoros	26 Sep 1978	7 Nov 1978	7 Dec 1978
Congo	27 Dec 1965	23 June 1966	14 Oct 1966
Congo, Democratic Republic of	29 Oct 1968	29 Apr 1970	29 May 1970
Costa Rica	29 Sep 1981	27 Apr 1993	27 May 1993
Côte d'Ivoire	30 June 1965	16 Feb 1966	14 Oct 1966
Croatia	16 June 1997	22 Sep 1998	22 Oct 1998
Cyprus	9 Mar 1966	25 Nov 1966	25 Dec 1966
Czech Republic	23 Mar 1993	23 Mar 1993	22 Apr 1993
Denmark	11 Oct 1965	24 Apr 1968	24 May 1968
Ecuador	15 Jan 1986	15 Jan 1986	14 Feb 1986
Egypt, Arab Republic of	11 Feb 1972	3 May 1972	2 June 1972
El Salvador	9 June 1982	6 Mar 1984	5 Apr 1984
Estonia	23 June 1992	23 June 1992	23 Jul 1992
Ethiopia	21 Sep 1965		
Fiji	1 July 1977	11 Aug 1977	10 Sep 1977

State	Signature	Deposit of Ratification	Entry into force of Convention
Finland	14 July 1967	9 Jan 1969	8 Feb 1969
France	22 Dec 1965	21 Aug 1967	20 Sep 1967
Gabon	21 Sep 1965	4 Apr 1966	14 Oct 1966
Gambia, The	1 Oct 1974	27 Dec 1974	26 Jan 1975
Georgia	7 Aug 1992	7 Aug 1992	6 Sep 1992
Germany	27 Jan 1966	18 Apr 1969	18 May 1969
Ghana	26 Nov 1965	13 July 1966	14 Oct 1966
Greece	16 Mar 1966	21 Apr 1969	21 May 1969
Grenada	24 May 1991	24 May 1991	23 June 1991
Guatemala	9 Nov 1995		
Guinea	27 Aug 1968	4 Nov 1968	4 Dec 1968
Guinea-Bissau	4 Sep 1991		
Guyana	3 July 1969	11 July 1969	10 Aug 1969
Haiti	30 Jan 1985		
Honduras	28 May 1986	14 Feb 1989	16 Mar 1989
Hungary	1 Oct 1986	4 Feb 1987	6 Mar 1987
Iceland	25 July 1966	25 July 1966	14 Oct 1966
Indonesia	16 Feb 1968	28 Sep 1968	28 Oct 1968
Ireland	30 Aug 1966	7 Apr 1981	7 May 1981
Israel	16 June 1980	22 June 1983	22 July 1983
Italy	18 Nov 1965	29 Mar 1971	28 Apr 1971
Jamaica	23 June 1965	9 Sep 1966	14 Oct 1966
Japan	23 Sep 1965	17 Aug 1967	16 Sep 1967
Jordan	14 July 1972	30 Oct 1972	29 Nov 1972
Kazakhstan	23 July 1992		
Kenya	24 May 1966	3 Jan 1967	2 Feb 1967
Kyrgyz, Republic of	9 June 1995		
Korea, Republic of	18 Apr 1966	21 Feb 1967	23 Mar 1967
Kuwait	9 Feb 1978	2 Feb 1979	4 Mar 1979
Latvia	8 Aug 1997	8 Aug 1997	7 Sep 1997
Lesotho	19 Sep 1968	8 July 1969	7 Aug 1969
Liberia	3 Sep 1965	16 June 1970	16 July 1970
Lithuania	6 July 1992	6 July 1992	5 Aug 1992
Luxembourg	28 Sep 1965	30 July 1970	29 Aug 1970
Macedonia, former Yugoslav Republic of	16 Sep 1998	27 Oct 1998	26 Nov 1998
Madagascar	1 June 1966	6 Sep 1966	14 Oct 1966
Malawi	9 June 1966	23 Aug 1966	14 Oct 1966
Malaysia	22 Oct 1965	8 Aug 1966	14 Oct 1966
Mali	9 Apr 1976	3 Jan 1978	2 Feb 1978
Mauritania	30 July 1965	11 Jan 1966	14 Oct 1966
Mauritius	2 June 1969	2 June 1969	2 July 1969
Micronesia	24 June 1993	24 June 1993	24 July 1993
Moldova	12 Aug 1992		
Mongolia	14 June 1991	14 June 1991	14 July 1991
Morocco	11 Oct 1965	11 May 1967	10 June 1967
Mozambique	4 Apr 1995	7 June 1995	7 July 1995

State	Signature	Deposit of Ratification	Entry into force of Convention
Namibia	26 Oct 1998		
Nepal	28 Sep 1965	7 Jan 1969	6 Feb 1969
Netherlands	25 May 1966	14 Sep 1966	14 Oct 1966
New Zealand	2 Sep 1970	2 Apr 1980	2 May 1980
Nicaragua	4 Feb 1994	20 Mar 1995	19 Apr 1995
Niger	23 Aug 1965	14 Nov 1966	14 Dec 1966
Nigeria	13 July 1965	23 Aug 1965	14 Oct 1966
Norway	24 June 1966	16 Aug 1967	15 Sep 1967
Oman	5 May 1995	24 July 1995	23 Aug 1995
Pakistan	6 July 1965	15 Sep 1966	15 Oct 1966
Panama	22 Nov 1995	8 Apr 1996	8 May 1996
Papua New Guinea	20 Oct 1978	20 Oct 1978	19 Nov 1978
Paraguay	27 July 1981	7 Jan 1983	6 Feb 1983
Peru	4 Sep 1991	9 Aug 1993	8 Sep 1993
Philippines	26 Sep 1978	17 Nov 1978	17 Dec 1978
Portugal	4 Aug 1983	2 July 1984	1 Aug 1984
Romania	6 Sep 1974	12 Sep 1975	12 Oct 1975
Russian Federation	16 June 1992		
Rwanda	21 Apr 1978	15 Oct 1979	14 Nov 1979
Samoa	3 Feb 1978	25 Apr 1978	25 May 1978
Saudi Arabia	28 Sep 1979	8 May 1980	7 June 1980
Senegal	26 Sep 1966	21 Apr 1967	21 May 1967
Seychelles	16 Feb 1978	20 Mar 1978	19 Apr 1978
Sierra Leone	27 Sep 1965	2 Aug 1966	14 Oct 1966
Singapore	2 Feb 1968	14 Oct 1968	13 Nov 1968
Slovak Republic	27 Sep 1993	27 May 1994	26 June 1994
Slovenia	7 Mar 1994	7 Mar 1994	6 Apr 1994
Solomon Islands	12 Nov 1979	8 Sep 1981	8 Oct 1981
Somalia	27 Sep 1965	29 Feb 1968	30 Mar 1968
Spain	21 Mar 1994	18 Aug 1994	17 Sept 1994
Sri Lanka	30 Aug 1967	12 Oct 1967	11 Nov 1967
St Kitts & Nevis	14 Oct 1994	4 Aug 1995	3 Sep 1995
St Lucia	4 June 1984	4 June 1984	4 July 1984
Sudan	15 Mar 1967	9 Apr 1973	9 May 1973
Swaziland	3 Nov 1970	14 June 1971	14 July 1971
Sweden	25 Sep 1965	29 Dec 1966	28 Jan 1967
Switzerland	22 Sep 1967	15 May 1968	14 June 1968
Tanzania	10 Jan 1992	18 May 1992	17 June 1992
Thailand	6 Dec 1985		
Togo	24 Jan 1966	11 Aug 1967	10 Sep 1967
Tonga	1 May 1989	21 Mar 1990	20 Apr 1990
Trinidad and Tobago	5 Oct 1966	3 Jan 1967	2 Feb 1967
Tunisia	5 May 1965	22 June 1966	14 Oct 1966
Turkey	24 June 1987	3 Mar 1989	2 Apr 1989
Turkmenistan	26 Sep 1992	26 Sep 1992	26 Oct 1992
Uganda	7 June 1966	7 June 1966	14 Oct 1966

Trade, commercial and investment protection dispute settlement bodies and rules

State	Signature	Deposit of Ratification	Entry into force of Convention
Ukraine	3 Apr 1998		
United Arab Emirates	23 Dec 1981	23 Dec 1981	22 Jan 1982
United Kingdom of Great Britain and Northern Ireland	26 May 1965	19 Dec 1966	18 Jan 1967
United States of America	27 Aug 1965	10 June 1966	14 Oct 1966
Uruguay	28 May 1992		
Uzbekistan	17 Mar 1994	26 July 1995	25 Aug 1995
Venezuela	18 Aug 1993	2 May 1995	1 June 1995
Yemen, Republic of	28 Oct 1997		
Yugoslavia, Socialist Federal Republic of	21 Mar 1967	21 Mar 1967	20 Apr 1967
Zambia	17 June 1970	17 June 1970	17 July 1970
Zimbabwe	25 Mar 1991	20 May 1994	19 June 1994

CHAPTER 7

International Court of Arbitration of the International Chamber of Commerce

INTRODUCTORY

General information

7.1 The International Court of Arbitration of the International Chamber of Commerce is a non-governmental entity based in Paris. Arbitration proceedings conducted under its auspices may take place at any location agreed upon by the parties to a dispute or, in the absence of such agreement, as determined by the ICC Court.[1] The headquarters of the International Court of Arbitration of the ICC ('ICC Court') and its Secretariat are at:

> ICC International Court of Arbitration
> 38, Cour Albert 1er
> Paris 75008
> France

> Tel: 33 1 49 53 28 28
> Fax: 33 1 49 53 29 33
> email: arb@iccwbo.org
> website: http://www.iccwbo.org/arb/index.htm

1 ICC Rules of Arbitration, in force as from 1 January 1998, art 14(1), ICC Publication no 581 10, ('Rules of Arbitration').

Description

7.2 Founded in 1923, the ICC International Court of Arbitration is a private arbitration body attached to the International Chamber of Commerce (ICC), which was founded four years earlier. The principal mission of the ICC is to promote international trade and investment, advocate the market economy system worldwide and regulate cross-border business. The establishment of a Court of Arbitration was intended to offer public and private parties to international business contracts an effective arrangement to settle any contractual disputes between them. It is to be emphasised that the ICC Court is not an ordinary standing court. Rather, the ICC Court supervises the establishment, operation and final decision of Arbitral Tribunals entrusted with responsibility for settling specific cases referred to them. ICC Tribunals are composed of independent arbitrators appointed or confirmed under the ICC Rules for each separate case before the ICC Court.

The ICC Court is an autonomous organisation consisting of more than 75 members (or alternate members) coming from almost 60 countries. Members of the court are appointed by the ICC Council for a renewable three-year term, upon nomination by a national committee of the ICC.[1] In addition, the ICC Council elects a chairman (upon recommendation of the ICC Executive Board) and vice-chairmen (at present there are 10 vice-chairmen). The court is assisted by a Secretariat, headed by a Secretary-General.

The main function of the ICC Court is to facilitate arbitration of international business disputes referred to it and ensure the application of the Rules of Arbitration of the ICC by the various arbitral tribunals established under its auspices. By way of example, at the end of the arbitration proceeding the court scrutinises all ICC Arbitral Awards before they become final and binding.

Since its establishment, the ICC Court has dealt with more than 10,000 arbitration cases. Each year arbitrations are held in some 40 different countries. In 1998, the most recent year for which information is available at the time of writing, 466 new requests for arbitration were filed with the ICC. These requests involved 1,151 parties from over 100 different countries. Of these cases, states (or state-controlled entities) were involved in 10 per cent of the cases. In approximately 60 per cent of the cases the amount in dispute exceeded one million US dollars.

In addition to its activities relating to arbitration, the ICC Court also oversees conciliation proceedings conducted in pursuance of the ICC Rules of Conciliation.[2]

1   ICC Rules of Arbitration, Appendix 1 Statutes of the International Court of Arbitration of the ICC, art 3, ICC Publication no 581 33 ('ICC Court Statutes').
2   ICC Rules of Optional Conciliation, in force as from 1 January 1988, ICC Publication no 581 46.

INSTITUTIONAL ASPECTS

Governing texts

Structure of the ICC Court

7.3   The ICC Court is regulated by two principal instruments: (1) Statutes of the International Court of Arbitration of the ICC,[1] which define the role, composition and functioning of the court; and (2) Internal Rules of the International Court of Arbitration of the ICC,[2] which provide for confidentiality, regulate the participation of court members in ICC Arbitral proceedings, state the independence of each member from the national committee of its country of origin, organises the committees of the court, contains provisions on the role of the Secretariat and defines the process of scrutiny of Arbitral Awards. The Statutes and the Internal Rules are appended to the ICC Rules of Arbitration (Appendix I and II, respectively).

1   ICC Rules of Arbitration, Appendix 1 Statutes of the International Court of Arbitration of the ICC.
2   Ibid, Appendix II Internal Rules of the International Court of Arbitration of the ICC.

Procedure of arbitration

7.4   The arbitration proceedings are governed by the ICC Rules of Arbitration. These rules have recently undergone a major revision.[1] Arbitrations commencing after 1 January 1998 are governed by the new rules; arbitrations initiated before that date are governed by a previous version of the rules (the 1988 Rules of Arbitration). While in normal practice the proceedings are governed by the rules in force at the time of commencement of the proceedings, parties may stipulate in their arbitration agreement that the prospective proceedings will be governed by the rules in force at the date on which they concluded their arbitration agreement.[2]

In all questions of procedure, not expressly regulated by the Rules or by way of agreement of the parties, the Court and Arbitral Tribunal are to act in the spirit of the Rules of Arbitration.[3]

1   Proposals for modification of the Rules of Arbitration are prepared by the ICC Commission on International Arbitration (acting inter alia upon an initiative of the court) and submitted to the Executive Board and Council of the ICC for approval.
2   Rules of Arbitration, art 6(1).
3   Ibid, art 35.

Substantive law of arbitration

7.5   ICC arbitration tribunals apply the choice of law agreed by the parties. If no agreement on applicable law has been entered into, the tribunal is expected to apply the rules of law it determines to be appropriate.[1] In all cases, the tribunal is to take into account relevant contractual provisions and trade usages.[2] Additionally, with the agreement of the parties, the tribunal may decide the dispute as an *amiable compositeur*, on the basis of equity (ie *ex aequo et bono*).[3]

1   Rules of Arbitration, art 17(1).
2   Ibid, art 17(2).
3   Ibid, art 17(3).

Organisation

Composition

ICC COURT OF ARBITRATION

7.6   The ICC Court consists of a chairman, vice-chairmen, members and alternate members. The ICC Council elects the court's chairman (upon recommendation of the Executive Board of the ICC) and the vice-chairmen of the court (either from among the members of the court or not).[1] In addition, the Council appoints the court's members, acting on proposals of ICC national committees (each committee is entitled to nominate one member); and alternate members, acting on the proposal of the chairman. The term of office for all members is three years.[2]

Members of the court (excluding the chairman) may be designated by a party to a case to serve as arbitrators, but cannot be selected by the court to serve in this position. As is the case with any other involvement of an ICC Court member in proceedings pending before the court, in whatever capacity, that member shall not participate in the discussions and decisions of the court concerning the same case.[3]

1   ICC Court Statutes, art 3.
2   Current membership is as follows (March 1999):
    Chairman: Robert Briner (Switzerland). **Vice-Chairmen:** Fali S Nariman (India); Toshio Sawada (Japan); Francis P Donovan (Australia); Carlos Henrique de C Fróes (Brazil); Richard W Hulbert (United States); Ottoarndt Glossner (Germany); Michel Aurillac (France); Piero Bernardini (Italy); Ahmed S El-Kosheri (Egypt); Michael J Mustill (United

Kingdom). **Members:** Sergio Le Pera (Argentina); Garry Downes (Australia); Waldemar Jud (Austria); Kamal Hossain (Bangladesh); Pierre Gabriel (Belgium); Luiz Fernando Teixeira Pinto (Brazil); Gaston Kenfack Douajni (Cameroon); Serge Gravel (Canada); Carlos Eugenio Jorquiera M (Chile); Francisco Ramirez Vasco (Colombia); Léon Boissier-Palun (Côte-d'Ivoire); Antis A Triantafyllides (Cyprus); P R Meurs-Gerken (Denmark); José Ramon Jimenez Carbo (Ecuador); Yehia El Gamal (Egypt); Robert Mattson (Finland); Patrice Level (France); Fabian von Schlabrendorff (Germany); Antonias Dimolitsa (Greece); Ivan Szasz (Hungary); Sarosh R Zaiwalla (India); Arnold Ahmad Baramuli (Indonesia); Mohammad H Tamaddon (Iran); Roderick H Murphy SC (Ireland); Michel A Calvo (Israel); Renzo Morera (Italy); Kazuo Takayanagi (Japan); Hatim Sharif Zu'bi (Jordan); Soo-Myung Min (Korea); Anwar Al-Fuzaie (Kuwait); Joseph S Takla (Lebanon); Pierre Seimetz (Luxembourg); Raymond Ranjeva (Madagascar); Julio C Treviño (Mexico); Hamid Andaloussi (Morocco); Sierk Bruna (Netherlands); Bola Ajibola (Nigeria); Gunnar Nerdrum (Norway); M A K Afridi (Pakistan); Jorge Avendaño V (Peru); Antonio Pires de Lima (Portugal); Hasan E Al-Mulla (Saudi Arabia); Jean Gabriel Benglia (Senegal); K S Chung (Singapore); Mervyn King SC (South Africa); Juan Antonio Cremades (Spain); C Chakradaran (Sri Lanka); Hans Bagner (Sweden); Pierre Neiger (Switzerland); Faez Anjak (Syria); Salah Mejri (Tunisia); Mahmut Birsel (Turkey); David St John Sutton (United Kingdom); Stephen R Bond (United States); Héctor Gros Espiell (Uruguay); James Otis Rodner (Venezuela); Dobrosav Mitrovic (Yugoslavia). **Alternate Members:** Ernesto O'Farrell (Argentina); Maximiano Mafra de Laet (Brazil); Joseph Helal (Egypt); Philippe Boivin (France); Michael Bühler (Germany); Mohsen Mohebi (Iran); Mahomed J Jaffer (Pakistan); João Luís Pinheiro Lopes dos Reis (Portugal); Saleh B Al Tayar (Saudi Arabia); Michael Lee (United Kingdom).

3   Internal Rules, art 2.

ARBITRAL TRIBUNALS

7.7 Subject to agreement between the parties to the contrary, disputes referred to ICC arbitration are normally to be settled by a sole arbitrator. However, where it appears to the ICC Court that the dispute warrants the appointment of three arbitrators, the court will take a decision to that effect.[1] In cases referred to a sole arbitrator, the parties are to agree on his or her identity within 30 days from the date on which the respondent received the Request for Arbitration (or within additional time designated by the Secretariat).[2] Upon failure of the parties to agree on the identity of the sole arbitrator within that time frame, or upon failure to agree upon the number of arbitrators, the ICC Court will appoint a sole arbitrator. In cases referred to three arbitrators, each party is entitled to appoint one arbitrator. If there is agreement between the parties on the number of arbitrators, each party nominates its arbitrator in either the Request for Arbitration or the Answer – submitted 30 days thereafter. If there is no such agreement, the court will allow the claimant 15 days to nominate an arbitrator, and allow the respondent 15 days after being notified of the first nomination to nominate its own arbitrator.[3] The third arbitrator (who is to be chairman of the tribunal) is to be appointed by the court, unless the parties have agreed upon an alternative procedure, which is to be carried out within time limits introduced by the court.

Appointments made by the parties are to be confirmed by the court or by the Secretary-General (the latter is authorised only to approve requests for confirmation; in case of refusal to confirm, the appointment will be brought before the court).[4] Before confirming or making an appointment, the court (or Secretary-General) is to verify that the prospective arbitrator has signed a statement of independence in which he or she is required to disclose any facts or circumstances that might compromise his or her independence.[5] In confirming or appointing an arbitrator, the ICC Court (or Secretary-General) will also, inter alia, take into account the nationality, residence and links of the prospective arbitrator to the nationality of the parties and other arbitrators. In appointing arbitrators, the ICC Court will generally act on a proposal of a relevant National Committee of the ICC (although in certain circumstances it may act in the absence of a National Committee proposal, or even select an arbitrator from a country that does not have a National Committee).[6]

1   Rules of Arbitration, art 8(1),(2).
2   Ibid, art 8(3).
3   Ibid, art 8(2),(4).
4   Ibid, art 9(1),(2).
5   Ibid, art 7(2).
6   Ibid, art 9.

DISQUALIFICATION OF ARBITRATORS

7.8   A party who wishes to challenge the appointment of an arbitrator must make a written submission to the Secretariat specifying the facts and circumstances indicating alleged lack of independence or other reason for disqualification.[1] The decision on the challenge shall be taken by the ICC Court after inviting the other party and all members of the tribunal (including the concerned arbitrator) for their views on the matter.

1   Rules of Arbitration, art 11. See para 7.21.

Plenary/chambers

THE ICC COURT

7.9   The ICC Court generally meets four times every month – once in plenary session and three times in committee sessions to which some of the court's decision making power has been delegated.[1] Plenary sessions (quorum of six members) are presided over by the chairman, or, in his absence, by a vice-chairman designated by him or her, and decisions are taken by a majority vote. In committee sessions, which comprise a chairman and two or more other members (quorum of two members), decisions are taken unanimously.

All sessions of the court are confidential and open only to court members and to the Secretariat.

1   Internal Rules, art 4(5); Rules of Arbitration, art 1(4); see also Robert Briner 'The Implementation of the 1998 ICC Rules of Arbitration' (1997) International Court of Arbitration Bulletin, Vol 8 No 2, p 7.

Appellate structure

7.10   The Rules of Arbitration of the ICC Court do not provide for an appellate procedure and awards by an ICC tribunal and subsequent decisions of the court are final and binding on the parties.[1]

1   Rules of Arbitration, arts 7(4), 28(6).

Technical/scientific experts

7.11   The tribunal may allow parties to an ICC case to present expert testimony.[1] In addition it may, after consulting with the parties, appoint one or more experts and instruct them to prepare a report.[2] The parties will have the opportunity to challenge such testimony. Arbitrators or parties in need of an expert opinion in specialised or technical fields may utilise the ICC International Centre for Expertise. This Centre has been active for more than 20 years in contributing expert services to ICC proceedings.[3]

1   Rules of Arbitration, art 20(3).
2   Ibid, art 20(4).
3   See ICC Rules for Expertise, in force as from 1 January 1993.

Secretariat

7.12   The ICC Court is assisted by a Secretariat located at ICC Headquarters in Paris. The Secretariat currently has a full-time, multilingual staff of about 40 persons, including 20 lawyers trained in the main legal traditions of the world. The Secretariat closely follows all ICC cases and is available to provide assistance and information when needed. At present, each case is followed by one of six teams headed by a counsel. The Secretariat is headed by the Secretary-General (currently Horacio A Grigera Naòn), assisted by his Deputy and a General Counsel.

Jurisdiction

Ratione personae

7.13   Any two (or more) parties to a dispute – natural persons, companies and other juridical persons or state entities can enter into an agreement to refer a case to the ICC Court. That agreement can take the form of an arbitration clause in a business contract or a separate agreement (ie *compromis*).[1]

In the case of a contractual arbitration clause, even if the contract as a whole is considered null and void, the agreement to arbitrate will normally continue to be regarded as valid for the purpose of determining by way of arbitration the respective rights and obligations of the parties (unless the parties agree otherwise).[2]

1   Standard ICC arbitration clauses in a number of languages are appended to the Rules of Arbitration.
2   Rules of Arbitration, art 6(4).

Ratione materiae

7.14   Disputes subject to ICC arbitration must be 'business disputes'.[1] Although the term 'business' is defined broadly in the practice of the ICC, jurisdiction over certain categories of disputes is excluded (eg divorce settlements, inheritance). While the ICC Court is primarily designed to address business disputes of an international character, business disputes not having such character may also be arbitrated under the ICC Rules provided the court is properly empowered by the relevant arbitration agreement.

1   Rules of Arbitration, art 1(1).

Ratione temporis

7.15   There are no procedural time limits in the Rules for bringing a claim to ICC arbitration. However, such limits may – and usually are – introduced in the arbitration clause or agreement or imposed by applicable rules of law.

Advisory jurisdiction

7.16 All proceedings before ICC Arbitral Tribunals are contentious and result in the rendering of a final and binding Award. Decisions of the ICC Court are also final and binding.

PROCEDURAL ASPECTS

Languages

7.17 The official languages of the ICC Court are English and French. However, arbitration proceedings may be conducted in any language agreed upon by the parties.[1] In the absence of agreement, the tribunal will determine the language (or languages) of the proceedings with due regard to all relevant circumstances (including the language of the contract).

Documents drafted in a language other than the ones used by the arbitrators and the court are translated as needed. The Secretariat normally offers linguistic assistance in relation to documents in English, French, German, Spanish, Italian and Arabic and, depending on staff availability, in Russian and Chinese.

1   Rules of Arbitration, art 16.

Instituting proceedings

7.18   A party wishing to have recourse to ICC arbitration submits a Request for Arbitration to the ICC Secretariat in Paris.[1] The Request must include the following information:

(a) the full name, description and address of each party to the dispute;
(b) the nature and circumstances of the dispute giving rise to the claim;
(c) a statement of the relief sought, including indication of the amounts claimed (to the extent possible);
(d) any relevant agreement, and, in particular, the arbitration agreement;
(e) all relevant particulars concerning the number and choice of arbitrators, and any nomination made in pursuance with arts 8–10 of the Rules of Arbitration;
(f) comments on the place of arbitration, applicable law and language of proceedings.[2]

The claimant must file the Request in a number of copies sufficient to provide one copy for each party, arbitrator, and the Secretariat.[3] The Request must be accompanied by a registration fee, constituting an advance payment on ICC administrative expenses.[4]

1   Rules of Arbitration, art 4(1).
2   Ibid, art 4(3).
3   Ibid, arts 3(1), 4(4).
4   The current registration fee is US$2,500. Rules of Arbitration, Appendix III Arbitration Costs and Fees, art 1(1) ('Arbitration Costs').

Financial assistance

7.19   The cost of ICC arbitration largely depends on the amount in dispute between the parties. The ICC Court does not have a financial assistance scheme.

Provisional measures

7.20 Unless the parties have agreed otherwise, an ICC arbitral tribunal may, at the request of a party, order any interim or conservatory measure it deems appropriate. This may be in the form of an order or an Award.[1] However, the requesting party may be required to provide an appropriate security, and mandatory rules may limit the tribunal's power to order such measures.

Before the file is transmitted to the arbitral tribunal (and in appropriate cases even thereafter), provisional measures may be requested from a competent judicial authority,[2] or from a Referee appointed under the ICC Rules for a Pre-Arbitral Referee Procedure.[3] This procedure, which the parties can adopt in advance (preferably as part of the arbitration clause),[4] involves the prompt appointment, upon request of a party, of a neutral person usually selected by the parties or the chairman of the ICC Court. The Referee is empowered to issue any urgent conservatory measure or measure of restoration necessary to prevent immediate damage or irreparable loss to the rights or property of the requesting party; order the making of a payment due; order the taking of steps that ought to be taken in accordance with the contract on hand; or order any measure necessary to preserve or establish evidence.[5] The orders of the Referee remain in force until he or she, or a competent authority (eg ICC arbitral tribunal) has decided otherwise.[6]

1   Rules of Arbitration, art 23(1).
2   Ibid, art 23(2).
3   ICC Rules for a Pre-Arbitral Referee Procedure, in force as from 1 January 1990, ICC Publication no 482 (1990) ('Pre-Arbitral Referee Rules').
4   Model arbitration clauses referring to the Pre-Arbitral Referee procedure are appended to the Pre-Arbitral Referee Rules.
5   Pre-Arbitral Referee Rules, art 2.1.
6   Ibid, art 6.3.

Preliminary objections/proceedings

7.21 Challenges concerning the existence, validity or scope of the arbitration agreement are initially dealt with by the ICC Court. If either party raises such a plea concerning the applicability of the arbitration agreement, or if the respondent fails to present an Answer (ie a written reply to the Request for Arbitration), the court may decide, without prejudice to the admissibility or merits of the plea, whether the arbitration should proceed. It will only do so if it is prima facie satisfied that an arbitration agreement under the ICC Rules may exist.[1] However, the final decision on the jurisdiction of the arbitral tribunal is to be taken by the tribunal itself.

If the court is not so satisfied that a prima facie valid and relevant agreement exists, the arbitration will not proceed. In that case, each party is entitled to seize any court having jurisdiction and obtain a ruling on whether there is or there is not a binding arbitration agreement.[2]

Another preliminary proceeding is in the case of challenge directed against an arbitrator. A party who wishes to disqualify an arbitrator on the basis of alleged lack of independence or another reason, shall submit to the Secretariat a written statement, specifying the facts and circumstances underlying the challenge. The statement must be presented within 30 days from notification of the appointment or confirmation of the arbitrator, or from the date on which the said facts and circumstances became known to it.[3] The court will decide on the challenge after the other party and the arbitrators (including the challenged arbitrator) have had a chance to submit written comments, within a period of time set by the Secretariat.[4]

Upon disqualification (and in other instances where replacement of an arbitrator is necessary) the court may decide whether to nominate a new arbitrator in accordance with the original nomination process, or otherwise. In addition, the court may decide (after hearing the view of the parties and the remaining arbitrators) that the arbitration shall proceed before a truncated tribunal.[5]

1   Rules of Arbitration, art 6(2).
2   Ibid.
3   Ibid, art 11(1),(2).
4   Ibid, art 11(3).
5   Ibid, art 12(4),(5).

Written pleadings

First stage

7.22   The arbitration proceedings begin on the date on which the Secretariat receives the Request of Arbitration submitted on behalf of the claimant. Upon receiving the Request, the Secretariat notifies the claimant and the respondent and sends the latter a copy of the Request. The respondent should file an Answer within 30 days from the receipt of the Request (however, the Secretariat may extend this period provided that the respondent has already communicated to it information on the number, choice and possible nomination of arbitrators).[1] The Answer should include the following information and be submitted in a number of copies identical to that of the Request:
(a) full name, description and address of the respondent;
(b) comments on the nature and circumstances of the dispute giving rise to the claim;
(c) response to the relief sought;
(d) comments on the number and choice of arbitrators, in light of the claimants proposals, and any nomination made in pursuance of arts 8–10 of the Rules of Arbitration;
(e) comments on the place of arbitration, applicable law and language of proceedings.
The Respondent may append to its Answer a Counter-Claim which shall include the following particulars:
(a) nature and circumstances of the dispute giving rise to the Counter-Claim;
(b) statement of the relief sought, including indications of the amounts claimed (to the possible extent).[2]
The claimant will then file a Reply to the Counter-Claim within 30 days from the date it received the Counter-Claim (although the Secretariat may extend this period of time).[3]

After it is constituted, the tribunal will receive a file from the Secretariat containing the initial submissions of the parties. The arbitral tribunal is then to prepare within two months the Terms of Reference for the proceedings. These Terms are based on the parties' most recent submissions, based on documents and/or in the presence of the parties.[4] The Terms shall include, inter alia, the names and addresses of the parties, a summary of the parties' respective claims and of the relief sought by each party, with an indication of the amounts involved. Unless the arbitral tribunal considers it inappropriate, the Terms will also include a list of issues to be determined. In addition, the Terms of Reference shall contain specific details on the applicable procedural rules. The Terms of Reference are to be signed by the parties to the dispute. If any of the parties refuses to sign the Terms, the tribunal will submit them for approval to the ICC Court.[5]

After the Terms of Reference have been signed by the parties, or approved by the court, new claims or Counter-Claims outside the limits of the Terms of Reference may not be made without the authorisation of the arbitral tribunal.[6]

1   Rules of Arbitration, art 5(1),(2).
2   Ibid, art 5(5).
3   Ibid, art 5(6).
4   Ibid, art 18(1),(2).
5   Ibid, art 19.
6   Ibid, arts 18(2),(3).

Merits stage

7.23   After completing the Terms of Reference, the Arbitral Tribunal proceeds to establish the facts of the case. It will do so on the basis of written submissions and documents provided by the parties. Additional written submissions, if necessary, can only be made with the approval of the tribunal in accordance with a provisional timetable established by it, and after consulting with the parties.[1]

1   Rules of Arbitration, art 18(4).

Oral arguments

7.24   The arbitral tribunal will hear the parties (or their representatives) in person if any of them so requests, or may provide for oral hearings of its own motion. In cases where no party requested a hearing, the tribunal may decide the case on the basis of written pleadings only.[1] In addition, the tribunal may decide to hear witnesses (including experts).

Persons other than the parties, their duly authorised representatives and legal advisers, and other persons involved in the proceedings, may not attend oral hearing sessions, except with the approval of the tribunal and the parties.[2]

1   Rules of Arbitration, art 20(2),(6).
2   Ibid, art 21(3).

Third-party intervention/multiple proceedings

7.25   Unless the parties have provided otherwise, third-party intervention in arbitral proceedings is only possible with the consent of all parties and the arbitral tribunal.

As to multiple proceedings, the Rules of Arbitration explicitly provide for the admissibility of multi-claimant or multi-respondent cases.[1] In the event of multiple proceedings, the appointment of the tribunal is to be conducted so that each group of claimants and/or respondents exercises jointly the right to nominate an arbitrator which exists under the ordinary procedure. Upon failure on the part of the parties to agree on a joint nomination or on the method of constitution of the tribunal, the ICC Court may appoint each member of the tribunal.[2]

1   Rules of Arbitration, art 2.
2   Ibid, art 10.

Amicus curiae

7.26   There is no provision in the Rules of Arbitration addressing the admissibility of amicus curiae briefs. Theoretically however, there is nothing in the Rules to prevent the tribunal from obtaining information from any third person.[1]

1   Rules of Arbitration, art 20(3).

Representation of parties

7.27   The parties may appear before the tribunal in person or through duly authorised representatives. They may be assisted by advisers.[1]

1   Rules of Arbitration, art 21(4).

Decision

7.28   The final decision of the arbitral tribunal on the merits of the case is rendered in the form of an Award. After the conclusion of the written and oral proceedings, the tribunal communicates to the Secretariat an approximate date by which the draft award will be submitted to the court.[1] Generally, an award must be rendered within six months from the signature or approval of the Terms of Reference. However, the court is free to extend this period if it decides that such extension is warranted.[2]

The award must state the reasons upon which it is based. It is deemed to have been made at the place of arbitration on the date indicated in it.[3] The award is binding upon the parties and they are deemed to have waived their right to any form of recourse against it.[4]

When the arbitral tribunal is composed of more than one arbitrator, an award is given by a majority decision. If no majority exists, the award is decided by the chairman of the arbitral tribunal alone.[5] If the parties reach a settlement agreement during the proceedings, the parties may request the tribunal to record their agreement in the form of an award.[6]

Finally, it should be emphasised that the ICC Court exercises powers of scrutiny over the award. Thus, before the final signing of the award, the tribunal must transmit the draft award to the court.[7] The latter shall decide whether to approve the form of the award, and may impose necessary modifications in form to that effect. As to the substantive contents of the award, the court may draw the attention of the arbitrators to certain points of substance (eg compatibility with requirement of applicable mandatory municipal law). The tribunal is not obliged to accept the view of the court on substance.

1   Rules of Arbitration, art 22(2).
2   Ibid, art 24.
3   Ibid, art 25(2),(3).
4   Ibid, art 28(6).
5   Ibid, art 25(1).
6   Ibid, art 26.
7   Ibid, art 27.

Revision of award

7.29 On its own initiative, the tribunal may correct within 30 days from the date the award was rendered any clerical, computational and typographical errors or any other such error contained it.[1] Alternatively, a party to the case may apply within the same 30-day period to the Secretariat and request correction of the award (referring to the aforementioned types of errors) or its interpretation.[2] The other party shall be accorded normally not more than 30 days to submit its comments on the request. The original tribunal is expected to render its decision on the request within 30 days of the last date on which the comments of the other party were due, or any other period determined by the court.

Any decision on correction or interpretaiion of the award must be approved by the court, and take the form of an Addendum to the original award.[3]

1 Rules of Arbitration, art 29(1).
2 Ibid, art 29(2).
3 Ibid, art 29(3).

Appeal

7.30 There is no possibility of appeal over an ICC Award. By submitting their dispute to ICC arbitration, the parties undertake to carry out any award without delay and are deemed to have waived their right to any form of appeal or challenge (insofar as such a waiver can validly be made).[1]

1 Rules of Arbitration, art 28(6).

Costs

7.31 The costs of ICC arbitration include the following components:
  (i) fees and expenses of arbitrators;
  (ii) administrative expenses of the ICC;
  (iii) fees and expenses of tribunal-appointed experts; and
  (iv) reasonable legal and other costs of the parties.[1]

The ICC Court fixes the fees of the arbitrators and the administrative expenses of the ICC at the end of the arbitration on the basis of a published scale attached to the ICC Rules.[2] Under that scale, the arbitrators' fees are fixed at a minimum and maximum rate with reference to the amount in dispute. In fixing the precise fee, the court considers, inter alia, the diligence of the arbitrators, the time spent, the rapidity of the proceedings and the complexity of the dispute.[3] However, the court may deviate from the scale when it is warranted by the special circumstances of the case. All costs and expenses not determined by the court are to be fixed by the arbitral tribunal.

Payments to the ICC Court are made upon initiation of proceedings, and on dates and in amounts fixed by the Secretary-General and/or the court, subject to future readjustments.[4] All advance payments are to be borne by the parties in equal shares.[5] However, the final award of the tribunal may allocate the costs of the proceedings between the parties in any proportion the tribunal deems proper.[6]

1 Rules of Arbitration, art 31(1).
2 Ibid, art 31(2); Arbitration Costs, art 2(1),(5).

3   Arbitration Costs, art 2(2).
4   Rules of Arbitration, art 30(1),(2).
5   Ibid, art 30(3).
6   Ibid, art 31(3).

Recognition and enforcement of awards

7.32   By submitting their dispute to ICC arbitration, the parties undertake to carry out any award without delay.[1] Although the Rules do not directly address recognition and enforcement of awards through municipal courts, the arbitral tribunal and the Secretariat shall assist the parties in complying with any formal legal requirement necessary to facilitate recognition and enforcement of ICC Awards.[2] In practice, recognition and enforcement will normally depend on the law of the place where the arbitration is conducted and the law of the place where recognition and enforcement is sought.[3]

1   Rules of Arbitration, art 28(6).
2   Ibid, art 28(5).
3   Under private international law, recognition and enforcement of arbitral awards is governed by the domestic law of the state in which recognition and enforcement are sought. However, over 120 states are parties to the 1958 New York Convention on the Recognition and Enforcement of Arbitral Awards, which obliges states to recognise and enforce awards that were rendered in the territory of the other signatory states.

REFERENCE

Case reports

Generally, ICC Awards are not published.[1] However, some ICC Awards are published in a form which does not allow the identification of the parties. Some cases are published in the following series:

J J Arnaldez, Y Derains, S Jarvin and D Hascher (eds) *ICC Arbitral Awards*, vols I–III (1974–95)

Procedural decisions can be found in D Hascher (ed) *Collection of ICC Procedural Decisions* (1993–96).

Yearbook of Commercial Arbitration Kluwer Law International.

1   Rules of Arbitration, art 28(1).

Selected bibliography

'The New 1998 ICC Rules of Arbitration: Proceedings of the ICC Conference presenting the Rules', Special Supplement (1997) International Court of Arbitration Bulletin.

The ICC International Court of Arbitration Bulletin (Periodical published by the ICC Court).

Stephen R Bond *Recent Developments in International Chamber of Commerce (ICC) Arbitration* (1988) 477 Practising Law Institute, Course Handbook Series 55.

W Laurence Craig, William W Park, Jan Paulsson *Annotated Guide to the 1998 ICC Arbitration Rules* (1998).

Trade, commercial and investment protection dispute settlement bodies and rules

W Laurence Craig, William W Park, Jan Paulsson *International Chamber of Commerce Arbitration* (1990).

W Laurence Craig, William W Park, Jan Paulsson *International commercial arbitration: International Chamber of Commerce Arbitration* (1984).

Derains & Schwartz *A Guide to the New ICC Rules of Arbitration* (1998).

Joachim Kuckenburg 'Presenting Claims in ICC Arbitration' (Spring 1997) 10 International Law Practicum 34.

Eric A Schwartz 'The Resolution of International Commercial Disputes under the auspices of the ICC International Court of Arbitration' (1995) 18 Hastings International and Comparative Law Review 719.

Regional economic integration bodies/ free trade arrangements

INTRODUCTION

The mechanisms addressed in this Part reflect the growing trend towards regional arrangements for economic co-operation and integration, and the consequential need for dedicated dispute settlement arrangements. The jurisdiction of the regional courts and tribunals in this Part generally includes:

- complaints against member states of the relevant community for non-compliance with its rules, which may generally be brought by community institutions or by other member states;
- complaints against the institutions of the community themselves, which may generally be brought by member states or other institutions established within the community;
- preliminary references by domestic courts of the member states for the interpretation of specific aspects of the law of the relevant the community.

The longest-standing and most experienced court addressed in this Part is the European Court of Justice (ECJ), the principal judicial organ of the European Communities. Others, such as the Court of Justice of the Common Market for Eastern and Southern Africa are newly-established and have yet to be utilised. The establishment of more courts of this type is envisaged, as regional economic co-operation expands. For example in 1991 the Economic Community of West African States (ECOWAS) adopted a protocol on a court of justice.[1] However, the court has yet to be established. Given the lengthy history of the ECJ, at this stage significantly more space is devoted to it in this manual than to the other courts addressed in this Part. It is anticipated, however, that as the work of these other courts expands in years to come their practice will require greater attention. In that regard, it will be of interest to see whether the courts of one region draw upon the practices of courts in another.

The ECJ is the first body considered in this Part. The court was first established in 1952, and in 1957 became the common judicial organ of the European Economic Community (EEC), the European Coal and Steel Community and the European Atomic Energy Community (Euratom). The principal function of the ECJ is to ensure the uniform interpretation and application of European Community (EC) law by EC member states and institutions. In 1989, a Court of First Instance (CFI) was established. The ECJ is among the busiest institutions considered in this manual – since its establishment it has dealt with more than 10,000 cases. In 1997 alone, 481 new

---

1 Official Journal of the Economic Community of West African States, Vol 19, July 1991, 4.

cases were submitted to the ECJ, and 238 to the CFI. The potential subject matter of disputes brought to the ECJ is delimited by the EC treaties and secondary Community legislation, but is vast in scope, and includes institutional issues such as the legal basis of Community legislation, and the proper exercise of powers by Community institutions. However, despite the apparently broad jurisdiction of the ECJ, the EC Treaty does impose significant limits on access to the court.

The second body considered in this Part is the Court of Justice of the European Free Trade Association, established in 1994. The subject-matter jurisdiction of the EFTA Court is linked to that of the ECJ, in that it applies the Agreement on the European Economic Area and certain EC legislation. The states parties to the Statute of the EFTA Court are Iceland, Liechtenstein and Norway.

Bodies similar to the ECJ have been established for the settlement of disputes in three other areas: the Andean Community (comprising Bolivia, Ecuador, Colombia, Peru and Venezuela); the Central American Integration System (comprising Costa Rica, El Salvador, Guatemala, Honduras, Nicaragua, and Panama);[2] and the Common Market for Eastern and Southern Africa (COMESA, comprising 21 African states – see Annex to Chapter 12). The categories of cases which these courts can hear is generally similar. It should be noted, however, that the subject-matter jurisdiction of the Central American Court of Justice is potentially broader in that it may hear *any* dispute between states parties to its statute. However, in relation to frontier, territorial or maritime cases, the consent of both parties to the dispute is required for the court to exercise its jurisdiction.

The final dispute settlement mechanisms considered in this Part are those established under the North American Free Trade Agreement (NAFTA) and the Agreement on Environmental Co-operation, concluded between Canada, Mexico and the USA in 1992 and 1993 respectively. These procedures differ significantly from those available in the other courts addressed in this Part. NAFTA provides for settlement through a panel system, similar to that established under the World Trade Organisation (see Chapter 5), for disputes between states parties concerning the interpretation or application of the NAFTA or allegations that the application of a measure taken by a party is inconsistent with its NAFTA obligations. Reports of dispute settlement panels under NAFTA are binding on the parties. A separate dispute settlement mechanism is established under NAFTA for the review of antidumping and countervailing duties adopted by the member states. In addition, NAFTA contains provisions relating to the settlement of investment disputes involving one state party and a national of another state party, which provides for arbitration through ICSID or the ICSID Additional Facility (see Chapter 6).

The 1993 North American Agreement on Environmental Co-operation provides dispute settlement procedures in the event that a state party alleges that another state party has demonstrated a persistent pattern of failure to enforce effectively its environmental laws relating to the manufacture of goods or services which are traded between the parties to the Agreement or which are in competition with traded goods or services. The Agreement

2   However, only El Salvador, Honduras and Nicaragua are subject to the court's compulsory jurisdiction.

provides for the establishment of an arbitral panel to resolve the dispute. So far, there have been no such inter-state disputes under the Agreement. In addition, the Agreement authorises the Secretariat of the Commission on Environmental Co-operation (which is established under the Agreement) to receive complaints from non-governmental organisations (NGOs) or persons established or residing in the territory of a state party alleging that a party has failed to enforce effectively its environmental laws. If the Secretariat considers the complaint admissible it will invite the state complained against to respond. By April 1999, 20 such submissions had been made to the Secretariat.

Overall, the bodies reviewed in this Part are notable for the sophisticated mechanisms they provide for the settlement of disputes in a specialised area of regional law, as well as for the mechanisms they provide, by way of preliminary references and opinions, for the uniform interpretation and application of regional economic law in the domestic legal systems of member states. While, in contrast to the WTO, a number of the courts reviewed here provide some direct recourse to dispute settlement procedures for natural and legal persons directly affected by the law in question, access is by no means unlimited. NGOs, for example, have been rebuffed in the ECJ in their efforts to gain standing to challenge acts of Community institutions under Community law. Unlike the North American Agreement on Environmental Co-operation, or even the Inspection Panels established by many of the multilateral development banks, the European system does not itself incorporate a procedure whereby NGOs can instigate complaints against member states for failure to enforce environmental and other laws addressing social matters.

CHAPTER 8
Court of Justice of the European Communities

INTRODUCTORY

Contact information

8.1 The Court of Justice of the European Communities, also known as the European Court of Justice ('ECJ' or 'the court') is located at:

> Court of Justice of the European Communities
> Palais de la Cour de Justice
> Boulevard Konrad Adenauer
> Kirchberg, L-2925
> Luxembourg

> Tel: 352 43 031
> Fax: 352 4303 2600
> website: http://europa.eu.int/cj/index.htm

Description

8.2 The ECJ forms part of the judicial branch of the European Communities, the economic pillar of the European Union (EU). The ECJ came into existence in 1952 as the adjudicative body attached to the first of the European Communities, the European Coal and Steel Community (ECSC). Following the establishment of the other two Communities in 1957, the European Economic Community (EEC) and the European Atomic Energy Community (Euratom), the ECJ became the common judicial organ of all three Communities (although the three Communities remain separate).[1] Throughout the transformation of the EEC into the European Community (EC), the establishment of the EU,[2] the expansion in the number of Community members (from the original six states to 15 states today) and the establishment of a Court of First Instance (see infra), the court has remained the principal judicial organ of the Communities. In that capacity, it plays an important role in respect of the activities of the EU, alongside the other principal institutions of the Union: the Commission (the executive branch), the Council (the main legislative and political organ) and the Parliament (a deliberative body invested with certain supervisory and legislative powers). The competence of the court is limited to those matters enumerated by the EC, ECSC and Euratom treaties, as amended.[3]

The ECJ's main task is to ensure the uniform interpretation and application of EC law by all Community member states and institutions including national courts and tribunals; to serve as a forum for the enforcement of EC law; and to settle disputes between the different actors in the Community (ie member states, Community institutions and, on occasion, private parties). Since 1989, a Court of First Instance (CFI) has operated under the ECJ, assuming the competence for some of its former caseload.[4] The CFI and the ECJ are not separate institutions, but rather the CFI is 'attached to' the ECJ.[5]

Since its establishment, the ECJ has dealt with more than 10,000 cases and the CFI with more than 2,800 cases. In 1998, 485 new cases were submitted to the ECJ and 238 cases were submitted to the CFI.

1   Convention on Certain Institutions Common to the European Communities, art 3, 25 March 1957, 298 UNTS 267.
2   Treaty Establishing the European Union, 7 February 1992, 1992 OJ (C224) 6 ('EU Treaty').
3   EU Treaty, art 46.
4   Treaty Establishing the European Community, 25 March 1957 (as amended by the EU Treaty), art 168a, 298 UNTS 3 ('EC Treaty'); Consolidated Version of the Treaty Establishing the European Community, 25 March 1957 (as amended by the 1997 Treaty of Amsterdam), art 225 ('New EC Treaty'). See also Treaty Establishing the European Coal and Steel Community, 18 April 1951, art 32d, 261 UNTS 140 ('ECSC Treaty'); Treaty Establishing the European Atomic Energy Community, 25 March 1957, art 140a, 298 UNTS 167 ('Euratom Treaty').
5   EC Treaty, art 225.

INSTITUTIONAL ASPECTS

Governing texts

8.3   The principal text governing the structure, role and powers of the ECJ is the Treaty establishing the European Community ('EC Treaty'), as amended by the 1992 Treaty on European Union – also known as the Maastricht Treaty ('EU Treaty') and the 1997 Amsterdam Treaty.[1] Additional functions and powers of the ECJ are enumerated in the constituent instruments of the other two Communities – the Treaty establishing the European Coal and Steel Community ('ECSC Treaty') and the Treaty establishing the European Atomic Energy Community ('Euratom Treaty').

More specific norms governing the operation of the ECJ are found in the following instruments:

- Statute of the Court of Justice of the European Coal and Steel Community ('ECSC Statute');[2]
- Statute of the Court of Justice of the European Economic Community ('EC Statute');[3]
- Statute of the Court of Justice of the European Atomic Energy Community ('Euratom Statute');[4] and
- Rules of Procedure of the Court of Justice of the European Communities.[5]

While the EC and Euratom Statutes are almost identical, there are several significant differences between these two statutes and the ECSC Statute. The Rules of Procedure of the ECJ are applicable to all procedures conducted under any of the different statutes of the court.

As to the CFI, the three aforementioned statutes govern its operations as well. The CFI has its own Rules of Procedure.[6]

It should be noted that some important powers are delegated to the ECJ by additional international treaties. Thus, for instance, Protocols appended to the Brussels Convention on Jurisdiction and the Enforcement of Judgments in Civil and Commercial Matters,[7] the Rome Convention on the Law Applicable to Contractual Obligations[8] and the Agreement on the European Economic

Area (EEA),[9] provide for the ECJ to have the power to issue interpretative rulings, upon request of a party to those agreements.

1 The Amsterdam Treaty entered into force in May 1999.
2 Protocol on the Code of the Court of Justice of the European Coal and Steel Community, 18 April 1951, 261 UNTS 140.
3 Protocol on the Statute of the Court of Justice of the European Economic Community, 17 April 1957, 298 UNTS 147 (as amended by Council Decision 88/591, 1989 OJ (C 215) 1) ('EC Statute').
4 Protocol on the Statute of the Court of Justice of the European Atomic Energy Community, 17 April 1957, 298 UNTS 176.
5 Rules of Procedure of the Court of Justice of the European Communities, 1974 OJ (L 350) 1, as revised in 1991 OJ (L 176) 7 ('Rules of Procedure').
6 Rules of Procedure of the Court of First Instance of the European Communities, 1990 OJ (C 136) 1, as revised in 1991 OJ (L 136) 1 ('CFI Rules of Procedure').
7 Convention on Jurisdiction and the Enforcement of Judgments in Civil and Commercial Matters, 27 September 1968, as amended, 1972 OJ (L 299) 32; Protocol on the Interpretation of the Convention on Jurisdiction and the Enforcement of Judgments in Civil and Commercial Matters, 3 June 1971, arts 1–4, 1975 OJ (L 204) 28.
8 First Protocol on the Interpretation by the Court of Justice of the European Communities of the Convention on the Law Applicable to Contractual Obligations, 19 June 1980, arts 1–3, 1989 OJ (L 48) 1.
9 Agreement on the European Economic Area, 2 May 1992, art 107, protocol 34, 1994 OJ (L 1) 3.

Substantive law

8.4 The substantive law to be applied by the ECJ is derived from the following sources:

- the constitutive treaties of the three communities (the most important of which is the EC Treaty);
- secondary Community legislation – regulations, directives and decisions;
- international treaties to which the Community is party; and
- general principles of Community law (largely derived from the constitutive treaties and the member states' national legal systems).[1]

It should also be noted that previous judgments of the ECJ, while not formally binding, are normally followed in subsequent cases of similar nature.

1 Note that under EC Treaty, art 220 the court 'shall ensure that in the interpretation and application of this Treaty the law is observed'.

Organisation

Composition

8.5 The ECJ is composed of 15 judges (equal in number to the number of member states).[1] The judges are appointed for a renewable six-year term through the common accord of all member states.[2] They must be qualified and independent persons (fit to serve in the highest judicial office of their home country or jurists of recognised competence). Although the treaties do not require that each member state shall have a representative on the bench, this has been the practice so far. The judges on the court elect a President for a three-year term.[3] For each case before the court, one of the judges will be appointed the judge-rapporteur, who prepares the synopsis for the other judges hearing the case.

Assisting the judges are eight advocates-general (a ninth advocate-general

126

is appointed to serve until October 2000). The advocates-general are entrusted with presenting the court with objective legal opinions on pending cases. Those opinions assist the court in deciding cases in accordance with EC law. The advocates-general meet the same service requirements as judges, and also serve a renewable six-year term.[4]

The CFI is also composed of 15 judges (coming from the 15 member states), appointed by the common accord of all member states for a six-year term.[5] CFI judges must meet similar service requirements to ECJ judges and advocates-general. Like their counterparts in the ECJ, the judges of the CFI elect a President for a three-year term.[6] However, unlike the ECJ, the CFI does not employ permanent advocates-general. In the past, in some complex cases, the President of the CFI has assigned the functions of an advocate-general to one of the judges.

1   EC Treaty, art 165 (New EC Treaty, art 221); ECSC Treaty, art 32; Euratom Treaty, art 137.
    The current composition of the court is:
        Giuseppe Federico Mancini (Italy); José Carlos de Carvalho Moitinho de Almeida (Portugal); Gil Carlos Rodríguez Iglesias (Spain); Paul J G Kapteyn (The Netherlands); Claus Christian Gulmann (Denmark); John Loyola Murray (Ireland); David Alexander Ogilvy Edward (UK); Jean-Pierre Puissochet (France); Günter Hirsch (Germany); Peter Jann (Austria); Hans Ragnemalm (Sweden); Leif Sevón (Finland); Melchior Wathelet (Belgium); Romain Schintgen (Luxembourg); and Vassilios Skouris (Greece). **Advocates-general:** Francis Jacobs (UK); Antonio Mario La Pergola (Italy); Georges Cosmas (Greece); Philippe Léger (France); Nial Fennelly (Ireland); Dámaso Ruiz-Jarabo Colomer (Spain); Siegbert Alber (Germany); Jean Mischo (Luxembourg); and Antonio Saggio (Italy).
2   EC Treaty, art 167 (New EC Treaty, art 223); ECSC Treaty, art 32b; Euratom Treaty, art 139.
3   Rules of Procedure, art 7(1).
4   EC Treaty, arts 166, 167 (New EC Treaty, arts 222, 223); ECSC Treaty, arts 32a, 32b; Euratom Treaty, arts 138, 139.
5   EC Treaty, art 168a (New EC Treaty, art 225); ECSC Treaty, art 32d; Euratom Treaty, art 140a.
    The current composition of the Court of First Instance is:
        Cornelis Paulus Briët (The Netherlands); Bo Vesterdorf (Denmark); Rafael García-Valdecasas y Fernández (Spain); Koenraad Lenaerts (Belgium); Christopher W Bellamy (UK); Andreas Kalogeropoulos (Greece); Virpi Tiili (Finland); Pernilla Lindh (Sweden); Josef Azizi (Austria); André Potockiv (France); Rui Manuel Gens de Moura Ramos (Portugal); John D Cooke (Ireland); Marc Jaeger (Luxembourg); Jorg Pirrung (Germany); and Paolo Mengozzi (Italy).
6   CFI Rules of Procedure, art 7(1).

INELIGIBILITY OF JUDGES

8.6   Judges who have been involved in a case pending before the ECJ in a previous capacity may not participate in the adjudication of the same case.[1] In addition, a judge who no longer meets the requirements for appointment, or fails to fulfil his or her official obligations may be removed from office by a unanimous decision of the court (including the advocates-general).[2]

The statutes specifically provide that a party to a case may not request changes to the composition of the court or the trial chamber on the grounds of the nationality of any of the judges (or the absence of a judge of its own nationality from the judicial panel).[3]

1   EC Statute, art 16; ECSC Statute, art 19; Euratom Statute, art 16.
2   EC Statute, art 6; ECSC Statute, art 7; Euratom Statute, art 6. Decisions regarding removal of CFI judges are also taken by the ECJ, after hearing the CFI: EC Statute, art 44; ECSC Statute, art 44; Euratom Statute, art 45.
3   EC Statute, art 16; ECSC Statute, art 19; Euratom Statute, art 16.

Plenary/chambers

THE ECJ

8.7 The court can sit in plenary sessions, or assign cases to chambers of three, five or seven judges. The use of chambers has developed steadily and today most cases are referred to a chamber, unless they are of exceptional difficulty or importance, involve particular circumstances, or if a member state or Community institution participating in the proceedings (even as a third-party intervenor) has requested hearings before the full court.[1] A chamber may refer a case back to the full court at any stage of the proceedings. The composition of the different chambers and the identity of their presidents (who exercise in chamber proceedings the powers of the President of the Court) are determined by the full court.[2]

1   EC Treaty, art 165 (New EC Treaty, art 221); ECSC Treaty, art 32; Euratom Treaty, art 137; Rules of Procedure, art 95.
2   Rules of Procedure, arts 9(1),(4), 10(1).

THE CFI

8.8 The CFI normally sits in chambers of three or five judges.[1] However, in cases of exceptional difficulty or importance, or involving special circumstances, the case may be referred to the plenary court (or in the alternative, transferred from a three-judge chamber to a five-judge chamber).[2] The decision to refer a case shall be taken by the full court, upon a proposal of the trial chamber (acting on its own initiative or following a request by one of the parties).[3] On 17 May 1999 the CFI Rules of Procedure were amended to the effect that a three judge chamber may now refer cases of limited importance to be heard before a single judge (unless this is objected to by a state or EC institution which is party to the proceedings).[4]

1   CFI Rules of Procedure, arts 10, 11.
2   Ibid, art 14.
3   Ibid, art 51.
4   Ibid, arts 11(1), 14(2).

Appellate structure

8.9 The ECJ sits as a court of appeal over judgments of the CFI on points of law only.[1] An appeal must allege one of the following grounds:
   (i) lack of competence of the CFI;
   (ii) breach of procedure which adversely affected the interests of the appellant; or
   (iii) infringement of Community law by the CFI.[2]
An appeal can be brought by any party to the original proceedings or any member state or Community institution (whether they intervened in the original case or not).[3] Private intervenors may appeal to the ECJ only if the CFI judgment in question directly affects them.

1   EC Treaty, art 168a (New EC Treaty, art 225); ECSC Treaty, art 32d; Euratom Treaty, art 140a.
2   EC Statute, art 51; Euratom Statute, art 53; ECSC Statute, art 51.
3   EC Statute, art 49; ECSC Statute, art 49; Euratom Statute, art 50.

Technical/scientific experts

8.10   The ECJ or CFI may order that an expert's report be obtained from any individual, body, authority, committee or other organisation, in any case before it.[1] The expert is to conduct his or her examination under the supervision of one of the judges (ie the judge-rapporteur).[2] The court may order that the expert shall be examined and the parties be given the opportunity to question him or her, subject to the control of the President of the Court (or Chamber). Parties may also present experts as witnesses on their behalf. The other parties to the case may object to such testimony on grounds of lack of expertise.[3]

1   EC Statute, art 22; ECSC Statute, art 25; Euratom Statute, art 23.
2   Rules of Procedure, art 49; CFI Rules of Procedure, art 70.
3   Rules of Procedure, art 50; CFI Rules of Procedure, art 73.

Secretariat

8.11   The ECJ is assisted in the conduct of its business by a Registrar appointed by it for a six-year term.[1] The Registrar is responsible for the court's administration, financial management and staff (including assistant-Registrars). The Registrar controls the court's Registry;[2] is responsible for all communication of parties with the court; draws minutes from hearings; and assists the judges in their official functions.[3]

   In addition to a Registry, the ECJ headquarters include (a) a library research and documentation directorate; (b) an information office; (c) a translation directorate; and (d) a department of administration.

   The CFI has its own Registrar, entrusted with similar responsibilities to the ECJ's Registrar.[4] However, the CFI relies on the ECJ for most administrative services (with the notable exception of an independent Registry).

1   EC Treaty, art 168 (New EC Treaty, art 224); ECSC Treaty, art 32c; Euratom Treaty, art 140; Rules of Procedure, art 12.
2   For more details, see Instructions to the Registrar, 1974 OJ L 350 33 and also 1982 OJ C 39 35.
3   Rules of Procedure, arts 16–18, 23.
4   CFI Rules of Procedure, arts 20–30.

Jurisdiction

General observations

8.12   The contentious jurisdiction of the court is divided into three principal categories of cases:
(a)   claims brought by the Community against member states, alleging non-compliance with EC law;
(b)   claims brought against one or more of the Community institutions; and
(c)   requests for preliminary rulings referred to the court by domestic courts of the member states concerning questions of EC law. In these cases, the court is requested to apply Community law to questions that arise in municipal proceedings.
Other less prominent heads of jurisdiction exercised by the ECJ are:
●   staff cases;[1]
●   inter-state disputes concerning one of the Treaties, brought by special agreement;[2]

- contractual disputes involving the Community as a party to a contract, on the basis of a compromissory clause;[3]
- interpretative rulings in pursuance of international treaties (including the European Economic Area Treaty); and
- appeals over decisions of intellectual property arbitration commissions established under art 18 of the Euratom Treaty.

The more important heads of jurisdiction will be discussed in more detail below.

1　EC Treaty, art 179 (New EC Treaty, art 236); Euratom Treaty 152. Under the ECSC Treaty, staff cases are treated as any other contractual claim brought on the basis of a compromissory clause under art 42 of that treaty.
2　EC Treaty, art 182 (New EC Treaty, art 239); Euratom Treaty, art 154. Under art 89 of the ECSC Treaty such procedure may be initiated unilaterally by any of the two concerned states if it concerns the application of that treaty, and cannot be settled by an alternative procedure.
3　EC Treaty, art 181 (New EC Treaty, art 238); ECSC Treaty, art 42; Euratom Treaty, art 153.

Ratione personae

CLAIMS AGAINST MEMBER STATES

8.13　Non-compliance claims intended to ensure compliance with Community law can be brought against any of the Community's member states. Claims under this head of jurisdiction may be brought by one or more member states[1] (rare) or by the European Commission (the usual case).[2]

1　EC Treaty, art 170 (New EC Treaty, art 227); ECSC Treaty, art 89; Euratom Treaty 142. To date only one such claim was submitted. Case 141/178, *France v UK* [1979] ECR 2923.
2　EC Treaty, art 169 (New EC Treaty, art 226); ECSC Treaty, art 88; Euratom Treaty 141. In addition, under art 180(a) of the EC Treaty (art 237(a) of the New EC Treaty), the Board of Directors of the European Central Bank ('ECB') may also present a claim against a member state for failure to comply with the Statute of the Bank. Furthermore, according to sub-s (d) of the same Article, the Council of the European Central Bank is authorised to bring non-compliance cases directly against the national banks of the member states for their failure to comply with the Statute of the ECB and the EC Treaty. In these cases, the Bank organs shall have the same powers as the EC Commission.

CLAIMS AGAINST COMMUNITY INSTITUTIONS

8.14　Under this head of jurisdiction the ECJ may review the legality of acts[1] and omissions of the EC Council, Commission, Parliament and the European Central Bank (ECB).[2] In appropriate cases, where the acts or omissions of the Community have resulted in damage giving rise to non-contractual liability (ie tortious liability), financial compensation may be ordered.[3]

Claims against Community institutions can be brought by any member state or by a Community institution, other than the institution subject of the complaint (ie the Commission, Council, Parliament, the Court of Auditors and the ECB).[4] In addition, the ECJ may be seized by a natural or legal person having a direct interest in the matter.[5] This last condition has been construed narrowly by the court (except in cases involving the non-contractual liability of the Community).[6]

Finally, it should be noted that indirect challenges against any Community legislation may be brought in any case in which such act is at issue, by any party to the proceedings.[7]

1　Acts (recommendations and opinions excluded) have been defined in the case law of the ECJ as 'measures intended to have legal effects': Case 22/70 *Commission v Council* [1971] ECR 263 at 277.
2　EC Treaty, arts 173, 175 (New EC Treaty, arts 230, 232); ECSC Treaty, arts 33, 35, 38; Euratom

Treaty, arts 146, 148. Similar powers of review exist in respect of measures taken by the principal organs of the European Investment Bank: EC Treaty, art 180(b),(c) (New EC Treaty, art 237(b),(c)). It should be noted that under the ECSC Treaty only acts of the Council and the Parliament, and not their omissions, are reviewable: ECSC Treaty, art 38.
3   EC Treaty, arts 178, 215 (New EC Treaty, arts 235, 288); ECSC Treaty, art 40; Euratom Treaty, arts 151, 188.
4   There are however, certain restrictions upon the right of institutions to bring claims. The Parliament, the Court of Auditors and the ECB may challenge acts only for the purpose of protecting their prerogatives (but under the Euratom Treaty, the latter two bodies cannot present such a challenge altogether); and the ECB may bring omission claims only in areas falling under its competence. Furthermore, under the ECSC the only Community organs that can bring a claim against Community institutions are the Commission and Council.
5   Under the ECSC the right of private challenge can only be exercised by directly affected undertakings and associations: ECSC Treaty, art 33.
6   The court has construed the latter alternative as applicable only to people with particular attributes, which differentiate them from all others affected by the decision: Case 25/62 *Plaumann v Commission* [1963] ECR 95 at 107.
7   EC Treaty, art 184 (New EC Treaty, art 241); Euratom Treaty, art 156. No equivalent provision exists under the ECSC Treaty.

PRELIMINARY RULINGS

8.15   The court may receive requests for the authoritative interpretation or as to the validity of Community law from the national courts of the member states (referred to as the art 177 procedure).[1] Such requests may be referred to the ECJ where a question involving the interpretation of Community law has arisen in domestic proceedings before a national court; however, when the question arises before a domestic court of last instance, a preliminary ruling must be sought (unless the matter is subject to the *acte clair* doctrine).[2] Although, the request is formally filed in the ECJ by the requesting national court, the parties to the domestic proceedings are entitled to participate in the preliminary ruling proceedings before the ECJ.[3]

Finally, similar procedures for reference of questions to the ECJ for binding interpretation were introduced by some of the international treaties mentioned above (eg the Brussels Judgment Convention, the Rome Convention on Contractual Obligations and the EEA Agreement).

1   EC Treaty, art 177 (New EC Treaty, art 234); ECSC Treaty, art 41; Euratom Treaty, art 150. Once a request is submitted, domestic proceedings are stayed (suspended) until the preliminary ruling is issued, and upon their renewal, the domestic court is obliged to implement the ruling in the case pending before it. An information note on references by national courts for preliminary rulings is available on the court's website: http://europa. eu.int/cj/en/txts/index.htm.
2   Case 283/31 *Clifit v Ministry of Health* [1982] ECR 3415 (holding that where the correct application of Community law is so obvious as to leave no scope for any reasonable doubt as to the manner in which the question is to be resolved, there is no obligation for the domestic court of last instance to refer the case to the ECJ).
3   EC Statute, art 20; Euratom Statute, art 21; Rules of Procedure, arts 103, 104.

Ratione materiae

CLAIMS AGAINST MEMBER STATES

8.16   The exclusive ground for presenting a non-compliance claim against a member state is failure to fulfil an obligation under the relevant treaties.[1] This obligation may be derived from the treaties themselves, from secondary Community legislation, from international treaties to which the Community is a party or from judgments of the ECJ (eg in cases involving that member state). Under the ECSC Treaty, inter-state disputes may be brought before the court in the case of any dispute concerning the application of that Treaty, provided that no alternative procedure exists under the Treaty.[2]

1   EC Treaty, arts 169, 170 (New EC Treaty, arts 226, 227); ECSC Treaty, art 88; Euratom Treaty arts 141, 142.
2   ECSC Treaty, art 89.

CLAIMS AGAINST COMMUNITY INSTITUTIONS

8.17   Challenges brought against an act adopted by a Community institution must allege one of the following grounds for review:
(a) lack of competence;
(b) infringement of an essential procedural requirement;
(c) infringement of the relevant treaty or any rule of law concerning its application; or
(d) misuse of power.[1]
On the other hand, claims directed against omissions to act need only establish that the failure to act constitutes an infringement of the relevant treaty.[2]

As indicated above, in cases where a Community act or omission has resulted in damage, a claim based on the non-contractual liability of the Community may be made (with or without bringing a claim intended to annul the said act or compel the taking of a necessary measure). A party claiming damages must establish a direct causal link between the wrongful act and the damage caused.[3]

1   EC Treaty, art 173 (New EC Treaty, art 230); ECSC Treaty, art 33; Euratom Treaty, art 146. Under art 38 of the ECSC Treaty a challenge against Council or Parliament acts can only allege one of the following two grounds: lack of competence, or infringement of an essential procedural requirement.
2   EC Treaty, art 175 (New EC Treaty, art 232); ECSC Treaty, art 35; Euratom Treaty, art 148.
3   See eg Joined Cases C-104/89, 37/90 *Mulder v Council* [1992] ECR I-3061.

PRELIMINARY RULINGS

8.18   Requests for preliminary rulings may be brought when a question has arisen in domestic proceedings concerning one of the following issues:
(a) interpretation of the treaties (ie primary legislation);
(b) validity or interpretation of acts of Community institutions (ie secondary legislation); or
(c) interpretation of statutes of subsidiary bodies (where the statutes provide so).[1]
As indicated above, the ECJ also has power to issue interpretative judgments (in a procedure similar to preliminary rulings) in cases where a question of interpretation of certain international treaties has arisen in domestic proceedings.

1   EU Treaty, art 177 (New EC Treaty, art 234); ECSC Treaty, art 41; Euratom Treaty, art 150. Under the ECSC Treaty, preliminary rulings can be sought only in cases where the validity of acts of the Commission or the Council is at issue.

Ratione temporis

CLAIMS AGAINST MEMBER STATES

8.19   As a preliminary stage to all non-compliance cases, the Commission must first issue a reasoned opinion addressing the compatibility with Community law of the challenged measure (or failure to act) of the respondent state.[1] Such an opinion will be prepared after the Commission has allowed the state complained against – and in cases brought by another state, that state as well – to submit observations on the claim of non-compliance. After receiving the opinion of the Commission a complainant state may then seize the ECJ. However, it may nevertheless approach the court if no reasoned opinion was made available to it within three months from the date it presented the complaint before the Commission.

In cases brought by the Commission, the court can be seized only after the period of time set in the opinion for compliance with Community law has expired and the state complained against has failed to take appropriate measures.

It should be noted that in some specific claims brought under the EC Treaty, a more expeditious procedure exists.[2]

The ECSC Treaty provides for a different non-compliance procedure. Under that treaty, the Commission issues a decision after receiving comments from the state whose compliance is questioned. If dissatisfied with the decision, the member state concerned must challenge it before the ECJ within two months, or be bound by it.[3] Furthermore, there are no temporal restrictions imposed upon inter-state non-compliance claims (or any other inter-state dispute concerning the application of the ECSC Treaty).[4]

1   EC Treaty, arts 169, 170 (New EC Treaty, arts 226, 227); Euratom Treaty arts 141, 142.
2   Those procedures pertain to 'state aid': EC Treaty, art 93 (New EC Treaty, art 88); and improper use by a state of the right of derogation from measures of harmonisation: EC Treaty, arts 100A(4), 225 (New EC Treaty, arts 95, 298).
3   ECSC Treaty, art 88.
4   Ibid, art 89.

CLAIMS AGAINST COMMUNITY INSTITUTIONS

8.20 Proceedings under this head of jurisdiction directed against an act must be initiated within two months from the date the measure in question was published or notified to the applicant – or in their absence, brought to its knowledge (one month in cases brought under the ECSC Treaty).[1]

Proceedings brought against a failure to act must be preceded by a call to act directed to the relevant Community institution. If the said institution fails to define its position regarding the demand for action within a period of two months, the applicant may bring the case to the court within the following two months (one month in cases brought under the ECSC Treaty).[2]

Claims for non-contractual damages must be brought within five years from the occurrence of the events giving rise to the claim.[3]

1   EC Treaty, art 173 (New EC Treaty, art 230); ECSC Treaty, art 33; Euratom Treaty, art 146.
2   EC Treaty, art 175 (New EC Treaty, art 232); ECSC Treaty, art 35; Euratom Treaty, art 148.
3   EC Statute, art 43; ECSC Statute, art 40; Euratom Statute, art 44. The period of limitations will be interrupted if application is made to the relevant Community institution. However, in that case, the ordinary time limits governing claims against Community institutions shall apply (ie one or two months to three or four months).

PRELIMINARY RULINGS

8.21 The only temporal condition placed on a request for a preliminary ruling is that the case giving rise to the question before the requesting domestic court must still be pending.[1]

1   EC Treaty, art 177 (New EC Treaty, art 234); ECSC Treaty, art 41; Euratom Treaty, art 150.

Advisory jurisdiction

8.22 The ECJ has two heads of advisory competence. First, it may review the compatibility of international treaties concluded between the Community and third parties with the treaties.[1] A request for the advisory opinion of the court can be presented by the Council, Commission or a member state. Second, the court may give its opinion on the need for amendment of the ECSC Treaty, upon the joint request of the Commission and the Council.[2]

1   EC Treaty, art 228 (New EC Treaty, art 300).
2   ECSC Treaty, art 95.

Division of jurisdiction between the ECJ and the CFI

8.23 Since the establishment of the CFI in 1989, a gradual process of transferring elements of the original jurisdiction of ECJ to the CFI has taken place. Decisions on referral of classes of cases to the CFI are taken by the Council, at the request of the ECJ, after consultation with the Commission and Parliament.[1] At present, the CFI is entrusted with handling staff, coal and steel, competition and certain trademark cases.[2] Furthermore, since 1994 all claims against Community institutions brought by natural or legal persons are initially submitted to the CFI.[3] It is expected that the process will continue and eventually result in the referral of all contentious cases (except art 177 cases) to the CFI.

1   EC Treaty, art 168a (New EC Treaty, art 225); ECSC Treaty, art 32d; Euratom Treaty, art 140a.
2   ECSC, EEC, Euratom Council Decision 88/591, 1988 OJ (L 319) 1; EC Regulation 40/94, art 63, 1994 OJ (L 11) 1.
3   ECSC, EEC, Euratom Council Decision 93/350, 1993 OJ (L 144) 21; ECSC, EEC, Euratom Council Decision of 7 March 1994, 1994 OJ (L 66) 29.

PROCEDURAL ASPECTS

Languages

8.24 The language of ECJ or CFI proceedings will normally be one of the twelve official languages of the EU, as chosen by the applicant.[1] However, in cases submitted against a member state (or a national thereof), or referred by a national court for preliminary ruling, the national language of that state must be selected by the applicant. In any event, member states intervening in a case may use their national language.

Any documents, testimony, reports before the court, or oral instructions or questions presented by the judges, which are not in the official language of the proceedings must be translated accordingly.

1   Rules of Procedure, art 29; CFI Rules of Procedure, art 35. The official languages of the EU are Danish, Dutch, English, Finnish, French, German, Greek, Irish, Italian, Portuguese, Spanish and Swedish. In exceptional cases, the court may authorise the use of additional languages.

Instituting proceedings

8.25 A case is brought before the ECJ or CFI by a written application to the relevant court's Registrar.[1] The application should be lodged together with five copies for the court and an additional copy for every other party to the case.[2] It should include the following information:
(a) name and address of applicant;

(b) designation of the party against whom the application is directed;

(c) subject matter of the proceedings and a summary of legal arguments;

(d) form of order sought by the applicant;

(e) where appropriate, nature of the evidence offered in support of the claim.[3]
The application should be accompanied by relevant documents (eg text of challenged act, request directed to a Community institution to adopt a measure, etc), although the Registrar shall prescribe, if necessary, a period of time for submitting any missing documents.[4]

Requests for preliminary rulings are initiated by the service of the decision of the domestic court, containing the question addressed by that court to the ECJ, to the ECJ's Registrar. The latter shall notify the immediate parties to the case, the member states, the Commission, and the Council, if necessary.[5]

1 EC Statute, art 19; ECSC Statute, art 22; Euratom Statute, art 19.
2 Rules of Procedure, art 37; CFI Rules of Procedure, art 43.
3 Rules of Procedure, art 38(1); CFI Rules of Procedure, art 44(1).
4 Additional requirements are a certificate of lawyer's entitlement to practise; proof of registration of incorporation of a juridical person; and proper authorisation granted by such person to the lawyer on its behalf: Rules of Procedure, art 38(3),(5),(7); CFI Rules of Procedure, art 44(3),(5),(7).
5 EC Statute, art 20; Euratom Statute, art 21; Rules of Procedure, art 103(3).

Financial assistance

8.26 A party who is unable to meet the full costs of ECJ or CFI proceedings may apply for legal aid.[1] The application to each court must be supported by evidence of the need for assistance provided by a competent authority and should indicate the subject of the proceedings, if these have not yet been initiated. The application is to be decided by a chamber, after considering the observations of the opposite party and hearing the view of the advocate-general. The decision whether to provide legal aid, in part or in full, is not subject to appeal.

If the application is approved in part or in full the court will advance funds to the requesting party. In addition, under the CFI Rules of Procedure, the court will order and facilitate the appointment of a lawyer for a person entitled to receive legal aid.[2] At the end of the proceedings, the court may decide to include the funds allocated for legal aid in the costs of the proceedings, borne by some or all the parties to the case.

1 Rules of Procedure, art 76; CFI Rules of Procedure, art 94.
2 CFI Rules of Procedure, art 95.

Provisional measures

8.27 The court is authorised to render interim measures of protection and suspend the operation of any measure adopted by a Community institution.[1] The party applying for such measures shall deposit with the court a separate written submission, meeting all the requirements of an application. The application should indicate, in particular, the subject matter of the proceedings, the circumstances giving rise to urgency and pleas of fact and law establishing a prima facie case.[2] An interim measure can be requested only if it relates to a case before the court.

The application is brought before the President of the Court, who shall prescribe a period of time for the other party to the case to submit its observations.[3] However, the President may indicate provisional measures on the basis of the application only (ie on an ex parte basis), subject to subsequent variation or cancellation. After receiving the observations of the other party the President shall decide upon the application, or refer the request to the court (in most cases to a chamber), which shall decide upon it promptly.[4] The requesting party can be required to deposit a security to meet expenses caused by the interim order.[5]

1   EC Treaty, arts 185, 186 (New EC Treaty, arts 242, 243); ECSC Treaty, art 39; Euratom Treaty, arts 157, 158; EC Statute, art 37; ECSC Statute, art 33; Euratom Statute, art 38.
2   Rules of Procedure, art 83; CFI Rules of Procedure, art 104.
3   Rules of Procedure, art 84; CFI Rules of Procedure, art 105.
4   Rules of Procedure, art 85; CFI Rules of Procedure, art 106.
5   Rules of Procedure, art 86(2); CFI Rules of Procedure, art 107(2).

Preliminary objections/proceedings

8.28   Preliminary objections concerning the admissibility of an application to initiate proceedings may be presented by the respondent party in a written document separate to its statement of defence.[1] The application may allege, inter alia, one of the following grounds of inadmissibility:
(a)   lack of jurisdiction;
(b)   lack of standing (in cases involving a private party);
(c)   prescription (or limitation bars);
(d)   failure to fulfil a preliminary procedure;
(e)   res judicata;[2] and
(f)   defective pleadings.
The application must state the relevant law and facts upon which the application is based, and include supporting documents. The President of the Court then grants the other party to the case a period of time to submit a reply drafted in like fashion to the application. Unless the court decides otherwise, oral hearings on the motion take place, and after receiving the Report of the advocate-general the court shall decide whether to accept or reject the application, or defer final decision to the merits stage.

In cases which properly fall under the competence of an instance of the court other than the one originally seized (ie CFI or ECJ), the first court may refer the case to the proper venue.[3] The court may consider whether there is an absolute bar to jurisdiction on their own initiative.[4]

1   Rules of Procedure, art 91; CFI Rules of Procedure, art 111.
2   Case 79, 82/63 *Reynier v Commission* [1988] ECR 4821. This is also the case with *lis alibi pendens* situations.
3   EC Statute, art 47, ECSC Statute, art 47; Euratom Statute, art 48; CFI Rules of Procedure, art 112.
4   Rules of Procedure, art 92(2); CFI Rules of Procedure, art 113.

Written pleadings[1]

8.29   Within a month of receiving the application initiating proceedings before the ECJ or CFI (or a longer period determined by the president), the defendant party must lodge a statement of defence including:
(a)   name and address of the defendant;
(b)   legal and factual arguments;
(c)   form of order sought by the defendant;
(d)   nature of any evidence offered by it.[2]
In addition, the defendant should include supporting documents (of the

same nature of those appended to the application).

The applicant may then file a reply and the defendant a rejoinder at times fixed by the president.[3] No new pleas of law may be raised after the lodging of the second round of written submissions (other than in exceptional circumstances).[4]

After evidence has been gathered during the preliminary inquiry stage of the proceedings (including the testimony of witnesses and experts), or at any other stage of the proceedings, the ECJ or CFI may fix the time for the parties to present their written observations.[5]

1 Notes for the Guidance of Counsel in written and oral proceedings before the ECJ are available on the court's website: <http://europa.eu.int/cj/en/txts/index.htm>.
2 Rules of Procedure, art 40; CFI Rules of Procedure, art 46.
3 Rules of Procedure, art 41; CFI Rules of Procedure, art 47.
4 Rules of Procedure, art 42; CFI Rules of Procedure, art 48.
5 Rules of Procedure, art 54. CFI Rules of Procedure, art 64(3)(b).

Oral arguments[1]

8.30   Oral hearings before the ECJ and CFI are normally conducted after evidence has been gathered during the preliminary inquiry stage (often in the presence of one judge only – ie the judge-rapporteur). However, the CFI may decide to conduct oral hearings without ordering a preliminary inquiry.[2] On the other hand, the ECJ may decide, with the consent of the parties (and after consulting with the judge-rapporteur and the advocate-general), to dispense with the oral stage of the proceedings.[3]

The oral procedure shall include a reading of the report of the judge-rapporteur, arguments of the legal representatives of the parties and reading of the advocate-general's submissions.[4] If the gathering of evidence has not been completed, witnesses and experts may also be heard. During the hearings the judges and the advocate-general may question the legal representatives of the parties.[5] The proceedings of the court are open to the public, unless the court decides otherwise.[6]

1 Note for the Guidance of Counsel before the Court of First Instance at the hearing of oral arguments and Notes for the Guidance of Counsel in written and oral proceedings before the ECJ are available on the ECJ website: http://europa.eu.int/cj/en/txts/index.htm.
2 CFI Rules of Procedure, art 53.
3 Rules of Procedure, art 44a.
4 EC Statute, art 18; ECSC Statute, art 21; Euratom Statute, art 18.
5 Rules of Procedure, art 57; CFI Rules of Procedure, art 58.
6 EC Statute, art 28; ECSC Statute, art 26; Euratom Statute, art 29.

Third-party intervention/multiple proceedings

Intervention

8.31   Under the three ECJ Statutes, member states and, in specified instances, Community institutions but always the Commission may intervene in all cases in support of the submissions of one of the parties to the case (except in inter-state cases brought under the ECSC Treaty, where only states may intervene).[1] Private parties may intervene only in cases involving other private parties (except under the ECSC, where there is no such limitation) and only if they can establish an interest in the result of the case.[2]

An application to intervene must be made within three months from the date of the publication of the Registration of the case in the Official Journal of

the European Communities. It shall include the following information:
(a) a description of the case;
(b) a description of the parties;
(c) the name and address of the the intervenor;
(d) the address for service at the place of the seat of the court;
(e) the form of order sought by one of the parties, in support of which leave to intervene is sought;[3]
(f) a statement of reasons establishing the intervenor's interest in the result of the case (but this latter only on an application made by private parties).[4]

The President of the Court shall decide on the application, after giving an opportunity to the parties to the case to submit their observations, or shall refer the matter to the court (or a chamber). If the intervention application is granted, the intervenor may submit to the court a statement including:
(a) form of order sought by the intervenor – in support of, or in opposition to, in whole or in part, an order sought by one of the parties;
(b) legal and factual arguments;
(c) nature of evidence offered (where appropriate).[5]

The parties shall be offered the chance to reply to the above statement. The right of intervention also exists in regard to some of the more particular ECJ procedures. Thus member states and Community institutions may submit a statement of case or written observations, within two months of being notified that a case has been presented to the ECJ for a preliminary ruling.[6] In addition, intervention is permitted in appeals against CFI judgments presented before the ECJ, by parties that were entitled to intervene in the lower instance but did not participate in those proceedings.[7] Such an application must be lodged within three months from the date the appeal was made.

Finally, as described below, it should be noted that the final judgment of the court may be challenged by parties that did not participate in the proceedings, if the judgment is deemed to be prejudicial to their rights.[8]

1 EC Statute, art 37; ECSC Statute, arts 34, 41; Euratom Statute, art 38. It should be noted that the ECSC statute refers only to a general right of intervention of natural and legal persons and states, but this has generally been interpreted to encompass Community institutions too.
2 EC Statute, art 37; ECSC Statute, art 34; Euratom Statute, art 38.
3 However, a private party intervenor may not raise an argument on the inadmissibility of a claim if that objection has not been taken by the defendant in the original proceedings.
4 Rules of Procedure, art 93; CFI Rules of Procedure, art 115.
5 Rules of Procedure, art 93(5); CFI Rules of Procedure, art 116.
6 EC Statute, art 20; Euratom Statute, art 21; Rules of Procedure, art 103(3).
7 Rules of Procedure, art 123.
8 EC Statute, art 39; ECSC Statute, art 36; Euratom Statute, art 40.

Multiple proceedings

8.32 As to multiple proceedings, the various instruments governing the work of the court do not specifically address multiple proceedings. There is no bar to proceedings involving more than one claimant or defendant, as long as jurisdictional requirements are met with regard to all parties cited in the application for commencement of the proceedings.

Amicus curiae

8.33 There is no provision in the various instruments governing the work of the court addressing the admissibility of amicus curiae briefs. Furthermore, it appears that the detailed rules on intervention provided by the Statutes and Rules preclude the admissibility of submissions on the part of persons who lack capacity to formally intervene in a case.[1]

1   See eg Case 6/64 *Costa v Enel* [1964] ECR 614 at 1194.

Representation of parties

8.34   Member states and institutions of the Community (or states parties to the European Economic Area Agreement) must be represented before the ECJ in each case by an agent, who may be assisted by an adviser or lawyer. Other parties to disputes before the ECJ must be represented by a lawyer. Only lawyers authorised to practice before a court of a member state (or a state party to the European Economic Area Agreement) may represent or assist a party before the ECJ. University teachers who are nationals of a member state whose law accords them a right to audience have the same rights before the ECJ as are accorded to lawyers.[1] The lawyer acting for a party in a case before the ECJ must lodge at the court's Registry a certificate that he or she is authorised to practise before a court of a member state or of another state which is party to the EEA Agreement.[2] The rights and obligations of agents, advisers and lawyers before the court are set out in the Rules of Procedure of the ECJ.[3] Similar provisions apply to the representation and assistance of parties before the CFI.[4]

1   EC Statute, art 17; ECSC Statute, art 20; Euratom Statute, art 17.
2   Rules of Procedure, art 38(3).
3   Rules of Procedure, Chapter 7.
4   EC Statute, art 46; EAEC Statute, art 47; ECSC Statute, art 46; CFI Rules of Procedure, art 44(3); CFI Rules of Procedure, Chapter 6.

Decision

8.35   The final decision of the court on the dispute before it is issued in the form of a judgment,[1] which will contain the following information:
(a)   date of delivery;
(b)   names of the judges that participated in the deliberation of the case;
(c)   name of the advocate-general;
(d)   name of the Registrar;
(e)   description of the parties;
(f)   names of the representatives of the parties;
(g)   form of order sought by the parties;
(h)   statement affirming that the advocate-general has been heard;
(i)   summary of facts;
(j)   reasons for decision;
(k)   operative part of decision, including decision on costs.[2]
Although decisions of the court are taken on the basis of a majority vote,[3] the final judgment is issued on behalf of the entire court (or chamber). No dissenting or individual opinions are published or otherwise indicated.

In claims against member states, an adverse judgment will require the defendant state to take the measures necessary to comply with the judgment (and the court may subsequently impose financial penalties for failing to comply with the judgment).[4] In claims against Community institutions, the court may declare the challenged acts to be void (although it can mitigate the

139

temporal effects of nullifying a regulation or a directive, in some cases),[5] or it may prescribe the taking of appropriate measures.[6] In appropriate cases, the ECJ may order Community institutions to pay compensation for damage and declare member states to be financially liable for non-compliance with judgments.

The judgment is binding on the parties to the case, and enforceable against them.

1 EC Statute, art 33; ECSC Statute, art 30; Euratom Statute, art 34.
2 Rules of Procedure, art 63; CFI Rules of Procedure, art 81.
3 Rules of Procedure, art 27(5); CFI Rules of Procedure, art 33(5).
4 EC Treaty, art 171 (New EC Treaty, art 228); Euratom Treaty, art 143.
5 EC Treaty, art 174 (New EC Treaty, art 231); ECSC Treaty, arts 37, 38; Euratom Treaty, art 147. EC Treaty, art 174 (New EC Treaty, art 231) in fact speaks of this mitigation power only with reference to a regulation, although the court has held the same power exists with respect to directives.
6 EC Treaty, art 176 (New EC Treaty, art 233); Euratom Treaty, art 149.

Revision of judgments

Rectification of errors

8.36 Acting upon an application of a party to the case submitted within two weeks from rendering the judgment, or acting of its own initiative, the court may correct any clerical or computational mistakes and obvious slips found in the judgment.[1] All parties to the cases will be invited to submit observations on the proposed rectification.

1 Rules of Procedure, art 66; CFI Rules of Procedure, art 84.

Omission to decide a claim

8.37 A party may submit within one month from the issue of the judgment an application to the court, alleging that the judgment omitted to indicate a decision on a specific head of claim, or on costs (the CFI Rules of Procedure allow only application on omission to decide costs).[1] The President shall prescribe a period of time within which the opposing party will be entitled to submit written observations. By the end of that period, the court, after hearing the advocate-general, shall decide on the application.

1 Rules of Procedure, art 67; CFI Rules of Procedure, art 85.

Interpretation

8.38 Any party to a case, or a Community institution with a sufficient interest in the case, may apply for interpretation of the meaning or scope of a judgment.[1] The application, which shall meet the formal requirements of an application to commence proceedings, must contain, in particular, information on the judgment in question and the passage the interpretation of which is sought.[2] The court, after allowing all parties to the case to submit their observations, and after hearing the advocate-general, shall issue a supplementary judgment.

1 EC Statute, art 40; ECSC Statute, art 37; Euratom Statute, art 41.
2 Rules of Procedure, art 102; CFI Rules of Procedure, art 129. The CFI may stay proceedings if an appeal on the same case is already pending.

Revision

8.39 Upon discovery of a fact of such a nature that could have been a decisive factor in the outcome of the case, a party may apply for the court to revise its judgment, provided that the contended fact was unknown at the time of the proceedings to the court and to the requesting party.[1] The application must be made within three months from the date the fact at issue became known to the requesting party.[2] In no case can a request for revision be made after the passage of ten years from the date of the judgment.

The request shall specify the following:
(a) the details of judgment contested;
(b) the points on which judgment is contested;
(c) the facts on which the application is based; and
(d) the nature of evidence showing that the requirements for a request of revision have been met.[3]

The application is to be communicated to all parties to the case, who will be invited by the court to submit their observations. After considering the views of the parties and of the advocate-general, the court shall decide on the application and, if necessary, issue a revising judgment.[4]

1 EC Statute, art 41; ECSC Statute, art 38; Euratom Statute, art 42.
2 Rules of Procedure, art 98; CFI Rules of Procedure, art 125.
3 Rules of Procedure, art 99; CFI Rules of Procedure, art 126.
4 Rules of Procedure, art 100; CFI Rules of Procedure, art 127. The CFI may stay proceedings on the application if an appeal is already pending: CFI Rules of Procedure, art 128.

Third party proceedings

8.40 Member states, Community institutions or legal or natural persons may initiate third-party proceedings to challenge a judgment which has been rendered without them being heard, and which is prejudicial to their rights.[1] In practice, the court admits only applications of parties who could and should have become parties to the original case, but were unable to do so for a good reason.[2]

An application to initiate third-party proceedings must be made within two months from the publication of the judgment in the Official Journal of the European Communities.[3] Such an application must be prepared in the same manner as an application to initiate proceedings. However, the application should also:
(a) give details of the judgment contested;
(b) state the way in which the judgment is prejudicial to that party's rights;
(c) indicate reasons why the requesting party was unable to participate in the original proceedings.

The application is presented to all parties to the original case. After receiving the observations of these parties, the court may amend the contested judgment, in accordance with the submissions of the third party.

1 EC Statute, art 39; ECSC Statute, art 36; Euratom Statute, art 40.
2 See eg Case C-147/87/TO/1 *Panhelinia Omospondia Idiokiton Frontistirion Xenon Glosson – POIFXG v Greece and Commission* [1989] ECR 4103.
3 Rules of Procedure, art 97; CFI Rules of Procedure, art 123.

Appeal

8.41 As mentioned above, since 1989 the ECJ has operated as a two-tier judicial body with the ECJ sitting in appeal over decisions of the CFI. Appeals

may challenge one of the following decisions of the CFI:
(a) judgments and other final decisions;
(b) decisions disposing of only some of the substantive issues in a case;
(c) decisions dismissing a procedural matter involving a plea of lack of competence or inadmissibility;
(d) decisions dismissing an application to intervene;
(e) decisions granting or denying interim relief or a stay of enforcement of a Council or Commission decision.[1]

The appeal is limited to questions of law and must allege one of the following grounds against the CFI decision:
(a) lack of competence;
(b) gross breach of procedure; or
(c) mistake in EC law.[2]

An appeal can be lodged by any party to the original case – including intervenors (whether unsuccessful in part or whole of its submissions), or by any member state of Community institution not party to the first-instance proceedings. Private party intervenors before the CFI may only lodge an appeal if the decision of the CFI directly affects them. The appeal must be lodged within two months of the notification of the decision (except in the case of denial of a request to intervene, which must be appealed within two weeks).

The appeal is lodged at the Registry of either the ECJ or CFI.[3] It should be prepared in a form similar to an application to initiate proceedings and should contain the following information:
(a) name and address of appellant;
(b) names of other parties to the CFI proceedings;
(c) pleas in law and legal arguments relied on; and
(d) form of order sought.[4]

The appellant must attach to the appeal the decision contested and indicate the date upon which it was rendered. Any party to the case may submit a reply within two months from being served with the notice of appeal.[5] The response should seek to dismiss or support the appeal, in whole or in part, and should not request a different form of order.[6] The response (which is in the form of an application) will include the following details:
(a) name and address of the respondent;
(b) date of service of notice of appeal;
(c) pleas in law and legal arguments relied on; and
(d) form of order sought.

The parties may further submit a written reply and/or rejoinder, with the permission of the President of the ECJ (which must be requested within seven days from receiving the relevant submission of the other party).[7]

The procedure before the ECJ when adjudicating an appeal generally follows the ordinary procedure of that court (with the notable exception of the preliminary inquiry).[8] An application to intervene can be brought within three months from the date the appeal was lodged.

After admitting the pleadings of the parties, reading the judge-rapporteur's report, and hearing the advocate-general, the ECJ will issue a judgment accepting or rejecting the appeal, or sending it back to the CFI for judgment.[9] In the latter case, the CFI will be bound by the ruling of the ECJ on matters of law.

1   EC Statute, arts 49, 50; ECSC Statute, arts 49, 50; Euratom Statute, arts 50, 51. The Statutes explicitly prohibit an appeal aimed only against a decision on payment of the costs of CFI proceedings.
2   EC Statute, art 51; ECSC Statute, art 51; Euratom Statute, art 52.

3   Rules of Procedure, art 111.
4   Ibid, art 112.
5   Ibid, art 115.
6   Ibid, art 116.
7   Ibid, art 117.
8   Ibid, art 118.
9   EC Statute, art 54; Euratom Statute, art 55; ECSC Statute, art 54.

Costs

8.42   Proceedings before the ECJ are normally free of charge. However, the court may require a party that has caused the court to incur avoidable costs or excessive translation expenses to reimburse the court.[1] Thus, in ordinary cases, the costs of the proceedings include only sums payable to witnesses and experts and the legal expenses of the parties (including enforcement-related expenses).[2]

The allocation of costs between the parties is determined by the court as part of the final judgment.[3] In the case of preliminary rulings, the costs before the ECJ of the parties to the national proceedings are left to the national court. All other parties who submit written observations or who appear before the ECJ in oral hearings bear their costs themselves. Normally, the unsuccessful party will bear the costs associated with the proceedings (excluding intervenors, who bear their own expenses, as a rule). However, the court may impose costs on the successful party as well, if that party has applied unreasonable or vexatious tactics which have resulted in unwarranted expenses.[4] Where both parties are successful and unsuccessful, and in other exceptional circumstances, the court may order that costs are to be shared (or that each party should bear its own costs). In cases where there are several unsuccessful parties, or where the case is terminated before judgment, the court will allocate costs at its discretion.

The parties are entitled to agree upon the allocation of costs before or during the proceedings, and the court shall respect such agreement. Disputes over recovery of costs can be referred back to the original chamber.[5]

1   Rules of Procedure, art 72; CFI Rules of Procedure, art 90.
2   Rules of Procedure, arts 71, 73; CFI Rules of Procedure, arts 89, 91.
3   EC Statute, art 35; ECSC Statute, art 32; Euratom Statute, art 36.
4   Rules of Procedure, art 69; CFI Rules of Procedure, art 87.
5   Rules of Procedure, art 74; CFI Rules of Procedure, arts 92.

Enforcement of judgments

8.43   The enforcement of ECJ and CFI judgments must be facilitated by a national authority of each member state designated under art 192 of the EC Treaty.[1] A party seeking to enforce a judgment is to petition the said authority, in accordance with the civil procedure of that country, and will only be required to present an authenticated copy of the judgment of the ECJ or CFI.

It should be noted that similar enforcement procedures may also be inferred from the Rules of Procedure with regard to the enforcement of orders for interim measures.[2]

1   EC Treaty, arts 187, 192 (New EC Treaty, arts 244, 256); ECSC Treaty, arts 44, 92; Euratom Treaty, art 164.
2   Rules of Procedure, art 86(2); CFI Rules of Procedure, art 107. However, there is no specific provision requiring states to enforce such orders.

REFERENCE

Case reports

ECJ judgments are published in a series titled 'Report of Cases before the Court of Justice and Court of First Instance' (ECR). Part I of the reports contains ECJ cases and Part II contains CFI cases. In addition, cases can be found in commercial publication such as 'Common Market Law Reports' (CMLR) and in computerised databases (CELEX, LEXIS, Westlaw). Recent cases are published on the EU's website at <http://europe.eu.int/abc/eur-lex/en/index.html>.

Finally, certain notices pertaining to the conduct of a case are published in the Official Journal of the European Communities.

Selected bibliography

Books

David W K Anderson *References to the European Court* (1995).

Gerald Barling and Mark Brealey (eds) *Practitioners' Handbook of EC Law* (1998).

George A Bermann, Roger J Goebel, William J Davey and Eleanor M Fox *Cases and Materials on European Community Law* (1993).

The British Institute of International and Comparative Law *The Roles and Future of the European Court of Justice* (1996).

N Brown and F Jacob *The Court of Justice of the European Communities* (1989).

Butterworths *European Court Practice* (1993).

Janet Dine, Sionaidh Douglas-Scott and Ingrid Persaud *Procedure and the European Court* (1991).

T C Hartley *The Foundations of European Community Law* (1994).

K P E Lasok *The European Court of Justice – Practice and Procedure*, 2nd edn (1994).

Neville March Hunnings *The European Courts* (1996).

T Millet *The Court of First Instance of the European Communities* (1989).

Richard Plender (ed) *European Courts, Practice and Precedents* (1997).

H G Schermers, C W A Timmermans and A E Kellerman *Article 177 EEC: Experiences and Problems* (1987).

H G Schermers and D Waelbroeck *Judicial Protection in the European Communities* (1992).

John A Usher *European Court Practice* (1983).

David Vaughn (ed) *Law of the European Communities* (1986).

Articles

Lisa Borgfeld White 'The Enforcement of European Union Law: The Role of the European Court of Justice and the Court's Latest Challenge' (1996) 18 Houston Journal of International Law 833.

T Kennedy 'Paying the Piper: Legal Aid in Proceedings before the Court of Justice' (1988) 25 Common Market Law Review 559.

Carl O Lenz 'The Role and Mechanism of the Preliminary Ruling Procedure' (1994) 18 Fordham International Law Journal 388.

Carl O Lenz 'The Court of Justice of the European Communities' (1989) 14 European Law Review 127.

T Millet 'The New European Court of First Instance' (1989) 38 ICLQ 811.

David O'Keefe 'Judicial Protection of the Individual by the European Court of Justice' 19 (1996) Fordham International Law Journal 901.

CHAPTER 9

Court of the European Free Trade Association

GENERAL INFORMATION

9.1 The European Free Trade Association (EFTA) is an international organisation established in 1960 in order to remove trade barriers between the states parties. The current membership of EFTA is Iceland, Liechtenstein, Norway and Switzerland.[1] In 1992, EFTA and the European Communities (EC) entered into an agreement intended to bring about the partial integration of EFTA into the EC through establishing the European Economic Area (EEA). The Agreement on the EEA entered into force on 1 January 1994, between the EC and two of the EFTA states (Iceland and Norway).[2] Liechtenstein became part of the EEA on 1 May 1995.

The EEA agreement provides for the creation of three independent EFTA organs – a Standing Committee, a Surveillance Authority and an EFTA Court (comparable to the EC Council, Commission and Court, respectively), and two collective EC-EFTA bodies – the EEA Council and Joint Committee. The EFTA Court is entrusted with monitoring the obligations of the participating EFTA states and the functioning of the Surveillance Authority under EEA law. Its work is governed by the EEA Agreement, by the Agreement on the Establishment of a Surveillance Authority and a Court of Justice (ESA/Court Agreement),[3] by the Statute of the Court,[4] and by the Rules of Procedure, which were adopted by the EFTA Court and approved by the three participating governments.[5] Generally speaking, the organisation, competence and procedure of the EFTA Court are modelled on the Court of Justice of the European Communities (ECJ).

The EFTA Court comprises three judges,[6] nominated by their respective governments and appointed by common accord of the three participating governments. They serve a renewable term of six years.[7] Unlike the ECJ, the EFTA Court does not employ advocates-general to assist it in its work. The EFTA Court is seated in Luxembourg (as is the ECJ) and its principal working language is English.[8] In adjudicating cases, the EFTA Court applies the EEA Agreement, other related agreements (ESA/Court Agreement and the Agreement on a Standing Committee of the EFTA states) and secondary EC legislation adopted by the EEA Joint Committee. When applying norms which also exist under EC law, the court must interpret these norms in conformity with the relevant practice of the ECJ, prior to the entry into force of the EEA Agreement.[9] Subsequent developments in EC case law should be accorded 'due account'.[10]

Since the establishment of the EFTA Court it has rendered decisions in over 30 cases.

1 The original members of EFTA were Austria, Denmark, Norway, Portugal, Sweden, Switzerland and the UK.

2 The Agreement on a European Economic Area, 2 May 1992, 1994 OJ (L 1) 60, 1 CMLR 921 (1992) ('EEA Agreement'). The Agreement harmonises the rules on free movement of goods, persons, services and capital and competition: EEA Agreement, art 1.
3 Agreement between the EFTA States on the Establishment of a Surveillance Authority and a Court of Justice, 2 May 1992, 1994 OJ (L 344) 1, as modified on 29 December 1994 ('ESA/Court Agreement').
4 Agreement on the Statute of the Court, ESA/Court Agreement, Protocol 5, ('EFTA Court Statute').
5 Rules of Procedure of the EFTA Court, 1994 Official Journal L278/1 <http://www.efta.int/structure/court/efta-crt.cfm>, ('EFTA Court Rules').
6 ESA/Court Agreement, art 28. The current judges are Bjørn Haug – President (Norway); Carl Baudenbacher (Liechtenstein); and Thór Vilhjálmsson (Iceland).
7 ESA/Court Agreement, art 30.
8 EFTA Court Rules, arts 25–27. In advisory opinion proceedings, however, the case runs in English and the language of the national court – Icelandic, German or Norwegian.
9 EEA Agreement, art 6; ESA/Court Agreement, art 3(1).
10 ESA/Court Agreement, art 3(2).

JURISDICTION

9.2 The competence of the EFTA Court is similar, in general terms, to that of the ECJ. It has jurisdiction over the following cases.

Claims brought against states

9.3 Claims against any of the three participating states may be brought by other states (although this has never occurred in practice) or by the Surveillance Authority.[1] In inter-state cases, the EFTA Court may address any dispute concerning the interpretation or application of the EEA Agreement and other two agreements (on ESA/Court and the Standing Committee). Cases brought by the Surveillance Authority must allege violation of the EEA or ESA/Court Agreement by a state party.[2] Before initiating a claim the Surveillance Authority will deliver its reasoned opinion to the state concerned and enable it to comply with the requirements of the opinion in a fixed period of time. There is no similar requirement for claims brought by a state.

1 ESA/Court Agreement, arts 31, 32.
2 Ibid, art 31: cf EC Treaty, art 169.

Claims brought against the Surveillance Authority

9.4 A case against the Surveillance Authority may be brought by any participating EFTA states or by natural or legal persons directly affected by an act or omission of the Surveillance Authority.[1] Claims against the Surveillance Authority must allege that an act adopted by the Surveillance Authority falls outside its competence, involves an infringement of an essential procedural requirement, constitutes an infringement of the EEA Agreement or ESA/Court Agreement (or any norm relating to their application) or is a misuse of powers. In the alternative, a claim may allege that a failure on the part of the Surveillance Authority to act constitutes an infringement of EEA law. The court also has jurisdiction to determine the non-contractual liability of the Surveillance Authority.[2] If 'general principles of law' support the issuance of remedies for damage caused by the Surveillance Authority or its staff, the court may award compensation. Unlike the ECJ, the EFTA Court lacks competence to review acts of legislation, since the EEA Joint Committee is not

147

subject to its jurisdiction. The ECJ alone is competent to review secondary EC legislation.

1   ESA/Court Agreement, arts 36, 37.
2   Ibid, arts 39, 46(2).

Advisory opinions

9.5   In similarity to the procedure of preliminary rulings employed by the ECJ, the EFTA Court may receive questions concerning the interpretation of the EEA Agreement from domestic courts of the participating EFTA states.[1] However, there is no obligation to make such a request under the EFTA system, and the decision of the EFTA Court constitutes an advisory opinion which the domestic court is not bound to apply. In practice, though, the advisory opinions are followed by the national courts.

1   ESA/Court Agreement, art 34.

CONTACT INFORMATION

The EFTA Court is located at:

> EFTA Court
> 1, rue du Fort Thüngen
> L-1499 LUXEMBOURG

> Tel: (+352) 42 10 81
> Fax: (+352) 43 43 89
> email: eftacourt@eftacourt.lu
> website: http://www.efta.int

REFERENCE

Sources of case law, including case reports

Decisions of the EFTA Court from 1994 to 1999 can be found on the EFTA website.

Selected bibliography

Books

N March Hunnings *The European Courts* (1996).

Articles

Carl Baudenbacher 'Between homogeneity and independence: the legal position of the EFTA Court in the European Economic Area' (1997) 3 Columbia Journal of Environmental Law 169.

P Christiansen 'The EFTA Court' (1997) European Law Review.

Vincent Kronenberger 'Does the EFTA Court interpret the EEA Agreement as if it were the EC Treaty? Some questions raised by the Restamark' (1996) 45 International and Comparative Law Quarterly 198.

CHAPTER 10

Court of Justice of the Andean Community

GENERAL INFORMATION

10.1 The Andean Community (previously known as the Andean Pact) is a sub-regional economic integration arrangement encompassing, at present, five South American states – Bolivia, Colombia, Ecuador, Peru and Venezuela. The Andean integration process began in 1969 with the signing of the Cartagena Agreement,[1] which created a custom union between the participating states and an institutional framework to monitor compliance with the Agreement and facilitate greater economic co-operation. Throughout the years the Cartagena Agreement has undergone a number of revisions, the most important of which has been the conclusion of the 1996 Protocol of Trujillo,[2] which strengthened economic integration and established a new institutional framework – the Andean Integration System. The principal institutions of the Andean Community are the Andean Presidential Council (the principal policy-making institution); the Council of Ministers of Foreign Affairs (a forum for political co-operation with legislative powers); the Commission (a legislative and supervisory body); the General Secretariat – previously known as the Junta (the executive body); the Parliament (a deliberative body with recommendatory powers); and the Court of Justice.

The court was established in 1979 by a special treaty ('Treaty Creating the Court')[3] and has its seat in Quito, Ecuador.[4] It comprises five judges from the five member states and elected by consensus of the five governments.[5] They serve a once-renewable term of six years.[6] The work of the court is governed by its constitutive Treaty, the Statute of the Court[7] and the Internal Regulations of Court.[8] In 1996, the parties concluded a Protocol Modifying the Treaty Creating the Court ('Modifying Protocol'), which, after entry into force, will significantly enhance the jurisdiction of the court (some provisions related to the recent reform in the structure of the Community order are already applied on a temporary basis).

The proceedings before the court include written and oral hearings and the introduction of evidence. They conclude with the issuance of a judgment, which is final and binding upon the parties.[9] The court receives administrative services from an independent Secretariat.[10]

1 Cartagena Agreement, 26 May 1969, 8 ILM 910 (1969).
2 Modifying Protocol of the Andean Subregional Integration Agreement (Cartagena Agreement), 10 March 1996, 273 Official Gazette of the Cartagena Agreement (1997) ('Protocol of Trujillo').
3 Treaty Creating the Court of Justice of the Cartagena Agreement, 28 May 1979, 17 ILM 1203 (1979) (unofficial translation) ('Treaty Creating the Court'). In 1996 a modifying protocol was concluded in Cochabamba, Bolivia: Modifying Protocol of the Treaty Creating the Court of

149

Justice of the Cartagena Agreement, 28 May 1996 ('Modifying Protocol').
4 Treaty Creating the Court, art 6 (Modifying Protocol, art 5).
5 Treaty Creating the Court, arts 7, 8 (Modifying Protocol, arts 6, 7).
6 Treaty Creating the Court, art 9 (Modifying Protocol, art 8). The current membership of the Court is Gualberto D Garcia, Roberto S Manrique, Patricio B Martinez, Juan Jose Calle Y Calle and Luis Enrique F Mata.
7 Statute of the Court of Justice of the Cartagena Agreement, 19 August 1983, 23 ILM 425 (1984) (unofficial translation).
8 Internal Regulations of the Court of Justice of the Cartagena Agreement, 8 Official Gazette of the Cartagena Agreement (1984) ('Internal Regulations').
9 Treaty Creating the Court, arts 22, 25, 31; Court Statute, art 58; Internal Regulations, arts 14–16.
10 Treaty Creating the Court, art 15 (Modifying Protocol, art 14); Court Statute, art 16.

JURISDICTION

10.2 The court may address complaints against member states and Andean Community institutions and receive requests for preliminary interpretive opinions.

Complaints against member states

10.3 A member state may bring a complaint against another member state for failure to comply with obligations under Andean Community law. The complaint must be brought first before the General Secretariat, which is expected to render its opinion on the matter within three months (60 days under the Modifying Protocol). If the General Secretariat does not issue an opinion on time, does not find a breach of Andean Community law, or finds non-compliance but fails to bring the case to the court within 60 days of publication of the opinion, the complaining state may seize the court.[1] The General Secretariat may also bring a case against a non-complying state to the court on its own initiative.[2] With the entry into force of the Modifying Protocol, natural or legal persons, whose rights are affected by a breach of Community law by a member state, will also be able to bring a complaint against that state to the court, subject to the same conditions governing inter-state complaints.[3]

1 Treaty Creating the Court, art 24 (Modifying Protocol, art 24).
2 Treaty Creating the Court, art 23 (Modifying Protocol, art 23).
3 Modifying Protocol, art 25.

Complaints against Community institutions

10.4 The court is authorised to declare the invalidity of Community legislation (Decisions adopted by the Council of Ministers of Foreign Affairs or the Commission and Resolutions of the General Secretariat) and, under the Modifying Protocol, also of side agreements adopted by the member states within the framework of the Andean integration process.[1] In addition, the court will be able, under the Modifying Protocol, to deal with complaints alleging inactivity on the part of the Council of Ministers for Foreign Affairs, the Commission, or the General Secretariat. The court will be able to order these institutions to perform any act which Community law specifically mandates.[2] Complaints against Community institutions can be brought by the other Community institutions, a member state (except in case of a

150

challenge to the validity of a Decision or agreement it previously subscribed to),[3] and natural and legal persons whose rights or legitimate interests are affected by the challenged act or omission.[4] Invalidity cases must be brought to the court within one year of enactment of the measure (although indirect challenge in domestic courts is possible at a later date).[5]

1 Treaty Creating the Court, art 17 (Modifying Protocol, art 17).
2 Modifying Protocol, art 37.
3 Treaty Creating the Court, art 18 (Modifying Protocol, art 18).
4 Treaty Creating the Court, art 19 (Modifying Protocol, arts 19, 37).
5 Treaty Creating the Court, art 20 (Modifying Protocol, art 20).

Preliminary interpretative opinions

10.5 In the event that a question which involves the application of Andean Community law arises before a national court, the national court may (or must, if there is no appeal over its decisions) stay the proceedings and refer the question to the Court of Justice.[1] The Court of Justice will render its opinion on the interpretation of the applicable norms of Community law, and the domestic court must then adopt the opinion of the Court of Justice and decide the case before it accordingly.[2]

1 Treaty Creating the Court, art 29 (Modifying Protocol, art 33).
2 Treaty Creating the Court, art 31 (Modifying Protocol, art 35).

Other heads of jurisdiction

10.6 Under the Modifying Protocol, the court will also be able to serve as an arbitral tribunal and settle disputes between Community institutions and between Community institutions and third parties in disputes concerning the interpretation or application of contracts or agreements. In addition, the court will deal with contractual disputes between private parties, if the relevant contract is governed by the Community legal order. In all cases, the parties to the arbitration will have to agree to refer the case to the court.[1] The court will also be authorised once the Modifying Protocol enters into force to handle labour disputes involving the staff of the Andean Integration System.[2]

To date, the court has decided ten cases brought against member states (one of the cases was brought by other member states), and 12 cases brought against Community institutions. It has also rendered some 150 preliminary interpretative opinions.

1 Modifying Protocol, art 38.
2 Modifying Protocol, art 40.

CONTACT INFORMATION

10.7 The headquarters of the Court of Justice are located at:

Court of Justice of the Andean Community
Calle Roca 450
Quito – Ecuador

Tel: (593-2) 529990/529998
Fax: (593-2) 565007/554533

email: tjca@impsat.net.ec
website: http:/www.altesa.net/tribunal.htm
community website: http:/www.communidadandina.org

REFERENCE

Sources of case law

The recent case law of the Andean Court of Justice can be found on its website.

Selected bibliography

Barlow Keener 'The Andean Common Market Court of Justice: its purpose, structure and future' (1997) 2 Emory Journal of International Law Dispute Resolutions 39.

Nicolas de Pierola 'The Andean Court of Justice' (1987) 2 Emory Journal of International Law Dispute Resolutions 11.

CHAPTER 11
Central American Court of Justice

GENERAL INFORMATION

11.1 The Central American Court of Justice (CACJ) is the principal judicial organ of the Central American Integration System (SICA). SICA is a framework for political co-operation and economic integration between six Central American states – Costa Rica, El Salvador, Guatemala, Honduras, Nicaragua and Panama. It was established in 1991 by the Protocol of Tegucigalpa,[1] which entered into force in 1993, replacing the more loosely structured Organisation of Central American States (ODECA), which had existed since 1962. The principal organs of SICA are the Meeting of Presidents (the principal policy-making and legislative body); the Council of Ministers (a policy-coordinating body); the Executive Committee (a permanent executive body composed of state representatives); the Secretary General (the top administrative position); the Central American Parliament; and the Court of Justice.[2]

The CACJ, which became operative in 1994, is seated in Managua, Nicaragua. To date, three SICA states, El Salvador, Honduras and Nicaragua, have ratified the court's Statute and become subject to its jurisdiction.[3] According to the court's Statute, an equal number of judges (and alternatives) from each of the participating member states is to be elected by the respective national supreme courts to serve on the CACJ.[4] The court is composed of two judges from each participating state.[5] In 1997 the Meeting of the Presidents considered certain reforms for the SICA's organs. They thought to reduce the number of judges at the court to one (and one alternate) per state, but this reform has not yet been approved or ratified. The judges serve a renewable period of ten years and the court may sit in plenary or in chambers.[6]

The work of the court is governed by its Statute, Regulations[7] and the Decree on Procedures.[8] Proceedings before the court consist of written and oral pleadings,[9] and the judgments of the court are final and binding.[10] The court receives administrative services from its own Secretariat and Administration headed by the court's Secretary General.[11]

To date, the court has received 16 cases (nine of which were requests for advisory opinions).

1 Protocol of Tegucigalpa of Reforms to the Charter of the Organisation of the Central American States, 13 December 1991, available at <http://www.ccj.org.ni/normjurd/prottegu.htm>.
2 Ibid, art 12.
3 Agreement on the Statute of the Central American Court of Justice, 10 December 1992, 34 ILM 921 (1995) (unofficial translation) ('CACJ Statute').
4 CACJ Statute, art 8.
5 The original composition of the court was Jorge Antonio Giammattei Avilés and Fabio

> Hércules Pineda Iel Salvador); Roberto Ramírez Ordoñez and Adolfo León Gómez (Honduras); Rafael Chamorro Mora and Orlando Trejos Somarriba (Nicaragua). The current membership is José Eduardo Gauggel Rivas, President (Honduras); Chamorro Mora, Vice-President; Giammattei Avilés; Hércules Pineda; León Gómez; Trejos Somarriba.

6 CACJ Statute, arts 7 and 11.
7 Regulations of the Central American Court of Justice, available at <http://www.ccj.org.ni/normjurd/reglam.htm> ('CACJ Regulations').
8 Decree on Procedures concerning the Object and Purpose of the Central American Court of Justice, available at <http://www.ccj.org.ni/normjurd/ordenanz.htm> ('CACJ Procedures').
9 CACJ Regulations, arts 9, 47, 48.
10 CACJ Statute, arts 24, 37, 38.
11 CACJ Regulations, arts 21, 22, 30.

JURISDICTION

11.2 The court enjoys competence over the following cases.

Inter-state disputes

11.3 The court may receive all disputes between the states parties to the Statute.[1] Proceedings before the CACJ can be initiated unilaterally, except in frontier, territorial or maritime disputes, where consent of all litigating parties is necessary. In addition, the court may hear cases between a SICA member state and a non-SICA state with the agreement of all concerned parties.[2]

1 CACJ Statute, art 22(a); CACJ Procedures, art 5(1).
2 CACJ Statute, art 22(h).

Complaints against states

11.4 Any interested party (state parties, SICA organs and natural or legal persons) may bring a case to the court against a state party that has adopted legal norms (laws, administrative provisions, etc), which are inconsistent with SICA law (including secondary legislation concluded by SICA organs).[1]

1 CACJ Statute, art 22(c).

Complaints against SICA organs

11.5 A state party and a natural or legal person may bring a case to the court against SICA organs challenging secondary legislation concluded by the latter, or non-fulfilment of an obligation under SICA law.[1] Individuals may challenge only decisions or resolutions which directly affect them.[2] The court also has competence over staff cases.[3]

1 CACJ Statute, art 22(b); CACJ Procedures, arts 60, 61.
2 CACJ Statute, art 22(g); CACJ Procedures, art 60(b).
3 CACJ Statute, art 22(j); CACJ Procedures, arts 51–53.

Constitutional controversies

11.6 The CACJ may adjudicate disputes that arise between the main branches of government of the states parties, including disputes over the implementation of judicial decisions.[1]

1 CACJ Statute, art 22(f); CACJ Procedures, arts 62, 63.

Arbitral competence

11.7   A dispute between a SICA state and an individual party may be referred to the court with the agreement of all parties.[1]

1   CACJ Statute, art 22(ch); CACJ Procedures, art 5(5).

Advisory competence

11.8   The court may provide advisory opinions on a variety of issues related to SICA law to the following bodies: the supreme courts of the states parties;[1] lower domestic courts (in a preliminary reference procedure similar to that of art 177 of the EC Treaty);[2] the organs of SICA;[3] and the states parties.[4]

1   CACJ Statute, art 22(d); CACJ Procedures, arts 54–56.
2   CACJ Statute, art 22(k); CACJ Procedures, arts 57–59.
3   CACJ Statute, art 22(e).
4   Ibid, art 23.

CONTACT INFORMATION

11.9   The court is located at:

Central American Court of Justice
Del porton del Hospital El Retiro 1 1/2 c.
al Lago Casa 1804
Apartado Postal 907
Managua, Nicaragua

Tel: (505) 2 66 62 73
Fax: (505) 2 66 84 86
email: cortecen@tmx.com.ni
website: http://www.CACJ.org.ni/

REFERENCE

Sources of case law

Case law of the Central American Court of Justice can be found on the court's website.

Selected bibliography

K Madlena *Zur Stellung der Obersten Gerichte in Mexico und Mittelamerika* (1995).

A Montiel-Argüello 'La Corte de Justicia Centroamericano y los Dere Chos Humanos' in *Liber Amicorum: Colleccion de Estudios Juridicas en Homenaje al Prof Dr José Perez Montero*, 3 vols (1988).

CHAPTER 12

Court of Justice of the Common Market for Eastern and Southern Africa (COMESA)

GENERAL INFORMATION

12.1   The Common Market for Eastern and Southern Africa (COMESA) was established in 1994, after the entry into force of its constitutive treaty,[1] and currently encompasses 21 African states (see Annex). The aim of COMESA is to increase economic co-operation, remove trade barriers and introduce a customs union between the member states.[2] The principal institutions are the Authority (the supreme policy organ composed of heads of states and governments); the Council of Ministers (the principal legislative organ); the Secretariat (the principal executive organ); and the Court of Justice.[3] The court became formally operational in 1998.

The task of the COMESA Court will be to supervise the interpretation and application of the COMESA Treaty.[4] Its operation will be governed by the COMESA Treaty and by the Rules of Court, which were adopted in September 1998.[5] The substantive law, which will be applied by the court, includes the COMESA Treaty and rules of law relating to its application (eg secondary legislation).

The court comprises seven judges,[6] appointed by the Authority for a renewable five-year term.[7] The court is to be temporarily seated in Lusaka, Zambia; and the Authority still has to decide on the location of the permanent seat of the court. The official languages of the court are English, French and Portuguese.[8]

1   Treaty Establishing the Common Market for Eastern and Southern Africa, 5 November 1993, 33 ILM 1067 (1994) ('COMESA Treaty').
2   COMESA Treaty, arts 3, 4.
3   Ibid, art 7.
4   Ibid, art 19.
5   Rules of the Court, 18 September 1998. Available on the COMESA website.
6   COMESA Treaty, art 20(1). The current judges are Josaphat L Kanywanyi – President (Tanzania); A M Akiwumi (Kenya); K R A Korash (Zimbabwe); Adrien Nyankiye (Burundi); James B Kalaile (Malawi); Ernest L Sakala (Zambia); and James M Ogoola (Uganda).
7   COMESA Treaty, arts 20, 21. Detailed rules on the appointment procedure were adopted by the Council of Ministers (Rules of Procedure for the Election of Judges and Nomination of the President of the COMESA Court of Justice).
8   COMESA Treaty, art 43.

JURISDICTION

12.2   The court will be able to exercise jurisdiction in the following cases.

Claims brought against states

12.3 A COMESA member state may bring to the court a claim against any other member state alleging that the respondent state has failed to fulfil an obligation under the COMESA Treaty or has infringed one or more of its provisions.[1] The Secretary-General of COMESA may also bring a claim against a state on similar grounds. However, the Secretary-General must provide the state concerned with his or her findings before initiating the claim. The state will be then granted two months to submit its observations. The Secretary-General, with the authorisation of the Council of Ministers (or the Council's Bureau), may seize the court only if the observations have not been submitted in time, or are unsatisfactory.[2] In addition, persons who reside in a COMESA member state may bring to the court a claim against any member state alleging that an act, regulation, directive or decision adopted by that state is unlawful or constitutes an infringement of the COMESA Treaty. However, the person in question must first exhaust local remedies available in the state complained against.[3]

1 COMESA Treaty, art 24(1).
2 Ibid, art 25.
3 Ibid, art 26.

Claims brought against the Council of Ministers

12.4 A COMESA member state or a person residing in a COMESA member state may challenge an act, regulation, directive or decision adopted by the Council of Ministers. The grounds for challenge in cases brought by a state are:
(a) ultra vires;
(b) unlawfulness;
(c) infringement of the COMESA Treaty and related law; or
(d) misuse or abuse of power.[1]
By contrast, claims presented by private persons may only allege unlawfulness or infringement of the COMESA Treaty.[2] A state may also bring to the court any failure on the part of the Council to fulfil an obligation under the COMESA Treaty, or of an infringement of the Treaty by the Council, in addition to the above-mentioned challenges (eg in the event of an omission to act).[3]

1 COMESA Treaty, art 24(2).
2 Ibid, art 26.
3 Ibid, art 24(1).

Preliminary rulings

12.5 A national court or tribunal may refer to the COMESA Court any question concerning the application or interpretation of the COMESA Treaty or the validity of secondary legislation (ie COMESA regulations, directives and decisions). If the question arises before a domestic court of last instance, that court must refer the question to the COMESA Court.[1]

1 COMESA Treaty, art 30.

Other heads of jurisdiction

12.6 The COMESA Court may receive cases referred to it by way of an arbitration clause or special agreement between the Common Market or one of its institutions and a third party; or between two or more member states.[1] It will also exercise jurisdiction over staff cases and over claims presented by any person against the Common Market or its institutions due to official acts of COMESA staff.[2] Finally, the court will be authorised to render advisory opinions at the request of the Authority, Council of Ministers or any member state, on any question of law arising from the COMESA Treaty and affecting the COMESA organisation.[3]

1   COMESA Treaty, art 28.
2   Ibid, art 27.
3   Ibid, art 32.

CONTACT INFORMATION

12.7   The Registrar of the COMESA Court is located at:

Registrar, COMESA Court of Justice
COMESA Centre
Ben Bella Road, PO Box 30051
10101 Lusaka
Zambia

Tel: (+260) 1 229 726 or 1 229 732
Fax: (+260) 1 225 107
email: rlimbambala@comesa.int
website: http://www.comesa.int

REFERENCE

Sources of case law

Since the court only became operational in 1998, there is as yet no case law. In future, case law should be available on the court's website.

Selected bibliography

Article

Kenneth Kiplagat 'Dispute recognition and dispute settlement in integration processes: the COMESA experience' (1995) 15 Northwestern Journal of International Law and Business 437.

ANNEX

List of COMESA member states

Angola, Burundi, Comoros, Democratic Republic of Congo, Djibouti, Egypt, Eritrea, Ethiopia, Kenya, Madagascar, Malawi, Mauritius, Namibia, Rwanda, Seychelles, Sudan, Swaziland, Tanzania, Uganda, Zambia, Zimbabwe.

CHAPTER 13

North American Free Trade Area dispute settlement procedures and Commission for Environmental Co-operation

NAFTA DISPUTE SETTLEMENT PROCEDURES

General information

13.1 In 1992 Canada, the USA and Mexico concluded the North American Free Trade Agreement (NAFTA),[1] establishing the North American Free Trade Area. The Agreement removes trade barriers and promotes economic co-operation between the three participating states. Supervision over the implementation of NAFTA is under the primary responsibility of a Free Trade Commission (comprising ministerial representatives of the parties) assisted by a permanent Secretariat.[2] Most disputes arising under NAFTA are to be assigned by the Free Trade Commission to ad hoc dispute settlement panels, roughly modelled on the GATT/WTO dispute settlement panels. Disputes concerning antidumping and countervailing duties are to be dealt with by different machinery involving bi-national panels.

1 North American Free Trade Agreement, 17 December 1992, 32 ILM 289 and 605 (1993) ('NAFTA').
2 NAFTA, arts 2001, 2002.

The general dispute settlement procedure (Chapter 20 of the NAFTA Agreement)

13.2 The dispute settlement provisions of NAFTA apply to any dispute between the states parties concerning: (1) the interpretation or application of NAFTA; or (2) allegations that the application of an actual or proposed measure taken by a party is inconsistent with its NAFTA obligations, or would cause impairment or nullification of certain benefits that the complaining party expects to attain under NAFTA.[1] Once a dispute has arisen the parties must first enter into consultations.[2] If no solution is found within a fixed period of time, the complaining party may request the convening of the Free Trade Commission, which will put its good offices at the disposal of the parties in order to facilitate a settlement.[3] If the parties fail to reach agreement within a fixed period of time, any party can request the Commission to establish an ad hoc arbitration panel.[4]

A panel comprises five independent experts. Each party is to select two persons, who are citizens of the other party to the dispute, and the chairperson is selected by agreement of the parties.[5] In order to facilitate the selection process, the parties maintain a permanent roster of potential arbitrators (comprising up to 30 qualified persons) appointed with the consent of all states parties.[6] The appointment of an arbitrator who is not on the roster may be challenged by the other party.[7]

The procedure taken by the panels follows closely that of GATT/WTO panels (see Chapter 5). After hearings conducted in pursuance of the Commission's Model Rules of Procedure[8] (from which the parties may agree to deviate), an initial report is published. The parties may submit their comments on the report and, subsequently, the panel issues a final report containing factual and legal findings.[9]

The reports are binding upon the parties. They are to be executed, preferably through non-implementation or removal of the unlawful measure, but alternatively through compensation. In case of failure to comply with the report, the complaining party may exercise trade sanctions against the recalcitrant party.[10] To date, two reports have been published under the general dispute settlement procedure outlined in Chapter 20 of the NAFTA Agreement; a few other cases are still pending.

1 NAFTA, art 2004.
2 Ibid, art 2006.
3 Ibid, art 2007.
4 Ibid, art 2008. The normal period before establishment of a panel is 30 days from the date the Commission was first convened to discuss the dispute.
5 NAFTA, art 2011. If no agreement is reached, one of the parties, designated by lot, will appoint the chair. However, the appointing party cannot select a person of its own nationality.
6 NAFTA, art 2009.
7 Ibid, art 2011.3.
8 Model Rules of Procedure for Chapter Twenty of the North American Free Trade Agreement and Supplementary Procedures Pursuant to Rule 35 on the Availability of Information, 13 July 1995, available on the NAFTA Secretariat's website.
9 NAFTA, arts 2016, 2017.
10 Ibid, arts 2018, 2019. The proportionality of trade sanctions may be subject of separate panel proceedings.

Antidumping and countervailing duties bi-national panels (Chapter 19 of the NAFTA Agreement)

13.3 Chapter 19 of NAFTA introduces a separate dispute settlement mechanism for review of antidumping and countervailing duties adopted by the three member states. The central feature of this mechanism is the establishment of ad hoc bi-national panels to review domestic administrative determinations relating to antidumping and countervailing duties. A special section of the Secretariat of the Free Trade Commission facilitates the operation of the bi-national panel system.[1]

A state party to NAFTA may request the establishment of a bi-national panel in two situations:

(1) if another party has adopted a statutory amendment which is inconsistent with the GATT (or certain specified side-agreements) or the object and purpose of NAFTA,[2] or has the function and effect of over-turning a bi-national panel decision (and is also inconsistent with the GATT and/or NAFTA);[3]

(2) if a determination of a competent domestic authority on antidumping or countervailing duties is incompatible with the domestic law of the importing state, as would have been applied by a domestic court of review.[4]

Such panels can also be established in relation to a dispute on antidumping or countervailing duties upon the request of the importing state, acting on its own initiative, or acting on the request of a person that would have had legal standing before equivalent domestic challenge procedures.[5] All state parties grant access to private litigants to bi-national panels and virtually all Chapter 19 cases until now involved a claim of private corporations from one state against the determination of a competent administrative authority of another state.

Bi-national panels comprise five independent and qualified experts, who are normally to be selected from a roster of at least 75 persons.[6] Each party is to select two panel members and the fifth is to be agreed upon or, failing agreement, nominated by a party chosen by lot.[7]

The procedure of bi-national panels requested to examine statutory amendments is governed by Annex 1903.2 to the NAFTA Agreement, which entails procedures similar to those of the general panel machinery (the panels, or the parties, acting jointly, are to decide on supplementary rules of procedure).[8] In the event of failure to comply with decisions of a bi-national panel on statutory amendments, the complaining state is free to adopt comparable legislation or equivalent executive action to the violating amendments, or even to terminate its participation in NAFTA.[9]

Bi-national panels established to review administrative determinations are to apply the same standards of review that a domestic court would have applied.[10] They conduct their business in accordance with fixed rules of appellate procedure that have been agreed upon by the states parties.[11] A private litigant is to have the same procedural rights before a bi-national panel as he or she would have had before a comparable domestic review tribunal.[12] The supervision of the mechanism of bi-national panels reviewing administrative determinations is assigned to two ad hoc bodies – the Extraordinary Challenge Committee (composed of three members, selected by the parties from a roster of 15 senior judges or former judges), which may be requested to review the integrity of the mechanism;[13] and a Special Committee (composed in a similar manner to the Extraordinary Challenge Committee), which oversees state compliance in relation to the operation of the mechanism. A Special Committee is to be established if one party alleges that the other party impeded the work of the bi-national panel or failed to comply with the panel's decision.[14] The Special Committee may approve sanctions against the non-complying party.

To date, nearly 50 cases have been referred to bi-national panels.

1 NAFTA, art 1908.
2 Ibid, arts 1902.2(d), 1903.1(a). Subs 2(d)(ii) defines the purpose and object of the NAFTA Agreement as: 'to establish fair and predictable conditions for the progressive liberalisation of trade among the Parties to this Agreement, while maintaining effective and fair disciplines on unfair trade practices.'
3 NAFTA, art 1903.1(b).
4 Ibid, art 1904.2.
5 Ibid, art 1904.5.
6 Ibid, Annex 1901.2. The parties may also select non-roster panel members; however, in this case, the other party has a right to disqualify up to four non-roster candidates.
7 NAFTA, Annex 1901.2, art 3.
8 NAFTA, Annex 1903.2, art 1.
9 NAFTA, art 1903.3(b).
10 Ibid, art 1904.3.
11 Ibid, art 1904 Panel Rules.

12 Ibid, arts 1904.5, 1904.7.
13 Ibid, art 1940.13. Grounds for extraordinary challenge (ECC) are: (1) gross misconduct, conflict of interest or other violation of rules of conduct by a panel member; (2) serious departure on the part of the panel from a fundamental rule of procedure; (3) if a panel manifestly exceeded its powers, authority or jurisdiction. Only states may initiate ECC proceedings.
14 NAFTA, art 1905. Grounds for a motion to establish a Special Committee are if a party has: (1) prevented the establishment of a panel; (2) prevented the panel from rendering its decision; (3) prevented the implementation of a panel decision; or (4) failed to provide an opportunity for panel or judicial review.

Investment disputes under NAFTA

13.4 Chapter 11 of the NAFTA sets out the applicable rules relating to investment. Within its framework it is also possible for an investor of a member state to institute arbitral proceedings for resolution of disputes which may arise with the host state. It is, however, first necessary to have attempted to settle the claim through consultation or negotiation,[1] and to have waited until at least six months have elapsed after the events giving rise to a claim.[2] Pursuant to the provisions of this section, an investor may submit the claim to arbitration under the ICSID Convention (if all parties concerned are parties to the ICSID Convention) or the Additional Facility Rules of ICSID. It is also possible to submit the dispute to arbitration under the UNCITRAL rules.[3]

1 NAFTA, art 1118.
2 Ibid, art 1120.
3 Ibid, art 1120(1). For ICSID arbitration see Chapter 6.

CONTACT INFORMATION

13.5 Contact details for the NAFTA Secretariat, which comprises Canadian, Mexican and US sections, are as follows:

> NAFTA Secretariat Canadian Section
> Royal Bank Centre
> 90 Sparks Street
> Suite 705
> Ottawa
> Ontario
> K1P 5B4
>
> Tel: 1 613 992 9388
> Fax: 1 613 992 9392
>
> Secretariado del TLCAN Sección Mexicana
> Blvd Adolfo López Mateos 3025
> 2° Piso
> Col Héroes de Padierna
> C P 10700
> Mexico DF

Tel: 525 629 9630
Fax: 525 629 9637

NAFTA Secretariat US Section
14th Street & Constitution Avenue NW
Room 2061
Washington DC 20230
USA

Tel: 1 202 482 5438
Fax: 1 202 482 0148
website: www.nafta.sec-alena.org

COMMISSION FOR ENVIRONMENTAL CO-OPERATION

General information

13.6 In 1993 Canada, Mexico and the US concluded the North American Agreement on Environmental Co-operation (NAAEC).[1] The Agreement, providing for stricter domestic environmental standards and increased environmental co-operation, was part of the movement towards North American economic integration culminating in the establishment of a North American Free Trade Area. The three states parties have established a Commission for Environmental Co-operation (CEC) in order to facilitate co-operation between them and monitor the implementation of the NAAEC.[2] The Commission comprises three organs – a Council (composed of cabinet-level state representatives), a Secretariat and a Joint Public Advisory Committee (composed of 15 members).

The role of the Council is, inter alia, to adopt recommendations on environmental standards and co-operation, supervise the work of the Secretariat and approve the annual budget and programme of the CEC. It is also entrusted with co-ordination of the settlement of inter-state disputes concerning the NAAEC. The Secretariat monitors the compliance of the states parties with the provisions of the NAAEC, provides technical, administrative and operational support to the Council,[3] and reports to the Council on a variety of environmental issues.[4] It also deals with submissions of persons and non-governmental organisations (NGOs) alleging that a state party has failed to effectively enforce its environmental laws, and it may present to the Council factual reports on such situations (which the latter may decide to publish). The official languages of the Commission are English, French and Spanish.[5]

1 North American Agreement on Environmental Cooperation, 14 September 1993, 32 ILM 1480 (1993) ('NAAEC').
2 NAAEC, art 10.
3 Ibid, arts 11(5), 12(2)(c).
4 Ibid, arts 12, 13.
5 Ibid, art 19.

Inter-state disputes

13.7 In the event that a state party alleges that another state party has demonstrated a persistent pattern of failures to enforce effectively its environmental laws,[1] it may initiate the dispute settlement procedures

163

prescribed in Part V of the NAAEC.[2] If direct consultations fail to resolve the matter, the complaining state may bring the matter before the Council, which is to attempt to facilitate a mutually acceptable solution.[3] If no settlement is reached within 60 days from the date in which the Council was first convened, each of the parties to the dispute may request the establishment of an arbitral panel. The request to establish a panel must be supported by two of the three members of the Council. However, a panel may only deal with cases involving environmental standards that relate to manufacturers of goods or services which are traded between the parties, or are in competition with traded goods or services.[4]

The panel is to be established by the disputing parties and is to include five independent experts (each party is to appoint two panellists and the Chair is normally selected by agreement).[5] In order to facilitate the selection process, the Council maintains a permanent roster of up to 45 individual experts in environmental law, international law or any other relevant area (the roster members are appointed by way of consensus).[6] Panel members should normally be selected from the roster.[7] The arbitration proceedings before the panel are to be conducted in accordance with Model Rules of Procedure (from which the parties may agree to deviate).[8] Until now, the Commission has not adopted Model Rules.

At the end of the hearings (generally within 180 days from the establishment of the panel), the panel is to issue an initial report, containing factual and legal findings and recommendations.[9] The parties may submit their comments on the initial report within 30 days. The panel will then render the final report, taking into consideration the comments of the parties, within 60 days from the date in which the initial report was issued.[10] In the event that a dispute concerning the implementation of the panel's report arises, the Council is to reconvene the panel, upon the request of a party.[11] The reconvened panel is to review compliance with the final report and may order payment of monetary enforcement costs, where warranted. Failure to comply with the decisions of the second panel may entitle the other party to suspend benefits due to the non-complying party under NAFTA (a panel may be reconvened once again by the Council in order to review the justification and proportionality of such counter-measures).[12]

To date, there have been no inter-state cases under Chapter V of the NAAEC.

1 Persistent pattern is defined under the Agreement as 'a sustained or recurring course of action or inaction' taking place during the life of the agreement: NAAEC, art 45.
2 NAAEC, art 22(1).
3 Ibid, art 23. The normal period of time between the initiation of direct consultations and the referral of the matter to the Council is 60 days. The Council will convene within 20 days from the date it was requested to address the dispute.
4 NAAEC, art 24(1).
5 Ibid, art 27. If no agreement on the identity of the Chair is reached, the party selected by lot will appoint a Chair who is not its citizen.
6 NAAEC, art 25.
7 Ibid, art 27(3). Parties may challenge the appointment of a non-roster panel member.
8 NAAEC, art 28.
9 Ibid, art 31.
10 Ibid, arts 31(4),(5), 32.
11 Ibid, arts 34, 35. The panel is to determine within 60 days from re-establishment whether measures taken by the state complained against has rectified the situation indicated in the final report.
12 NAAEC, art 36.

Submissions on enforcement measures

13.8 The NAAEC authorises the Secretariat to receive complaints from any NGO or person established or residing in the territory of a state party, alleging that a state party is failing to enforce effectively its environmental laws.[1] The procedure governing such complaints is regulated by arts 14–15 of the NAAEC and the Guidelines for Submissions on Enforcement Matters adopted by the Council.

The submission is to be made in writing and contain the necessary supporting information.[2] The Secretariat will examine the submission (eg whether it is frivolous or of an harassing nature and whether prior communication to the authorities of the state concerned was made) and determine whether it merits response from the state party complained against, in light of any harm allegedly caused to the author of the submission, the importance of the issues raised, the availability of alternative remedies and the nature of the source of information.[3] If the Secretariat is convinced that the submission warrants response, it will invite the state party complained against to provide its response.[4] On the basis of the information presented by the parties the Secretariat may request the approval of the Council for further investigation of the matter. If approval is granted, the Secretariat is to prepare a factual record on the matter, based, inter alia, on information presented by NGOs, persons, the Joint Public Advisory Committee, or the Parties, or developed by the Secretariat or independent experts.[5] The factual record is then to be submitted to the Council, which may decide to make it available to the public.[6]

As of 1 April 1999, the CEC Secretariat has received a total of 20 submissions on enforcement matters. There are currently 11 submissions under review. One Factual Record has been prepared and made public. The Secretariat is currently (April 1999) developing a Factual Record for another submission, as instructed by the Council.

1 NAAEC, art 14(1); Guidelines for Submissions on Enforcement Matters under arts 14 and 15 of the North American Agreement on Environmental Cooperation, paras 3.1, 7.1, Council Res 95/10 ('Guidelines').
2 NAAEC, art 14(1)(a),(c); Guidelines, paras 2.1, 4.3.
3 NAAEC, art 14(2); Guidelines, para 9.
4 NAAEC, art 14(3); Guidelines, para 11.
5 NAAEC, art 15(4); Guidelines, paras 12–14.
6 NAAEC, art 15(5)–(7); Guidelines, para 15.

CONTACT INFORMATION

13.9 The Secretariat of the CEC is located at:

Secretariat of the CEC
393 rue St-Jacques Ouest, bureau 200
Montreal, Quebec
H2Y 1N9 Canada

Tel: 1 514 350-4300
Fax: 1 514 350-4314
email: msilva@ccemtl.org
website: http://www.cec.org/

REFERENCE

Selected bibliography

Book

Trakman and Jadeja *Dispute settlement under the NAFTA: manual and source book* (1997).

Articles

J Bialos and D Siegel 'Dispute resolution under NAFTA: the improved model' (1993) 27 The International Lawyer.

Robert Cassidy 'Dispute resolution under NAFTA: a United States perspective' (1997) 23 Canada-United States Law Journal 147.

Harry Endsley 'Dispute settlement under CFTA and NAFTA: from eleventh-hour innovation to accepted institution' (1995) 18 Hasting International and Comparative Law Review.

Gary Horlik and Amanda Debusk 'Dispute resolution under NAFTA: building on the United States-Canada FTA, GATT and ICSID' (1993) 36 Private Investment Abroad.

Homer E Moyer 'Chapter 19 of the NAFTA: binational panels as the trade courts of last resort' (1993) 27 The International Lawyer.

Kristin L Oelstrom 'A treaty for the future: the dispute settlement mechanisms of the NAFTA' (1994) 25 Law and Policy in International Business.

Simon Potter 'Dispute resolution under NAFTA: a Canadian perspective' (1997) 23 Canada-United States Law Journal 151.

J Renya 'NAFTA Chapter 19 binational panel review in Mexico: a marriage of two distinct legal systems' (1997) 5 United States-Mexico Law Journal 65.

Hector V Royas 'Dispute resolution under the NAFTA' (1993) 1 United States-Mexico Law Journal.

Human rights bodies

INTRODUCTION

This Part of the manual has been prepared with the assistance of INTERIGHTS, the international centre for the legal protection of human rights, and addresses four regional and four international bodies established to oversee the implementation of human rights norms. All eight bodies have been established since the end of the Second World War, and illustrate the growing concern with human rights at the international and regional level in this period. The bodies covered in this Part generally provide for the establishment of committees or commissions to review periodic reports by states parties on their implementation of obligations under the covered agreements, as well as additional optional procedures for inter-state and individual complaints alleging non-compliance by a state with its human rights obligations under the relevant treaty.

The first body reviewed is the UN Human Rights Committee, established under the 1966 International Covenant on Civil and Political Rights. The Covenant entered into force in 1976 and has now been ratified by 144 states. The Committee receives and studies periodic reports from states parties as to their implementation of the standards set out in the Covenant, and may issue general comments on the provisions of the Covenant. Where a state party has accepted its competence to do so, the Committee may also receive communication from states and/or individuals alleging violations of human rights by that state party. So far 96 states have accepted the competence of the Committee (under the Optional Protocol) to receive communications from individuals, and 47 have authorised it to receive inter-state communications. The Committee has received over 850 individual complaints and has issued views on some 300 cases. However, no inter-state communications have been lodged.

The two other Committees reviewed in this Part have been established to monitor compliance with particular human rights treaties, the 1966 International Convention on the Elimination of All Forms of Racial Discrimination (CERD Committee) and the 1984 Convention Against Torture and other Cruel, Inhuman or Degrading Treatment or Punishment (CAT Committee). The CERD Committee examines periodic reports of the 155 states parties to the CERD Convention. It may also address complaints presented against states parties by other states or by individuals or groups of individuals. Inter-state complaints are permitted under the Convention itself, while the submission of complaints by individuals or groups requires prior acceptance by the state concerned of the competence of the CERD Committee to receive such complaints. To date the CERD Committee has received eight individual complaints, and no inter-state communications. The CAT Committee may hear inter-state or individual complaints provided the states parties concerned have accepted the jurisdiction of the CAT Committee to receive such complaints. In addition the CAT Committee considers periodic reports by the states parties on measures taken to implement the CAT Convention, and it may also investigate situations where information on the systematic practice of torture has been received from reliable sources, without any formal complaint. A protocol establishing an individual complaints mechanism is expected to be adopted shortly in relation to the Committee on the Elimination of Discrimination Against Women.

The fourth global mechanism reviewed here is the representation and complaint procedure of the International Labour Organisation (ILO). ILO member states report periodically on measures taken to implement the various ILO Conventions to which they are party and these are reviewed by a Committee of Independent Experts. In addition, representations or complaints may be made to the ILO alleging failure of member states to comply with relevant ILO Conventions or freedom of association standards. These complaints, which may be made by states, delegates to the ILO General Conference, and domestic and international employers' or workers' associations are dealt with by the ILO Governing Body, or subsidiary bodies established by it.

The regional mechanisms reviewed in this Part generally comprise a commission and/or a court entrusted with receiving and investigating and/or adjudicating complaints. The first to be established was the European Court of Human Rights ('EHR Court'), which is entrusted with monitoring the compliance of member states of the Council of Europe with their obligations under the European Convention on Human Rights. Under the original text of the Convention, a two-tier enforcement mechanism was established, consisting of two organs – the European Commission on Human Rights ('Commission') and the European Court of Human Rights. Under this system, petitions from individuals, NGOs or states alleging violations of the Convention had to be brought initially before the Commission. The Commission examined the admissibility of the petition, attempted to find a friendly settlement and could refer the case, under certain conditions, to the Court on behalf of the complainant. Following the entry into force of the 11th Protocol to the Convention on 1 November 1998, the Commission was abolished and most of its functions have been transferred to the Court. As a result, claimants (states and individuals) can now submit applications directly to the Court.

The EHR Court deals with complaints by states and individuals concerning the protection of human rights by the 41 states parties to the Convention. Upon receipt of an application, the court determines its admissibility and, if admissible, attempts to secure a friendly settlement of the dispute on the basis of respect for the human rights set out in the Convention and Protocols thereto. If no settlement is reached, a chamber of the court is to hear the case and issue a binding judgment, which in exceptional cases may be referred for second review before an enlarged chamber. Since its establishment, the court has dealt with over 1,000 petitions.

The Inter-American human rights system incorporates a two-tier system similar to that originally utilised under the European Convention. Thus, the Inter-American Commission on Human Rights and the Inter-American Court of Human Rights are entrusted with monitoring and adjudicating the human rights practices of 25 states parties to the 1969 American Convention on

Human Rights. All complaints are first brought to the Commission, which examines the admissibility of the complaint, investigates the allegations against the state party concerned, makes recommendations to states parties, and, if appropriate, prepares a report on the case. The Commission may decide to pursue the complaint by bringing a claim before the court against a state party. The court has both advisory and contentious jurisdiction. Since 1979 the court has decided more than 25 cases, while the Commission has dealt with more than 12,000 complaints since 1965.

The African Commission on Human Rights is an expert body intended to ensure compliance with the 1981 African Charter on Human and People's Rights, which functions under the institutional framework of the Organisation of African Unity. It disseminates information on human rights in Africa, and receives periodic reports from the states parties to the African Charter. The Commission is also authorised to receive communications from state and non-state actors alleging violation of the human rights guaranteed by the African Charter. The procedure for handling communications involves investigation by the Commission of the factual claims of the parties and the issue of recommendations on the merits, in the form of observations or a report. Where a case brought by a person or entity other than a state party alleges the existence of a series of serious and massive violations of human and peoples' rights or an emergency, an in-depth study (involving active investigation on the part of the Commission) can be undertaken with the approval of the Assembly of Heads of State and Government of the OAU.

Since its establishment, the African Commission has received more than 200 communications from individuals and NGOs. By contrast, the inter-state communication procedure before the Commission has been hardly used. In June 1998, the member states of the OAU adopted a Protocol on the establishment of a Court of Human and People's Rights. The court will become operational only after the Protocol enters into force – still some time in the future.

The final mechanism reviewed in this Part is that established under the European Social Charter, which was concluded in 1961 within the framework of the Council of Europe, and entered into force on 26 February 1965. Under the Charter and its 1988 Additional Protocol, states parties have undertaken to aim at the attainment of conditions in which a detailed list of economic and social human rights enumerated in Part I of the Charter may be effectively realised. The states parties have undertaken to consider some of these rights as legally binding upon them. At present, there are 24 states parties to the Social Charter (eight of which are also parties to the 1988 Additional Protocol). The Social Charter is supervised mainly through a system of regular state reports, which are examined by the European Committee of Social Rights (formerly called the Committee of Independent Experts). The Committee communicates its conclusions on the degree of state compliance with the political organs of the Council of Europe (the Governmental Committee and the Committee of Ministers). In 1995, a new Protocol was concluded (the 'Collective Complaints Protocol'), granting the Committee quasi-judicial responsibilities. The Protocol entered into force on 1 July 1998 and eight states have ratified it to date. Under the Protocol, the Committee may receive complaints alleging unsatisfactory application of the Charter on the part of states parties to the Protocol. To date, one complaint has been submitted under the Protocol.

CHAPTER 14

Human Rights Committee

INTRODUCTORY

Name and seat of the body

14.1   The Human Rights Committee (HRC or 'the Committee') is an independent expert body established to monitor compliance with the International Covenant on Civil and Political Rights (ICCPR).[1] It is located in the UN headquarters in Geneva:

> Human Rights Committee
> Centre for Human Rights
> Palais des Nations, United Nations
> 8–14 Avenue de la Paix
> 1211 Geneva 10
> Switzerland
>
> Tel: (41) 22 917 3965
> Fax: (41) 22 917 0099
> website: http://www.unhchr.ch

1   International Covenant on Civil and Political Rights, 16 December 1966, art 28, UN GA Res 2200 A (XXI), GAOR, 21st Session, Supp No 16 (A/6316) 52, reprinted in UN Doc A/CONF 32/4 ('ICCPR').

Description

14.2   The HRC was established under the 1966 ICCPR, which entered into force in 1976. It is an independent expert body, entrusted with powers of supervision over the implementation of the ICCPR, which has been ratified by 144 states. The HRC reports to the General Assembly of the UN (through the Economic and Social Council), conducts its sessions in UN facilities, is financed by the UN budget and receives all administrative services from the UN Secretariat.

The Committee serves three main functions. It receives periodic reports from the states parties to the ICCPR on their compliance with the human rights standards set out in the Covenant and issues observations therein. It also issues 'general comments' on the provisions of the Covenant.[1] In addition, the HRC may receive communications from individuals and/or states alleging violation of human rights by states parties to ICCPR that have accepted the competence of the HRC to review such petitions.[2] So far, 96 states have accepted the jurisdiction of the HRC to receive individual communications and 47 states have authorised the HRC to receive inter-state complaints. The procedure for dealing with communications is essentially quasi-judicial (although in inter-state cases, the HRC primarily provides its good offices in an attempt to find an amicable solution or facilitate conciliation). The HRC admits evidence, receives submissions and makes its views available to the parties. These views are not binding upon the states parties.

To date the HRC has received 862 individual complaints. It has considered a communication on the merits and issued its views on some 317 cases, finding a breach of the ICCPR in 245 cases. The rest of the communications have been found inadmissible, were discontinued or are still pending before the HRC. By contrast, no inter-state communication has ever been lodged with the HRC.

1   ICCPR, art 40.
2   Ibid, art 40; Optional Protocol to the International Covenant on Civil and Political Rights, UN GA Res 2200 A (XXI), GAOR, 21st Session, Supp No 16 (A/6316) 59 ('Optional Protocol').

INSTITUTIONAL ASPECTS

Governing texts

14.3   The principal texts governing the structure, responsibilities and competence of the HRC are the ICCPR and the Optional Protocol. The Optional Protocol authorises the HRC to address individual communications and outlines the procedure for handling such complaints. As indicated above, the Optional Protocol has been adopted by 96 of the states parties to the ICCPR. Other rules governing the work of the HRC are to be found in the HRC Rules of Procedure.[1]

1   Rules of Procedure of the Human Rights Committee, UN Doc CCPR/C/3/Rev 5, 11 August 1997 ('Rules of Procedure').

Substantive law

14.4   The substantive law to be applied by the HRC comprises the human rights provisions found in Parts I–III of the ICCPR. Additionally, for the 38 state parties that have adopted the Second Optional Protocol on Abolishing the Death Penalty, the provisions of that Protocol will also be applicable.[1]

1   Second Optional Protocol to the International Covenant on Civil and Political Rights, Aiming at the Abolition of the Death Penalty, 15 December 1989, GA Res 128 (44), UN Doc A/RES/44/128.

Organisation

Composition

14.5   The HRC comprises 18 independent experts, who are nationals of different states parties to the ICCPR.[1] The members of the Committee are nominated and elected by the states parties (each party may nominate two of its nationals) for a renewable period of four years.[2] They should be persons of high moral character having recognised competence in the area of human rights.[3] The composition of the entire Committee should reflect equitable geographical distribution and represent the variety of forms of civilisation and legal systems;[4] it is also desirable that some members will have some legal background.[5]

171

The Committee elects from within its members a Chairman, three Vice-Chairmen and a Rapporteur.[6] The officers serve a renewable two-year term.[7] The Committee meets three times a year in either Geneva or New York.

1 ICCPR, arts 28, 31(1). The current membership of the HRC is Mr Abdel Fattah Amor (Tunisia); Mr Nisuke Ando (Japan); Mr Prafullachandra Natwarlal Bhagwati (India); Mr Thomas Buergenthal (US) Mrs Christine Chanet (France); Lord Colville (UK); Mrs Elizabeth Evatt (Australia); Mr Eckart Klein (Germany); Mr David Kretzmer (Israel); Ms Pilar Gaitan De Pombo (Colombia); Mr Rajsoomer Lallah (Mauritius); Mrs Cecilia Medina Quiroga (Chile); Mr Abdallah Zakhia (Lebanon); Mr Fausto Pocar (Italy); Mr Martin Scheinin (Finland); Mr Roman Wieruszewski (Poland); Mr Maxwell Yalden (Canada); Mr Hipólito Solari Yrigoyen (Argentina).
2 ICCPR, arts 29, 30(4), 32(1).
3 Ibid, art 28(2).
4 Ibid, art 31(2).
5 Ibid, art 28(2).
6 Rules of Procedure, r 17.
7 ICCPR, art 39(1); Rules of Procedure, r 18.

DISQUALIFICATION OF COMMITTEE MEMBERS

14.6 An HRC member is expected not to participate in a case involving an individual communication if he or she has a personal interest or previous involvement in the case in any capacity.[1] In this event, the member is to withdraw voluntarily or be removed from sitting on that case, by a decision of the Committee.[2]

If a member of the Committee has ceased to carry his or her official functions, the other members may decide unanimously to remove him or her from office. In this case, the Chairman will notify the Secretary-General of the UN accordingly, and the latter will declare the seat vacant.[3]

1 Rules of Procedure, r 84(1).
2 Ibid, rr 84(2), 85.
3 ICCPR, art 33(1); Rules of Procedure, r 13(1).

Plenary/chambers

14.7 The HRC sits in plenary (a quorum of 12 members is required).[1] Nonetheless, the Committee may establish subsidiary bodies and delegate parts of its functions to such bodies.[2] For instance, the admissibility of individual communications to the HRC may be determined by a working group of five members.[3]

1 ICCPR, art 39(2)(a); Rules of Procedure, r 37.
2 Rules of Procedure, r 62.
3 Ibid, rr 87(2), 89.

Appellate structure

14.8 The ICCPR does not have an appellate structure and there is no avenue for recourse against recommendations of the HRC.

Technical/scientific experts

14.9 There is no explicit provision under the various instruments governing the work of the HRC that permit involvement by experts, other than the Committee members, in the proceedings.

Secretariat

14.10 Responsibility for administration of the HRC lies with the Secretary-General of the UN.[1] The Secretary-General provides the Committee with the staff and facilities that comprise the HRC's secretariat.[2] The secretariat, inter alia, arranges for the meetings of the HRC;[3] receives communications to the Committee and registers them; circulates documents between the members of the HRC, as required;[4] requests additional information from the complainant (if necessary);[5] and informs the concerned parties of various procedural decisions taken by the Committee.[6] Since 1997, overall responsibility for the administration of the HRC (and the other treaty bodies) has been assigned by the UN General Assembly to the Office of the High Commissioner for Human Rights.

1 ICCPR, art 36; Rules of Procedure, r 23(2).
2 Rules of Procedure, r 23.
3 Ibid, r 25.
4 Ibid, rr 73, 78–79.
5 Ibid, r 80.
6 Ibid, rr 77C, 93.

Jurisdiction

Ratione personae

14.11 The HRC may receive communications relating to states parties that have accepted the jurisdiction of the Committee. Under the ICCPR and Optional Protocol, a separate declaration is required for each of the two heads of jurisdiction of the HRC – ie involving inter-state and individual communications. A declaration made by a state party under art 41 of the ICCPR (recognising the inter-state competence of the Committee) enables the HRC to receive communications against that state, if presented by another state which has also made an art 41 declaration.[1] In addition, the HRC may receive individual communications directed against states that have accepted the Optional Protocol.[2] Individual communications may be brought only by individuals who are subject to the jurisdiction of the state complained against and claim to be victim of a human rights violation under the Covenant.[3]

1 ICCPR, art 41(1).
2 Optional Protocol, art 1.
3 Ibid, arts 1, 2. See *A Group of Associations for the Defence of the Rights of Disabled and Handicapped Persons in Italy v Italy*, Comm No 163/1984, GAOR, 39th Session, Supp No 40, at 198 (holding that an NGO can bring a communication only if the organisation itself was a victim of a human rights violation).

Ratione materiae

14.12 Communications to the HRC can address any failure to fulfil the obligations of the ICCPR (in the case of an inter-state communication);[1] or any violation of the rights enumerated in the ICCPR (in the case of individual communication).[2] A complaint against a state that has adopted the Second Optional Protocol may also allege breach of a relevant provision thereunder (unless, upon ratification, the ratifying state has restricted the application of the communication mechanism in cases involving the Second Optional Protocol).[3]

1 ICCPR, art 41(1).
2 Optional Protocol, art 1.
3 Second Optional Protocol, arts 4, 5.

Ratione temporis

14.13   As a general rule, the HRC will only consider an alleged violation of human rights that has occurred on or after the date of entry into force of the Covenant and the First Optional Protocol in the territory of the state complained against, unless the alleged violation is one which, despite occurring before this date, continues to have effect.

The HRC can deal with any communication only after available domestic remedies have been exhausted (unless such remedies are unreasonably prolonged).[1] The other temporal conditions governing the admissibility of complaints depend on whether the communication was lodged by a state or an individual. Where inter-state communications are involved, a state may present a communication against another state only after the expiration of six months from the date of notifying the state complained against, by way of an initial written communication, that it has failed, in the opinion of the complainant, to give effect to a provision of the Covenant.[2]

Where individual communications are involved, no limitation period is provided.

1   ICCPR, art 41(1)(c); Optional Protocol, arts 2, 5(2)(b).
2   ICCPR, art 41(1)(a),(b).

Other international claims

14.14   An individual communication may be presented only if the same matter is not pending at the same time before another international procedure of investigation.[1]

1   Optional Protocol, art 5(2)(a). This excludes procedures reviewing the general human rights situation in a particular country.

Advisory jurisdiction

14.15   Generally speaking the HRC does not have an advisory jurisdiction. The Committee has, however, issued 26 'general comments' on the Covenant, which serve as important interpretative pronouncements on the meaning and scope of the provisions of the Covenant.[1]

1   Compilation of General Comments and General Recommendations Adopted by Human Rights Treaty Bodies, UN Doc HRI/GEN/1/Rev1 (1994) (General Comments 1–23); General Comment 24 (52), UN Doc CCPR/C/21/Rev 1/Add 6 (1994); General Comment 25 (57), UN Doc CCPR/C/21/Rev1/Add 7 (1996); General Comment 26 (61), <http://www1.umn.edu/humanrts/gencomm/hrcom26.htm>.

PROCEDURAL ASPECTS

Languages

14.16   The official languages of the HRC are Arabic, Chinese, English, French, Russian and Spanish (ie the official languages of the UN).[1] All official languages, except Chinese, are also the working languages of the Committee. Discussions in the HRC are translated into all working languages. A person who addresses the Committee in a non-official language must arrange for translation into one of the working languages.[2]

1   Rules of Procedure, r 28.
2   Ibid, rr 29, 30.

Instituting proceedings

14.17   A case is brought before the HRC by way of a written communication. An inter-state communication alleging failure to comply with the Covenant should include, inter alia, the following information:

(a)   details on the steps taken to ensure settlement of the dispute prior to the reference to the HRC, including the text of the initial communication made directly to the state complained against, and any subsequent explanations or statements relevant to the matter;

(b)   steps taken to exhaust domestic remedies;

(c)   any other international investigation or settlement procedures resorted to by the parties.[1]

Communications submitted by individuals under the Optional Protocol should include the following information:

(a)   name, address, age and occupation of the author and verification of his or her identity;

(b)   the object of the communication;

(c)   provisions of the Covenant which allegedly have been violated;

(d)   facts of the claim;

(e)   steps taken to exhaust domestic remedies; and

(f)   the extent to which the same matter is the subject of another international procedure of investigation or settlement.[2]

If the communication is lacking in details or unclear (including doubts as to whether the author intends to bring the matter before the HRC), the Secretary-General of the UN may request additional information or clarifications from the author.[3] In doing so, the Secretary-General will prescribe time limits for the response of the author.

1   Rules of Procedure, r 72.
2   Optional Protocol, art 5(2)(a); Rules of Procedure, r 80(1). This excludes procedures reviewing the general human rights situation in a particular country.
3   Rules of Procedure, rr 79(2), 80(1),(2).

Financial assistance

14.18   Financial assistance is not available for participants in HRC proceedings.

Interim measures

14.19   In cases involving individual communications, the HRC may, at any time during the proceedings, inform the state party concerned of the view of the Committee on whether interim measures are desirable in order to prevent irreparable damage to the alleged victim.[1] Any such recommendation is not binding upon the state party concerned.

1   Rules of Procedure, r 86. It is the practice of the HRC that interim measures can be recommended even before a decision on admissibility has been taken.

Preliminary proceedings

14.20   The Committee is to decide as soon as possible on the admissibility of the complaint.[1] In inter-state cases, the Committee must make the following determinations:

(a)   that both involved states made appropriate declarations under art 41 of the ICCPR;

(b)   that the six months time limit from the date of the initial communication has expired;

(c)   that domestic remedies have been exhausted, as required by international law, or that their application is unreasonably prolonged.[2]

In the case of individual communications, the question of admissibility is handled by the full Committee or by a working group of no more than five members. A working group is to recommend to the HRC a decision on the question of admissibility; however, it may also declare a communication admissible (if it comprises five members and all of them support such a decision).[3] The Committee may also designate members as special rapporteurs to prepare the consideration of communications by the Committee. The full Committee or working groups must confirm that:

(a)   the communication is not anonymous and emanates from an individual (or individuals) subject to the jurisdiction of a state party to the Optional Protocol;

(b)   the individual in question has sufficiently substantiated that he or she has been a victim of a violation by that state party of a human right prescribed by the Covenant – in cases where the alleged victim is unable to submit the communication himself or herself, the communication may be submitted on his or her behalf;

(c)   the communication does not constitute an abuse of the right of submission;

(d)   the communication is not incompatible with the provisions of the ICCPR;

(e)   the same matter is not the subject of another pending international procedure of investigation or settlement;

(f)   the individual has exhausted all available domestic remedies, or the application of these remedies is unreasonably prolonged.[4]

In relation to individual communications, the 1997 Rules of Procedure of the HRC provide for the submission of written explanations and statements by the state party concerned that address both admissibility and merits of the communication[5] unless, due to the exceptional nature of the case, the Committee, working group or special rapporteur decides to request a written reply on admissibility only. A state party that receives a request for a written reply on admissibility and merits may apply in writing, within two months, for the communication to be rejected as inadmissible, setting out the grounds of inadmissibility. The Committee, working group or special rapporteur may decide, because of the special circumstances of the case, to extend the time for the submission of the reply until the Committee has ruled on the question of admissibility.[6] The procedure of requesting a state party to reply on admissibility and merits does not imply that any decision has been taken on the question of admissibility.[7]

1   ICCPR, art 41(1)(c); Optional Protocol, art 5(2).
2   Rules of Procedure, r 76.
3   Ibid, rr 87(2), 89(1).
4   Optional Protocol, art 5(2), Rules of Procedure, r 90.

5 Rules of Procedure, r 91(2).
6 Ibid, r 91(3).
7 Ibid, r 91(5).

Written pleadings

Inter-state communications

14.21 States which are parties to a dispute before the HRC are entitled to present written submissions on their behalf when the communication involving them is being considered.[1] The Committee will determine the procedure for making these submissions, after consulting with the parties.[2] Furthermore, during its handling of the communication, the Committee may request the involved states to supply it with additional relevant information, including written observations on their behalf.[3] Such request will be made through the Secretary-General and will indicate a time limit for the submission of the information.

1 ICCPR, art 41(1)(g); Rules of Procedure, r 77C(1).
2 Rules of Procedure, r 77C(3).
3 ICCPR, art 41(1)(f); Rules of Procedure, r 77B.

Individual communications

14.22 After the communication has been received, the state complained against will be given six months to submit to the Committee written explanations or statements. The Committee, working group or special rapporteur may request the state party or author of the communication to submit, within specified time limits, additional written information or observations relevant to the admissibility or merits of the communication.[1] Within fixed time limits, each party may be given an opportunity to comment on submissions made by the other party.[2]

1 Rules of Procedure, r 91(4).
2 Ibid, r 91(6).

Oral arguments

14.23 The parties to an inter-state case before the HRC are entitled to make oral representations before the Committee.[1] The Committee will determine the procedure for making such submissions, after having consulted with the parties.[2] The HRC may also request the introduction of additional oral information or observations by the parties, within fixed time limits.[3] There are no provisions for oral proceedings under the Optional Protocol or the Rules of Procedure governing the consideration of individual communications. The meetings of the HRC in which communications are being considered are not public.[4]

1 ICCPR, art 41(1)(g); Rules of Procedure, r 77C(1).
2 Rules of Procedure, r 77C(3).
3 Ibid, r 77B.
4 ICCPR, art 41(1)(d); Optional Protocol, art 5(3); Rules of Procedure, r 81.

Third-party intervention/multiple proceedings

14.24 The various instruments governing the work of the HRC do not provide for intervention. As to multiple proceedings, the Optional Protocol allows for communications to be presented by more than one person adversely affected by violation of human rights.[1] Furthermore, the Committee may consider two or more communications jointly, if it deems this to be appropriate.[2]

1　Optional Protocol, art 1.
2　Rules of Procedure, r 88(2).

Amicus curiae

14.25　There is no explicit provision in the any of the relevant instruments permitting the submission of amicus curiae briefs to the HRC. So far the Committee has not admitted such submissions.

Representation of parties

14.26　The Communication should be submitted personally by the individual claiming to be a victim, or by that individual's representative. Additionally, a communication may be submitted on behalf of an alleged victim when it appears that the individual in question is unable to submit the communication personally.[1]

1　Rules of Procedure; r 90(b).

Decision

14.27　In inter-state cases, the HRC must prepare a report within 12 months of the date in which the communication has been brought before it.[1] If a friendly settlement has been reached, the report should briefly describe the facts of the case and the solution reached. If no solution was agreed upon, the report will state the facts of the case and will have attached to it the written and oral submissions of the parties. The HRC may then appoint a Conciliation Committee, with the agreement of the parties, to continue to deal with the dispute.[2]

In cases brought by individual complainants, where the Committee has received information from the parties on both admissibility and merits, after considering the communication in the light of all written information the HRC formulates its views on the matter.[3] Normally, such views include the details of the complaint; the submissions of the parties; any interim decisions taken by the Committee; the facts as proven before the Committee; conclusions as to whether any provisions of the ICCPR were violated; the legal reasoning; and in some cases, an operative part indicating the actions necessary to restore compliance with the ICCPR. In relation to individual complaints, where the Committee decides that a communication is inadmissible under the Protocol, it communicates its decision to the author of the communication and to the state party concerned through the Secretary-General as soon as possible.[4]

The decisions of the HRC are taken by a majority of the members,[5] although, generally speaking, the HRC operates by way of consensus. Members of the HRC may append to the views of the Committee their individual opinions.[6] The views of the Committee are communicated to the individual and to the state party concerned.[7]

1　ICCPR, art 41(1)(h); Rules of Procedure, r 77D(1).
2　ICCPR, art 42; Rules of Procedure, r 77E.

3 Optional Protocol, art 5(4); Rules of Procedure, r 94(2).
4 Rules of Procedure, r 92(1).
5 ICCPR, art 39(2)(b); Rules of Procedure, r 51.
6 Rules of Procedure, r 94(3).
7 Ibid, r 94(4).

Interpretation and revision of judgments

14.28 The relevant instruments regulating the work of the HRC do not permit requests for interpretation or revision of the views of the Committee. It should be noted that a communication declared inadmissible by the HRC may be resubmitted to the Committee if the reasons for inadmissibility are no longer applicable.[1]

1 Rules of Procedure, r 92(2).

Appeal

14.29 There is no appeal in respect of decisions of the HRC.

Costs

14.30 Proceedings before the HRC are free of charge. However, the parties must bear their own expenses.

Enforcement of decisions

14.31 The decisions of the Committee are not binding upon the parties, and as a result cannot be enforced without their consent. However, the HRC designates a special rapporteur for follow-up to ascertain measures taken by states parties to give effect to the Committee's views.[1] The special rapporteur may make such contacts and take such action as appropriate for the due performance of the follow-up mandate, and is to make such recommendations for further action by the Committee as may be necessary.

1 Rules of Procedure, r 95.

REFERENCE

Case reports

The views of the Committee on the merits and admissibility of communications are normally made public.[1] They are published in the annual report of the HRC to the General Assembly of the UN (UN Doc Supp 40). The decisions can be found in *Selected Decisions under the Optional Protocol* (UN, 1985–) and in *Official Records of the Human Rights Committee* (UN, 1993–). Many decisions can be found on the University of Minnesota Human Rights Library's website: <http://www.umn.edu/humanrts/undocs/undocs.htm>.

1 Rules of Procedure, r 96(4),(5).

Selected bibliography

Books

Yearbook of the Human Rights Committee (UN, 1986–).

Human rights bodies

Marc J Bossuyt *Guide to the 'Travaux Préparatoires' of the International Covenant on Civil and Political Rights* (1987).

M O'Flaherty *Human Rights and the United Nations: Practice before the treaty bodies* (1996).

P R Gandhi *The Human Rights Committee and the Right of Individual Communication – Law and Practice* (1988).

Dominic McGoldrick *The Human Rights Committee* (1991).

Manfred Nowak *A Commentary on the UN Covenant on Civil and Political Rights* (1993).

Henry J Steiner and Philip Alston *International Human Rights in Context – Law, Politics, Morals* 522 (1996).

Articles

P S Brar 'The Practice and Procedures of the Human Rights Committee under the Optional Protocol of the International Covenant on Civil and Political Rights' (1983) 26 Indian Journal of International Law 506.

K Das 'United Nations Institutions and Procedures Founded on Conventions on Human Rights and Fundamental Freedoms' in K Vasak and P Alston (eds) *The International Dimension of Human Rights* 303 (1982).

A De Zayas, J Th Moller and T Opsahl 'Application of the International Covenant on Civil and Political Rights under the Optional Protocol by the Human Rights Committee' (1989) 26 Comparative Judicial Review 3.

S Davidson 'The Procedure and Practice of the Human Rights Committee under the First Optional Protocol on Civil and Political Rights' (1991) 4 Canterbury Law Review 337.

P R Gandhi 'The Human Rights Committee and the Right of Individual Petition' (1986) 57 British Yearbook of International Law 173.

A H Robertson 'The Implementation System: International Measures' in Louis Henkin (ed) *The International Bill of Rights – the Covenant on Civil and Political Rights* (1981).

D Shelton 'Individual Complaint Machinery under the United Nations 1503 Procedure and the Optional Protocol to the International Covenant on Civil and Political Rights' in H Hannum (ed) *Guide to International Human Rights Practices* 59 (1984).

ANNEX

List of 144 states parties to the ICCPR

Afghanistan, Albania, Algeria, Angola, Argentina, Armenia, Australia, Austria, Azerbaïjan, Barbados, Belarus, Belgium, Belize, Benin, Bolivia, Bosnia and Herzegovina, Brazil, Bulgaria, Burkina Faso, Burundi, Cambodia, Cameroon, Canada, Cape Verde, Central African Republic, Chad, Chile, Colombia, Congo, Costa Rica, Côte d'Ivoire, Croatia, Cyprus, Czech Republic, Democratic Republic of the Congo, Denmark, Dominica,

Dominican Republic, Ecuador, Egypt, El Salvador, Equatorial Guinea, Estonia, Ethiopia, Finland, France, Gabon, Gambia, Georgia, Germany, Greece, Grenada, Guatemala, Guinea, Guyana, Haiti, Honduras, Hungary, Iceland, India, Iran, Iraq, Ireland, Israel, Italy, Jamaica, Japan, Jordan, Kenya, Democratic People's Republic of Korea, Kuwait, the Kyrgyz Republic, Latvia, Lebanon, Lesotho, Libya, Liechtenstein, Lithuania, Luxembourg, the former Yugoslav Republic of Macedonia, Madagascar, Malawi, Mali, Malta, Mauritius, Mexico, Monaco, Mongolia, Morocco, Mozambique, Namibia, Nepal, Netherlands, New Zealand, Nicaragua, Niger, Nigeria, Norway, Panama, Paraguay, Peru, Philippines, Poland, Portugal, Republic of Korea, Republic of Moldova, Romania, Russian Federation, Rwanda, Saint Vincent and the Grenadines, San Marino, Senegal, Seychelles, Sierra Leone, Slovakia, Slovenia, Somalia, South Africa, Spain, Sri Lanka, Sudan, Suriname, Sweden, Switzerland, Syria, Tajikistan, Thailand, Togo, Trinidad and Tobago, Tunisia, Turkmenistan, Uganda, Ukraine, United Kingdom, United Republic of Tanzania, United States, Uruguay, Uzbekistan, Venezuela, Vietnam, Yemen, Yugoslavia, Zambia and Zimbabwe.

List of 96 states parties to the Optional Protocol[1]

Algeria, Angola, Argentina, Armenia, Australia, Austria, Barbados, Belarus, Belgium, Benin, Bolivia, Bosnia and Herzegovina, Bulgaria, Burkina Faso, Cameroon, Canada, Central African Republic, Chad, Chile, Colombia, Congo, Costa Rica, Côte d'Ivoire, Croatia, Cyprus, Czech Republic, Democratic Republic of the Congo, Denmark, Dominican Republic, Ecuador, El Salvador, Equatorial Guinea, Estonia, Finland, France, Gambia, Georgia, Germany, Greece, Guinea, Guyana, Honduras, Hungary, Iceland, Ireland, Italy, the Kyrgyz Republic, Latvia, Libya, Liechtenstein, Lithuania, Luxembourg, the former Yugoslav Republic of Macedonia, Madagascar, Malawi, Malta, Mauritius, Mongolia, Namibia, Nepal, Netherlands, New Zealand, Nicaragua, Niger, Norway, Panama, Paraguay, Peru, Philippines, Poland, Portugal, Republic of Korea, Romania, Russian Federation, Saint Vincent and the Grenadines, San Marino, Senegal, Seychelles, Sierra Leone, Slovakia, Slovenia, Somalia, Spain, Sri Lanka, Suriname, Sweden, Tajikistan, Togo, Trinidad and Tobago, Turkmenistan, Uganda, Ukraine, Uruguay, Uzbekistan, Venezuela, and Zambia.

1   Jamaica withdrew from the Optional Protocol in 1997.

List of 47 states that made ICCPR, art 41 declarations accepting the competence of the HRC to receive inter-state complaints

Algeria, Argentina, Australia, Austria, Belarus, Belgium, Bosnia and Herzegovina, Bulgaria, Canada, Chile, Congo, Croatia, Czech Republic, Denmark, Ecuador, Finland, Gambia, Germany, Guyana, Hungary, Iceland, Ireland, Italy, Republic of Korea, Liechtenstein, Luxembourg, Malta, Netherlands, New Zealand, Norway, Peru, Philippines, Poland, Russian Federation, Senegal, Slovakia, Slovenia, South Africa, Spain, Sri Lanka, Sweden, Switzerland, Tunisia, Ukraine, United Kingdom, United States and Zimbabwe.

CHAPTER 15

Committee on the Elimination of Racial Discrimination

NAME AND SEAT OF THE BODY

15.1   The Committee on the Elimination of Racial Discrimination ('CERD Committee' or 'the Committee') is an independent expert body established to monitor compliance with the 1965 International Convention on the Elimination of All Forms of Racial Discrimination ('CERD').[1] It is located at:

> Committee on the Elimination of Racial Discrimination
> Centre for Human Rights
> Palais des Nations, United Nations
> 8–14 Avenue de la Paix
> 1211 Geneva 10
> Switzerland

> Tel: (41) 22 917 3965
> Fax: (41) 22 917 0099
> website: http://www.unhchr.ch

1   International Convention for Elimination of All Forms of Racial Discrimination, 21 December 1965, UN GA Res 2106A (XX), GAOR, 12th Session, Supp No 14 (A/6014) 47, UN Doc A/CONF 32/4 ('CERD').

DESCRIPTION

15.2   The CERD Committee begun began its operation in 1969, following the entry into force of CERD. The states parties to the Convention agree to undertake appropriate measures to eliminate racial discrimination and promote understanding between different races. The CERD Committee is entrusted with monitoring compliance of the 155 states parties with the provisions of CERD.

The Committee comprises 18 independent experts elected by the states parties for four-year terms.[1] It examines periodic reports of the states parties on the implementation of CERD and submits its general suggestions and recommendations to the General Assembly of the UN.[2] In addition, the Committee may address complaints presented against states parties to CERD by other states and, in some cases, individuals or groups of individuals.[3] The complaints procedures involve quasi-judicial investigation of allegations of non-compliance with the Convention, which results in the preparation of a report by the CERD Committee containing non-binding recommendations. The work of the CERD Committee is governed by Part II of CERD and by the

Rules of Procedure adopted by the Committee.[4] According to the Rules, complaint proceedings are generally closed to the public.[5] The official languages of the CERD Committee are Chinese, English, French, Russian and Spanish (all but Chinese are also working languages).[6] The administrative needs of the Committee are provided by the Secretary-General of the UN;[7] the UN also provides its premises for the sessions of the Committee.[8]

1   CERD, art 8. The current membership is Mahmoud Abdoul-Nasr (Egypt), Michael Parker Banton (UK), Régis de Gouttes (France), Ion Diaconu (Romania), Eduardo Ferrero Costa (Peru), Ivan Garvallov (Bulgaria), Carlos Lechuga Hevia (Cuba), Gay J McDougall (US), Peter Nobel (Sweden), Yuri A Rechetov (Russia), Shanti Sadiq Ali (India), Agha Shahi (Pakistan), Michael E Sherifis, (Cyprus), Luis Valencia Rodriguez (Ecuador), Theordor van Boven (Netherlands), Rüdiger Wolfrum (Germany) Mario Jorge Yutzis (Argentina) and Deci Zou (China).
2   CERD, art 9.
3   Ibid, arts 11, 14.
4   Rules of Procedure, as revised on 1 January 1989, UN Doc CERD/C/35/Rev 3 ('CERD Rules').
5   CERD Rules, r 88.
6   Ibid, r 26.
7   CERD, art 10(3); CERD Rules, rr 21, 23. These responsibilities were assigned to the Office of the High Commissioner for Human Rights.
8   CERD, art 10(4); CERD Rules, r 5.

INTER-STATE COMMUNICATIONS

15.3   Any state party to CERD may bring a complaint against any other state party, which has allegedly failed to give effect to the provisions of the Convention (without need for an additional manifestation of consent by the respondent state).[1] The communication is then to be transmitted to the state complained against and the latter must provide written explanations or statements to the CERD Committee within three months from receiving the complaint.[2] In the event that the states concerned have been unable to settle the dispute between them within six months from the date in which the state complained against received the communication, either state may refer the matter again to the Committee.[3]

The Committee will address the matter only if available domestic remedies have been exhausted, or their application is unreasonably prolonged.[4] It may request further information from the states concerned[5] and it must invite them to participate in the sessions in which the communication is being considered.[6] After verifying the admissibility of the communication, the Committee is to refer the case to a five-member ad hoc conciliation commission (comprising nationals of states parties other than the parties to the dispute; they may or may not be members of the Committee). The composition of the commission is to be agreed upon by the states parties concerned or, in the absence of such agreement, determined by the CERD Committee (which in this case elects five of its members to serve on the commission).[7] The commission will attempt to secure a friendly settlement of the dispute and, in the event of failure to reach a solution, it will send to the Committee a report containing its factual and legal findings.[8] The Committee will then forward the report to the parties, and they must declare to the Committee within three months whether they intend to comply with the recommendations of the commission.[9] After the expiry of three months the Chairman of the Committee will circulate the commission's report and the declarations of the states parties concerned to all states parties to CERD.[10] Ongoing inter-state disputes may then be referred to the ICJ for judicial settlement.[11]

So far there have been no inter-state cases under this procedure.

1 CERD, art 11(1).
2 Ibid; CERD Rules, r 69. The Rules suggest that the Committee may decide not to transfer the communication for comments in an appropriate case (eg when the complaint is patently ill-founded).
3 CERD, art 11(2).
4 Ibid, art 11(3).
5 Ibid, art 11(4); CERD Rules, r 70.
6 CERD, art 11(5); CERD Rules, r 71.
7 CERD, art 12(1),(2); CERD Rules, rr 72–74.
8 CERD, art 12(1)(a), 13(1).
9 Ibid, art 13(2); CERD Rules, r 78(1),(2).
10 CERD, art 13(3); CERD Rules, r 78(3).
11 CERD, art 22.

INDIVIDUAL COMMUNICATIONS

15.4 Since 1982 the CERD Committee has been authorised to receive communications from individuals and groups of individuals who claim to be victims of a violation of CERD by a state party, to which jurisdiction they are subject.[1] However, complaints can only be filed against states that have accepted the competence of the Committee to receive individual communications, by way of a declaration deposited with the UN Secretary-General. To date, 27 states have made such a declaration.

Any state party which makes a declaration accepting the competence of the Committee to hear individual complaints may establish or indicate a national body competent to receive communications alleging violations of CERD[2] after exhaustion of all other domestic remedies. Where such national bodies exist, the complainant may only bring the case before the CERD Committee if the designated national body fails to resolve the matter.[3]

The complainant should bring the case before the CERD Committee within six months from the exhaustion of domestic remedies or, where a body has been designated to hear such complaints, six months from the failure of that body to resolve the matter.

The Committee must first ascertain the admissibility of the communication, the conditions for which are:[4]

(i) it is not anonymous;
(ii) it emanates from individuals subject to the jurisdiction of a state party that has made a declaration under art 14 (accepting the competence of the Committee to receive such communications);
(iii) the individual complainant claims to be a victim of a violation of CERD (but in exceptional cases the communication can be submitted on behalf of such a victim);
(iv) the communication is compatible with the provisions of CERD;
(v) it is not an abuse of right;
(vi) the individual has exhausted all domestic remedies (including national review body), except when their application is unreasonably prolonged; and

(vii) the communication was submitted within six months of the exhaustion of domestic remedies (except in the event of exceptional circumstances). The Committee may request additional information, clarifications and observations related to the question of admissibility from the parties.[5] If it finds a communication to be admissible, it will give the state party an opportunity to submit, within three months, its written observations and statements on the matter (including information on possible remedies); the individual will be then given the opportunity to respond to the state's contentions.[6] If deemed necessary, the Committee may invite the petitioner and the state concerned to appear before the Committee and provide additional information or answers to questions.[7] The Committee will then formulate its opinion on the case, taking into consideration all relevant information presented to it. The opinion will contain the suggestions and recommendations of the Committee, and the state party will be invited to inform the Committee, at a later date, on whether it has taken measures to implement the Committee's views.[8] A summary of the submissions of the parties and the opinion of the Committee is published in the Committee's annual report to the General Assembly and in press communiqués.[9]

To date, the Committee has received nine individual communications. Of these, three were declared inadmissible, and two others are still pending. In three cases the Committee has found a violation of CERD.

1   CERD, art 14(1). The Committee became competent to review individual communications immediately after 10 states declared their acceptance of this power of the Committee.
2   CERD, art 14(2)
3   Ibid, art 14(5).
4   CERD, art 14(2),(5),(6)(a),(7)(a); CERD Rules, r 91.
5   CERD Rules, r 92. A communication cannot be declared admissible unless the state complained against was given an opportunity to comment upon it.
6   CERD, art 14(6); CERD Rules, r 94(1),(2),(4).
7   CERD Rules, r 94(5).
8   CERD, art 14(7)(b); CERD Rules, r 95.
9   CERD, art 14(8); CERD Rules, rr 96, 97. Selected opinions are published on the CERD Committee's website.

REFERENCE

Sources of case law, including case reports

Relevant materials can be found on the Committee website.

Selected bibliography

Official publications

The Reports Series of the Committee on the Elimination of Racial Discrimination is published by the UN.

Books

M Banton *International action against racial discrimination* (1996).

UN Centre for Human Rights *The Committee on the Elimination of Racial Discrimination* (1991).

ANNEX

List of 155 states parties to CERD

Afghanistan, Albania, Algeria,* Antigua and Barbuda, Argentina, Armenia, Australia,* Austria, Azerbaïjan, Bahamas, Bahrain, Bangladesh, Barbados, Belarus, Belgium, Bolivia, Bosnia and Herzegovina, Botswana, Brazil, Bulgaria,* Burkina Faso, Burundi, Cambodia, Cameroon, Canada, Cape Verde, Central African Republic, Chad, Chile,* China, Colombia, Congo, Democratic Republic of the Congo, Costa Rica,* Côte d'Ivoire, Croatia, Cuba, Cyprus,* Czech Republic, Denmark,* Dominican Republic, Ecuador,* Egypt, El Salvador, Estonia, Ethiopia, Fiji, Finland,* France,* Gabon, Gambia, Georgia, Germany, Ghana, Greece, Guatemala, Guinea, Guyana, Haiti, Holy See, Hungary,* Iceland,* India, Indonesia, Iran, Iraq, Israel, Italy,* Jamaica, Japan, Jordan, Kazakhstan, Korea,* Kuwait, Kyrgyzstan, Laos, Latvia, Lebanon, Lesotho, Liberia, Libya, Lithuania, Luxembourg,* former Yugoslav Republic of Macedonia, Madagascar, Malawi, Maldives, Mali, Malta,* Mauritania, Mauritius, Mexico, Moldova, Monaco, Mongolia, Morocco, Mozambique, Namibia, Nepal, Netherlands,* New Zealand, Nicaragua, Niger, Nigeria, Norway,* Pakistan, Panama, Papua New Guinea, Peru,* Philippines, Poland,* Portugal, Qatar, Romania, Russia,* Rwanda, Saint Lucia, Saint Vincent and the Grenadines, Saudi Arabia, Senegal,* Seychelles, Sierra Leone, Slovakia,* Slovenia, Solomon Islands, Somalia, South Africa,* Spain,* Sri Lanka, Sudan, Suriname, Swaziland, Sweden,* Switzerland, Syria, Tajikistan, Tanzania, Togo, Tonga, Trinidad and Tobago, Tunisia, Turkmenistan, Uganda, Ukraine,* United Arab Emirates, United Kingdom, United States of America, Uruguay,* Uzbekistan, Venezuela, Vietnam, Yugoslavia, Zambia, Zimbabwe.

* States that have recognised the competence of the CERD Committee to receive individual communications.

CHAPTER 16

Committee against Torture

INTRODUCTORY

Name and seat of body

16.1 The UN Committee against Torture ('CAT Committee' or 'the Committee') is authorised to monitor compliance with the UN Convention against Torture and other Cruel, Inhuman or Degrading Treatment or Punishment ('CAT'), to receive applications from complainants in respect of violations of the Convention and to conduct ex officio inquiries into the practice of torture.
   The CAT Committee is located at:

> Committee against Torture
> Centre for Human Rights
> Palais des Nations, United Nations
> 8–14 Avenue de la Paix
> 1211 Geneva 10
> Switzerland

> Tel: (41) 22 917 3965
> Fax: (41) 22 917 0099
> website: http://www.unhchr.ch

Description

16.2 CAT was concluded in 1984 and entered into force in 1987.[1] To date, 117 states have ratified or acceded to the Convention (see Annex) and another 66 are signatories. Under CAT, states have undertaken to take all measures to prevent torture in their territory and/or involving any person subject to their jurisdiction. The Convention provides for the establishment of the CAT Committee in order to monitor the compliance of the states parties with their obligations under CAT.[2]
   The Committee comprises 10 independent experts elected by the states parties to CAT for renewable four-year terms.[3] In electing experts, factors for consideration include geographical distribution and the usefulness of some members of the Committee having legal experience, as well as of their being serving members of the Human Rights Committee.[4] There may be no more than one member per country.
   The Committee considers periodic reports submitted by the states parties on the measures taken by them to implement the Convention and may issue general comments thereon.[5] The Committee can also receive communications

from individuals or from the states parties alleging non-compliance with CAT by a state party which has accepted the jurisdiction of the CAT Committee to investigate such complaints.[6] In addition, the Committee may investigate situations in respect of which information on the systematic practice of torture has been received from reliable sources.[7] As in relation to its powers governing inter-state and individual communications, in the consideration of periodic reports the CAT Committee may consider information from NGOs, amongst others.[8] All investigation procedures involve the exercise of quasi-judicial powers by the Committee and the formulation of its findings in the form of a non-binding report.

The procedure applied by the CAT Committee is governed by Part II of CAT and by the Rules of Procedure adopted by the Committee. The Secretary-General of the UN provides the CAT Committee with secretarial services and the sessions of the Committee are held in UN facilities.[9] The official and working languages of the Committee are English, French, Russian and Spanish.[10] The meetings of the CAT Committee in which communications or information on systematic practice of torture are considered are normally closed to the public.[11] The Committee normally holds two working sessions every year, usually in April/May and November, in Geneva.[12]

1 Convention against Torture and Other Cruel, Inhuman or Degrading Treatment or Punishment, 10 December 1984, GA Res 39/46, 39 UN GAOR Supp (No 51), UN Doc A/39/51, at 197 (1984), 23 ILM 1027 (1984).
2 CAT, art 17.
3 Ibid, art 17(1),(5). The current membership is Peter Thomas Burns (Canada); Guibril Camara (Senegal); Sayed Kassem El Masry (Egypt); Poblete Alejandro Gonzales (Chile); Gaspar Antonio Silva Henriques (Portugal); Georghios M Pikis (Cyprus); Bent Sorensen (Denmark); Alexander M Yakovlev (Russia); Mengjia Yu (China); and Bostjan M Zupancic, (Slovenia).
4 CAT, art 17(1),(2).
5 Ibid, art 19. Unlike other treaty bodies, the Committee has no power to issue general comments or recommendations addressed to all states parties.
6 CAT, arts 21, 22.
7 Ibid, art 20.
8 UN Doc CAT/C/3/Rev 3 as revised on 13 July 1998 ('CAT Rules'), r 62.
9 CAT, arts 18(3), 23; CAT Rules, rr 4, 21, 23. Since 1997 administrative responsibility for the functioning of the CAT Committee has been in the hands of the Office of the UN High Commissioner for Human Rights.
10 CAT Rules, r 26.
11 CAT, arts 20(5), 21(1)(d), 22(6), CAT Rules, rr 73, 89, 101.
12 CAT Rules, rr 2, 4.

Inter-state communications (Article 21 procedure)

16.3 A state party to CAT may present to the Committee a communication against another state party if both states have accepted, by way of declaration, the jurisdiction of the CAT Committee to receive inter-state complaints.[1] To date, 44 states have accepted this head of jurisdiction of the Committee (see Annex). The communication must allege that the respondent state has failed to fulfil its obligations under CAT.[2] The complaining state must initially forward the complaint to the state complained against, and the latter is to respond in writing within three months. If no friendly settlement is reached within six months from the date on which the initial communication was received by the respondent state, either state may refer the matter to the CAT

Committee.[3] Before considering the merits of the case, the Committee must verify the admissibility of the complaint, especially whether domestic remedies have been exhausted (unless their application is unreasonably prolonged or likely to be ineffective).[4]

The CAT Committee will offer its good offices to the parties, with a view to facilitating amicable settlement based on respect for the obligations under CAT, and may establish an ad hoc conciliation commission for this purpose.[5] The parties are entitled to make oral and/or written submissions before the Committee, which may request from the parties additional information or observations, orally or in writing.[6] Within twelve months from the date on which the dispute was referred to the CAT Committee, the Committee will publish a report; where no settlement was reached this will contain a brief statement of facts, the written submissions and a summary of the oral submissions of the parties.[7] Where settlement is reached, the report would be limited to a brief statement of the facts and the solution reached. The report will be communicated to the concerned state parties. Unsettled inter-state disputes may be submitted eventually to arbitration or to the ICJ.[8]

So far there have been no inter-state cases before the CAT Committee.

1   CAT, art 21(1).
2   Ibid.
3   Ibid, art 21(1)(b).
4   Ibid, art 21(1)(c); CAT Rules, r 91.
5   CAT, art 21(1)(e); CAT Rules, r 92.
6   CAT, art 21(1)(f),(g); CAT Rules, rr 93, 94.
7   CAT, art 21(1)(h); CAT Rules, r 95. If a solution was found, the report will indicate its terms.
8   CAT, art 39.

Individual communications (Article 22 procedure)

16.4   The CAT Committee may also receive communications from individuals subject to the jurisdiction of a state party that has declared its acceptance of the competence of the Committee to receive individual complaints.[1] To date, 41 states have recognised this competence of the CAT Committee (see Annex).

A communication must be submitted to the Committee by or on behalf of any person who claims to be a victim of a violation of the CAT by the state complained against.[2] This includes a relative or designated representative of the victim or any other person when it appears that the alleged victim is unable to submit the communication and the author of the communication justifies his or her acting on the victim's behalf.[3]

The Committee must first determine whether the communication is admissible.[4] This will include verification that the complainant has exhausted domestic remedies (unless their application is unreasonably prolonged or likely to be ineffective).[5] It will also require confirmation that another international dispute settlement procedure has not been invoked in relation to the same case. This appears not to refer to the non-conventional mechanisms of the UN, such as the special rapporteurs.[6] The Committee will not accept anonymous communications, although it may accept a request by the author of the communication to have his or her name withheld if so required by the circumstances.[7] The alleged violation must have occurred on or after the date when art 22 of CAT came into force for the state concerned.[8]

The Committee may then allocate the case to a member of the Committee who will serve as a rapporteur, seeking further information and referring the case to the state party concerned. If necessary, the rapporteur or the Committee may take interim action requesting the state party to take measures to protect the victim.[9] The Committee may require from the individual and state concerned additional information, clarifications and observations on the issue of admissibility.[10]

In the event that the Committee finds the communication admissible, it will allow the state concerned six months to submit written observations and statements on the merits of the complaint.[11] The author of the communication will be then given the opportunity to respond to the state's submissions. The Committee may invite the individual and state concerned to appear before it to provide clarifications or answer questions.[12] It may also address matters which it considers of relevance, notwithstanding the fact that no submissions as to such matters have been made by the parties. It may refer to information supplied to it by UN bodies or specialised agencies which may assist in the disposal of the case.[13]

After receiving the submissions of the parties, the Committee formulates its views on the matter. Although the Committee's practice is to do so by consensus, members may append summaries of their individual views to those of the Committee.[14] The views will be forwarded to the parties to the dispute and the Committee may subsequently invite the state concerned to report on whether it has implemented the Committee's recommendations.[15] Summaries of the submissions of the parties and the views of the Committee are published in its annual report to the states parties to CAT and to the General Assembly.[16]

So far, the CAT Committee has dealt with 133 individual communications. In 34 of these cases, the Committee submitted its views on the merits (finding a violation in 16 cases); 28 cases were found inadmissible, 38 cases were discontinued; and 33 cases are still pending.

1 CAT, art 22(1).
2 Ibid.
3 CAT Rules, r 107(b).
4 CAT, art 22(5); CAT Rules, r 107.
5 If a communication is found inadmissible on this ground, it may be resubmitted later when remedies can be shown to have been exhausted, unreasonably prolonged or ineffective: see CAT Rules, r 109.
6 Communication No 1, 2, 3/1988, reported in UN Doc 1/45/44 and *Mutombo v Switzerland*, Communication No 13/1993, reported in UN Doc A/49/44, Annex VI.
7 CAT, art 22(2); CAT Rules, r 107. The other requirements of admissibility are that: it emanates from a person subject to the jurisdiction of a state that recognised the competence of the Committee to receive individual communications; it is not an abuse of right; and it is not incompatible with the provisions of CAT.
8 See Comm No 1, 2, 3/1988, reported in UN Doc A/45/44
9 CAT Rules, rr 108(9) and 110(3). Also see *Mutombo v Switzerland* (see n 6 above); Communication No 1/1994, reported in UN Doc A/50/44, Annex V.
10 CAT Rules, r 108(6). A communication cannot be declared admissible unless the state complained against was given an opportunity to comment upon it.
11 CAT, art 22(3); CAT Rules, r 110.
12 CAT Rules, r 110(5).
13 Ibid, r 111.
14 Ibid.
15 CAT, art 22(7); CAT Rules, r 111.
16 CAT, art 24; CAT Rules, r 112. Selected views are published on the CAT Committee's website and on <http://www.umn.edu/humanrts/catdecisions.html>.

Investigation of systematic practice of torture (Article 20 procedure)

16.5 The CAT Committee may also investigate allegations of the systematic practice of torture in the territory of any state party without being prompted by a formal complaint. If reliable information on the existence of such a situation is brought to the attention of the Committee by any source, it may initiate examination of the matter and invite the state concerned to submit its observations within a limited period.[1] There is no requirement regarding the exhaustion of domestic remedies in respect of such allegations before they may be submitted to the Committee.[2] The Committee may obtain additional information from a variety of sources (eg intergovernmental organisations, NGOs and individuals).[3] Where necessary, the Committee may authorise one or more of its members to conduct a confidential inquiry.[4]

In conducting the inquiry, the Committee shall seek the co-operation of the state party concerned.[5] The inquiry may include, with the consent of the state concerned, a visit to the territory of the state concerned and hearings of witnesses and other individuals.[6] The Committee may request the concerned government to ensure that there is no interference with such proceedings and no intimidation of any witnesses.[7] The findings of the inquiry will be presented to the Committee, which will examine these and then transmit them along with its own comments and suggestions, as appropriate, to the state concerned, inviting it to suggest any action which it might take.[8] A summary account of the investigation proceedings may be published in the annual report of the Committee to the General Assembly.[9] The proceedings will remain confidential until this stage.[10]

A state may, upon its signature, ratification or accession to CAT, declare that it does not recognise the competence of the CAT Committee under article 20.[11] To date, 11 states parties maintain such declarations (see Annex). In such cases, the Committee will not be able to pursue any investigation of information received against such a state without its consent.[12] To date, an investigation has been concluded and summary accounts of the proceedings published on two occasions;[13] several other cases are pending before the Committee.

1 CAT, art 20(1); CAT Rules, r 76.
2 See Andrew Byrnes 'The Committee against Torture' in P Alston (ed) *The United Nations and Human Rights* (1992) pp 530–533.
3 CAT Rules, rr 76(4), 77.
4 CAT, art 20(2); CAT Rules, r 78.
5 CAT, art 20(3).
6 Id; CAT Rules, rr 80, 81.
7 CAT Rules, r 81.
8 CAT, art 20(4); CAT Rules, r 83.
9 CAT, art 20(5); CAT Rules, r 84. The Committee must consult with the state concerned before deciding to publish the summary account.
10 CAT, art 20(5).
11 Ibid, art 28(2).
12 Ibid, art 28(1); CAT Rules, r 69(2).
13 UN Doc A/48/44 Add 1(Turkey) and UN Doc A/51/44 (Egypt).

REFERENCE

Sources of case law, including case reports

Relevant materials can be found on the CAT website.

Selected bibliography

UN Centre for Human Rights *The Committee against Torture* (1992).

A Byrnes 'The Committee against Torture' in P Alston (ed) *The United Nations and Human Rights* (1992).

ANNEX

List of 117 states parties to CAT

Afghanistan,* Albania, Algeria, Antigua and Barbuda, Argentina, Armenia, Australia, Austria, Azerbaïjan, Bahrain,* Bangladesh, Belarus,* Belgium, Belize, Benin, Bolivia, Bosnia and Herzegovina, Brazil, Bulgaria,* Burkina Faso, Burundi, Cameroon, Cambodia, Canada, Cape Verde, Chad, Chile, China,* Colombia, Democratic Republic of the Congo, Costa Rica, Côte d'Ivoire, Croatia, Cuba, Cyprus, Czech Republic, Denmark, Ecuador, Egypt, El Salvador, Estonia, Ethiopia, Finland, France, Georgia, Germany, Greece, Guatemala, Guinea, Guyana, Honduras, Hungary, Iceland, Indonesia, Israel,* Italy, Japan, Jordan, Kazakhstan, Kenya, Korea, Kuwait,* Kyrgyzstan, Latvia, Libya, Liechtenstein, Lithuania, Luxembourg, former Yugoslav Republic of Macedonia, Malawi, Mali, Malta, Mauritius, Mexico, Moldova, Monaco, Morocco,* Namibia, Nepal, Netherlands, New Zealand, Niger, Norway, Panama, Paraguay, Peru, Philippines, Poland,* Portugal, Romania, Russia, Saudi Arabia,* Senegal, Seychelles, Slovakia, Slovenia, Somalia, South Africa, Spain, Sri Lanka, Sweden, Switzerland, Tajikistan, Togo, Tunisia, Turkey, Turkmenistan, Uganda, Ukraine,* United Kingdom, United States of America, Uruguay, Uzbekistan, Venezuela, Yemen, Yugoslavia, Zambia.

* States that have excluded the competence of the CAT Committee to investigate systematic practice of torture under Article 20 of CAT.

List of states parties to CAT that recognise the competence of the Committee to receive inter-state communications

Algeria, Argentina, Australia, Austria, Belgium, Bulgaria, Canada, Croatia, Cyprus, Czech Republic, Denmark, Ecuador, Finland, France, Greece, Hungary, Iceland, Italy, Japan, Liechtenstein, Luxembourg, Malta, Monaco, Netherlands, New Zealand, Norway, Poland, Portugal, Russia, Senegal, Slovakia, Slovenia, South Africa, Spain, Sweden, Switzerland, Togo, Tunisia, Turkey, United Kingdom, United States of America, Uruguay, Venezuela, Yugoslavia.

List of states parties to CAT that recognise the competence of the Committee to receive individual communications

Algeria, Argentina, Australia, Austria, Belgium, Bulgaria, Canada, Croatia, Cyprus, Czech Republic, Denmark, Ecuador, Finland, France, Greece, Hungary, Iceland, Italy, Liechtenstein, Luxembourg, Malta, Monaco, Netherlands, New Zealand, Norway, Poland, Portugal, Russia, Senegal, Slovakia, Slovenia, South Africa, Spain, Sweden, Switzerland, Togo, Tunisia, Turkey, Uruguay, Venezuela, Yugoslavia.

CHAPTER 17

Representation and complaint procedures of the International Labour Organisation

GENERAL INFORMATION

17.1   The International Labour Organisation ('ILO') was established in 1919 in order to promote, at the international level, domestic working conditions and social justice with a view to contributing thereby to world peace.[1] The Organisation has 174 state members. It comprises three principal organs:

(1)   a General Conference of representatives of the member states (each national delegation including two government representatives, an employers' representative and a workers' representative);

(2)   a Governing Body (comprising 28 governmental representatives, 14 employers' representatives and 14 workers' representatives); and

(3)   the International Labour Office, which is the organisation's secretariat.

The central function of the ILO is the adoption of international labour standards by way of conventions (open to ratification by the member states) and non-binding instruments (recommendations, resolutions, declarations). In order to ensure compliance of member states with ILO standards, the ILO employs several supervisory procedures. Each state reports periodically to the ILO on the measures taken to give effect to ILO Conventions it has ratified[2] and the reports are reviewed by a special Committee of Independent Experts appointed by the Governing Body.[3] In addition, states, delegates to the General Conference and domestic and international employers' and workers' associations may communicate to the ILO representations or complaints alleging failure of a member state to comply with applicable ILO Conventions or required freedom of association standards. The communications are dealt with by the Governing Body itself, or by subsidiary bodies established by it.

1   Constitution of the International Labour Organisation, 9 October 1946, Preamble, 15 UNTS 40 ('ILO Constitution').
2   ILO Constitution, art 22.
3   See generally, ILO, *Handbook of Procedures relating to International Labour Conventions and Recommendations*, Rev 2/1998, at pp 21–23.

REPRESENTATION PROCEDURE

17.2   In accordance with Article 24 of the ILO Constitution any employers' or workers' industrial association (eg labour union) may submit a written representation to the International Labour Office alleging that a member state has failed to secure in any respect the effective observance within its jurisdiction of an ILO Convention, to which it is party.[1] The Office will forward the representation to the Governing Body.[2] If the Officers of the Governing Body (the Chairman and the two Vice-Chairmen) find the representation admissible, the Governing Body will set up a subsidiary tripartite committee, composed of non-involved members of the Governing Body, to examine the matter. The Governing Body may also refer the case, where appropriate, to the Committee on Freedom of Association. The tripartite committee may invite the concerned association and government to provide it with information and statements.[3] After examining the representation, the tripartite committee is to deliver a report to the Governing Body containing the committee's conclusions and recommendations.[4] The reports of the tripartite committee are normally published. The Governing Body will consider the report (in the presence of the government concerned, if not represented in the Governing Body) and decide whether to adopt any decisions on the basis of the committee's recommendations. The Governing Body may also decide to publish the representation and the government's response thereto.[5]

During 1997, the Governing Body adopted eight reports of tripartite committees, established four new tripartite committees and has taken procedural decisions in relation to three other representations. In 1998 four more reports were adopted and examination of four other representations was authorised.

1 ILO Constitution, art 24. The representation must indicate that the author is an industrial association; explicitly refer to Article 24 of the Constitution; refer to the Convention to which the relevant ILO member state is party; and provide details on the alleged non-compliance. Governing Body Standing Orders concerning the procedure for the examination of representations under Articles 24 and 25 of the Constitution of the International Labour Organisation, arts 1, 2, 64 ILO Official Bulletin (ser A) No 1, at 93–95 (1981) ('Standing Orders').
2 ILO Constitution, art 24.
3 Standing Orders, arts 4, 5. The government has a right to be heard in an oral session, while the appearance of representatives of the association before the committee is in the latter's discretion.
4 Standing Orders, art 6.
5 ILO Constitution, art 25; Standing Orders, art 8.

COMPLAINT PROCEDURE

17.3 Article 26 of the Constitution of the ILO authorises a state party to bring a complaint against another member state that has allegedly failed to secure the effective observance of any ILO Convention to which both the complaining state and the state complained against are parties.[1] The complaint is to be filed with the International Labour Office, which will refer the case to the Governing Body. The complaint procedure may also be initiated by a complaint made by a delegate to the Conference to the Governing Body, or upon the latter body, acting on its own motion.[2]

The Governing Body will normally establish a Commission of Inquiry to investigate the complaint. However, it may, at its discretion, decide to give the government complained against an opportunity to reply to the allegations before appointing the Commission of Inquiry (and may decline to appoint one if the response of the said government is considered satisfactory).[3] The respondent government is entitled to participate in the meetings of the Governing Body in which the complaint is being considered.[4]

Commissions of Inquiry are composed of three independent experts.[5] There are no standing orders governing the procedure of the Commissions and every Commission determines its own procedure (subject to the ILO Constitution and general guidance from the Governing Body). In practice, the proceedings are of a judicial nature (involving gathering of evidence, presentation of written and/or oral arguments and, on occasion, on-site visits: the last of these need consent, but this tends to be granted, notwithstanding the seriousness of the allegations concerned). The Commissions of Inquiry prepare a report containing factual findings and recommendations, and submit the report to the Governing Body.[6] The reports are published by the International Labour Office.[7]

After the report is concluded the states involved in the proceedings will inform the International Labour Office within three months from receiving the report whether they intend to comply with it, or, if not, whether they agree to refer the case to the International Court of Justice.[8] The Governing Body may recommend to the Parties' General Conference to take appropriate implementation measures against a state party which fails to implement a report (or a judgment of the ICJ on the same matter).[9] The Governing Body may also appoint another Commission of Inquiry, upon the request of the defaulting government, in order to verify compliance with the report (or the ICJ judgment).[10] During 1998 two new complaints were made and one Commission of Inquiry report adopted.

1 ILO Constitution, art 26(1).
2 Ibid, art 26(4).
3 Ibid, art 26(2),(3).
4 Ibid, art 26(5).
5 Although there is no formal requirement as to the composition of the Commission of Inquiry, is has been the unchanged practice of the Governing Body to appoint three persons thereto.
6 ILO Constitution, art 28.
7 Ibid, art 29(1).
8 Ibid, art 29(2).
9 Ibid, art 33.
10 Ibid, art 34.

COMPLAINTS ON INFRINGEMENT OF FREEDOM OF ASSOCIATION

17.4 In 1951 the Governing Body established a mechanism to supervise the implementation of labour standards relating to freedom of association. An employers' or workers' organisation or a government may bring a complaint against any ILO member state alleging infringement of freedom of association by that state (even if it is not a party to one of the ILO Conventions on freedom of association).[1] An employers' or workers' association must meet one of the following conditions:

(1) it is a directly interested domestic organisation;
(2) it is an international organisation with consultative status with the ILO; or
(3) it is an international organisation to which a domestic organisation directly affected is affiliated.[2]

The communication is to be made in writing to the International Labour Office, which may request additional information.[3]

The International Labour Office will communicate the complaint and the reply of the concerned government to a permanent subsidiary committee of the Governing Body – the Committee on Freedom of Association. The Committee comprises nine members of the Governing Body and an independent Chairman.[4] The Committee is authorised to investigate complaints (including the conduct of oral hearings and on site visits, if necessary)[5] and submit its recommendations to the Governing Body. The Governing Body may then approve the recommendations of the Committee. The reports of the Committee are published; and the Committee may take follow-up action, where needed (eg when the member state is not subject to a relevant ILO Convention that introduces periodic reporting duties).[6] The Freedom of Association Committee meets three times every year and deals with over 30 cases at each meeting. To date it has examined some 2,000 complaints. The Committee gives priority to cases involving human life or personal freedom and those effecting the trade union movement as a whole, or involving states of emergency.

In appropriate cases, the Governing Body, acting upon the recommendation of the Committee on Freedom of Association may refer specific complaints for further investigation to a permanent nine-member independent Fact-finding and Conciliation Commission (which normally works in panels of three members).[7] The procedure of the latter body is generally similar to that of the Commission of Inquiry (but there is no right of appeal to the ICJ), and its reports are also published. However, if the government complained against is not a party to any ILO freedom of association Convention, its consent to the process is required.

1   Function of the ILO and Mandate of the Committee on Freedom of Association, Doc 101, para 5, Committee on Freedom of Association Digest of Decisions (1996)
2   Procedures of the Fact-Finding and Conciliation Commission and the Committee on Freedom of Association for the Examination of Complaints alleging Violations of Freedom of Association, Doc 1901, para 34, Committee on Freedom of Association Digest of Decisions (1996) ('CFA Procedures').
3   CFA Procedures, para 47.
4   Ibid, para 10. See generally, ILO, *Handbook of Procedures relating to International Labour Conventions and Recommendations*, Rev 2/1998, at pp 30–31.
5   CFA Procedures, para 66.
6   Ibid, para 21.
7   Ibid, para 22.

CONTACT INFORMATION

17.5   The International Labour Office of the International Labour Organisation is located at:

> International Labour Office
> Department of Labour Standards
> 4, route de Morillons
> CH-1211 Geneva 22
> Switzerland
>
> Tel: (41) 22 799 61 11
> Fax: (41) 22 799 69 26
> email: infleg@ilo.org
> website: http://www.ilo.org/

REFERENCE

Sources of case law, including case reports

Relevant materials can be found on the ILO website.

Selected bibliography

Books

V Y Ghebali *The ILO: A Case Study on the Evolution of UN Specialised Agencies* Nijhoff (1989).

E A Landy *The Effectiveness of International Supervision* Stevens and Sons (1966).

Articles

E Landy 'The implementation procedures of the ILO' (1980) 20 Santa Clara Law Review 633.

B H Simamba 'The jurisdiction of the ILO to hear complaints regarding trade union freedom' (1988) Comparative and International Journal of Southern Africa.

N Valticos 'Les Commissions d'enquête de l'Organisation Internationale du Travail' (1987) Revue Générale de Droit Internationale Public.

N Valticos 'Les conventions de l'Organisation Internationale du Travail à la croisée des anniversaires' (1996) 100 Revue Générale de Droit Internationale Public 5.

N Valticos 'Once more about the ILO system of supervision: in what respect is it still a model?' in N Blokker and S Muller (eds) *Towards More Effective Supervision by International Organisations* Nijhoff (1994).

N Valticos 'Les commissions d'enquête de l'OIT' 91 Revue Générale de Droit Internationale Public 847.

ANNEX

List of ILO member states

Afghanistan, Albania, Algeria, Angola, Antigua and Barbuda, Argentina, Armenia, Australia, Austria, Azerbaïjan, Bahamas, Bahrain, Bangladesh, Barbados, Belarus, Belgium, Belize, Benin, Bolivia, Bosnia and Herzegovina, Botswana, Brazil, Bulgaria, Burkina Faso, Burundi, Cambodia, Cameroon, Canada, Cape Verde, Central African Republic, Chad, Chile, China, Colombia, Comoros, Congo, Democratic Republic of the Congo, Costa Rica, Côte d'Ivoire, Croatia, Cuba, Cyprus, Czech Republic, Denmark, Djibouti, Dominica, Dominican Republic, Ecuador, Egypt, El Salvador, Equatorial Guinea, Eritrea, Estonia, Ethiopia, Fiji, Finland, France, Gabon, Gambia, Georgia, Germany, Ghana, Greece, Grenada, Guatemala, Guinea, Guinea-Bissau, Guyana, Haiti, Honduras, Hungary, Iceland, India, Indonesia, Iran,

Human rights bodies

Iraq, Ireland, Israel, Italy, Jamaica, Japan, Jordan, Kazakhstan, Kenya, Korea, Kuwait, Kyrgyzstan, Laos, Latvia, Lebanon, Lesotho, Liberia, Libya, Lithuania, Luxembourg, the former Yugoslav Republic of Macedonia, Madagascar, Malawi, Malaysia, Mali, Malta, Mauritania, Mauritius, Mexico, Moldavia, Mongolia, Morocco, Mozambique, Myanmar, Namibia, Nepal, Netherlands, New Zealand, Nicaragua, Niger, Nigeria, Norway, Oman, Pakistan, Panama, Papua New Guinea, Paraguay, Peru, Philippines, Poland, Portugal, Qatar, Romania, Russian Federation, Rwanda, Saint Kitts and Nevis, Saint Lucia, Saint Vincent and the Grenadines, San Marino, Sao Tome and Principe, Saudi Arabia, Senegal, Seychelles, Sierre Leone, Singapore, Slovakia, Slovenia, Solomon Islands, Somalia, South Africa, Spain, Sri Lanka, Sudan, Suriname, Swaziland, Sweden, Switzerland, Syria, Tajikistan, Tanzania, Thailand, Togo, Trinidad and Tobago, Tunisia, Turkey, Turkmenistan, Uganda, Ukraine, United Arab Emirates, United Kingdom, United States, Uruguay, Uzbekistan, Venezuela, Vietnam, Yemen, Yugoslavia, Zambia, Zimbabwe.

CHAPTER 18

European Court of Human Rights

INTRODUCTORY

Name and seat of the court

18.1   The European Court of Human Rights ('EHR Court' or 'the court') is a permanent court entrusted with monitoring the compliance of member states of the Council of Europe with their obligations under the European Convention on Human Rights. The Registry of the court operates within the organisational framework of the Council of Europe and is located at:

> European Court of Human Rights
> Conseil de l'Europe
> F-67075 Strasbourg CEDEX
> France

> Tel: 33 3 88 41 20 18
> Fax: 33 3 88 41 27 30
> website: http://www.dhcour.coe.fr

Description

18.2   The European Convention of Human Rights ('the Convention') was created within the framework of the Council of Europe in 1950,[1] an organisation designed to bring European states into closer association.[2] The institutional link between the Council of Europe, based in Strasbourg (France), and the EHR Convention has remained until today. The Council's Committee of Ministers is responsible for monitoring the implementation of judgments of the European Court of Human Rights ('the court'). States interested in joining the Council of Europe must undertake a political commitment to ratify the Convention.

The Convention and the Protocols thereto, which have been adopted subsequently, enumerate fundamental rights and freedoms which the contracting parties undertake to respect and secure. The original text of the Convention introduced a two-tier enforcement mechanism, intended to ensure compliance with the prescribed human rights standards. This mechanism consisted of two organs – the European Commission of Human Rights ('Commission') and the European Court of Human Rights.

Under the original system, petitions from individuals, NGOs or states alleging violations of the Convention had to be brought initially before the Commission. The Commission examined the admissibility of the petition, attempted to find a friendly settlement and could refer the case, under certain conditions, to the court on behalf of the complainant. Following the entry into force of the 11th Protocol to the Convention on 1 November 1998, the Commission was abolished and most of its functions have been transferred to the court. As a result, claimants (states and individuals) can now submit applications directly to the court.[3]

The court deals with complaints by states and individuals concerning the protection of human rights by the 41 states parties to the Convention. Upon receipt of an application, the court determines its admissibility and, if admissible, attempts to secure a friendly settlement of the dispute on the basis of respect for the human rights set out in the Convention and Protocols thereto.[4] If no settlement is reached, a chamber of the court is to hear the case and issue a binding judgment, which in exceptional cases may be referred for second review before an enlarged chamber. Since its establishment, the court has dealt with over 1,000 petitions, nearly all of which were initiated by private parties. More than 670 of these petitions were adjudicated on the merits, and in over 460 of these cases a violation of the Convention was found. In the first five months of 1999 the court received some 10,000 applications and has made final or interim decisions in over 1,300 cases.[5]

1   Convention for the Protection of Human Rights and Fundamental Freedoms, 4 November 1950, ETS 5 (1950); 213 UNTS 221, as amended by Protocol No 11, 11 May 1994, ETS 155 (1994) ('EHR Convention'). The original text of the EHR Convention will be referred to hereinafter as 'original EHR Convention'.
2   Statute of the Council of Europe, 5 May 1949, preamble, ETS 1.
3   EHR Convention, arts 33, 34.
4   Ibid, arts 38, 39.
5   This sharp increase can be explained by the fact that the court now receives cases which were previously screened by the Commission.

INSTITUTIONAL ASPECTS

Governing texts

18.3   The principal text governing the operation of the EHR Court is the EHR Convention, as amended by the 11th Protocol. The Convention establishes the court and determines its composition, jurisdiction and the general contours of its procedure. The rules of procedure are enumerated in the Rules of Court, adopted in November 1998,[1] though the court may derogate from these rules, where appropriate, after consulting with the parties.[2] In addition, an agreement has been concluded on the treatment to be accorded by states to persons participating in proceedings before the court, designed to guarantee to such persons certain immunities and facilitate their access to the court.[3]

1   Rules of Court, 4 November 1998 ('Rules of Court').
2   Rules of Court, r 31.
3   European Agreement relating to Persons Participating in Proceedings of the European Court of Human Rights, 5 March 1996, ETS 161 (1996).

Substantive law

18.4   The substantive law to be applied by the EHR Court consists of the rights and freedoms listed in Section I of the EHR Convention and in Protocols 1,[1] 4,[2] 6,[3] and 7[4] to the Convention.

1   Protocol to the Convention for the Protection of Human Rights and Fundamental Freedoms, 20 March 1952, ETS 9 (1952).

2 Protocol No 4 to the Convention for the Protection of Human Rights and Fundamental
   Freedoms, 16 September 1963, ETS 46 (1963).
3 Protocol No 6 to the Convention for the Protection of Human Rights and Fundamental
   Freedoms, 28 April 1983, ETS 114 (1983).
4 Protocol No 7 to the Convention for the Protection of Human Rights and Fundamental
   Freedoms, 22 November 1984, ETS 155 (1984).

Organisation

Composition, appointment and disqualification

18.5 The court is composed of judges, equal in number to the number of
states parties to the Convention.[1] At present there are 40 judges (a 41st judge
is about to be appointed).[2] Judges must be persons of high moral character
who possess qualifications required for appointment to a high judicial
domestic office or are considered to be juriconsults of recognised
competence.[3] Each state party is entitled to nominate three candidates for
service on the court (who may or may not be its nationals), and the
Parliamentary Assembly of the Council of Europe elects one judge in respect
of a given country.[4] Despite their nomination by states (normally their state
of nationality) the judges serve on the bench in their individual capacity.[5] The
term of office is a renewable six-year period (except at the first election, where
half of the judges are elected for a three-year term) and retirement age is 70.[6]
The court is headed by a President and two Vice-Presidents elected for three-
year terms.[7] The quorum for plenary sessions of the court is two-thirds of the
judges.[8]

1 EHR Convention, art 20.
2 A Russian judge has not yet been appointed.
3 EHR Convention, art 21(1).
4 Ibid, art 22(1). The current composition of the court is:
   President: Luzius Wildhaber (Switzerland). **Vice-Presidents:** Elisabeth Palm (Sweden);
   Christos Rozakis (Greece). **Chamber Presidents:** Sir Nicolas Bratza (UK); Matti
   Pellonpää (Finland). **Judges:** Benedetto Conforti (Italy); Antonio Pastor Ridruejo (Spain);
   Luigi Ferrari Bravo (for San Marino); Gaukur Jorundsson (Iceland); Georg Ress
   (Germany); Giovanni Bonello (Malta); Lucius Caflisch (for Liechtenstein); Loukis
   Loucaides (Cyprus); Jerzy Makarczyk (Poland); Pranas Kuris (Lithuania); Ireneu Cabral
   Barreto (Portugal); Riza Türmen (Turkey); Jean-Paul Costa (France); Françoise Tulkens
   (Belgium); Viera Stráznická (Slovakia); Corneliu Bîrsan (Romania); Peer Lorenzen
   (Denmark); Willi Fuhrmann (Austria); Karel Jungwiert (Czech Republic); Marc
   Fischbach (Luxembourg); Volodymyr Butkevych (Ukraine); Josep Casadevall (Andorra);
   Boštjan Zupancic (Slovenia); Nina Vajic (Croatia); John Hedigan (Ireland); Wilhelmina
   Thomassen (Netherlands); Margarita Tsatsa-Nikolovska (former Yugoslav Republic of
   Macedonia); Tudor Pantiru (Moldavia); Hanne Sophie Greve (Norway); András Baka
   (Hungary); Rait Maruste (Estonia); Egils Levits (Latvia); Kristaq Traja (Albania); Snejana
   Botoucharova (Bulgaria); Mindia Urgekhelidze (Georgia).
5 EHR Convention, art 21(2).
6 Ibid, art 23(1),(6).
7 EHR Convention, art 26(a); Rules of Court, r 8.
8 Rules of Court, r 20(2).

Disqualification of judges

18.6 A judge may not participate in a case in which he or she has personal
interest or was previously involved as representative of one of the parties or
another interested person, or as member of a dispute settlement or
investigation body.[1] If the President of a Chamber becomes aware of a reason
which warrants the withdrawal of a judge from the case, he or she may

request the concerned judge to do so, and bring the case to the decision of the chamber in the event of disagreement.[2]

Judges must refrain from engaging in any activity which is incompatible with their independence, impartiality or the demands of their office. Judges are to report to the President any additional activity they engage in, and the latter may request the judge concerned to forgo that activity or bring the matter to the decision of the plenary court.[3] Any judge may bring to the plenary court a motion against another judge who has allegedly ceased to fulfil the conditions for service on the bench. A two-thirds majority of the judges is required in order to dismiss a judge in these circumstances.[4]

1 Rules of Court, r 28(2).
2 Ibid, r 28(4).
3 EHR Convention, art 21(3); Rules of Court, r 4.
4 EHR Convention, art 24; Rules of Court, r 7.

Plenary/chambers

18.7 The court hears cases in committees of three judges (reviewing the admissibility of applications), in chambers of seven judges or in the Grand Chamber, comprising seventeen judges and three substitute judges.[1] The plenary court determines the composition of the Grand Chamber, of the four or more Sections, from which ad hoc seven-judge chambers are formed for each case (with the other judges of the Section sitting as substitutes), and the Presidency of these Sections ('Presidents of Chambers').[2] The Sections are composed with due regard to the need for geographical and gender balance and are to be representative of the different legal systems of the states parties.[3] The Grand Chamber is to include ex officio the President and Vice-Presidents of the court and the Presidents of the different chambers. When the Grand Chamber is dealing with a case as a second instance review chamber (see para 18.8 below), judges who sat on the first chamber that reviewed the case may not sit on the Grand Chamber (with the exception of chamber presidents and the judges elected in respect of the states concerned).[4] All chambers will include the judges elected in respect of the state party concerned.[5] If no such judge is available, the state concerned may appoint an ad hoc judge meeting the qualifications for appointment to the court.[6] The various Sections establish committees from within their members for one-year terms.[7]

Cases will normally be heard before a seven-judge chamber. However, when a case raises a serious question affecting the interpretation of the Convention or Protocols, or one which might result in a judgment inconsistent with a previous judgment of the court, the chamber may relinquish its jurisdiction in favour of the Grand Chamber. This is possible only if none of the parties to the case submits a reasoned objection within one month from being notified of the intent to relinquish jurisdiction.[8]

1 EHR Convention, art 27(1).
2 Ibid, art 26(b),(c); Rules of Court, rr 8, 24–26. The Rules provide that Vice Presidents of Chambers are also to be elected and will replace the Presidents of the Chambers if they cannot preside over a case (eg in a case involving the President's state of nationality or the state that nominated him or her to the court): Rules of Court, rr 12–13, 25(5)(a). When appointing Presidents and Vice-Presidents, the court will strive to reach balanced representation of the sexes in those positions: r 14.
3 Rules of Court, rr 24(3), 25(2).
4 EHR Convention, art 27(3).

5   Ibid, art 27(2); Rules of Court, rr 24(4), 26(2).
6   EHR Convention, art 27(2); Rules of Court, r 29. If several state parties involved in the case
    have a common interest, the President of the Court will invite them to appoint an ad hoc
    judge in common: Rules of Court, r 30.
7   EHR Convention, art 27(1); Rules of Court, r 27.
8   EHR Convention, art 30; Rules of Court, r 72.

Appellate structure

18.8   The Grand Chamber can hear cases as a second instance at the request
of a party to a case decided by a seven-judge chamber. However, the Grand
Chamber will grant a request for referral of a case already decided to the
Grand Chamber only in exceptional cases which raise a serious question
affecting the interpretation of the Convention or Protocols, or a serious issue
of general importance.[1]

1   EHR Convention, art 43; Rules of Court, r 73.

Scientific and technical experts

18.9   The parties to a case before the court may ask to introduce the testimony of expert witnesses. The court may also summon experts on its own
initiative, or following a request by a third party.[1] A party may object to the
invitation of a specific expert witness.[2] The judges and parties may question
experts appearing before the court (the parties may do so subject to the
control of the President of the Chamber).[3]

The court can also resort to other measures to obtain expert opinion. It may
approach any person or institution and request it to provide the court with
information, an opinion, or a report on a specific issue.[4] In addition, the court
may set up a delegation comprising one or more judges to conduct investigation related to a case pending before the court and appoint independent
external experts to assist that delegation.[5]

1   Rules of Court, rr 42, 65(1).
2   Ibid, r 67.
3   Ibid, r 68.
4   Ibid, r 42(3).
5   Ibid, r 42(2).

Registry

18.10   The administration of the court is facilitated by its Registry, headed by
the Registrar.[1] The Registrar is elected by the plenary court for a renewable five-
year term[2] and is assisted by two Deputy Registrars[3] and by Section Registrars
and Deputy Registrars appointed for each Section of the court.[4] The Registrar
is responsible for the work of the Registry and for the court's archives,
communications with the court and dissemination of information concerning
the court.[5] The staff of the Registry is to be designated by the Secretary-General
of the Council of Europe with the agreement of the court's President or
Registrar.[6] The current Registrar is Michele de Salvia (Italy). His deputies are
Paul Mahoney (UK) and Maud De Boer-Buquicchio (Netherlands).

1   EHR Convention, art 25.
2   Rules of Court, r 15(1),(2).
3   Ibid, r 16.

4   Ibid, r 18.
5   Ibid, r 17.
6   Ibid, r 18(3).

Jurisdiction of and access to the court

Ratione personae

18.11   Any state party to the Convention may bring to the court a case against any other state party, which is alleged to have breached the provisions of the Convention or the Protocols.[1] Individuals, NGOs and groups of individuals, who claim to have been victims of a human rights violation,[2] may also bring a case against the state party which has committed the alleged violation.[3]

1   EHR Convention, art 33.
2   The EHR Court and Commission have construed the term 'victim' narrowly. The court has held that an individual cannot bring an *actio popularis* against a law *in abstracto*: *Klass v Germany* (1978) 2 EHRR 214. In addition, the EHR Commission has declined on several occasions to regard organisations bringing complaints on behalf of their members, specific persons or the general public, as victims under the Convention: eg *Church of X v UK* (1969) App No 3798/68, 12 Yearbook of the European Convention on Human Rights 306.
3   EHR Convention, art 34. Under the old system, complaints presented to the Commission by individuals could be brought to the court by the Commission, or an interested state party. Only individuals from states parties to Protocol 9 could forward the complaint to the court after it had been dealt with by the Commission: Original EHR Convention, art 48; Protocol no 9 to the European Convention for the Protection of Human Rights and Fundamental Freedoms, 6 November 1990, ETS 140 (1994).

Ratione materiae

18.12   In inter-state cases, the court may address any complaint alleging a breach by a state party of the provisions of the Convention and Protocols.[1] In cases brought by private parties, the court has jurisdiction to receive claims alleging violation of the rights enumerated in the Convention and Protocols.[2]

1   EHR Convention, art 33.
2   Ibid, art 34.

Ratione temporis

18.13   A case must be presented to the EHR Court within six months from the date in which domestic remedies were exhausted and the final decision of the competent domestic authorities rendered ('the six months rule').[1] Only violations committed by a state after the entry into force of the EHR Convention with respect to it may be alleged.

1   EHR Convention, art 35(1).

Advisory jurisdiction

18.14   The court may render an advisory opinion on the interpretation of the Convention and Protocols, at the request of the Committee of Ministers.[1] However, opinions can only deal with procedural questions and may not deal with matters concerning the scope of the substantive rights and freedoms enumerated in the Convention and Protocols, or any other matter which may be raised in ordinary proceedings before the court.[2]

A request for advisory opinion is to be filed with the Registry and should contain the following information:

(a) the date in which the Committee of Ministers decided to request the opinion;

(b) names and addresses of the representatives of the Committee before the court;

(c) the question on which the opinion of the court is sought; and

(d) all relevant documents.[3]

The states parties are then invited to submit their comments on the matter to the court, within time limits fixed by the President.[4] The Registry communicates all submissions to the Committee of Ministers and to the states parties.[5] The President may invite the parties who have submitted written comments to present oral arguments before the Grand Chamber, which renders the opinions.[6]

Opinions must be reasoned and can include, where relevant, the separate or dissenting opinions.[7]

1 EHR Convention, art 47(1). The power to issue advisory opinions was granted to the court in Protocol no 2 to the Convention for the Protection of Human Rights and Fundamental Freedoms, 6 May 1963, ETS 44 (1963).
2 EHR Convention, art 47(2).
3 Rules of Court, r 83.
4 Ibid, rr 84, 85(1).
5 Ibid, r 85(1).
6 Ibid, rr 86, 88(1).
7 EHR Convention, art 49; Rules of Court, r 88(2).

PROCEDURAL ASPECTS

Languages

18.15 The official languages of the court are English and French.[1] However, correspondence with the court before the adoption of the decision on admissibility (including the initial applications) may be submitted in any of the official languages of the states parties.[2] In addition, the President of the Chamber may authorise the use of a non-official language. In that case, the requesting party will normally be responsible for providing interpretation or translation of the pleadings.[3] The court may also invite the respondent state to provide an applicant of the same nationality with a translation of the state's submissions in that state's official language in order to facilitate better understanding of the state's position by the applicant.[4]

Witnesses, experts and other persons appearing before the court may use their own language if they do not possess sufficient knowledge of the official languages. In that event, the Registrar will arrange for interpretation or translation.[5]

1 Rules of Court, r 34(1).
2 Ibid, r 34(2).
3 Ibid, r 34(3),(4). When the original application was in a non-official language and the applicant requests to continue and use an official language of a state party, the President may instruct the Registry to provide translation services.
4 Rules of Court, r 34(5).
5 Ibid, r 34(6).

Instituting proceedings

18.16   All cases before the court are initiated by way of a written application.[1] In inter-state cases, the application must include the following details:

(a) name of state party against which the application is made;
(b) statement of the facts;
(c) statement of the alleged violations of the Convention and relevant arguments;
(d) statement on compliance with admissibility requirements (exhaustion of domestic remedies and the six months rule);
(e) object of the application and indication of any claims for just satisfaction to the injured party;
(f) name and address of applicant's agent; and
(g) copies of relevant documents (in particular decisions relating to the object of the application).[2]

An application filed by a natural or legal person should contain the following information:

(a) name, date of birth, nationality, sex, occupation and address of applicant;
(b) name, occupation and address of the representative;
(c) name of state party against which the application is made;
(d) succinct statement of the facts;
(e) succinct statement of the alleged violations of the Convention and relevant arguments;
(f) succinct statement of compliance with conditions of admissibility (including information on whether other international investigation or settlement procedures have been previously invoked);
(g) object of the application and indication of claims for just satisfaction to the applicant; and
(h) copies of relevant documents (in particular, decisions relating to the object of the application).[3]

1   Rules of Court, r 45(1).
2   Ibid, r 46.
3   Ibid, r 47.

Financial assistance

18.17   The President of the Chamber may grant free aid to an applicant in pursuance of a request by the applicant or on the President's own motion.[1] However, the President must be satisfied that the proper conduct of a case before the court justifies legal aid and that the applicant has insufficient means to meet the costs entailed by the proceedings.[2] The latter determination will be based on a financial statement on the means available to the applicant to be submitted by him or her and upon which the respondent state may comment.[3] The decision to grant legal aid can only be adopted after the respondent state has submitted its observations on the admissibility of the case (or has failed to do so within the fixed time limit).

Once a decision to grant legal aid has been adopted, the Registrar will fix a rate of legal fees in accordance with a pre-existing legal aid scale and is to determine the level of other expenses to be paid.[4] The grant will also cover, where necessary, representation before the Grand Chamber.[5] The President may revoke or modify a grant of legal aid in case of a change in the circumstances underlying the previous decision.[6]

1 Rules of Court, r 91.
2 Ibid, r 92.
3 Ibid, r 93.
4 Ibid, rr 94, 95.
5 Ibid, r 91(2).
6 Ibid, r 96.

Interim measures

18.18 The chamber, or its President, may indicate to the parties interim measures which should be adopted. It may do so at the request of a party, any other concerned person or acting *proprio motu*.[1] The adoption of interim measures must be justified by the interests of the parties or the proper conduct of the proceedings. The court has construed the indication of interim measures as lacking formally binding power.[2] However, in practice, states have almost always demonstrated compliance with them.

The chamber will notify the Committee of Ministers of the interim measures it has indicated and may request information from the parties on their implementation.[3] In all urgent cases, the Registrar, acting with authorisation of the President, will inform the state party concerned as soon as possible that an application aimed to secure an object that needs urgent protection has been filed.[4]

1 Rules of Court, r 39(1).
2 *Cruz Varas v Sweden* (1991) 14 EHRR 1.
3 Rules of Court, r 39(2)–(3).
4 Ibid, r 40.

Preliminary proceedings

Initial examination by a judge rapporteur

18.19 Before reviewing the merits of an application, the court must ascertain the admissibility of the case. The initial examination of the application is undertaken by a judge rapporteur, appointed by the chamber (in inter-state cases) or the President of the section to which the case was assigned (in individual applications).[1] In cases brought before the Grand Chamber, the judge rapporteur is to be appointed by its President.[2] The judge rapporteur receives the written observations of the parties to the case and submits a report to the relevant chamber on the admissibility of the case, which must include the following information:

(a) a statement of the relevant facts;
(b) an indication of the issues arising under the Convention;
(c) a proposal on admissibility and, where needed, a provisional opinion on the merits.[3]

In cases submitted by individuals, the judge rapporteur may request the parties to offer additional information or evidence within fixed time limits. If the judge rapporteur considers the individual application to be inadmissible, he or she may decide (subject to the directions of the President of the Section) not to refer the case to a chamber, but rather to a three-judge committee.[4] In this event, the judge rapporteur will submit to the committee a report including a brief statement of the relevant facts and the reasons for his or her proposal to dismiss the case.[5]

1 Rules of Court, rr 48(1), 49(1).
2 Ibid, r 50.
3 Ibid, rr 48(2), 49(4).
4 Ibid, r 49(2).
5 Ibid, r 49(3).

Proceedings on admissibility

18.20 In inter-state cases the decision on admissibility is to be taken by the chamber designated by the President of the section to which the case was assigned. The President of the section will also invite the respondent party to submit to the Registrar written observations on the question of admissibility, which are to be communicated to the applicant for a reply in writing.[1] The chamber may request additional written observations from the parties within time limits fixed by the President of the Chamber after consulting with the parties.[2] The chamber will hold oral hearings if one or more of the parties so request, or on its own motion.[3] The chamber is then to decide the question of admissibility on the basis of the proceedings before it and the report of the judge rapporteur.[4]

In individual applications referred to a committee, the latter may declare the application inadmissible only by a unanimous vote, after considering the judge rapporteur's report (the judge rapporteur may be invited to attend the deliberations of the committee). It may adopt such a decision if it is convinced that further examination of the case is unnecessary.[5] If the committee is not unanimous that the case should be dismissed, it will refer the case to a chamber to decide the question of admissibility.[6] The chamber may strike the case out of the list of cases at once, or decide to conduct proceedings on admissibility. In this event, it may request more information from the parties and invite one or all of them to submit written observations within time limits fixed by the President of the Chamber.[7] Where appropriate, the chamber may invite the parties, at their request or on its own motion, to participate in oral hearings (which may also include reference to issues concerning the merits of the case).[8] Before deciding the motion, the chamber will consider the report of the judge rapporteur.[9]

The grounds for inadmissibility of an application to the court (from any source) are the following:
(a) failure to exhaust domestic remedies in accordance with the rules of international law;
(b) failure to submit the case within six months from the date on which the final decision of the competent domestic authorities was adopted (the six months rule).[10]

In individual applications, the court will also refuse to entertain cases for the following reasons:
(c) the application is anonymous;
(d) the application is substantially the same as one which has been examined by the court or submitted to another international investigation or settlement procedure and contains no new relevant information;
(e) the application is incompatible with the provisions of the Convention or Protocols, manifestly ill-founded or an abuse of right.[11]

A chamber decision on admissibility must provide reasons and indicate the majority by which it was rendered.[12] The court may decide in exceptional cases to join the decision on admissibility to the merits stage.[13] In cases where a finding of admissibility was reached, the court may adopt a finding of inadmissibility at any subsequent stage of the proceedings.[14]

1 Rules of Court, r 51(3).
2 Ibid, r 51(4),(6).
3 Ibid, r 51(5).
4 EHR Convention, art 29(2); Rules of Court, r 51(7).
5 EHR Convention, art 28; Rules of Court, r 53(1),(3).
6 EHR Convention, art 29(1); Rules of Court, r 53(4).
7 Rules of Court, r 52(3),(5).
8 Ibid, r 54(4).
9 Ibid, r 54(1).
10 EHR Convention, art 35(1).
11 Ibid, art 35(2),(3);
12 Rules of Court, r 56(1).
13 EHR Convention, art 29(3).
14 Ibid, art 35(4).

PROCEEDINGS

Written pleadings

18.21 After a case has been declared admissible the President of the Chamber will fix time limits and the order for the filing of written pleadings and additional evidence (in inter-state cases, after consulting with the parties).[1] In inter-state applications the President may, with the agreement of the parties, order that written pleadings will be dispensed with.[2] Claims for just satisfaction for injury are to be set out in the written observations on the merits or, if no such observations are filed, in a separate document presented within two months from the date the application was held to be admissible.[3] The claim for just satisfaction must enumerate the particulars of the damage, costs and expenses and include supporting documents.[4] The chamber may invite the parties to submit comments on the claim for just satisfaction at any stage of the proceedings.[5]

1 Rules of Court, rr 58(1), 59(1),(3).
2 Ibid, r 58(1).
3 Ibid, r 60(1).
4 Ibid, r 60(2).
5 Ibid, r 60(3).

Oral pleadings

18.22 A hearing is to take place if the chamber decides it is necessary, or if one of the parties to the case so requests. However, in cases initiated by an individual application the chamber may decide not to conduct hearings if the merits of the case have been addressed at hearings held in the admissibility stage or, in exceptional cases, where the chamber considers hearings to be unnecessary for examination of the matter.[1] Once it is decided that oral hearings will be held, the President of the Chamber is to fix the relevant procedure.[2]

In oral proceedings, the parties or their representatives may make statements to the court and summon witnesses and experts on their behalf.[3] The judges may then question the parties' representatives, witnesses and experts.[4] In addition, the representatives of the parties may question, subject to the control of the President of the Chamber, witnesses and experts introduced by the other party or by the chamber.[5]

Oral hearings before the court are public, unless, in exceptional circumstances, the court decides otherwise.[6] The court may decide to hold hearings in camera following a reasoned request of a party or any other person concerned, or of its own motion.[7] The circumstances, which the court may consider, must relate to the interests of morals, public order or national security in a democratic society, interests of juveniles, the protection of private lives or other interests of justice.[8]

1　Rules of Court, rr 58(2), 59(2).
2　Ibid, rr 58(2), 59(3).
3　Ibid, r 65(1).
4　Ibid, r 68(1).
5　Ibid, r 68(2).
6　EHR Convention, art 40(1); Rules of Court, r 33(1).
7　Rules of Court, r 33(1),(4).
8　Ibid, r 33(2).

Third party intervention

Intervention by the applicant's state of nationality

18.23　Once a case submitted by an individual applicant has been declared admissible by the court, the Registrar will notify the state of nationality of the applicant accordingly.[1] The latter is entitled to intervene in the case (if it is not the defendant), submit written comments and participate in the oral proceedings.[2] The President of the Chamber will establish detailed procedures for the intervention. The parties to the case may submit written observations on any written comments submitted by the intervening state.[3]

1　Rules of Court, r 61(1).
2　EHR Convention, art 36(1).
3　Rules of Court, r 61(2),(5).

Intervention by other entities

18.24　The President of the Court may also invite a state party (other than the applicant's state of nationality) or any person concerned with the outcome of the case to participate in the proceedings as third party intervenors (or as amicus curiae of the court), if the interest of the proper administration of justice supports such intervention.[1] NGOs and other interested natural or legal persons may submit information to the court through this procedure.[2] A third party seeking permission to intervene may submit to the court a reasoned request indicating the nature of its interest in the case within a reasonable time from the date in which the written procedure was fixed. Permission may be granted subject to conditions and time limits set by the President of the Chamber.[3] The intervening party may submit written comments, and, in exceptional cases, participate in oral hearings. As is the case with intervention by the applicant's state of nationality, the original parties to the case are entitled to respond to any comments submitted by the third party intervenor.[4]

1　EHR Convention, art 36(2).
2　See eg *Malone v UK* (1984) 7 EHRR 14.
3　Rules of Court, r 61(3),(4).
4　Ibid, r 61(5).

Multiple proceedings

18.25 The Rules of Court clearly permit the submission of applications by more than one applicant party or against more than one respondent party.[1] Furthermore, the court may order, at the request of the parties, or on its own motion, to join the consideration of two or more applications or to join hearings related to these applications.[2]

1 See eg Rules of Court, r 30(1) (appointment of common ad hoc judge to more than one applicant or respondent state party); see also rr 46, 47(1)(c).
2 Rules of Court, r 43.

LEGAL REPRESENTATION

Amicus curiae

18.26 As indicated above (para 18.24), the court may permit any person concerned with the outcome of the case (including NGOs) to intervene as amicus curiae and submit written comments to the court.[1]

1 EHR Convention, art 36(2); Rules of Court, r 61(3)–(5).

Representation of parties

18.27 States parties are to be represented by agents, who may have the assistance of advocates or counsel.[1]

Persons, non-governmental organisations or groups of individuals may initially present applications under art 34 of the EHR Convention themselves or through a representative. Such a representative for an applicant shall be an advocate authorised to practise in any of the states parties to the EHR Convention and resident in the territory of any of them, or any other person approved by the President of the Chamber.[2] An applicant must be so represented at any hearing decided on by the chamber or for the purposes of the proceedings following a decision to declare the application admissible, unless the President of the Chamber decides otherwise.[3] The President of the Chamber may, however, give leave to the applicant to present his or her own case. In exceptional circumstances, and at any stage, the President of the Chamber may direct that a representative of an applicant be replaced, where the President considers that the circumstances or the conduct of the advocate or other representative so warrant.[4]

1 Rules of Court, r 35.
2 Ibid, r 36(4)(a).
3 Ibid, r 36(3).
4 Ibid, r 36(4)(c).

Decision

18.28 The decisions of the EHR Court are issued in the form of legally binding judgments. They are to contain the following information:
(a) names of the judges of the chamber and the Registrar and Deputy Registrar;
(b) date in which judgment was adopted and delivered;
(c) description of the parties;
(d) names of the legal representatives of the parties;

(e) account of the procedure;
(f) facts of the case;
(g) summary of the parties' submissions;
(h) reasons in point of law;
(i) operative provisions;
(j) decision on costs (if one has been adopted);
(k) number of judges constituting the majority; and
(l) if necessary, a statement as to which text is authentic.[1]

Any judge on the bench may append his or her separate or dissenting opinion to the judgment.[2] The judgment is read at a public hearing and is to become available to the general public.[3]

Where just satisfaction is properly requested and raised in the proceedings, the court may include in the judgment a ruling on that matter. Just satisfaction will only be awarded if the domestic law of the state party fails to afford satisfaction to the injury suffered. Alternatively, the court may reserve its decision on remedies and order the conduct of further proceedings, preferably before the same chamber.[4] The court may encourage the parties to the judgment to negotiate a settlement on the issue of just satisfaction and the equitability of such settlement will be reviewed by the court.[5]

1   EHR Convention, art 45(1); Rules of Court, r 74(1).
2   EHR Convention, art 45(2); Rules of Court, r 74(2).
3   EHR Convention, art 44(3); Rules of Court, rr 76(1), 77(2), 78.
4   EHR Convention, art 41; Rules of Court, r 75(1),(2).
5   Rules of Court, r 75(3),(4).

Interpretation and revision of judgment

18.29 A party to a case decided by the EHR Court may request interpretation of the judgment within one year from its delivery.[1] The request must state the exact points in the operative provisions of the judgment which require interpretation. The request is to be filed with the Registrar and presented before the original chamber (or, if impossible, before the available judges of that chamber with other judges selected by the President of the Court by a draw of lots).[2] The chamber may reject the motion on the grounds that there is no reason warranting its consideration, or it may invite the other parties to the case to submit written comments within fixed time limits. If necessary, the chamber may hold oral hearings. The decision on interpretation will be rendered in the form of a new judgment.[3]

If a clerical error, error in calculation or another obvious mistake has been found in the judgment, the court on its own motion, or at the request of a party, may rectify the error. Such a request must be submitted within one month from the delivery of judgment.[4]

If a fact which might have had a decisive influence on the outcome of the case is discovered after the judgment has been rendered, any party may request the court to revise the judgment. The request must be made within six months from discovery of the new fact and will be reviewed only if that fact was unknown to the court and the requesting party at the time when the judgment was delivered and could not have reasonably been discovered then.[5] The request must:
(a) identify the judgment to be revised;
(b) contain information necessary to show the existence of the conditions of admissibility of the request for revision; and

(c) be supported by relevant documents.

The request for revision is to be filed with the Registrar and will be referred to the original chamber if possible.[6] The chamber may reject the request at once, or invite comments from the other parties and hold hearings where necessary. The final decision on the motion is to be issued in the form of a new judgment.[7]

1   Rules of Court, r 79(1).
2   Ibid, r 79(2),(3).
3   Ibid, r 79(4).
4   Ibid, r 81.
5   Ibid, r 80(1).
6   Ibid, r 80(2),(3). Here too, the President will select by lot judges to complete the composition of the original chamber, if necessary.
7   Rules of Court, r 80(4).

Appeal

18.30   A party to a case that has been decided by a seven-judge chamber may request, in exceptional circumstances, that the case be referred to the Grand Chamber. The request must be made in writing and filed with the Registry within three months from the date of delivery of the judgment.[1] It must demonstrate that the judgment raises a serious question affecting the interpretation of the Convention or Protocols or a serious issue of general importance which merits consideration by the Grand Chamber. The request is to be referred to a panel of five Grand Chamber judges. They are to examine the application on the basis of the existing case file. Reasons need not be given for the refusal of the request.[2] If the panel accepts the request, the Grand Chamber will hear the case in accordance with the ordinary procedure of the court and will render a new judgment.[3]

1   EHR Convention, art 43(1); Rules of Court, r 73(1).
2   EHR Convention, art 43(2); Rules of Court, r 73(2).
3   EHR Convention, art 43(3); Rules of Court, rr 71, 73(3).

Costs

18.31   The operational costs of the court are covered by the Council of Europe.[1] Each party to a case is responsible for costs associated with the summoning of witnesses and experts on his or her behalf and with other measures for taking evidence adopted by the court at his or her request. Nonetheless, the court may decide to allocate these costs otherwise (ie order the other party, a third party or the Council of Europe to bear them).[2] As to legal costs and other expenses, the court may award them to the applicant if a request for their reimbursement is included within the claim for just satisfaction.[3]

1   EHR Convention, art 50.
2   Rules of Court, rr 42(5), 65(3).
3   See eg *Castells v Spain* (1992) 14 EHRR 445.

Enforcement of judgments

18.32   Once final, the judgments of the court are binding upon the states parties.[1] All judgments of the Grand Chamber are final. Judgments of

ordinary chambers are final if:
(a) the parties waive the right to request referral to the Grand Chamber;
(b) no request for reference to the Grand Chamber was filed within three months from the date of delivery of the judgment; or
(c) a Grand Chamber panel has rejected the request for reference.[2]
The states parties must execute the judgment subject to supervision by the Committee of Ministers of the Council of Europe.[3]

1 EHR Convention, art 46(1).
2 Ibid, art 46(2).
3 Ibid.

REFERENCE

Sources of case law

The judgments of the EHR Court are published by the court's Registry in *Publications of the European Court of Human Rights, Judgments and Decisions.* Decisions of the former Commission were reported in a series titled *Decisions and Reports of the European Commission on Human Rights*. Recent decisions of the court can be found on the court's website.

Judgments of the court can also be found in *European Human Rights Reports* (EHRR) (European Law Centre Ltd, 1979–) and the *Yearbook of the European Convention on Human Rights*/European Commission and European Court of Human Rights (Martinus Nijhoff, 1960–) (selected decisions only).

Selected bibliography

Ralph Beddard *Human Rights and Europe*, 3rd edn (1993).

Luke Clements *European Human Rights – Taking a Case under the Convention* (1996).

P van Dijk and G H J van Hoof *Theory and Practice of the European Convention on Human Rights*, 3rd edn (1998).

J E S Fawcett *The Application of the European Convention on Human Rights*, 2nd edn (1987).

D J Harris, M O'Boyle and C Warbrick *Law of the European Convention on Human Rights* (1995).

Francis G Jacobs and Robin C A White *The European Convention on Human Rights*, 2nd edn (1996).

Mark W Janis & Richard S Kay *European Human Rights Law* (1990).

A H Robertson and J G Merrills *Human Rights in Europe – a Study of the European Convention on Human Rights* (1994).

Tom Zwart *The Admissibility of Human Rights Petitions: the Case Law of the European Commission of Human Rights and the Human Rights Committee* (1994).

ANNEX

List of states parties to the EHR Convention

Albania, Andorra, Austria, Belgium, Bulgaria, Croatia, Cyprus, Czech Republic, Denmark, Estonia, Finland, France, Georgia, Germany, Greece, Hungary, Iceland, Ireland, Italy, Latvia, Liechtenstein, Lithuania, Luxembourg, the former Yugoslav Republic of Macedonia, Malta, Moldova, Netherlands, Norway, Poland, Portugal, Romania, Russia, San Marino, Slovak Republic, Slovenia, Spain, Sweden, Switzerland, Turkey, Ukraine, United Kingdom.

CHAPTER 19

Inter-American Commission and Court of Human Rights

INTRODUCTORY

Name and seat of the court

19.1 The Inter-American Court of Human Rights ('IAHR Court' or 'the court') is a body with advisory jurisdiction to interpret human rights treaties to which member states of the Organisation of American States ('OAS') are parties and with contentious jurisdiction to establish international responsibility of states parties to the American Convention on Human Rights 1969 and to other inter-American treaties which grant jurisdiction to it. It is located in San José, Costa Rica, at:

> Inter-American Court of Human Rights
> Apdo 6906-1000
> San José
> Costa Rica
>
> Tel: (506) 234-0581 or 225-3333
> Fax: (506) 234-0584
> email: corteidh@sol.racsa.co.cr
> website: http://corteidh-oea.nu.or.cr/ci/

The Inter-American Commission on Human Rights ('IAHR Commission') is a main organ of the OAS with the mandate to promote and protect the fundamental rights of persons under the jurisdiction of OAS member states. Amongst other functions it prepares and publishes reports on the situation of human rights in particular member states, special thematic reports, and reports on individual cases that it may decide to refer to the IAHR Court for adjudication. The Commission is located in Washington DC, at:

> CIDH-OEA
> 1889 F St, NW
> Washington, DC
> USA 20006
>
> Tel: (202) 458-6002
> Fax: (202) 458-3992
> website: http://www.oas.org/

Description

19.2 The IAHR Court is the principal judicial body entrusted with monitoring and adjudicating the human rights practices of states parties to the 1969 American Convention on Human Rights,[1] which was concluded under the organisational framework of the OAS. The Convention entered into force in 1978 and the Court was officially inaugurated in 1979.

The Inter-American Commission on Human Rights operates alongside the Court. The Commission predates the Court and has been active since 1959.

Once the Commission decides to open a case regarding the alleged violation of the Declaration or the Convention it determines whether it satisfies the admissibility requirements. If it does, it places itself at the disposal of the parties to reach a friendly settlement. If there is *no* friendly solution it issues a confidential report on the merits including its conclusions on whether the Declaration and/or the Convention have been violated and issues a number of recommendations, which it sends to the state. The state has three months to comply with the recommendations. During that period either the Commission or the state may decide to refer the case to the court whenever it involves an alleged violation of the Convention by a state party that has accepted the jurisdiction of the court or is willing to accept it for the particular case.

The Court has advisory[2] and contentious[3] jurisdiction. Any member state can request an advisory opinion from it on any matter relating to human rights in the Americas. The Court has contentious jurisdiction only over the 21 states parties to the American Convention that have declared their acceptance ipso facto of the its compulsory jurisdiction. In contentious cases the Court, which is not bound to accept the facts as found by the Commission, investigates and determines whether or not the defendant state has violated the human rights of the victim or victims. If the Court finds a violation, it may decide to award reparations. To date, 32 cases have been referred to the contentious jurisdiction of the court and it has issued 15 judgments on the merits. The Commission has opened more than 12,000 cases since 1965 and has issued nearly 600 reports on individual cases.

1 American Convention on Human Rights, 22 November 1969, OASTS 36; OAS Off Rec OEA/Ser L/V/II 23, doc 21, rev 6 (1979); reprinted in 9 ILM 673 (1970) ('American HR Convention').
2 Ibid, art 64.
3 Ibid, art 62.

INSTITUTIONAL ASPECTS

Governing texts

19.3 The principal text governing the structure, role and powers of the IAHR Court is Chapter VIII of the American Convention on Human Rights. The Convention establishes the court, determines its composition and jurisdiction and outlines its procedure. Other more specific rules regulating the operation of the court can be found in the following instruments:

• Statute of the Inter-American Court on Human Rights ('the Statute');[1]
• Rules of Procedure of the Inter-American Court on Human Rights ('Rules of Procedure').[2]

The IAHR Commission has its own Statute and Regulations.[3]

1 Statute of the Inter-American Court on Human Rights, OAS Res 448 (IX-O/79), OAS Official Records OEA/Ser P/IX.0.2/80, Vol 1, at 98 ('IAHR Court Statute').
2 Rules of Procedure of the Inter-American Court on Human Rights, Annual Report of the

Inter-American Court of Human Rights, 1991, OAS Doc OEA/Ser L/V/III 25 doc 7 at 18 (1992) ('IAHR Court Rules of Procedure'). The 1996 Rules of Procedure, which came into effect on 1 January 1997 replaced the previous version of the Rules that were adopted in 1992.

3 Statute of the Inter-American Commission on Human Rights, OAS Res 447 (IX), OAS Official Records OEA/Ser P/IX.0.2/80, Vol 1 ('IAHR Commission Statute') available on website: http://www1.umn.edu/humanrts/iachr/iachr.html; Regulations of the Inter-American Commission on Human Rights, OAS Official Records OAS/Ser L V/II, doc 31, rev 3 ('IAHR Commission Regulations').

Substantive law

19.4 The substantive law to be applied by the IAHR Court, when exercising its contentious jurisdiction, is to be found in Part I of the American Convention on Human Rights, its Protocols, the Inter-American Convention to Prevent and Punish Torture and the Inter-American Convention on Forced Disappearance of Persons.[1] When exercising its advisory competence, the court may interpret any other human rights treaties that the OAS member state is party to.[2] The IAHR Commission may also review complaints involving the human rights practices of OAS member states that are not parties to the American Convention on Human Rights.[3] In cases brought against such states, the Commission applies the American Declaration of the Rights and Duties of Man, which is considered to be part of the definition of human rights included in the OAS Charter and therefore binding on member states by reference to it.[4]

1 Additional Protocol to the American Convention on Human Rights in the area of Economic, Social and Cultural Rights, 7 November 1988, art 8(a) (not yet in force), arts 13, 19(6), OAS Official Records OAS/Ser L V/II 92, doc 31 rev 3; Inter-American Convention on Forced Disappearance of Persons, 9 June 1994, 33 ILM 1529 (1994).
2 American HR Convention, art 64(1).
3 IAHR Commission Statute, art 20.
4 American Declaration of the Rights and Duties of Man, OAS Res XXX, adopted by the Ninth International Conference of American States (1948), reprinted in Basic Documents Pertaining to Human Rights in the Inter-American System, OEA/Ser L V/II 82 doc 6 rev 1 at 17 (1992). The Commission must give particular attention to arts 1–4, 18, 25, 26 of the Declaration: IAHR Commission Statute, art 20(a). See also Advisory Opinion OC-10 of the IAHR Court.

Organisation

Composition

19.5 The IAHR Court comprises seven judges, who are nationals of different OAS states (not necessarily states which are parties to the Convention).[1] They are elected by the states parties to the American Convention on Human Rights for a renewable six-year term.[2] Judges should be jurists of the highest moral authority, of recognised competence in the area of human rights, and must have the required qualifications for service in the highest judicial office of their state of nationality (or in the state that proposed them as candidates). In the event that a state party to a case does not have a judge of its nationality on the bench, it may appoint an ad hoc judge.[3]

The court elects a President and Vice-President for a renewable two-year term.[4]

1 American HR Convention, art 52; IAHR Court Statute, art 4. The current composition of the court is:
    President: Hernán Salgado Pesantes (Ecuador). **Vice President:** Antonio A Candado Trindade (Brazil). **Judges:** Carlos Vicente de Roux Rengifo (Colombia); Sergio Garcia

Ramirez (Mexico); Máximo-Pacheco Gomez (Chile); Oliver Jackman (Barbados) and
Alirio Abreu-Burelli (Venezuela).
2   American HR Convention, arts 53, 54; IAHR Court Statute, arts 5(1), 7.
3   Ibid, art 55; IAHR Court Statute, art 10; IAHR Court Rules of Procedure, art 18.
4   IAHR Court Statute, art 12; IAHR Court Rules of Procedure, art 3.

IAHR COMMISSION

19.6   The Commission comprises seven members of high moral character and
recognised competence in the field of human rights.[1] They are elected by the
member states of the OAS for a term of four years, which is renewable once.[2]
No two commissioners can be of the same nationality.[3] The Commission elects
a Chairman and two Vice-Chairmen for one-year terms (renewable once every
four-year period).[4]

1   American HR Convention, art 34; IAHR Commission Statute, art 2. The current membership
    of the Commission is:
    Chairman: Professor Robert Ko god Goldman. **First Vice-Chairman:** Dr Helio Bicudo.
    Second Vice-Chairman: Claudio Grossman; **Commissioners:** Dr Alvaro Tirado Mejía;
    Dr Jean Joseph Exumé; Sir Henry Forde; Professor Carlos Manuel Ayala Corao. As from
    1 January 2000 Marta Altoleguirre, Julio Prado Vallejo and Juan E Mendez will replace
    Tirado Mejía, J J Exumé and Ayala Corao.
2   American HR Convention, arts 36, 37; IAHR Commission Statute, arts 3, 6.
3   American HR Convention, art 37(2); IAHR Commission Statute, art 7.
4   IAHR Commission Statute, art 14; IAHR Commission Regulations, arts 6, 8.

DISQUALIFICATION OF JUDGES

19.7   Judges cannot sit in a case pending before the court if they (or their
family members) have direct interest in it, or had previously taken part in it
(as lawyers, members of a dispute settlement body or in any other capacity).[1]
If the judge in question refuses to withdraw from the case, the court may
decide to disqualify him or her.[2] In the event that a judge has become unfit to
serve (ie if he or she takes certain positions in a domestic executive branch or
in an international organisation, or is in a situation that might prevent him or
her from discharging a judge's official functions, or that might affect his or her
independence or impartiality or the dignity or prestige of the office), the court
can decide to remove the judge from a specific case and recommend to the
General Assembly of the OAS Assembly of the States Parties to remove that
judge from office.[3]

Similarly, members of the Commission who fail to fulfil the duties of their
office or engage in functions which are incompatible with their service in the
Commission may be removed from office by the General Assembly of the
OAS, acting upon the recommendation of five other Commission members.[4]

1   IAHR Court Statute, art 19(1),(3). The President, acting on his or her own initiative, or on a
    motion of a party, may advise a judge to disqualify himself or herself for the above reasons
    or for some other pertinent reason: IAHR Court Rules of Procedure, art 19.
2   IAHR Court Statute, art 19(2),(3).
3   American HR Convention, art 73; IAHR Court Statute, art 18.
4   American HR Convention, art 73; IAHR Commission Statute, arts 8, 10; IAHR Commission
    Regulations, art 4.

Plenary/chambers

19.8   The IAHR Court sits in plenary. The quorum for deliberation consists
of five judges.[1] The Commission also decides in plenary (quorum of four

members), although it may conduct some preparatory parts of its work in working groups of not more than three members.[2]

1   IAHR Court Statute, art 21(1); IAHR Court Rules of Procedure, art 13.
2   IAHR Commission Statute, art 17; IAHR Commission Regulations, arts 17, 18.

Appellate structure

19.9   The inter-American human rights system does not have an appellate structure and decisions of the Court are final and binding.[1] However, a case dealt with by the Commission may be brought by a dissatisfied state party to the Court for additional review.

1   American HR Convention, art 67.

Technical/scientific experts

19.10   The court may hear, on its own motion, any evidence it considers helpful. This includes obtaining the opinion of an expert witness or any other relevant entity.[1] A party who believes that the expert appointed by the court (or his or her family member) has a direct interest in the outcome of the case, or was previously involved in the dispute in any capacity, may ask for the expert to be disqualified within 15 days from his or her appointment.[2] The court will rule on the challenge. The court can also allow the parties to introduce expert witnesses on their behalf.[3] In that case, the other party may object to the qualifications of the expert before testimony is given.[4]

1   IAHR Court Rules of Procedure, art 44(1),(3).
2   Ibid, art 49.
3   Ibid, arts 44(2), 46.
4   Ibid, art 48.

Secretariat

19.11   The administrative needs of the court are served by the Secretariat of the Court headed by a Secretary.[1] The court elects the Secretary for a renewable five-year term,[2] and the rest of the staff of the Secretariat is appointed by the Secretary-General of the OAS, in consultation with the Secretary of the Court. The Secretary is responsible, inter alia, for communicating the decisions of the court; taking minutes at its meetings; dealing with the correspondence of the court; directing the administration of the court (in pursuance of the instructions of the President); preparing draft rules, programmes and budget; and supervising the work of the court staff.[3]

The IAHR Commission receives secretarial services from a special unit in the General Secretariat of OAS, headed by an Executive Secretary.[4] The Secretariat of the Commission is responsible, inter alia, for preparing draft reports and resolutions; distributing documents among the members of the Commission; receiving petitions; requesting information from governments; and assisting the Commission in the performance of its functions.[5]

1   American HR Convention, art 59; IAHR Court Statute, art 14. The current Secretary of the Court is Manuel E Ventura Robles (Costa Rica).
2   IAHR Court Rules of Procedure, art 7.
3   Ibid, art 10.
4   American HR Convention, art 40; IAHR Commission Statute, art 21.
5   IAHR Commission Regulations, arts 13, 14.

Jurisdiction (including admissibility)

Ratione personae

IAHR COMMISSION

19.12   Any person, group of persons or NGO (recognised under the laws of at least one member state of the OAS) may submit a petition to the Commission alleging a violation of the American Convention on Human Rights by a state party.[1] Any state party may accept, by way of a declaration, the competence of the Commission to receive claims against it from another member state.[2] Such declarations (submitted under art 45(1) of the Convention) may be unrestricted, or for limited period, or a specific case. In any event, only states that have also made declarations under art 45(1) may bring communications to the Commission.[3] Persons, groups of persons and NGOs may also present to the Commission communications against OAS member states not parties to the Convention, alleging violation of fundamental human rights.[4] Only complaints brought against state parties to the Convention have the option of being subsequently forwarded to the Court.

1   American HR Convention, art 44.
2   Ibid, art 45.
3   Ibid, art 45(2).
4   IAHR Commission Statute, art 20.

IAHR COURT

19.13   The IAHR Court has jurisdiction over claims against states that have accepted its jurisdiction. Consent to the jurisdiction of the court can be expressed through a general declaration of acceptance ipso facto of jurisdiction, pursuant to art 62(1) of the Convention or through ad hoc declarations or a special agreement.[1] As mentioned above, 19 states parties to the Convention have made general declarations accepting the court's jurisdiction.

Only states parties and the Commission may bring a case before the court.[2] Where declarations of acceptance of jurisdiction under art 62(1) require reciprocity, only states that have also made a declaration under the same article may present a claim against the respondent state.

Petitioners and/or representatives of the victims assist the Commission in the filing and litigation of a case before the court. In practice, they participate in the preparation of briefs and the delivery of some of the oral arguments on the merits.[3] In the reparation stage they have standing to present their own arguments and evidence.[4]

1   American HR Convention, art 62.
2   Ibid, art 61.
3   IAHR Court Rules of Procedure, art 22(2).
4   Ibid, art 23.

Ratione materiae

19.14   The IAHR Court and Commission are competent to address all questions concerning the alleged violation or the interpretation and application of the human rights enumerated in the American Human Rights Convention and some relevant provisions found in the Protocols thereto, the Inter-American Convention to Prevent and Punish Torture, the Inter-American Convention on Forced Disappearance of Persons and, only in the case of the Commission, the Inter-American Convention for the Eradication of Violence against Women.[1] With regard to OAS member states not parties to the American Convention, the IAHR Commission may review the observation of fundamental human rights standards, under general international law, with particular reference to the American Declaration of the Rights and Duties of Man.[2]

1 American HR Convention, arts 44, 45(1), 62(3); Economic, Social and Cultural Rights Protocol, art 19(6); Inter-American Convention On Forced Disappearance of Persons, 9 June 1994, art XIII.
2 IAHR Commission Statute, art 20.

Admissibility [1]

IAHR COMMISSION

19.15 The Commission may admit cases under the Convention only if the following conditions have been met:
(a) the individual whose rights have been violated has exhausted the remedies existing under domestic law of the state concerned, in accordance with international law (except in cases where the defendant state failed to observe due process in its domestic procedures; prevented the exhaustion of remedies; or if there has been unwarranted delay in providing a final judgment under domestic procedures);
(b) the petition has been lodged within six months from the date the individual whose rights had been violated has been notified of the final judgment in his or her case;
(c) the petition or inter-state communication is not pending before another international dispute settlement procedure.[2]
(d) the alleged violation is attributable or imputable to the state.

1 See also para 19.24 below.
2 American HR Convention, art 46. It is also necessary that the alleged violation took place at a time when the Convention (or relevant Protocol) was in force with respect to the state concerned.

IAHR COURT

19.16 The IAHR Court can receive cases only after proceedings at the Commission have failed to yield an appropriate result.[1]

1 American HR Convention, art 61(2). See eg *In the Matter of Viviana Gallardo*, No G 101/81, Decision of 13 November 1981 and Decision of 8 September 1983, I/A Court HR, Ser A (1984), reprinted in (1981) 2 Human Rights Law Journal 108, and in (1984) 5 Human Rights Law Journal 77 (involving rejection by the court of an attempt of a state accused of a human rights violation to bring a case on its own initiative directly to the court).

Advisory jurisdiction

19.17 The IAHR Court may render non-binding advisory opinions at the request of any OAS member state (including, inter alia, on the compatibility of domestic legislation with the Convention), or an authorised OAS organ, within the scope of its competence.[1] The subject matter of such an opinion can encompass the interpretation of the American Convention on Human Rights and other human rights treaties applicable in the territory of the member states to the OAS.

The request for an advisory opinion should specify with precision the question on which the opinion of the court is sought; the considerations giving rise to the request; and names and addresses of representatives.[2] Requests submitted by OAS organs other than the Commission must also specify the relation between the question and their sphere of competence. If the request pertains to a treaty other than the American Convention on Human Rights, the request should also include the name of the treaty and a list of parties thereto.[3] Where the compatibility of domestic legislation with the Convention is at issue, the request should refer to the provisions of the law to which the advisory opinion should relate and a copy of the legislation must be attached to the request.[4]

Upon initiation of advisory proceedings, the Secretary will send copies of the request to all OAS member states, the Commission, the Secretary-General of OAS and all relevant OAS organs. The President will fix time limits for submission of written observations[5] and the court will decide whether to hold oral proceedings on the request. The advisory opinion will be delivered in a manner similar to the delivery of judgment.[6] The opinion will include the following information:

(a) names of judges who participated in the opinion and the Secretary and Deputy Secretary;
(b) issues presented to the court;
(c) description of the steps in proceedings;
(d) the legal arguments;
(e) the opinion of the court;
(f) statement indicating which text is authentic.[7]

Dissenting or separate opinions may be published in addition to the opinion of the majority.[8] To date, some 15 advisory opinions have been rendered by the court.

1   American Convention, art 64.
2   IAHR Court Rules of Procedure, art 59.
3   Ibid, art 60(1).
4   Ibid, art 61.
5   Ibid, art 62.
6   Ibid, art 64(1).
7   Ibid, art 64(2).
8   Ibid, art 64(3).

PROCEDURAL ASPECTS

Languages

19.18   The official languages of the Court, Commission and the OAS are Spanish, English, French and Portuguese.[1] The Court and Commission may select any of the official languages to be its working language (or languages).[2] The working languages are English and Spanish. However, the court may replace the working language for each specific case with the language of one of the parties to the case (provided that it is also an official language). In cases where a person appearing before the court is not fluent in the working language, the court can authorise him or her to use another language and it will arrange for a translator and interpreter.[3]

1   IAHR Court Rules of Procedure, art 20(1); IAHR Commission Regulations, art 25(1).
2   IAHR Court Rules of Procedure, art 20(2); IAHR Commission Regulations, art 25(1). The court's decision is to be reviewed each year and the Commission's every two years.
3   IAHR Court Rules of Procedure, art 20(4).

Instituting proceedings

IAHR Commission

19.19 Petitions to the Commission are to be made in writing and are to include the following information:

(a) name, nationality, profession or occupation, postal address or domicile and signature of the petitioner (in cases presented by an NGO – the name and signature of its representatives);

(b) account of the act or situation which is denounced, specifying place and date of the alleged violation, and, if possible, name of victims and any officials that might have appraised the act or situation;

(c) indication of the state responsible by act or omission for a violation of a human right protected under the American Convention on Human Rights (it is not necessary to cite a specific article);

(d) whether domestic remedies have been exhausted or it has been impossible to exhaust them.[1]

The Secretariat or the Commission may ask the petitioner to complete any information omitted from its petition.[2] If the Commission finds the petition prima facie admissible it will require the government concerned to provide information on the case within 90 days (which may be extended by the Commission to not more than 180 days).[3] In urgent cases, the Commission will ask the government concerned to provide it with information in the promptest manner.[4]

1 IAHR Commission Regulations, art 32.
2 Ibid, arts 30, 33.
3 Ibid, art 34(1),(5),(6).
4 Ibid, art 34(2).

IAHR Court

19.20 A case is brought before the IAHR Court by a written application prepared in all of the working languages.[1] The application will contain the following information:

(a) names of parties to the case;

(b) purpose of the application;

(c) statement of the facts;

(d) supporting evidence and the facts they bear upon;

(e) particulars of witnesses and expert witnesses;

(f) legal arguments;

(g) conclusions reached; and

(h) names of agents and delegates.[2]

Applications presented by the Commission shall also include a copy of the Commission's report.

After a preliminary review of the application, the President may instruct the applicant to correct deficiencies in the application within 20 days.[3] The Secretary will forward a notice of the application to the judges of the court, the respondent state, the Commission (if it is not the applicant), the victim or his or her next of kin and the original claimant (if other than the victim; and if their identity is known).[4] The fact that an application has been filed will also be communicated to the states parties

to the Convention and the Secretary-General of the OAS.
The respondent state will have four months to reply to the application.[5]

1 IAHR Court Rules of Procedure, art 32. In the event that a party submits the application only in one of the working languages, it must provide translated copies in the other official languages within 30 days from the date of filing of the original application.
2 IAHR Court Rules of Procedure, art 33.
3 Ibid, art 34.
4 Ibid, art 35.
5 Ibid, art 37.

Financial assistance

19.21   There is no programme of financial assistance under the framework of the American Human Rights system.

Precautionary and provisional measures

IAHR Commission

19.22   In urgent cases, when irreparable harm to persons is likely, the Commission may request the concerned government to take provisional precautionary measures until it is decided whether the facts alleged in the petition or communication are true.[1] The decision to request such measures is to be taken by the Commission as a whole or, when it is not in session, by the Chairman, after consulting with the other members of the Commission.[2]

1 IAHR Commission Regulations, art 29(2).
2 Ibid, art 29(3).

IAHR Court

19.23   The court is authorised to order provisional measures in cases of extreme gravity and urgency, if such measures are necessary to avoid irreparable harm to persons.[1] The court may order measures at the request of a party, at the request of the Commission (in matters not yet submitted to the court), or acting on its own initiative.[2] The request is to be submitted by any means of communication to any judge or to the Secretariat, and transmitted to the President. The latter (after consulting with some or all of the judges) may call upon the government concerned to adopt the necessary temporary measures to ensure the effectiveness of any order that the court may issue at a later date in pursuance of the request for provisional measures.[3]

1 American HR Convention, art 63(2); IAHR Court Rules of Procedure, art 25(1).
2 American HR Convention, art 63(2); IAHR Court Rules of Procedure, art 25(1),(2).
3 IAHR Court Rules of Procedure, art 25(3),(4).

Preliminary questions

IAHR Commission

19.24   Before reviewing the merits of a petition or inter-state communication, the Commission considers first the admissibility of the complaint. The following questions are considered:
(a) whether domestic remedies have been exhausted and, if not, whether there are grounds to exempt the petition from this requirement;[1]

(b) whether the deadline for presentation of a petition (six months after the conclusion of domestic proceedings) has elapsed;[2]

(c) whether the petition is also pending before another international settlement procedure to which the state complained against is subject, or constitutes a duplication of a petition pending or settled in the past by the Commission or another international organisation;[3]

(d) whether there are other grounds for inadmissibility; and

(e) whether grounds for the petition exist or subsist.[4]

The Commission may or may not issue a preliminary decision on admissibility. In some cases it issues a single report including findings on both admissibility and merits.

1   IAHR Commission Regulations, arts 35(a), 37.
2   Ibid, art 38. Where no prompt and effective domestic remedies are available, the Commission will verify whether the petition has been filed within reasonable time under the circumstances of the case.
3   IAHR Commission Regulations, art 39.
4   Ibid, art 35(b),(c).

IAHR Court

19.25   Within two months from the date of the application, a party to a case may file a preliminary objection to the admissibility of the case or to the jurisdiction of the court.[1] The objection should include the following information:

(a) facts on which the objection is based;

(b) legal arguments;

(c) conclusions reached;

(d) supporting documents;

(e) any evidence professed.[2]

The other party may present a brief responding to the objections to the court's jurisdiction within 30 days.[3] The filing of preliminary objections does not suspend the proceedings on the merits. The parties may request or the court may convene a hearing on the objection and decide upon it.[4]

As indicated above, a party to a case may request the disqualification of a judge. Such a request must be filed with the court before the first hearing of the case, or, if the relevant facts become known subsequently, at the first possible opportunity.[5]

1   IAHR Court Rules of Procedure, art 36(1).
2   Ibid, art 36(2).
3   Ibid, art 36(5).
4   Ibid, art 36(4),(6).
5   Ibid, art 19.

Written pleadings

IAHR Commission

19.26   After receiving the response of the government accused of violation of the Convention, the Commission will forward pertinent parts of that response to the petitioner and allow him or her 30 days to comment in writing and submit relevant evidence pertaining to the position of the government in question.[1] The government will then be given 30 days to respond to the comments and evidence of the petitioner. During hearings on the merits, the

Commission may receive further written statements from the parties.[2] In practice, the processing and requests for information extend for as long as the Commission considers pertinent.

1 IAHR Commission Regulations, art 34(7).
2 Ibid, art 43(2).

IAHR Court

19.27 Within four months from receiving the application, the respondent shall provide an answer in writing to the application.[1] The answer will address the same issues as the application and will be prepared in a similar format. The parties may request the President of the Court, at any time before the opening of the oral proceedings, to allow them to present additional written pleadings. The President may permit such pleadings and fix time limits for their presentation.[2]

1 IAHR Court Rules of Procedure, art 37.
2 Ibid, art 38.

Oral arguments

IAHR Commission

19.28 The Commission may request the representatives of the state concerned to provide it with information on the complaint at the regularly scheduled biannual hearings or at an extraordinary session, if deemed necessary. In addition, any of the parties may request a formal oral hearing on the case.[1]

1 IAHR Commission Regulations, art 43(2).

IAHR Court

19.29 The President of the IAHR Court will call oral hearings if necessary, and prescribe the order of the presentations.[1] The judges may question all persons appearing before the court. In addition, the representatives of the parties (including the Commission in cases other than those brought by it) and the representatives of the alleged victim may question any witness, expert or other person that the court decides to hear.[2] Such questioning is subject to the control of the President of the Court (although the court can overrule him or her on some issues). Minutes of the hearing are taken and distributed to the parties (relevant parts of the minutes are also made available to other persons appearing before the court).[3] The hearings of the court are public, unless the court decides otherwise due to exceptional circumstances.[4]

1 IAHR Court Rules of Procedure, arts 39, 40.
2 Ibid, art 41.
3 Ibid, art 43.
4 IAHR Court Statute, art 24(1).

Third-party intervention/multiple proceedings

19.30 There is no explicit provision for intervention in any of instruments governing the operation of the IAHR Court or Commission. As to multiple proceedings, there is no bar against the bringing of a complaint on behalf of more than one person and/or state to the Commission or to the court (provided that jurisdictional conditions have been met). Furthermore, the Commission may combine and process petitions dealing with the same facts and persons in a single file,[1] and the court may order the joinder of inter-related cases.[2]

1 IAHR Commission Regulations, art 40(2).
2 IAHR Court Rules of Procedure, art 28.

Amicus curiae

19.31 Although there is no explicit provision in the various instruments governing the work of the court addressing the admissibility of amicus curiae briefs,[1] amici curiae have been particularly relevant to the court in the exercise of its advisory jurisdiction, and the court has developed a practice of receiving amicus curiae briefs relating to contentious cases.

1 IAHR Court Rules of Procedure, art 44(1),(3).

Representation of parties

19.32 States parties to come before the court are to be represented by an agent, who may be assisted by any persons of his choice.[1]

The Commission shall be represented by the delegates it has designated, who may be assisted by any persons of their choice, who may include the original claimant or the representatives of victims or their next of kin.[2]

At the reparation stage of proceedings, the representatives of the victims or of their next of kin may independently submit their own arguments and evidence.[3]

1 IAHR Court Rules of Procedure, art 21.
2 Ibid, art 22.
3 Ibid, art 23.

Decision

IAHR Commission

19.33 The Commission issues a report on the merits including its conclusions of fact and law and determination on whether the Declaration, the Convention or another instrument has been violated.[1] In that case it issues a number of recommendations. In the case of OAS member states the examination of the case concludes with the publication of this report together with an assessment of whether the state has complied with the recommendations. In the case of states parties the decision on the merits – known as an 'Article 50 Report' – is transmitted to the state, which has three months to implement the recommendations and inform the Commission. In the case of states parties that have accepted or are willing to accept the jurisdiction of the court, the Commission may – during this period – refer the case for adjudication. If the case has not been referred to the court, the Commission publishes a final decision – known as an 'Article 51 Report' – in its Annual Report to the General Assembly of the OAS.

The court has declared that states parties to the American Convention have the obligation to make every effort to apply the recommendations of a protection organ such as the Commission.[2]

1   American HR Convention, art 50(1); IAHR Commission Regulations, art 46(2).
2   *Loayza Tamayo Case*, judgment of 17 September 1997, para 80 (IAHR Ct).

IAHR Court

19.34   The final decision of the court on the dispute before it is issued in the form of a judgment. A judgment must include the following particulars:

(a)   the names of judges who participated in the judgment and the Secretary and Deputy Secretary;
(b)   the identity of parties and their representatives (including representatives of the victim);
(c)   a description of the steps in proceedings;
(d)   the facts of the case;
(e)   the conclusions of the parties;
(f)   the legal arguments;
(g)   the ruling of the court;
(h)   the decision, if any, on costs;
(i)   the result of the voting;
(j)   a statement indicating which text is authentic.[1]

The judgment is decided by a majority of the judges.[2] Judges may append to the judgment dissenting or separate opinions.[3] If a violation of the Convention was found, the court will order the respondent state to take measures so that the injured party be ensured the enjoyment of the rights or freedoms which were violated.[4] In appropriate case, where the judgment failed to address the question of reparations, the court will set time limits and procedure for proceedings aimed at securing a separate judgment on the question of reparations to the injured party.[5] If the parties have reached an agreement on reparations, the court is to verify the fairness of the agreement.[6]

1   IAHR Court Rules of Procedure, art 55(1).
2   IAHR Court Statute, art 23(2).
3   IAHR Court Rules of Procedure, art 55(2).
4   American HR Convention, art 63(1).
5   IAHR Court Rules of Procedure, art 56(1).
6   Ibid, art 56(2).

Interpretation and revision of judgments

19.35   In the event of disagreement over the meaning or scope of the judgment, any party to a case may request the court to interpret it.[1] The request must be filed with the secretariat within 90 days from the date of notification of the judgment and will state with precision the issues which require interpretation.[2] The Secretary will transmit the request to the states parties to the case and the Commission and invite them to submit written comments within a time limit fixed by the President of the Court.[3] The court (preferably at the same composition that rendered the original judgment) will determine what procedure to take on the request and will deliver interpretation of the request in the form of a judgment.[4] The Convention and other relevant instruments do not address the possibility of a revision of the judgment.

1   American HR Convention, art 67.
2   Ibid, art 67; IAHR Court Rules of Procedure, art 58(1).

3 IAHR Court Rules of Procedure, art 58(2).
4 Ibid, art 58(3),(5).

Appeal

19.36 There is no appeal over judgments of the IAHR Court. The judgments are final and binding.[1]

1 American HR Convention, art 67.

Costs

19.37 Proceedings before the Court and Commission are free of charge for the parties. They will normally bear their own expenses, including the cost of production of evidence they request.[1] The court may determine an amount to cover expenses incurred before both the domestic courts and the organs of the Inter-American system by the victims, as well as attorney's fees.[2]

1 IAHR Court Rules of Procedure, art 45.
2 Ibid, art 55(1)(h).

Enforcement of judgments

19.38 The states parties participating in a case before the IAHR Court must comply with its judgment.[1] In the event that the court awards damages against a state party, this part of the judgment may be enforced in the state concerned by the same domestic procedures governing the execution of judgments against the state.[2] The reports of the Commission are not formally binding and, as a result, cannot be enforced.

1 American HR Convention, art 68(1).
2 Ibid, art 68(2).

REFERENCE

Case reports

Judgments of the IAHR Court are published in a series titled *Inter-American Court of Human Rights Reports* and are available on the internet.

Reports of the Commission can be found in the annual reports of the Commission and in two commercial publications: the *Inter-American Yearbook on Human Rights* (Martinus Nihoff, 1992–98) and Buergenthal & Norris's *Human Rights: The Inter-American System*.

Selected bibliography

Books

Association of the Bar of the City of New York *The Inter-American Commission on Human Rights: a promise unfulfilled* – a report by the Committee on International Human Rights (1993).

Thomas Buergenthal et al *Protecting Human Rights in the Americas: Selected Problems*, 3rd edn (1990).

Scott Davidson *The Inter-American Human Rights System* (1997).

David J Harris & Stephen Livingstone (eds) *The Inter-American System of Human Rights* (1998).

Richard B Lillich *International Human Rights: Problems of Law, Policy and Practice*, 2nd edn (1991).

Frank Newman & David Weissbrodt *International Human Rights: Law, Policy and Process* (1990).

Articles

Thomas Buergenthal 'The Inter-American Court of Human Rights' (1982) 76 American Journal of International Law 231.

Claudio Grossman 'Proposals to Strengthen the Inter-American System of Human Rights' 32 German Year Book of International Law 264 at 274.

C Medina 'The Inter-American Commission on Human Rights and the Inter-American Court of Human Rights: Reflections on a Joint Venture' (1990) 12 Human Rights Quarterly 439.

Juan E Mendez & José Migual Vivanco 'Disappearances and the Inter-American Court: Reflections on a Litigation Experience' (1990) 13 Hamline Law Review 507.

Robert E Norris 'Bringing Human Rights Petitions Before the Inter-American Commission' (1980) 20 Santa Clara Law Review 733.

David J Padilla 'The Inter-American Commission on Human Rights of the Organisation of American States: A Case Study' (1993) 9 American University Journal of International Law and Policy 95.

Dinah Shelton 'Improving Human Rights Protections: Recommendations for Enhancing the Effectiveness of the Inter-American Commission and Inter-American Court of Human Rights' (1988) 3 American University Journal of International Law and Policy 323 at 332.

Manuel D Vargas 'Individual Access to the Inter-American Court of Human Rights' (1984) 16 New York University Journal of International Law and Politics 601.

William M Walker 'A Litigator's Look at the Inter-American Commission on Human Rights' (1993) 2 ACLU International Civil Liberties Report 38.

J Lauchlan Wash et al 'Conference Report, The Inter-American Human Rights System: Into the 1990s and Beyond' (1988) 3 American University Journal of International Law and Policy 517 at 551–556.

ANNEX

List of states parties to the American Convention on Human Rights[+]

Argentina;* Barbados; Bolivia;* Brazil;* Chile;* Colombia;* Costa Rica;* Dominica; Dominican Republic;* Ecuador;* El Salvador;* Grenada;

Guatemala;* Haiti; Honduras;* Jamaica; Mexico;* Nicaragua;* Panama;* Paraguay;* Peru;‡ Suriname;* Uruguay;* Venezuela.*

† Trinidad and Tobago have withdrawn from the American Convention, effective 26 May 1999.
* States that recognise the competence of the IAHR Court.
‡ Peru has recently announced its intention to withdraw its recognition of the competence of the IAHR Court.

OAS member states not parties to the American Convention on Human Rights

Antigua and Barbuda, Bahamas, Belize, Canada, Cuba, Guyana, Saint Lucia, Saint Vincent and the Grenadines, St Kitts and Nevis, Trinidad and Tobago, United States of America.

CHAPTER 20

African Commission and Court on Human and Peoples' Rights

INTRODUCTORY

Name and seat of the body

20.1   The African Commission on Human and Peoples' Rights ('Commission') is an expert body intended to ensure compliance with the African Charter on Human and Peoples' Rights ('African Charter').[1] The headquarters of the Commission are at:

> African Commission on Human and Peoples' Rights
> Kairaba Avenue
> PO Box 673
> Banjul
> The Gambia
>
> Tel: 220 392962
> Fax: 220 390764
> email: achpr@achpr.gm

The Commission does not yet have a website but instruments related to its work can be found on <http://www.oau-oua.org/oau-info/commis.htm>.

Sessions of the Commission are alternated between Banjul and other venues offered by different states parties to the Charter. The African Court on Human and Peoples' Rights has not yet been established.

1   African Charter on Human and People's Rights, 27 June 1981, OAU Doc CAB/LEG/67/3 Rev 5, 21 ILM 58 (1982) ('African HR Charter').

Description

20.2   The African Commission was established under art 30 of the 1981 African Charter and began its operation in November 1987. It has certain supervisory powers over all 53 states parties to the African Charter. The Commission functions under the institutional framework of the Organisation of African Unity.

The Commission's task is to promote and ensure respect for human rights in Africa. It disseminates information on human rights in Africa (inter alia, through sponsoring research and conferences);[1] and receives periodic reports from the states parties to the African Charter on measures taken to give effect to the human rights obligations prescribed thereby.[2] Furthermore, the Commission is authorised to receive communications from state and non-state actors alleging violation of the human rights guaranteed by the African

Charter. The procedure for handling communications involves investigation by the Commission of the factual claims of the parties and the issue of recommendations on the merits, in the form of observations or a report. Where a case brought by a person or entity other than a state party alleges the existence of a series of serious and massive violations of human and peoples' rights or an emergency, an in-depth study (involving active investigation on the part of the Commission) can be undertaken with the approval of the Assembly of Heads of State and Government of the OAU (Assembly). An in-depth study will also lead to the writing of a report. The observations or reports of the Commission are not binding upon the states parties.

Since its establishment, the Commission has received more than 200 communications from individuals and NGOs. The inter-state communication procedure before the Commission has been hardly used, although the Commission has recently received a complaint by the Democratic Republic of the Congo (DRC) against Rwanda and Uganda. By the end of 1997, the Commission had considered some 25 applications on their merits, and the rest of the communications were either still pending, declared inadmissible, or voluntarily withdrawn.

In June 1998, the member states of the OAU adopted a Protocol on the establishment of a Court of Human and Peoples' Rights ('Protocol on the Court').[3] The Court will become operative only after the Protocol enters into force – still some time in the future.

1 African HR Charter, art 45(1)(a).
2 Ibid, art 62.
3 Protocol to the African Charter on Human and Peoples' Rights on the Establishment of an African Court of Human and Peoples' Rights, June 1998 (not in force) ('Court Protocol'). To date, two states have ratified the Protocol.

INSTITUTIONAL ASPECTS

Governing texts

20.3 The principal text governing the composition, mandate and procedure of the African Commission is Part II of the African Charter. Other provisions regulating the work of the Commission are to be found in the Rules of Procedure of the Commission.[1] The operation of the African Court will be governed by the Protocol on the Court and by Rules of Procedure, which will be adopted by the court.[2]

1 Rules of Procedure of the African Commission on Human and Peoples' Rights, ACHPR/ RP/XIX, 19th Ordinary Session, 26 March–4 April 1996, Ouagadougou, Burkina Faso.
2 Court Protocol, art 33.

Substantive law

20.4 When handling communications, the Commission reviews compliance of states with the provisions of the African Charter. In construing the Charter, the Commission is instructed to draw inspiration from other sources of international human rights law including, inter alia, the Charters of the UN and the OAU, the Universal Declaration of Human Rights, and also African, UN and other instruments on human rights to which African states are parties (or members of UN specialised agencies that sponsored such instruments).[1] The Commission is also to take into consideration other international conventions setting out norms recognised by OAS member states, African practices (which are in conformity with the international human rights standards), customs generally accepted as law, general principles of law recognised by African states and legal precedents and doctrine.[2]

Under the Protocol on the Court, the court is to apply the Charter and any relevant human rights instruments adopted by the states concerned.[3]

1 African HR Charter, art 60.
2 Ibid, art 61.
3 Court Protocol, art 7.

Organisation

Composition

20.5 The Commission comprises 11 persons, who are nationals of different states parties to the African Charter.[1] The members of the Commission are nominated by the states parties (each party may nominate two candidates – at least one of whom must be its national) and elected by the OAU Assembly for a renewable period of six years.[2] Members of the Commission must be persons of the highest reputation, known for their high morality, integrity, impartiality and competence in the field of human and peoples' rights (preferably, equipped with legal experience).[3] The members sit on the Commission in their private capacity.[4] The Commission elects a Chairman and a Vice-Chairman from within its ranks. These officers serve for a renewable two-year period.[5]

The future Court will comprise 11 judges, who are to be nationals of different OAU states.[6] Judges should be jurists of high moral character with recognised practical, judicial or academic ability in the field of human and peoples' rights. They will be elected by the Assembly upon nominations of the states parties to the Protocol on the Court (each state may propose three candidates, at least two of whom are to be its nationals).[7] In selecting the judges the Assembly must ensure that the bench as a whole is representative of the main different regions and legal traditions in Africa[8] and that adequate gender representation is achieved.[9] The judges will serve a once renewable six-year term and they will elect a President and Vice-President for a once renewable two-year period.[10]

1 African HR Charter, arts 31(1), 32, 34. The present composition of the Commission is:
   Professor Isaac Nguema (Gabon); Professor E V O Dankwa (Ghana); Mr Atsu Koffi Amega (Togo); Ambassador Mohammed Hatem Ben Salem (Tunisia); Ambassador Ibrahim Badawi (Egypt); Dr Vera Duarte Martins (Cape Verde Islands); Mr Youssoupha Ndiaye (Senegal); Mrs Julienne Ondziel-Gnelenga (Congo); Mr Kamel Rezzag-Bara (Algeria); and Dr Nyameko Barney Pityana (SA).
   The vacancy created by the death of Mr Alioune Blondin Beye (Mali) in 1998 will be filled during the Summit meeting of the Assembly in June 1999.
2 African HR Charter, arts 33, 34, 36; Rules of Procedure, rr 11, 13.
3 African HR Charter, art 31(1).
4 Rules of Procedure, r 11(2).
5 African HR Charter, art 42(1); Rules of Procedure, r 17.
6 Court Protocol, art 11.
7 Ibid, arts 12, 14.
8 Ibid, art 14(2).
9 Ibid, arts 12(2), 14(3).
10 Ibid, arts 15, 21.

DISQUALIFICATION OF COMMISSION MEMBERS

20.6 A Commission member must not participate in the consideration of a communication in which he or she has a personal interest or has participated in any previous capacity in the adoption of a decision relating to the same case.[1] In such circumstances the member concerned should voluntarily withdraw or be removed from the case by a decision of the Commission.[2] If a member of the Commission has ceased to carry out his or her official functions, the other members may decide unanimously to remove that member from office. In this case, the Chairman will notify this decision to the Secretary-General of the OAU, who will then declare the seat vacant.[3]

Under the new Protocol on the Court, a judge may not participate in a case in which his or her state of nationality is involved.[4] In addition, a judge may not sit in a case in which he or she was involved as a party representative, a member of another dispute settlement body or in any other capacity.[5] The court may decide unanimously (with the exception of the judge concerned) to suspend or remove a judge from office if his or her activities interfere with the judge's independence or impartiality, or are incompatible with the requirements of the office.[6] However, the Assembly may overrule such a decision.[7]

1 Rules of Procedure, r 109(1).
2 Ibid, rr 109(2), 110.
3 Ibid, r 14(1).
4 Court Protocol, art 22.
5 Ibid, art 17(2).
6 Ibid, arts 18, 19(1).
7 Ibid, art 19(2).

Plenary/chambers

20.7 The Commission conducts most of its business in plenary (the quorum is seven members).[1] However, the Commission may create subsidiary bodies – ie committees, sub-commissions and working groups, and delegate some of its functions to those bodies.[2] In reviewing communications, the Commission may establish working groups (each including three members) to make recommendations to the plenary session of the Commission on the admissibility of the communications or on the contents of the Commission's observations and reports.[3] The prospective Court will also sit in plenary and seven judges are to constitute the necessary quorum.[4]

1 African HR Charter, art 42(3); Rules of Procedure, r 43.
2 Rules of Procedure, rr 28, 29.
3 Ibid, rr 115, 120(1),(3).
4 Court Protocol, art 23.

Appellate structure

20.8 There is no possibility of appeal under the existing African human rights system. However, with the establishment of the Court, it will become possible in some cases to submit matters already reviewed by the Commission to an additional review by the Court.

Technical/scientific experts

20.9 There is no explicit provision under the various instruments governing the work of the Commission that addresses participation of experts in communication proceedings. However, it appears that parties can introduce expert opinions as part of the evidence they submit to the Commission.[1] The Charter authorises the Commission to invite any organisation or persons capable of enlightening it to participate in its sessions.[2]

1 See Court Protocol, art 26(2).
2 African HR Charter, art 46.

Secretariat

20.10 The administrative needs of the Commission are fulfilled by the Secretary-General of the OAU, who provides the Commission with the necessary staff, means and services.[1] The head of the secretariat of the Commission is the Secretary, appointed by the Secretary-General, in consultation with the Chairman of the Commission. The Secretary, inter alia, assists the members of the Commission in the exercise of their functions; serves as a channel of communication to and from the Commission; is the custodian of the archives of the Commission; keeps a record of all communications; notifies the members of the Commission on issues submitted to him or her; and makes arrangements (under the instructions of the Secretary-General) for the meetings of the Commission.[2]

The new Court, once established, will have its own registry and staff, headed by a Registrar.[3]

1 African HR Charter, art 41; Rules of Procedure, r 22(3).
2 Rules of Procedure, rr 22(4), 23, 27.
3 Court Protocol, art 24.

Jurisdiction

Ratione personae

20.11 The Commission may receive communications against states parties to the African Charter, if submitted by: (1) another state party,[1] or (2) any other source.[2] In the latter case, the Commission may consider the communication only if the majority of its members so decide.[3]

1 African HR Charter, arts 47, 49.
2 Ibid, art 55.
3 Ibid, art 55(2).

AFRICAN COURT

20.12 The future Court will have jurisdiction over cases brought by the following claimants:
(1) the Commission;
(2) the state party that lodged a complaint to the Commission;
(3) the state party against which the complaint has been lodged;
(4) the state party whose citizen is a victim of human rights violations; and
(5) any African inter-governmental organisation.[1]
Although the Protocol does not explicitly require that the claim be presented against a state which is a party to the Protocol, such interpretation is sensible, since only such states will be bound by the judgments of the court.[2]

The court will also be able to receive cases brought by individuals or NGOs with observer status before the Commission, if the state against which the complaint is made has submitted a declaration under art 34(6) of the Protocol, recognising the competence of the court to receive such claims.[3]

1 Court Protocol, art 5(1).
2 Ibid, art 30.
3 Ibid, arts 5(3), 34(6).

Ratione materiae

20.13 The jurisdiction of the Commission encompasses all cases where a state party has good reasons to believe that another state has violated the provisions of the Charter.[1]

A communication lodged by 'other sources' (not by a state party) must also assert a violation of the Charter. However, for the purpose of conducting an in-depth study of the communication (as opposed to the ordinary review procedure resulting in the Commission's observations), the communication must indicate, on its own, or together with other communications, the existence of a series of serious or massive violations of human rights, or a state of emergency. In this case, the Commission will refer the case to the Assembly, to obtain its authorisation to conduct an in-depth study.[2]

1 African HR Charter, arts 47, 49, 55–56. The Charter is not clear on the subject-matter of complaints submitted by persons or bodies other than state parties. Nonetheless, in practice, these communications should address human rights violations under the Charter.
2 African HR Charter, art 58.

AFRICAN COURT

20.14 Under the Protocol, the court's jurisdiction will extend to all cases and disputes concerning the interpretation and application of the African Charter, the Protocol on the Court, or any human rights instrument ratified by the states concerned.[1]

1 Court Protocol, art 3(1).

Ratione temporis

20.15 The Commission may normally deal with an inter-state communication only after the complaining state has addressed a written communication to the other state concerned and drawn its attention to the possible violation.[1] The Commission can be seized only after the expiration of three months from the date on which the original communication was received by the state complained against, if the matter has not been settled. However, in cases of patent violations the state complainant may refer the case to the Commission immediately. In all events, the communication must be filed only after the exhaustion of available domestic remedies, unless the application of such remedies is unduly prolonged.[2]

In cases involving communications from other sources, the complaint must also be made only after the exhaustion of domestic remedies (unless, the procedure is unduly prolonged).[3] Moreover, the communication is to be submitted within reasonable time from the date on which local remedies were exhausted.[4]

1 African HR Charter, art 48.
2 Ibid, art 50.

3   Ibid, art 56(5).
4   Ibid, art 56(6).

20.16   In principle, the same requirement of admissibility applicable to the Commission should also apply to the Court.[1] This includes exhaustion of domestic remedies and probably an obligation to file a claim within a reasonable time after exhausting domestic remedies. The precise division of labour between the Court and the Commission will be addressed in the Rules of Procedure of the Court. Given the complementarity between the Court and the Commission it might be expected that a case will be brought before the Court only after it has been dealt with by the Commission.[2]

1   Court Protocol, art 6(2).
2   Ibid, arts 2, 6(3), 8.

Advisory jurisdiction

20.17   The Commission is authorised to interpret the provisions of the African Charter at the request of a state party, an OAU institution or an African organisation recognised by the OAU.[1] The Rules of Procedure fail to specify a procedure for consideration of requests for interpretation.[2] The court will have similar powers to render advisory opinions, provided that the same matter is not being dealt with by the Commission. Such an opinion is to be reasoned and every judge may produce his or her dissenting opinion.[3]

1   African HR Charter, art 45(3).
2   In practice, the Commission has adopted, on its own initiative, several resolutions aimed to elucidate unclear provisions of the Charter without, however, suggesting that this was an exercise of its advisory jurisdiction under the Charter.
3   Court Protocol, art 4.

PROCEDURAL ASPECTS

Languages

20.18   The working languages of the Commission and the OAU are Arabic, English, French and Portuguese.[1] All working languages may be used before the Commission and translated into all other working languages. A person who addresses the Commission in a language which is not a working language must arrange for translation into one of the working languages.[2]

1   Rules of Procedure, r 34.
2   Ibid, r 35.

Instituting proceedings

20.19   A case is initiated before the Commission by way of a written communication. A communication must contain a detailed and comprehensive statement on (a) the actions denounced; and (b) provisions of the Charter allegedly violated.[1] In inter-state cases, the communication must normally be made first to the state party complained against, with a copy to the Secretary-General and the Chairman of the Commission.[2] After a period of three months in which no settlement has been reached (except in cases of clear violation), the complaining state must send a notification of its intent to submit the dispute to the Commission. The notification is to be sent to the Secretary-General and the Chairman and a copy must be sent to the other state involved.[3] A notification will include the following information:

(a) measures taken to settle the dispute before resorting to the Commission, including the text of the original communication and the correspondence between the two states;

(b) measures taken to exhaust local remedies (or assertion that their application is unduly prolonged);

(c) any other international procedure for investigation or settlement to which the parties have resorted.[4]

Communications submitted by other sources should contain the following details:

(a) name, address, age and profession of the author and verification of his or her identity;

(b) name of state party concerned;

(c) the purpose of the communication;

(d) provisions of the Charter which allegedly have been violated;

(e) facts of the claim;

(f) measures taken to exhaust local remedies, or explanation why they will be futile; and

(g) the extent to which the same matter has been settled by another international procedure of investigation or settlement.[5]

If the applicability of the African Charter to the communication is in doubt, the Commission, through its Secretary, may request clarifications or additional information from the author within fixed time limits.[6]

1 Rules of Procedure, r 88(2).
2 Ibid, r 88(1).
3 African HR Charter, art 48; Rules of Procedure, r 92.
4 Rules of Procedure, r 93(2)(a),(c)
5 Ibid, r 104(1).
6 Ibid, r 104.

Financial assistance

20.20 Financial assistance is not available for participants in proceedings before the Commission. However, under the Protocol on the Court, the new court will provide free legal representation to a party to a case before it, when the interests of justice so require.[1]

1 Court Protocol, art 10(2).

Provisional measures

20.21 During proceedings involving individual communications, the Commission may indicate its views on whether interim measures are needed to avoid irreparable damage to the alleged victim.[1] The Commission (or the Chairman when the Commission is not at session) may also indicate other desirable interim measures necessary to protect the interests of the parties or the proper conduct of the proceedings.[2] Provisional (or interim) measures will not be binding upon the parties.

The Protocol establishing the court allows it to adopt provisional measures in cases of extreme gravity and urgency, if such measures are needed to avoid irreparable harm to persons.[3]

1   Rules of Procedure, r 111(1).
2   Ibid, r 111(2),(3).
3   Court Protocol art 27(2).

Preliminary proceedings

20.22   Before reviewing the merits of a communication, the Commission must take a decision on the question of admissibility.[1] In cases brought by states, the Committee must be satisfied that the following conditions have been met:

(a)   the preliminary stage of direct communications between the two states (in accordance with art 47 of the Charter) has been exhausted;
(b)   the three months time limit from the date of the original communication has expired;
(c)   domestic remedies have been exhausted, in accordance with the principles of international law, unless it is obvious that their application will be unreasonably prolonged or if there are no effective domestic remedies.[2]

In the case of a communication presented by another source, the Commission must verify the following requirements for the admissibility of the communication:

(a)   it indicates the name of the authors (even if they wish the Commission to protect their anonymity);
(b)   it is compatible with the Charter of the OAU or with the African Charter on Human and Peoples' Rights;
(c)   it is not written in a disparaging or insulting language directed at the state concerned (or its institutions), or the OAU;
(d)   it is not based exclusively on mass media reports;
(e)   local remedies have been exhausted, unless the application of such remedies is clearly unduly prolonged;
(f)   it is submitted within reasonable time after the exhaustion of local remedies, or after the Commission became seized of the matter;
(g)   it does not deal with matters already settled by the states involved in accordance with the Charters of the UN or OAU or the African Charter on Human and Peoples' Rights.[3]

The Commission may be assisted in its consideration of the admissibility of the complaint by working groups composed of three members of the Commission (or less). Working groups may recommend to the plenary Commission whether to admit the communication on hand.[4] The Commission (or working group) may request the state concerned or the author of the communication for additional written information or observations on admissibility within fixed time limits.[5] In any event, the Commission cannot declare a communication admissible unless the state party has received an opportunity to make its observations on the question of admissibility (within not more than three months from receiving the communication).[6]

1   African HR Charter, arts 50, 56; Rules of Procedure, r 118.
2   Rules of Procedure, r 97.
3   African HR Charter, art 56; Rules of Procedure, r 116.
4   Rules of Procedure, r 115.

5   Ibid, r 117(1).
6   Ibid, r 117(2),(4).

Written pleadings

Inter-state communications

20.23   Upon receipt of the original communication (before the seizing of the Commission), the state complained against must present a written reply to the complaining state within three months.[1] The reply must include the following information:

(a)   written explanations, declarations or statements relating to the issues raised;
(b)   possible indications and measures that are to be taken to end the situation denounced;
(c)   indication of the applicable laws and rule of procedure;
(d)   indication of appellate procedures in use or still available.[2]

After the Commission has been seized of the communication, by way of notification (see supra, para 20.19), both parties are entitled to submit written observations, according to a procedure determined by the Commission.[3] In addition, the Commission may request the parties to provide further information or observations in writing, within fixed time limits.[4]

1   African HR Charter, art 47; Rules of Procedure, r 90(1).
2   African HR Charter, art 47; Rules of Procedure, r 90(2).
3   African HR Charter, art 51(2); Rules of Procedure, r 100.
4   African HR Charter, art 51(1); Rules of Procedure, r 99.

Other communications

20.24   In the event that the Commission decides that the communication is admissible, the state complained against will be given three months to submit in writing its explanation or statement clarifying the issue under consideration, and indicating, if possible, remedial measures it intends to apply.[1] The explanation and the statement will then be made available to the author of the communication, who will be entitled to submit, within fixed time limits, a written response including additional information and observations.[2]

1   Rules of Procedure, r 119(2).
2   Ibid, r 119(3).

Oral arguments

20.25   The parties to a case brought by a state may present their oral submissions before the Commission.[1] The Commission may also, on its own initiative, request the parties (through the Secretary) to appear before it and provide information or comments.[2] Such presentation is to be made within fixed time limits and according to a procedure determined by the Commission.[3] The Commission has evolved a practice of affording oral hearings as well in communications received from other sources. Prior to the session in which it proposes to take the oral hearing, the Commission issues hearing notices to the parties notifying them of the venue and time for the hearing. The consideration of communications by the Commission is conducted in private sessions, not open to the public.[4] In contrast, the proposed new court will normally sit in public.[5]

1 African HR Charter, art 51(2); Rules of Procedure, r 100.
2 African HR Charter, art 51(1); Rules of Procedure, r 99.
3 Rules of Procedure, r 100(3).
4 Ibid, rr 96(1), 106.
5 Court Protocol, art 10(1).

Third-party intervention/multiple proceedings

20.26 The various instruments regulating the work of the Commission do not specifically provide for or exclude third-party intervention and the Commission has yet to receive or consider any such request or application. However, under the Protocol on the Court, any state party with an interest in a case will be able to make a request to join the proceedings.[1] Under the African Charter there is no impediment to two or more parties filing a communication together against a state party. In cases brought by persons or entities other than states parties, the Commission may decide to consider two or more communications jointly, if it deems this to be useful.[2]

1 Court Protocol, art 5(2).
2 Rules of Procedure, r 114(2).

Amicus curiae

20.27 In investigating a communication the Commission may receive information from the Secretary-General of the OAU or from any person capable of enlightening it.[1] A similar power can be found in regard to interested states and specialised institutions of the OAU.[2] Any procedures regarding the role of intervenors or amici curiae in communications before the Commission will, however, be subject to the overriding consideration that all measures taken by the Commission with respect to the communications are confidential.[3]

1 African HR Charter, art 46.
2 Rules of Procedure, rr 71, 73.
3 African HR Charter, art 59(1).

Representation of parties

20.28 States parties to the Charter concerned have the right to be represented during the consideration of a relevant issue by the Commission and to submit observations orally and in writing.[1] The Commission also authorises authors of other communications to be represented if they so choose. Under the new court, any party to a case shall be entitled to be represented by a legal representative of the party's choice. Free legal representation may be provided where the interests of justice so require.[2]

1 Rules of Procedure, art 100.
2 Court Protocol, art 10(2).

Decision

20.29 In cases brought by states, if no amicable settlement has been reached, the Commission will prepare a report within 12 months from the date it was seized by way of notification.[1] The report will include the decisions and conclusions of the Commissions on the merits of the case.[2]

In cases brought by other complainants, the Commission will normally prepare observations, made on the basis of the information submitted to it by the parties.[3] In cases where the Commission believes that the communication, alone or together with other communications, reveals a series of serious or massive human rights violations or a case of emergency, it may notify the Assembly accordingly.[4] The Assembly may then request the Commission to conduct an in-depth study of the situation. The factual findings of such study, as well as the recommendations of the Commission, will be made in the form of a report.[5]

Decisions of the Commission are not binding. The reports of the Commission are to remain confidential unless the Assembly decides to publish them. However, the Commission may issue, through the Secretary, press releases on its activities, which include, inter alia, information on the decisions of the Commission on communications presented before it.[6]

The new court will present its decisions within 90 days from the end of deliberations. The decision will be prepared in the form of a reasoned judgment, which is to be publicised.[7] Any judge may deliver his or her separate or dissenting opinion with the judgment.[8]

1   African HR Charter, art 52; Rules of Procedure, r 101(1).
2   Rules of Procedure, r 101(3).
3   Ibid, r 120.
4   African HR Charter, art 58.
5   Ibid, art 58(2); Rules of procedure, r 120(3).
6   African HR Charter, art 59(2); Rules of Procedure, r 108.
7   Court Protocol, art 28(1),(5)–(6).
8   Ibid, art 28(7).

Interpretation and revision of judgments

20.30   There are no explicit provisions under the instruments governing the work of the Commission that allow for interpretation or revision of observations or reports adopted by the Commission. An exception is found in regard to a decision on admissibility of other complaints, allowing the Commission to reconsider its decision at a later date, if requested to do so.[1] Under the new Protocol on the Court, parties to a case may request interpretation of a judgment, or its revision, in the light of new evidence.[2]

1   Rules of Procedure, r 118(2).
2   Court Protocol, art 28(3),(4).

Appeal

20.31   There is no appeal over decisions of the Commission. The exact relations between the prospective court and the Commission – including whether the court will have any appellate jurisdiction over decisions of the Commission – has yet to be determined.[1]

1   Court Protocol, art 8.

Costs

20.32   Proceedings before the Commission (and the Court) are free of charge, but the parties must bear their own expenses.

Enforcement of decisions

20.33 Decisions of the African Commission are not binding and thus are not subject to enforcement procedures. Judgments of the prospective court will be binding upon the parties and states will have to comply with judgments within time periods fixed by the court. Moreover, states parties to the Protocol on the Court will be obliged to guarantee the execution of the court's judgments.[1]

1 Court Protocol, art 30.

REFERENCE

Case reports

The observations of the Commission are published in the *Review of the African Commission on Human & Peoples' Rights* (seven volumes to date) and in the Annual Activity Reports (1987–).

Selected bibliography

Books

Evelyn A Ankumah *The African Commission on Human and Peoples' Rights* 18–20 (1996).

Thomas Buergental *International Human Rights* 228–247 (1995).

Shadrack B O Gutto *ICJ workshops on NGO participation in the African Commission on Human and Peoples' Rights 1991 to 1996: a critical evaluation*, Geneva (1996).

Jean Matringe *Tradition et modernité dans la Charte Africaine des Droits de l'Homme et des Peuples: étude du contenu normatif de la Charte et de son apport à la théorie du droit international des droits de l'homme*, Bruylant (1996).

Fatsah Ouguergouz *La Charte Africaine des Droits de l'Homme et des Peuples: une approche juridique des droits de l'homme entre tradition et modernité*, PUF (1993).

N S Rembe *The System of Protection of Human Rights under the African Charter on Human and Peoples' Rights: Problems and Prospects* (1991).

U Oji Umozurike *The African Charter on Human and Peoples' Rights* (1997).

Eteka Yemet Valere *La Charte Africaine des Droits de l'Homme et des Peuples: etude comparative*, Ed l'Harmattan (1996).

Articles

Amoah 'The African Charter on Human and People's Rights – An Effective Weapon for Human Rights?' (1992) 4 African Journal of International & Comparative Law 226.

Arthur E Anthony 'Beyond the Paper Tiger: The Challenge of a Human Rights Court in Africa' (1997) 32 Texas International Law Journal 511.

Ibrahim A Badawi El-Sheikh 'The African Commission on Human and Peoples' Rights: A Call for Justice' in Kalliopi Koufa (ed) (1997) *International Justice* – XXVI Thesaurus Acroasium.

Hamid Boufrik 'La Cour Africaine des Droits de l'Homme et des Peuples: un organe judiciaire au service des droits de l'homme et des peuples en Afrique' (1998) Revue africaine de droit international et comparé, Vol 10/1.

Khadija El Madmad 'Les droits des femmes dans la Charte Africaine des Droits de l'Homme et des Peuples' (1993) Afrique 2000.

Gino J Naldi & Konstantinos Magliveras 'Reinforcing the African System of Human Rights: The Protocol on the Establishment of a Regional Court of Human and Peoples' Rights' 16 (1998) Netherlands Human Rights Quarterly 431–456.

Mutoy Mubiala 'La Cour Africaine des Droits de l'Homme et des Peuples: mimétisme institutionnel ou avancée judiciaire?' (1998) Revue générale de droit international public.

Rachel Murray 'Decisions by the African Commission on Individual Communications under the African Charter in Human and People's Rights' (1997) 46 ICLQ 412 at 422–423.

Chidi Anselm Odinkalu & Camilla Christensen 'The African Commission on Human and Peoples' Rights: The Development of its Non-State Communication Procedures' (1998) 20 Human Rights Quarterly, 235–280.

Obinna Okere 'The Protection of Human Rights in Africa and the African Charter on Human and People's Rights: Comparative Analysis with the European and American Systems' (1984) 6 Human Rights Quarterly 141.

ANNEX

List of 53 states parties to the African Charter on Human and Peoples' Rights

Algeria; Angola; Benin; Botswana; Burkina Faso; Burundi; Cameroon; Cape Verde; Central African Republic; Chad; Comoros; Congo; Democratic Republic of Congo; Côte d'Ivoire; Djibouti; Egypt; Equatorial Guinea; Eritrea; Ethiopia, Gabon; The Gambia; Ghana; Guinea; Guinea-Bissau; Kenya; Lesotho; Liberia; Libya; Madagascar; Malawi; Mali; Mauritania; Mauritius; Mozambique; Namibia; Niger; Nigeria; Rwanda; Sao Tome and Principe; Senegal; Seychelles; Sierra Leone; Somalia; South Africa; Sudan; Swaziland; Tanzania; Togo; Tunisia; Uganda; Western Sahara (Sahrawi Arab Democratic Republic); Zambia; Zimbabwe.

CHAPTER 21

Collective complaint system under the European Social Charter

GENERAL INFORMATION

21.1 The European Social Charter was concluded in 1961 within the framework of the Council of Europe, and entered into force on 26 February 1965.[1] Under the Charter and its 1988 Additional Protocol states parties have undertaken to accept as the aim of their policy the attainment of conditions in which a detailed list of economic and social human rights enumerated in Part I the Charter may be effectively realised. The states parties have undertaken to consider some of these rights as legally binding upon them.[2] At present, there are 24 states parties to the Social Charter and the Revised Social Charter (11 of which are also parties to the 1988 Additional Protocol).

The Social Charter is supervised mainly through a system of regular state reporting. The examination of reports is carried out by the Committee of Independent Experts ('CIE') – which in November 1998 renamed itself the European Committee of Social Rights ('ECSR' or 'the Committee') – established thereunder. The Committee comprises nine experts of the highest integrity with recognised competence in international social questions, elected by the Council of Europe's Committee of Ministers from a list nominated by the states parties to the Charter.[3] The experts serve on the Committee a renewable six-year term.[4] The Committee receives administrative services from a section of the Secretariat of the Council of Europe (the Directorate of Human Rights).

The states parties submit to the ECSR periodic reports on the implementation of the Social Charter and the Committee communicates its conclusions on the degree of state compliance to the political organs of the Council of Europe (the Governmental Committee and the Committee of Ministers).[5] In 1995, a new Protocol was concluded ('Collective Complaints Protocol'), granting the ECSR quasi-judicial responsibilities. The new Protocol provides for a system of collective complaints by certain domestic and international NGOs to the ECSR.[6] The Protocol entered into force on 1 July 1998 and nine states are now bound by it.

Under the Collective Complaints Protocol the ECSR may receive complaints alleging unsatisfactory application of the Charter on the part of states parties to the Protocol.[7] The procedure is governed by the 1998 Protocol and by the Rules of Procedure adopted by the Committee.[8] Complaints are to be made using one of the official languages of the Council of Europe or, in the case of domestic NGO complainants, any other language.[9] The Committee will receive written pleadings from the complainant, the state complained against and third parties (other states parties to the Collective Complaints Protocol and international organisations of employers or trade unions with observer status before the Governmental Sub-Committee).[10] The ECSR may hold oral hearings on the case, either at its own initiative or at the request of one of the parties.[11]

At the end of the proceedings, the Committee is to prepare a report on the compliance of the state complained against with the applicable Charter (or Protocol) obligations.[12] The report is then communicated to the Committee of Ministers and the Parliamentary Assembly of the Council of Europe and will be published within four months from its conclusion.[13] If the Committee finds that the Charter has not been applied in a satisfactory manner, the Committee of Ministers shall adopt a recommendation by a majority of two-thirds of those voting.[14] In that event, the state concerned is expected to inform the ECSR in its next periodic report on the measures it has taken to give effect to the recommendations of the Committee of Ministers.[15]

To date, one complaint has been submitted to the ECSR by the International Commission of Jurists, directed against the Government of Portugal. It was declared admissible by the Committee in March 1999.[16]

1 European Social Charter, 18 October 1961, 529 UNTS 89, ETS 35 ('Social Charter'). A revised version of the Social Charter and amending Protocols entered into force on 1 July 1999: European Social Charter (Revised), 3 May 1996, ETS 163 ('Revised Social Charter').

2 Part I of the Social Charter lists broad rights and principles which need to be pursued as a matter of policy. Part II enumerates rights with greater detail, and the parties undertake to accept 10 articles (or 45 numbered paragraphs) as binding upon them (including at least five basic rights): Social Charter, art 20(1). In addition, parties to the Additional Protocol to the Social Charter undertake to implement at least one more right: Additional Protocol to the European Social Charter, 5 May 1988, ETS 128. Under the Revised Social Charter, each state party is bound by six or more basic rights and a total of at least 16 articles (or 63 numbered paragraphs).

3 Social Charter, art 25(1). The original number of experts on the Committee was seven. It was subsequently agreed to increase that number to nine: Protocol amending the European Social Charter, 10 October 1991, art 3, ETS 142. The current membership of the Committee of Experts is:
   President: Matti Mikkola (Finland). **Vice-Presidents:** Rolf Birk (Germany) and Stein Evju (Norway). **General Rapporteur:** Suzanne Grevisse (France). **Members:** Konrad Grillberger (Austria); Tekin Akillioglu (Turkey); Nikitas Aliprantis (Greece); Alfredo Bruto da Costa (Portugal) and Micheline Jamoulle (Belgium).

4 Social Charter, art 25(2).

5 Ibid, arts 21, 22, 27 (Revised Social Charter, art C).

6 Additional Protocol to the European Social Charter providing for a System of Collective Complaints, 9 November 1995, ETS 158 ('Complaints Protocol').

7 Complaints Protocol, arts 1, 11.

8 Rules of Procedure of the Committee of Independent Experts for the Examination of Collective Complaints, Council of Europe, Social Charter Fact Sheet no 7 (May 1998) ('Rules of Procedure'). These rules are currently being reviewed.

9 Rules of Procedure, r 2.

10 Complaints Protocol, arts 6, 7.

11 Ibid, art 7(4); Rules of Procedure, r 10.

12 Complaints Protocol, art 8(1).

13 Ibid, art 8(2).

14 Ibid, art 9(1).

15 Ibid, art 10.

16 See decision on admissibility, http://www.dhdirhr.coe.fr/socialcharter/collectivecomplaints.

JURISDICTION

21.2 The ECSR may receive complaints alleging unsatisfactory application of the Social Charter or the 1988 Protocol filed against states parties to these instruments and to the Collective Complaints Protocol by any of the following organisations:

   (i) international organisations of employers and trade unions;[1]

  (ii) international NGOs which have consultative status with the Council of Europe if included on a list drawn up by the Governmental Committee, and then only in respect of matters in which they have 'particular competence'; inclusion on the list is valid for four years, but can be renewed upon application;[2]

 (iii) 'representative' national organisations of employers and trade unions;[3] whether they are 'representative' or not is to be decided in the admissibility proceedings;

 (iv) other types of 'representative' national NGOs only after a special optional declaration by the respective respondent government allowing such complaints and again only in respect of matters in which those NGOs have 'particular competence'.[4]

1   Complaints Protocol, art 1(a).
2   Ibid, art 1(b).
3   Ibid, art 2(c).
4   Ibid, art 2(1).

CONTACT INFORMATION

21.3

      Directorate of Human Rights
      Conseil de l'Europe
      Point I, F-67075 Strasbourg CEDEX,
      France

      Tel: (33) 388 412 000
      Fax: (33) 388 4127 81
      email: point_i@coe.int
      website: www.dhdirhr.coe.fr/socialcharter/index.html

REFERENCE

Sources of jurisprudence

The conclusions of the European Committee of Social Rights (formerly Committee of Independent Experts) are published at the end of each supervision cycle (last published: *Committee of Independent Experts Conclusions XIV-2 vols 1 and 2*, Council of Europe publishing, December 1998, ISBN 92-871-3792-7).

The reports of the Governmental Committee to the Committee of Ministers concerning each cycle are published periodically (latest reports are *Governmental Committee 13th report (IV) and 13th report (V)* published in a single volume, August 1998, ISBN 92-871-3701-3).

Reports on non-accepted provisions of the Charter are published in separate volumes: the latest covers Articles 5 and 6 (the right to organise and to bargain collectively), *Sixth report on certain provisions of the Charter which have not been accepted*, September 1998, ISBN 92-871-3732-3).

The Charter texts are published in several forms, including a comprehensive volume of basic texts and separate treaties in small format. These as well as other information are available from the Social Charter, Directorate of Human Rights Council of Europe, 67075 Strasbourg, Cedex, http://www.dhdirhr.coe.fr. Tel: 33 3 88 41 22 57; Fax: 33 3 41 37 00; email: Social Charter@coe.int.

Selected bibliography

David Harris *The European Social Charter*, University Press of Virginia, Charlottesville (1984).

Donna Gomien, David Harris, Leo Zwaak *Law and practice of the European Convention on Human Rights and the European Social Charter*, Council of Europe (1996) ISBN 92-871-2956-8.

The Social Charter publishes a series of pocket paperbacks, including *European Social Charter, Collected texts* (1997) and *Fundamental Social Rights, Case law of the Committee of Independent Experts* (1997); new editions of both publications are forthcoming. It also produces a series of 'monographs' with focus on particular topics in relation to the Charter, the latest being a new edition of *Monograph No 2 – Equality between men and women in the European Social Charter* ISBN 92-871-3777-3, and *Monograph No 7 – Social Protection in the European Social Charter*. A new edition of Monograph No 6 on conditions of employment is forthcoming.

An NGO Action Pack on the Social Charter has just been launched for use by non-governmental organisations and is also available from the Social Charter Section.

ANNEX

States parties to the Social Charter 1961 and to the Revised Social Charter

Austria; Belgium; Cyprus; Denmark; Finland; France;[†] Germany; Greece; Iceland; Ireland; Italy;[†] Luxembourg; Malta; Netherlands; Norway; Poland; Portugal;[†] Romania;[†] Slovakia;[†] Slovenia;[†] Spain; Sweden;[†] Turkey; United Kingdom.

[†] States parties to the Revised Social Charter.

States parties to the Collective Complaint Protocol

Cyprus; Finland;[*] France; Greece; Italy; Norway; Portugal; Sweden.

[*] States that have accepted the competence of the CIE to receive complaints from representative national NGOs other than employers and trade union organisations.

List of international NGOs entitled to file a complaint under the collective complaints system

Conference of European Churches; Eurolink Age; European Antipoverty Network; European Centre of the International Council of Women; European

Council of Police Trade Unions; European Ecumenical Commission for Church and Society; European Federation of Employees in Public Services (EUROFEDOP); European Federation of National Organisations Working with the Homeless; European Forum for Child Welfare; European Movement; European Regional Council of the World Federation for Mental Health; International Association Autism-Europe; International Centre for the Legal Protection of Human Rights (INTERIGHTS); International Commission of Jurists; International Council of Nurses; International Council on Social Welfare; International Federation of Educative Communities; International Federation of Human Rights Leagues; International Federation for Hydrocephalus and Spina Bifida; International Federation of Settlements and Neighbourhood Centres; International Movement ATD – Fourth World; International Road Safety; Public Services International; Quaker Council for European Affairs; Standing Committee of the Hospitals of the European Union; World Confederation of Teachers.

International criminal tribunals

INTRODUCTION

This Part of the manual considers three tribunals established in recent years as the international community attempts to bring to account individuals alleged to have committed acts in violation of international humanitarian law, particularly during periods of international or civil strife. Developments in this area are controversial, but have culminated in 1998 with the adoption of the Statute of the International Criminal Court (ICC). The Statute of the Court will enter into force once it has been ratified by 60 states, and marks the culmination of efforts since the close of the Second World War, and the Nuremberg and Tokyo trials, to establish a standing international court with jurisdiction over the most serious violations of internationally protected human rights. Prior to the entry into force of the ICC Statute, a preparatory Commission has been established to carry out work required for the establishment of the Court. The Commission is scheduled to meet three times during 1999.

The International Criminal Court will be a permanent and independent court with criminal jurisdiction over natural persons accused of one or more of the four crimes identified in the ICC Statute: genocide, crimes against humanity, war crimes or aggression. In contrast to the Rwandan and Yugoslav Tribunals which have primacy over national courts in relation to crimes within their jurisdiction, the ICC will exercise its jurisdiction only where national courts are unable or unwilling to try an accused person. The ICC will only be empowered to deal with crimes committed after the entry into force of its Statute. Several aspects of the procedural and substantive law of the ICC remain to be elaborated, initially through the Preparatory Commission and subsequently through the Assembly of States Parties to its Statute.

The two other tribunals dealt with in this Part are unusual in that they were established by way of resolution of the Security Council, acting under Chapter VII of the Charter of the United Nations. The jurisdiction of the Rwandan and Yugoslav Tribunals is defined by their respective Statutes as incorporated into the Security Council Resolutions under which the tribunals are established.[1] Both tribunals have jurisdiction over genocide and crimes against humanity. In addition the Yugoslav Tribunal has jurisdiction over grave breaches of the Geneva Conventions of 12 August 1949 and violations

---

1 Security Council resolution 827, 25 May 1993, UN Doc S/RES/827 (1993) (Yugoslav Tribunal); Security Council resolution 955, 8 November 1994, UN Doc S/RES/955 (1994) (Rwanda Tribunal).

of the laws or customs of war. The Rwandan Tribunal has jurisdiction over violations of art 3 common to the Geneva Conventions and of Additional Protocol II to the Geneva Conventions. As in the case of the ICC, each tribunal has jurisdiction over natural persons accused of crimes falling within its respective Statute, and has no jurisdiction over states, legal persons, or organisations. The jurisdiction of both tribunals is time-limited. The Rwandan Tribunal has jurisdiction over crimes committed between 1 January 1994 and 31 December 1994. The Yugoslav Tribunal has jurisdiction over crimes committed after 1 January 1991. However, the Statute of the Yugoslav Tribunal does not specify a date by which crimes must have been committed in order to fall within the jurisdiction of the tribunal. It is therefore conceivable that any serious violations which fall within the subject-matter of the tribunal may in due course be tried before the ICTY.

By the middle of 1999, 12 trials had been initiated before the ICTY and four judgments handed down. Some 23 other individuals alleged to have committed crimes within the Statute of the ICTY are being held in custody. The Rwandan Tribunal has handed down four judgments to date, and further public indictments have been issued or confirmed. As of April 1999, 34 individuals are detained and four other suspects are in custody pending extradition.

Given the adoption of the Statute of the International Criminal Court it remains open to question whether the Security Council will in future decide to establish further dedicated tribunals to deal with violations of international humanitarian law occurring during particular incidents and conflicts. Given the present opposition of some states to the International Criminal Court, this cannot be ruled out.

CHAPTER 22

International Criminal Court

INTRODUCTORY

Name and seat of the court

22.1   The International Criminal Court ('ICC' or 'the court') is established under the 1998 Rome Statute of the International Criminal Court ('Statute'),[1] which has not yet entered into force. Once active, the court will have the power to try persons for the most serious international crimes. The seat of the court will be in the Hague, The Netherlands, at a location yet to be determined. The Statute will enter into force 60 days after the deposit of the 60th instrument of ratification or accession with the Secretary-General of the UN. Information on the establishment of the ICC can be found at the following web-site:

> http://www.un.org/icc

1   Rome Statute of the International Criminal Court, 17 July 1998, UN Doc A/Conf 183/9 ('ICC Statute'). To date, three states have ratified the statute.

Description

22.2   The ICC will be a permanent and independent court entrusted with criminal jurisdiction over persons accused of committing one or more of the crimes enumerated in the Statute (genocide, crimes against humanity, war crimes and aggression). The judicial activities of the court will complement national courts – ie the ICC will exercise its jurisdiction only when national courts are unable or unwilling to bring to justice a person accused of the crimes defined under the Statute.[1] Once a case is handled by the court, all states parties to the Statute must co-operate with the investigation and prosecution.[2]

The prosecution of cases before the court will fall under the responsibility of the Office of the Prosecutor, which is to constitute a separate organ of the court, headed by a Prosecutor elected by the states parties.[3] The Prosecutor will receive cases on referral from the states parties to the Statute or the Security Council; he or she may also initiate investigation on the basis of information received from other sources.[4] The Prosecutor will investigate the criminal allegations and prosecute all cases before the court. In addition, the Prosecutor (with the assistance of Deputy Prosecutors) will be responsible for the management and administration of his or her Office.

The Assembly of States Parties (Assembly) will supervise the work of the ICC. It will review the administration of the court, approve its budget, receive reports on its operation and may decide to introduce changes in its structure and procedure (eg alteration to the number of judges or amendment of the Rules of Procedure and Evidence).[5] The Assembly will also address instances of failure on the part of states parties to co-operate with the court. A Bureau (including 20 members of the Assembly, representing the legal and geographical diversity of the states parties, elected for a period of three years) will assist the Assembly in performing its functions.[6] The Assembly may create other subsidiary bodies, as necessary.[7]

The court is expected to have significant links to the UN. The precise terms of the relationship will be set out in an agreement which will be concluded between the UN and the court (and approved by the Assembly).[8] The Statute already provides that the UN will participate in the funding of the court, together with the states parties, especially in relation to expenses incurred in cases initiated through referral by the Security Council.[9]

Resolution F of the Rome Final Act established a Preparatory Commission for the Establishment of an International Criminal Court. The Preparatory Commission met for the first time from 16 to 26 February 1999, and will hold two further meetings in 1999. The mandate of the Commission includes the preparation of draft Rules of Procedure and Evidence for the ICC and of elements of crimes.[10]

1 ICC Statute, arts 1, 17.
2 Ibid, art 86.
3 Ibid, art 42.
4 Ibid, art 13.
5 Ibid, arts 36(2), 51(2), 112 (2),(4).
6 Ibid, art 112(3).
7 Ibid, art 112(4).
8 Ibid, art 2.
9 Ibid, art 115.
10 Resolution F, *Final Act of the UN Diplomatic Conference of Plenipotentiaries on the Establishment of an International Criminal Court*, UN Doc A/CONF 183/10, 37 ILM 999.

INSTITUTIONAL ASPECTS

Governing texts

22.3   The principal text governing the establishment, structure, jurisdiction and procedure of the ICC is the Statute.[1] The court will also follow the Rules of Procedure and Evidence, to be adopted by the Assembly (by a vote of two-thirds);[2] and the Regulations of the Court (governing the routine operation of the court), which will be adopted by the court (and enter into force if the majority of states parties do not raise an objection).[3]

1 See para 22.1 n 1.
2 ICC Statute, art 51.
3 Ibid, art 52.

Substantive law

22.4   The substantive law to be applied by the ICC primarily consists of the Statute and an additional instrument on Elements of Crimes (assisting the court in the interpretation of the crimes that fall under the court's jurisdiction), which will be adopted by a two-thirds majority of the Assembly.[1]

Secondary sources of law to be applied by the court are applicable treaties, principles and rules of international law and of armed conflict;[2] general principles of law accepted by municipal systems, including the state which has jurisdiction over the crime[3] and, to some extent, previous case law of the ICC.[4] In any event, norms applied by the ICC must be in conformity with internationally recognised human rights standards and must be of a non-discriminatory nature.[5]

1 ICC Statute, arts 9, 21(1)(a). To the extent that they raise substantive law issues, the court will also apply the Rules of Procedure and Evidence.
2 ICC Statute, art 21(1)(b).
3 Ibid, art 21(1)(c).
4 Ibid, art 21(2).
5 Ibid, art 21(3).

Organisation

Composition

22.5 The ICC will comprise 18 judges, nominated and elected by the states parties for a non-renewable term of nine years.[1] Judges should be persons of high moral character, impartiality and integrity who possess the qualifications required for appointment to the highest judicial office in their own countries.[2] At least nine of the judges must have established competence and experience in criminal law, and at least five of the judges must have competence and relevant experience in international humanitarian law and human rights law.[3] The judges will be nationals of states parties, and no two judges can be nationals of the same state.[4] The composition of the entire bench should reflect equitable geographical distribution and represent the different legal systems of the world. When composing the bench, the need for adequate gender representation must also be taken into account.[5]

The judges will elect a President and First and Second Vice-Presidents for a once renewable three-year term. The three officers will constitute the Presidency of the court and will be responsible, inter alia, for the court's administrative functions.[6]

1 ICC Statute, art 36(1),(6),(9). At the first election, one-third of the judges will serve three years, another third, six years and the others, nine years. Judges who serve three years will be eligible for re-election to a full term.
2 ICC Statute, art 36(3)(a).
3 Ibid, art 36(3)(b),(5).
4 Ibid, art 36(4)(b),(7).
5 Ibid, art 36(8).
6 Ibid, art 38.

DISQUALIFICATION OF JUDGES

22.6 A judge may not participate in a case where his or her impartiality may be questioned (eg if he or she has been involved in a previous capacity in a case involving the defendant). The Prosecutor or the accused person may request disqualification of a judge for lack of impartiality, or any other ground specified by the Rules of Procedure and Evidence.[1] The other members of the court will decide the motion after hearing the judge in question. A defendant may also raise challenges against the Prosecutor or a Deputy Prosecutor for lack of impartiality. In that event, the decision will be taken by the Appeals Chamber of the court, after hearing the officer under consideration.[2]

The court may also determine whether the activities or additional occupations of a judge are compatible with the office he or she holds.[3] If the court finds that a judge has committed serious misconduct or serious breach of his or her official duties, or that the judge is unable to exercise the official functions required by the Statute, it may recommend to the Assembly the removal of that judge from office.[4] Such a decision of the court must be taken by a majority of two-thirds of the other judges.

1 ICC Statute, art 41(2).
2 Ibid, art 42(7),(8).
3 Ibid, art 40(2)–(4).
4 Ibid, art 46. The Assembly may also remove from office the Prosecutor, a Deputy Prosecutor (in pursuance of a recommendation by the Prosecutor) and the Registrar or Deputy Registrar of the court (in pursuance of a recommendation by the court).

Plenary/chambers

22.7 The ICC will be composed of three Divisions – a Pre-Trial Division, a Trial Division and an Appeals Division.[1] The Pre-Trial and Trial Division will each comprise six judges or more, and the Appeals Division will comprise five judges (including the President). The assignment of judges to Divisions is to be determined by the court and be based on the qualifications of the judges, the nature of the functions of each Division and the need to preserve an appropriate combination of judges with expertise in criminal law and international law.[2] The court is to deal with cases in chambers. The Appeals Division will constitute a single chamber; the Trial Division will sit in three-judge chambers; and cases brought before the Pre-Trial Division will be heard by a single judge or a three-judge chamber.[3]

1 ICC Statute, art 34(b).
2 Ibid, art 39(1). Judges assigned to the Appeals Division will serve there for their entire term. Other judges can change Divisions after the end of three years: art 40(3).
3 ICC Statute, art 39(2).

Appellate structure

22.8 Decisions of the Pre-Trial and the Trial Chamber may be appealed before the Appeals Chamber. The appeal may challenge either a decision of acquittal or conviction, a decision on the sentence of a convicted person or other important interim decisions (eg admissibility of case; jurisdiction of the court; and release or detention of a person subject to investigation or prosecution).[1] An appeal may be brought before the Appeals Chamber by the prosecutor or the defendant and, in some cases, by others involved in the proceedings (eg a state party investigating the same case, representatives of the victim). The Appeals Chamber may affirm, amend or reverse the original decision, order a new trial or send the case back on remand to the trial chamber.[2]

1 ICC Statute, arts 81, 82.
2 Ibid, art 83(1)–(3).

Technical/scientific experts

22.9 The Statute clearly envisages the use of experts by the parties to the proceedings[1] and by the court (eg request for an expert opinion or report).[2]

Moreover, it specifically authorises the Pre-Trial Chamber to appoint an expert (normally, upon request of the prosecutor), in order to assist in the examination or testing of evidence in the pre-trial stage, if it is feared that the evidence might not be available at the time of the trial.[3]

The ICC will have general competence to employ experts made available to it ex gratis by states parties, international organisations and NGOs, in order to assist the court or the prosecution in its work. The terms of their employment are to be determined by the Assembly.[4]

1   See eg ICC Statute, arts 48(4), 93(1)(b),(2),(10)(b)(ii),(2).
2   ICC Statute, art 100(1)(d).
3   Ibid, art 56(2)(c).
4   Ibid, art 44(4).

Secretariat

22.10   The Registry of the court will bear responsibility for the administration and provision of secretarial services to the ICC.[1] The Registry is to be headed by a Registrar (assisted by a Deputy Registrar) elected by the court for a once renewable five-year term.[2] The Registrar will maintain the records of the court,[3] and will assume responsibility over the work of the staff of the Registry. The employment of the staff of the Registry and the Office of the Prosecutor will be regulated by Staff Regulations to be drafted by the Registrar (with agreement of the Presidency and the Prosecutor) and approved by the Assembly.[4]

A Victims and Witnesses Unit will operate within the Registry and provide protective measures, security arrangements, counselling and other assistance to witnesses and victims that appear before the court.[5]

1   ICC Statute, art 43(1).
2   Ibid, art 43(2),(4),(5).
3   Ibid, art 64(10).
4   Ibid, art 44(1)–(3).
5   Ibid, art 43(6).

Jurisdiction

22.11   The court must satisfy itself that it has jurisdiction over a case which comes before it.[1]

1   ICC Statute, art 19(1).

Ratione personae

22.12   All cases before the court are to be brought by the Prosecutor, at his or her discretion.[1] A situation in which one or more crimes has been committed will be referred to the attention of the Prosecutor by a state party to the Statute or by the Security Council, acting under Chapter VII of the UN Charter.[2] The Prosecutor will also be able to initiate a case *proprio motu*, on the basis of information he or she receives on crimes within the jurisdiction of the court.[3] The *proprio motu* exercise of power of the Prosecutor is subject to review by the Pre-Trial Chamber.[4]

The ICC will have jurisdiction over persons accused of a crime under the Statute, only if either:

(1)   the state on whose territory the crime was committed (or aboard a ship

or aircraft registered under its name) is a party to the Statute or has agreed to the jurisdiction of the court; or

(2) the state of nationality of the accused is a party to the Statute or has agreed to the jurisdiction of the court.[5]

Agreement of a state not party to the Statute to the jurisdiction of the court must be made by way of a declaration deposited with the Registrar.[6] An exception to the general rule on personal jurisdiction is found in cases referred to the Prosecutor by the Security Council, acting under Chapter VII of the UN Charter. In that event, a case can be brought against any person, regardless of his or her nationality or the place in which the alleged crimes were committed.[7]

1   ICC Statute, art 53.
2   Ibid, arts 13(a),(b), 14(1).
3   Ibid, arts 13(c), 15(1).
4   Ibid, art 15(4).
5   Ibid, art 12.
6   Ibid, art 12(3).
7   Ibid, art 12(2).

Ratione materiae

22.13 The court will have jurisdiction over four categories of crimes: genocide, crimes against humanity, war crimes and the crime of aggression.[1] Genocide involves certain serious crimes committed with intent to destroy, in whole or in part, a national, ethnic, racial or religious group;[2] crimes against humanity involve certain serious crimes knowingly committed against civilian populations, as part of a widespread or systematic attack;[3] and war crimes include grave breaches of the 1949 Geneva Conventions and other serious violations of the laws of war.[4] The court will deal with crimes which fall under its jurisdiction only in cases of sufficient gravity.[5] Upon ratification of the Statute, a state party can exclude, by way of a declaration, the jurisdiction of the court over war crimes committed by its nationals or in its territory. Such declaration will be in effect for seven years from the date in which the Statute will enter into force for the state concerned (or a shorter period of time prescribed by the reserving state).[6] Jurisdiction over the crime of aggression will be exercised only after an agreed definition of the crime has been adopted by the states parties.[7]

1   ICC Statute, art 5.
2   Ibid, art 6. The acts enumerated in the Statute are killing, causing serious harm, inflicting condition of life calculated to bring about physical destruction, preventing birth and forcibly transferring children from one group to another.
3   ICC Statute, art 7. The acts enumerated in the Statute are murder, extermination, enslavement, deportation or forcible transfer, unlawful deprivation of liberty, torture; rape and other forms of serious sexual violence; collective persecution; enforced disappearances of persons; apartheid; and other similar inhumane acts causing great suffering or serious injury.
4   ICC Statute, art 8. The crimes enumerated in the Statute are, inter alia, wilful killing, torture or inhuman treatment, wilfully causing great suffering or serious injury, extensive and unjustified destruction of property, compelling a prisoner of war to serve in the forces of an hostile army, wilful deprivation of the right to a fair trial from prisoners of war or other protected persons, unlawful deportation, transfer or confinement and taking of hostages.
5   ICC Statute, art 17(1)(d).
6   Ibid, art 124.
7   Ibid, art 5(2).

Ratione temporis

22.14 The ICC will only be able to deal with crimes committed after the entry into force of the Statute.[1] The court will also lack jurisdiction over crimes committed in the territory of a state party, or by a national of a state party if the crimes took place before the entry into force of the Statute for that state. However, the concerned state may declare its acceptance of the jurisdiction of the court over such crimes (in the same way as states not parties to the Statute).[2]

The Security Council may request the court to suspend any investigation or prosecution for twelve months. Such a request must be made through a resolution adopted under Chapter VII of the UN Charter.[3] After the expiration of 12 months, the request may be submitted anew under the same conditions. The court will be obliged to comply with the request of the Security Council.

1   ICC Statute, art 11(1).
2   Ibid, art 11(2).
3   Ibid, art 16.

COMPLEMENTARITY

22.15 The jurisdiction of the court is complementary to that of national courts.[1] The ICC will not have jurisdiction if a case that was brought before it is dealt with by a national legal system in one of these alternative ways:
(a) the case is being investigated or prosecuted in a national legal system;
(b) the case has been investigated in a national legal system and a decision not to prosecute has been adopted; or
(c) the case has been tried before a national court.[2]
However, the court will be able to exercise jurisdiction if it considers the national authorities to be unwilling or unable to carry out a genuine investigation and/or prosecution (eg if the proceedings were or are intended to shield the accused person from criminal responsibility or were or are not independent and impartial, or if the national legal system has collapsed).[3]

1   ICC Statute, preamble, art 1.
2   Ibid, arts 17(1)(a),(c), 20(3).
3   Ibid, arts 17, 20(3).

Advisory jurisdiction

22.16 The ICC will not have advisory jurisdiction.

PROCEDURAL ASPECTS

Languages

22.17 The official languages of the ICC will be Arabic, Chinese, English, French, Russian and Spanish (ie the official languages of the UN). All main decisions will be published in these languages.[1] The working languages of the court are to be English and French. The Rules of Procedure and Evidence will determine under what circumstances other official languages may be used as working languages.[2] The court will allow the use of languages other than the working languages, if it finds a request to this effect to be justified.[3]

1   ICC Statute, art 50(1).
2   Ibid, art 50(2).
3   Ibid, art 50(3).

Instituting proceedings

22.18 Proceedings before the ICC will begin with a request for authorisation of investigation, submitted by the prosecutor to the Pre-Trial Chamber. The request will be accompanied by supporting evidence.[1] The prosecutor may request additional information needed to substantiate the information in his or her possession from any reliable source (eg states, international organisations or NGOs).[2]

The prosecutor may decide not to pursue a case if he or she considers that:
(a) the case falls outside the jurisdiction of the court;
(b) the case is inadmissible;
(c) there is no legal basis for an arrest warrant or summons to appear; or
(d) prosecution would not serve the interests of justice.

However, this decision may be appealed by the entity that referred the situation to the prosecutor (a state party or the Security Council), or reviewed by the Pre-Trial Chamber, on its own motion (if the prosecutor's decision is based on the last ground).[3]

1 ICC Statute, art 15(3).
2 Ibid, art 15(2).
3 Ibid, art 53.

Financial assistance

22.19 If a person that is the subject of investigation or prosecution does not have legal representation, he or she is entitled to have legal assistance assigned to him or her, where the interests of justice so require. If the person lacks sufficient means to pay for the legal assistance, the court will fund it.[1] In addition, where standards of fairness so demand, the accused is entitled to receive, free of charge, the assistance of an interpreter and any necessary translation services.[2]

1 ICC Statute, arts 55(2)(c), 67(1)(d).
2 Ibid, arts 55(1)(c); 67(1)(f).

Provisional measures

Warrants of arrest

22.20 A Pre-Trial Chamber may order the arrest of a person, acting upon an application by the prosecutor. An arrest will be ordered if the court is satisfied that there are reasonable grounds to believe that the person committed a crime falling under the jurisdiction of the ICC and that the arrest is necessary to achieve one of the following goals:
(a) to ensure that person's appearance in trial;
(b) to prevent that person from obstructing or endangering the investigation; or
(c) to prevent that person from continuing to commit the same crime or a related crime arising out of the same circumstances (which is also within the jurisdiction of the court).[1]

The application for arrest must include the following information:
(a) the name of the person and other identifying information;
(b) a specific reference to the crimes which fall under the court's jurisdiction that the person is alleged to have committed;

(c) a concise statement of facts which constitute the said crimes;

(d) a summary of evidence and other information which establish reasonable grounds to believe that the person committed the crimes attributed to him or her; and

(e) the reason why the prosecutor believes that the arrest of the person is necessary.[2]

The warrant to be issued by the court will specify the above particulars (a)–(c), to the extent that the Pre-Trial Chamber is convinced by the evidence presented by the prosecutor (for instance, the court may issue a warrant for only some of the crimes advanced by the prosecutor).[3] At a later date, the prosecutor may request the chamber to modify or add to the contents of the warrant of arrest.[4] A request to arrest and surrender a person, based on the warrant of arrest, issued by the court, will be binding upon the states parties and they will be obliged to take immediate measures to bring the person into custody and subsequently deliver him or her to the seat of the court.[5] In urgent cases, the court may request provisional arrest of a person, for whom a warrant of arrest has been issued, until the court files with the state concerned a formal request for arrest and surrender.[6]

A person subject to an arrest warrant may apply at any time for interim release pending trial. The decision of the Pre-Trial Chamber on the motion will be subject to periodic review, and may also be re-examined at the request of the concerned person or the prosecutor.[7] If the Pre-Trial Chamber will consider that the person in question has been detained before trial for an unreasonable period of time, due to inexcusable delay on the part of the prosecutor, it may order release of the person – with or without conditions.[8]

1   ICC Statute, art 58(1).
2   Ibid, art 58(2).
3   Ibid, art 58(3).
4   Ibid, art 58(6).
5   Ibid, arts 59, 89, 91.
6   Ibid, art 92.
7   Ibid, art 60(2),(3).
8   Ibid, art 60(4).

UNIQUE INVESTIGATIVE OPPORTUNITY

22.21   The prosecutor may request the Pre-Trial Chamber to order measures necessary to take advantage of a unique opportunity to take testimony or statement from a witness, or to examine, collect or test evidence, which might not be available at the time of the trial.[1] The decision of the Pre-Trial Chamber will normally be taken after hearing the accused person.[2] The chamber may order any necessary action, taking into consideration the efficiency and integrity of the proceedings and the rights of the defendant. These orders may, inter alia, provide for a record to be made of the investigative proceedings, for representatives of the defence to attend them, or may involve the appointment of an ICC judge to supervise the questioning or gathering of evidence.[3] In appropriate cases, the Pre-Trial Chamber may order any of the above measures on its own initiative (even against the wishes of the prosecutor – who may bring an appeal against such a decision), or at the request of the accused person.[4]

A similar motion for provisional measures may be made in some cases by the prosecutor, pending a decision on a challenge to admissibility or to jurisdiction. While normally investigation is to be suspended upon the institution of such a challenge, if presented by a state, the prosecutor may seek author-isation from the court to continue with the investigation in exceptional cases. These are cases involving:

(a) investigative measures in respect of evidence which might not be avail-able later;

(b) completion of an investigative step which has already begun (eg taking of testimony); or

(c) prevention of the absconding of persons who are subject of a request submitted by the prosecutor for an arrest warrant.[5]

1   ICC Statute, art 56(1).
2   Ibid, art 56(1)(c).
3   Ibid, art 56(2).
4   Ibid, arts 56(3), 57(3)(b).
5   Ibid, art 19(8).

Preliminary objections and proceedings

22.22   A challenge to the admissibility of a case or to the jurisdiction of the court can be made by the following persons:

(a) an accused person (or a person for whom an arrest warrant or summons to appear have been issued);

(b) a state with jurisdiction over the case that is investigating and/or prosecuting the case, or has already done so;

(c) a state from which acceptance of jurisdiction is required under art 12 of the Statute (ie not party to the Statute at the time of the crime).[1]

The prosecutor may also seek a ruling from the court on admissibility or jurisdiction;[2] and the court may determine admissibility on its own motion (if involving questions of complementarity).[3]

Challenges should be raised before the commencement of the trial and only once.[4] However, in exceptional circumstances the court may allow more than one challenge or hear a challenge made after the beginning of the trial (in the latter case, only if the challenge alleges that the accused has already been tried for the same offence).[5] Challenges on behalf of states must be raised at the earliest opportunity and the prosecutor will suspend the investigation until the court renders its decision on such challenges.[6] Challenges made before the confirmation of charges (see infra) are to be brought before the Pre-Trial Chamber, while subsequent challenges will be presented to the Trial Chamber. In any event, decisions on challenges may be appealed before the Appeals Chamber.[7]

If the prosecutor informs a state that he or she intends to investigate crimes which fall under its jurisdiction, that state may request the prosecutor to defer his or her investigation, since the case is being investigated or has already been investigated by that state. The request must be made within one month from receiving notice from the prosecutor's office.[8] If the prosecutor believes that the requesting state is unwilling or unable to carry out the investigation, he or she may apply to the Pre-Trial Chamber for authorisation of investi-gation despite the request for deferment.[9] The state concerned, or the prosecutor, may appeal before the Appeals Chamber against a decision of the Pre-Trial Chamber on the application for authorisation of investigation.[10]

As indicated above, all proceedings must begin with authorisation of investigation. The Pre-Trial Chamber, acting on a request of the prosecutor, will grant such authorisation only if satisfied that the material submitted to it constitutes a reasonable basis for investigation proceedings and that the case seems to fall under the jurisdiction of the court.[11] Furthermore, at the end of the investigation, the prosecutor will present the charges against the accused person to the Pre-Trial Chamber for confirmation.[12] If the Pre-Trial Chamber finds, after hearing the prosecution and the accused person, that the evidence establishes substantial grounds to believe that the person has committed the crimes charged, it will confirm the charges and enable the case to be brought before the Trial Chamber.[13] At confirmation hearings, the prosecutor must support each charge with sufficient evidence; it is not necessary at this stage to call witnesses. The accused may object to the charges, challenge the evidence, and present evidence on his or her own behalf.[14] The chamber may confirm or decline to confirm the charges, in part or in whole, and may suggest to the prosecutor to gather more evidence or amend the charges.[15] The prosecutor may request the Pre-Trial Chamber, at a later date, to permit modification of the charges.[16]

1 ICC Statute, art 19(2).
2 Ibid, art 19(3).
3 Ibid, art 19(1).
4 Ibid, art 19(4)
5 Ibid, art 19(4).
6 Ibid, art 19(5).
7 Ibid, art 19(6).
8 Ibid, art 18(1),(2).
9 Ibid, art 18(2).
10 Ibid, art 18(4).
11 Ibid, art 15(4).
12 Ibid, art 61.
13 Ibid, art 61(1),(7).
14 Ibid, art 61(5),(6).
15 Ibid, art 61(7).
16 Ibid, art 61(9).

Written pleadings

22.23 The charges raised by the prosecutor will be presented to the court and to the defendant in the form of a document.[1] According to the Statute, the defence is entitled to submit to the court a written statement in reply to the charges.[2]

1 ICC Statute, art 61(3)(a).
2 Ibid, art 67(1)(h).

Oral arguments

22.24 The trial begins with the reading of the charges and a plea of guilty or not guilty by the accused person.[1] If the accused person admits his or her guilt, the court may convict him or her after being satisfied that the person understands the charges and the implication of admission, that the admission was made voluntarily and is supported by evidence.[2] If the accused person pleads not guilty, hearings will take place under conditions of equality between the parties and each party will submit evidence relevant to the case, including its witnesses.[3] The court can order, on its own initiative, that further evidence be produced.[4] The Statute explicitly provides that the accused will be given the opportunity to introduce witnesses on his or her behalf and to examine the witnesses against him or her.[5] Furthermore, the prosecutor must disclose the evidence in his or her possession to the defence, as soon as practicable.[6] The accused will be able to make an unsworn oral statement in his or her defence,[7] although he or she has the right to refuse to testify and remain silent without this conduct being held against the defence.[8]

The specific procedures of the trial are to be determined by the Trial Chamber, after consulting with the parties.[9] However, the chamber must ensure that the trial takes place without undue delay.[10] Trials will be held in public, unless special circumstances require that some of the session will be closed to the public (in order to protect victims, witnesses or confidential or sensitive information offered as evidence).[11]

1 ICC Statute, art 64(8)(a).
2 Ibid, art 65.
3 Ibid, art 69(3).
4 Ibid, arts 64(6)(d), 69(3).
5 Ibid, art 67(1)(e).
6 Ibid, art 67(2).
7 Ibid, art 67(1)(h).
8 Ibid, art 67(1)(g).
9 Ibid, art 64(3)(a).
10 Ibid, art 67(1)(c).
11 Ibid, art 64(7).

Third-party intervention/multiple proceedings

22.25 The Statute permits states and certain interested persons to intervene in certain stages of the proceedings, in connection with decisions that affect their interests. A state with jurisdiction over the crime, which is investigating and/or prosecuting the same matter or has already done so, and any state the consent of which is required for investigation (the state in which the crime took place and the state of nationality of the suspect, if they were not parties to the Statue at the time of the crime) may challenge the admissibility of the case or the jurisdiction of the court.[1] These states may also bring an appeal against a decision on admissibility or jurisdiction to the Appeals Chamber.[2] In the event that the prosecutor requests from the Pre-Trial Chamber authorisation to take investigative steps in the territory of a state party without its co-operation because that state is clearly unable to execute a request for co-operation, the state concerned will be heard before the chamber. It will also be entitled to submit an appeal to the Appeals Chamber against the decision of the Pre-Trial Chamber.[3] If a state believes that disclosure of certain information or documents is prejudicial to its national security interests, it may intervene in the proceedings and notify the prosecutor or the court of its objection to disclosure.[4] Upon failure to reach an agreement on the matter, the court will decide whether refusal to co-operate is in accordance with the concerned state's obligations under the Statute.[5] Representatives of the victim and other interested persons should be heard before the ICC rules on the issue of reparations to the victim.[6] The representatives of the victim, as well as bona fide owners of property adversely affected by forfeit of the convicted person's proceeds, property or assets, may appeal an order for reparations.[7]

As to multiple proceedings, the Statute envisages charges being brought in the same proceedings against multiple defendants, and the court is authorised to join or sever charges brought against more than one accused person.[8]

1 ICC Statute, art 19(2)(b),(c).
2 Ibid, arts 18(4), 19(6), 82(1)(a).
3 Ibid, arts 57(3)(d), 82(2).
4 Ibid, art 72(4)–(6).
5 Ibid, art 72(7). If the court finds that the state concerned violated its obligations under the Statute it may order disclosure of the information, make appropriate inference in the trial of the accused and bring the matter to the attention of the Assembly or the Security Council.
6 ICC Statute, art 75(3).
7 Ibid, art 82(4).
8 Ibid, art 64(5).

Amicus curiae

22.26   There are no explicit provisions in the Statute of the ICC concerning the introduction of amicus curiae briefs. However, the court can ask for information and documents from an intergovernmental organisation,[1] and arguably from other sources as well (particularly during pleadings on the issue of reparations).[2] It should also be kept in mind that investigation by the prosecutor could be prompted by any information delivered to him or her.

It is conceivable that the ICC Rules of Procedure and Evidence, which have yet to be adopted, will explicitly address the issue of amicus curiae briefs.

1 ICC Statute, art 87(6).
2 Ibid, arts 69(3) 75(3).

Representation of parties

22.27   A person to be questioned regarding a crime within the jurisdiction of the ICC has the right to have legal assistance of his or her choosing, or if he or she does not have legal assistance, to have legal assistance assigned in any case where the interests of justice so require. If the person concerned does not have sufficient means to pay for such assistance, it shall be provided free of charge.[1] In trials conducted under the Statute, the accused shall be entitled to conduct his or her defence in person or through legal assistance of the accused's choosing. Where the accused does not have legal assistance, this may be assigned by the court where the interests of justice so require, without payment if necessary.[2]

1 ICC Statute, art 55(2)(c).
2 Ibid, art 67(1)(d).

Decision

22.28   The decision of the Trial Chamber on the merits of the case will be based on evaluation of the evidence submitted and discussed before the court and upon assessment of the entire proceedings.[1] In order to convict the accused the court must be convinced of his or her guilt beyond reasonable doubt.[2] The decision will be given in writing and read in public (in full, or in a summary version).[3] It is to contain findings on the evidence presented and the chamber's conclusions.[4] If no unanimity is achieved, the decision will be taken by a majority vote and the opinion of the minority judges will be append to the decision.[5]

The decision cannot exceed the facts and circumstances alleged in the charges.[6] If the accused is convicted, the court will also consider the sentence to be imposed upon him or her. The sentence will be determined on the basis of the evidence and submissions made during trial or during a special session, convened by the court, in which evidence and submission relevant to the sentence will be presented.[7] When deciding the sentence, the court will consider, inter alia, the gravity of the crime and the individual circumstances of the convicted person (including time already served for the same crime).[8] In addition, the court may decide, if requested, or acting *proprio motu* in exceptional circumstances, to order reparations to be made to the victims of the crimes. Such a decision will be taken after hearing the convicted person, representatives of the victims and other interested persons and states. The reparations will be collected from the convicted person or, where appropriate, from a special trust fund maintained by the Assembly.[9]

1   ICC Statute, art 74(2).
2   Ibid, art 66(3).
3   Ibid, art 74(5).
4   Ibid, art 74(5).
5   Ibid, art 74(3),(5).
6   Ibid, art 74(2).
7   Ibid, art 76(1),(2). The sentences that the court may impose are imprisonment of up to 30 years or life imprisonment, a fine and forfeit of proceeds or property derived from the crime (without affecting the rights of third parties). If a person is found guilty for more than one crime, the court will impose a separate penalty for each crime and a cumulative penalty which cannot exceed 30 years or life imprisonment (nor fall short of the highest separate sentence pronounced): art 78(3).
8   ICC Statute, art 78(1),(2).
9   Ibid, arts 75(1)–(3), 79.

Revision of judgments

22.29   The convicted person – or if dead, another person on his or her behalf – or the prosecutor, acting on behalf of the convicted person, may apply to the Appeals Chamber to review a final judgment if one of the following has occurred:
(a) new evidence has been discovered which –
      (i) was not available at the time of the trial for reasons that cannot be attributed to the applying party; and
      (ii) is sufficiently important to have probably influenced the verdict;
(b) it has been newly discovered that decisive evidence relied upon in trial was false, forged or falsified;
(c) one or more of the judges committed in relation to the case a serious act of misconduct or a serious breach of duty, which could justify their removal from office.[1]
If the Appeals Chamber finds merit in the application it may reconvene the original Trial Chamber, refer the case to a new Trial Chamber or retain jurisdiction. The proceedings will then be resumed, and after hearing the parties the court will decide whether the judgement should be revised.[2] If the court finds that a miscarriage of justice has occurred, it may award compensation to the person who suffered punishment due to the conviction.[3]

1   ICC Statute, art 84(1).
2   Ibid, art 84(2).
3   Ibid, art 85(2).

Appeal

22.30 An appeal over a decision of the Trial Chamber on the guilt or acquittal of the accused person can be brought by the prosecutor or the convicted person (or the prosecutor acting on that person's behalf). The appeal must allege one of the following flaws in the decision:
  (i) procedural error;
  (ii) error of fact;
  (iii) error of law; or
  (iv) any other ground that affects the fairness or reliability of the proceedings or decision (this can be advanced only on behalf of the convicted person).[1]
The prosecutor or the convicted person may also appeal against a sentence, arguing that the sentence is disproportionate to the crime,[2] and the convicted person may also appeal against an order for reparations.[3] In addition, a party to a case may appeal against the following decisions of the Pre-Trial or Trial Chamber:
(a) decision on admissibility or jurisdiction;
(b) decision granting or denying release to a person investigated or prosecuted;
(c) decision of the Pre-Trial Chamber, acting *proprio motu*, to order measures in relation to a unique investigative opportunity (only the prosecutor can appeal on this ground);
(d) any decision that might significantly affect the fair and expeditious conduct of the proceedings or the outcome of the trial, in relation to which the Pre-Trial or Trial Chamber is of the opinion that an appeal may materially advance the proceedings.[4]
In addition, an appeal can be presented by other interested states and persons in the following cases:
(a) a state may appeal a decision to authorise investigation within its territory without its co-operation;
(b) states challenging the admissibility of the case or the jurisdiction of the court may appeal a relevant decision of the Pre-Trial or Trial Chamber;
(c) the representatives of the victim and a bona fide owner of property adversely affected by a forfeit of the convicted persons proceeds, property or assets may appeal an order on reparations.[5]
On appeal, the Appeals Chamber will have all of the powers of the Trial Chamber.[6] If it finds that the proceedings below were unfair in a way that affected the reliability of the decision or the sentence, or if it finds a factual, legal or procedural error, which materially affected the decision or the sentence, it may order one of the following:
(a) reversal or amendment of the decision or sentence;
(b) a new trial before a different Trial Chamber.[7]
If necessary, the Appeals Chamber may permit the introduction of new evidence before it, or send the case on remand to the original Trial Chamber to determine factual issues and report back to the Appeal Chamber accordingly.[8] If during an appeal against the sentence the court finds grounds to set aside the conviction, in part or in whole, or if during appeal against the conviction, the court finds grounds to reduce the sentence, it may invite the parties to submit their arguments on the issue, and may decide the matter.[9] However, in no case will an appeal submitted by one party only result in that party's detriment.[10]
The judgment of the Appeals Chamber will state the reasons on which it is

based, and will be delivered in public. If no unanimity is reached between the judges, the view of the minority will be indicated and judges may append their separate or dissenting opinions on questions of law.[11]

A convicted person will normally remain in custody during the appeal, and in exceptional circumstances an acquitted person will also remain in detention.[12] The execution of other aspects of the sentence will be suspended for the duration of the appeal.[13]

1 ICC Statute, art 81(1).
2 Ibid, art 81(2)(a).
3 Ibid, art 82(4).
4 Ibid, art 82(1).
5 Ibid, arts 19(6), 82(2),(4).
6 Ibid, art 83(1).
7 Ibid, art 83(2).
8 Ibid, art 83(2).
9 Ibid, art 81(2)(b),(c).
10 Ibid, art 83(2).
11 Ibid, art 83(4).
12 Ibid, art 81(3).
13 Ibid, art 81(4).

Costs

22.31 Every party to criminal proceedings before the ICC bears its own expenses. As indicated above, the accused will be provided with legal and linguistic assistance free of charge, if necessary. The costs of the activities of the court conducted in the territory of a state, in co-operation with it, will normally be incurred by that state, except for certain expenses that will be borne by the court.[1]

1 ICC Statute, art 100(1). The measures that the court will fund are travel and security of witnesses, experts and persons in custody of the state concerned; translation, interpretation and transcription; travel and subsistence of court and prosecution personnel; expert opinion or report requested by the court; transport of person surrendered to the jurisdiction of the court; and extraordinary costs. In the event that a state will request co-operation from the court in relation to proceedings conducted under that state's laws, the court will bear all ordinary expenses: arts 93(10), 100(2).

Enforcement of sentences

22.32 A sentence of imprisonment will be served in the territory of a state, designated by the court, which has volunteered to accept sentenced persons.[1] If no state is designated, the sentence will be carried out in The Netherlands. The court may, however, transfer a convicted prisoner to any state other than that originally or subsequently designated (or the host state).[2] The state in which the sentence of imprisonment is being carried out is bound by the decision of the court and cannot modify the sentence, nor extradite the convict to a third state that wishes to prosecute or punish him or her (without the court's approval).[3] The conditions of imprisonment must conform to the relevant international standards and will be supervised by the court.

The court will review an imprisonment sentence after two-thirds of the sentence has been served (or 25 years in the case of life imprisonment), and at subsequent dates to be determined by the Rules of Procedure and Evidence. In reviewing the sentence, the court will consider the level of co-operation of the convicted person with the court and other factors indicating clear and significant change of circumstances justifying the reduction of the sentence.[4]

Fines and forfeits ordered by the court will be recognised and enforced in the territory of the states parties in accordance with their laws, and without prejudice to the rights of bona fide third parties. The property forfeited, or, where appropriate, the proceeds of its sale (or the sale of other property of the convicted person of comparable value) will be transferred to the court.[5]

After a person is convicted or acquitted by the ICC, he or she may not be tried again for the same conduct before another court or before the ICC itself.[6]

1   ICC Statute, art 103. When designating a state the court will take into account the principle of equitable distribution of responsibilities by states; the conformity of prison conditions to international standards; the views of the sentenced person; and his or her nationality.
2   ICC Statute, art 104.
3   Ibid, arts 105, 108.
4   Ibid, art 110.
5   Ibid, art 109.
6   Ibid, art 20(1),(2).

REFERENCE

Selected bibliography

Book

M Cherif Bassiouni *The Statute of the International Criminal Court: a Documented History* (1998).

Articles

Mahnoush H Arsanjani 'The Rome Statute of the International Criminal Court' (1999) 93 American Journal of International Law 22.

M Cherif Bassiouni 'From Versailles to Rwanda in 75 Years: The Need to Establish a Permanent International Criminal Court' (1997) 10 Harvard Human Rights Yearbook 11.

M Cherif Bassiouni 'The Time has Come for an International Criminal Court' (1991) 1 Indiana International and Comparative Law Review 1.

Bradley E Berg 'The 1994 ILC Draft Statute for an International Criminal Court: A Principled Appraisal of Jurisdictional Structure' (1996) 28 Case Western Reserve Journal of International Law 221.

James Crawford 'A Permanent International Criminal Court: A Proposal that Overcomes Past Objections' (1995) 89 American Journal of International Law 404.

Christopher Keith Hall 'The First Two Sessions of the UN Preparatory Committee on the Establishment of an International Criminal Court' (1997) 91 American Journal of International Law 177.

Philippe Kirsch and John T Holmes 'The Rome Conference on an International Criminal Court: The Negotiating Process' (1999) 93 American Journal of International Law 2.

Bryan F MacPherson 'Building an International Criminal Court for the Twenty-First Century' (1998) 13 Connecticut Journal of International Law 1.

Mathew D Peter 'The Proposed International Criminal Court: A Commentary on the Legal and Political Debates Regarding Jurisdiction that Threaten the Establishment of an Effective Court' (1997) 24 Syracuse Journal of International Law and Commerce 177.

Darryl Robinson 'Defining "Crimes against Humanity" at the Rome Conference' (1999) 93 American Journal of International Law 43.

David J Scheffer 'The United States and the International Criminal Court' (1999) 93 American Journal of International Law 12.

Robert B Rosenstock 'The Proposal for an International Criminal Court, McLean Lecture on World Law' (1994) 54 University of Pittsburg Law Review 271.

Michael P Scharf 'Getting Serious About an International Criminal Court' (1994) 6 Pace International Law Review 103.

CHAPTER 23

International Criminal Tribunal for the former Yugoslavia

INTRODUCTORY

Name and seat of the body

23.1 The International Tribunal for the Prosecution of Persons Responsible for Serious Violations of International Humanitarian Law Committed in the Territory of the former Yugoslavia since 1991 (International Criminal Tribunal for the former Yugoslavia, hereinafter 'the tribunal' or 'ICTY') is seated in The Hague, The Netherlands. The address of the tribunal is:

> International Criminal Tribunal for the former Yugoslavia
> Churchillplein 1
> 2517 JW The Hague
> PO Box 13888
> 2501 EW The Hague
> The Netherlands
>
> Tel: 31 70 416 5233
> Fax: 31 70 416 5355
> website: http://www.un.org/icty

Although the headquarters of the ICTY are located in The Hague, a Trial Chamber may exercise its functions at another place if so authorised by the President of the tribunal in the interests of justice.[1]

1 Rules of Procedure and Evidence, *International Tribunal for the Prosecution of Persons Responsible for Serious Violations of International Humanitarian Law Committed in the Territory of the former Yugoslavia since 1991*, UN Doc IT/32 (1993) ('Rules of Procedure'), r 4. Amendments to the Rules of Procedure are reported in the Judicial Supplement to the ICTY Bulletin.

Introductory description

23.2 The ICTY is an ad hoc international criminal tribunal, mandated to prosecute persons responsible for serious violations of international humanitarian law committed in the territory of the former Socialist Federal Republic of Yugoslavia since 1 January 1991. The tribunal was established pursuant to a Security Council resolution[1] under Chapter VII of the UN Charter as an enforcement measure, and its jurisdiction is limited to crimes enumerated in arts 2–5 of the Statute of the tribunal.[2] Although the ICTY and national courts have concurrent jurisdiction over the crimes specified in the Statute, the ICTY has primacy over national courts: at the request of the ICTY national courts must defer to competence of the tribunal.[3] As the mandate of the tribunal is based on a Security Council resolution, all states are bound by it and obliged to comply with the requests and decisions of the tribunal.[4] In case of non-compliance the President of the ICTY may refer the case to the Security Council.[5]

The prosecution of cases before the tribunal falls within the responsibility of the Prosecutor, an independent and separate organ of the tribunal. The Prosecutor ex officio investigates all matters falling within the jurisdiction of the ICTY, regardless of the source of information and of any parallel national proceedings, and pursues the cases before the tribunal.[6] The cases are dealt with by the Trial Chambers, whose decisions – subject to restrictions – may be challenged before the Appeals Chamber.

By July 1999, 12 trials had been initiated before the ICTY and four judgments handed down. Sixty-five indictments have been issued and 23 accused persons are currently held in custody awaiting trial.

1　SC Res 827, 25 May 1993, UN Doc S/RES/827 (1993).
2　Statute of the International Tribunal, *International Tribunal for the Prosecution of Persons Responsible for Serious Violations of International Humanitarian Law Committed in the Territory of the former Yugoslavia since 1991*, adopted by SC Res 827 ('ICTY Statute' or the 'Statute').
3　ICTY Statute, art 9(2).
4　UN Charter, art 25.
5　Rules of Procedure, r 11.
6　ICTY Statute, art 18(1).

INSTITUTIONAL ASPECTS

Governing texts

Procedural law

23.3　The principal texts governing the activities of the tribunal are the Statute of the International Tribunal[1] and the Rules of Procedure and Evidence.[2] Other texts concerning proceedings before the tribunal include the Rules governing the Detention of Persons awaiting Trial and Appeal before the Tribunal or otherwise Detained on the Authority of the Tribunal (Rules of Detention),[3] Directive on the Assignment of Defence Counsel (Defence Counsel Directive),[4] the Regulations to govern the Supervision of Visits to and Communications with Detainees[5] and the Code of Professional Conduct for Defence Counsel appearing before the International Tribunal.[6] The above procedural rules, except for the Statute, have been adopted by the tribunal and have been amended or revised on several occasions.

1　See para 23.2 n 2.
2　See para 23.1 n 1.
3　UN Doc IT/38/Rev 7.
4　UN Doc IT/73/Rev 1 (Dir No 1/94).
5　UN Doc IT/98/Rev 2.
6　UN Doc IT/125.

Substantive law

23.4　The substantive law to be applied by the tribunal is set forth in arts 2–5 of its Statute. This includes the fundamental rules of international humanitarian law, the violation of which entails individual criminal responsibility (grave breaches of the 1949 Geneva Conventions, war crimes, genocide and crimes against humanity). In determining the substantive law to be applied, the tribunal may look at previous international practice and case law.

Organisation

23.5 The tribunal consists of three Trial Chambers, an Appeals Chamber, the Prosecutor's Office and a Registry servicing both the Chambers and the Prosecutor.[1]

1   ICTY Statute, art 11.

Composition

23.6 The tribunal comprises 14 judges, three judges serving in each Trial Chamber and five judges in the Appeals Chamber.[1] The judges are elected for a renewable term of four years by the UN General Assembly from a list of candidates prepared by the Security Council from the nominees of the states.[2] The judges must be persons of high moral character, impartiality and integrity. They must possess qualifications required for the highest judicial offices in their respective countries. The judges must have established competence in criminal law and international law, including international humanitarian and human rights law. Due account must be taken of the adequate representation of the principal legal systems of the world.[3] No two judges can be nationals of the same state.[4]

The judges of the tribunal elect a President and a Vice-President[5] (currently President Kirk McDonald and Vice-President Shahabuddeen) both of whom may be re-elected once. The President is generally responsible for the administrative functions of the tribunal, in which capacity he or she, inter alia, co-ordinates the work of the chambers, supervises the activity of the Registry and presides at the plenary meeting as well as in the Appeal Chamber.[6]

The President, after consultation with the judges, assigns judges to the Appeals Chamber and to the Trial Chambers.[7] Under the Rules of Procedure and Evidence, judges are required to rotate on a regular basis between the Trial Chambers and the Appeals Chamber.[8]

1   ICTY Statute, art 12. Currently, the judges are:
  President: Gabrielle Kirk McDonald (United States). **Vice-President:** Mohamed Shahabuddeen (Guyana). **Judges:** Antonio Cassese (Italy), Claude Jorda (France); Richard George May (United Kingdom); Florence Ndepele Mwachande Mumba (Zambia); Rafael Nieto Navia (Colombia); Fouad Abdel-Moneim Riad (Egypt); Almiro Simoes Rodrigues (Portugal); Lal Chand Vohrah (Malaysia); Tieya Wang (China); David Anthony Hunt (Australia); Mohamed Bennouna (Morocco) and Patrick Lipton Robinson (Jamaica).
2   ICTY Statute, art 13(2).
3   Ibid, art 13(2).
4   Ibid, art 12.
5   Ibid, art 14(1), Rules of Procedure, r 20.
6   Rules of Procedure, r 19(A).
7   ICTY Statute, art 14(3).
8   Rules of Procedure, r 27(A).

DISQUALIFICATION OF JUDGES

23.7 A judge may not sit on a trial or appeal in a case in which he or she has a personal interest or where his or her impartiality can be otherwise questioned. In any such circumstance the judge must withdraw or may be disqualified by the Bureau (the internal consulting organ of the tribunal)[1] at the motion of the prosecutor or the defendant.[2] No judge can sit on a trial for which he or she has reviewed the indictment or on an appeal in a case in which that judge has already participated. Similarly, no former member of a Trial Chamber may sit on review proceedings in a matter in which he or she has been previously involved.[3]

1 Rules of Procedure, r 23.
2 Ibid, r 15(A),(B).
3 Ibid, r 15(D).

Plenary/chambers

23.8 The tribunal deals with cases in chambers. The judges meet in plenary only to elect the President and the Vice-President; to adopt and amend the Rules of Procedure and Evidence; to adopt the Annual Report of the tribunal; to determine or supervise the conditions of detention; or to decide upon matters relating to the internal functioning of the tribunal.[1]

The pre-trial proceedings are conducted by a duty judge (eg review of indictment, handling applications for warrant) designated by the President,[2] or by a Trial Chamber. For the co-ordination of pre-trial proceedings the Trial Chamber may designate from among its members a pre-trial judge.[3] The pre-trial judge may be entrusted with some of the Trial Chamber's pre-trial functions, such as handling motions, conducting pre-trial and pre-defence conferences.[4]

The trials are dealt with by three-judge Trial Chambers and appeals are heard by the five-judge Appeals Chamber.

1 Rules of Procedure, r 24.
2 Ibid, r 28(A),(C).
3 Ibid, r 65*ter*(A),(B).
4 Ibid, r 65*ter*(D).

Appeals structure

23.9 A Trial Chamber decision of acquittal or conviction, or a decision on the sentence can be challenged before the Appeals Chamber by the prosecutor or the convicted person. The grounds of challenge have been narrowly formulated: an appeal lies against the decision where an error of law invalidates the decision or an error of fact that has resulted in miscarriage of justice.[1] Some interlocutory decisions can also be challenged, but normally appeal in these cases is subject to a leave granted by the Appeals Chamber (see para 23.31, infra). The Appeals Chamber may affirm, reverse or revise the decision of the Trial Chambers.[2] Moreover, a state directly affected by an interlocutory decision of a Trial Chamber may seek review of that decision if it concerns issues of general importance relating to the powers of the tribunal. The Appeals Chamber may suspend the execution of the attacked decision.[3]

1 ICTY Statute, art 25(1).
2 Ibid, art 25(2).
3 Rules of Procedure, 108*bis*.

Technical/scientific experts

23.10 The Rules of Procedure and Evidence envisage the broad use of experts. The Trial Chamber may order the medical, psychiatric or psychological examination of the accused *proprio motu* or at the request of either party. Such examinations are conducted by one or more experts entrusted by the Registrar, selected from a list of experts maintained by the Registry.[1] The parties may also present statements of experts as evidence.[2]

1 Rules of Procedure, r 74*bis*.
2 For the rules governing disclosure of evidence given by experts see Rules of Procedure, r 94*bis*.

Secretariat

23.11 The Registry of the tribunal is responsible for providing secretarial services to the chambers as well as the prosecutor.[1] The Registry is headed by the Registrar appointed by the Secretary-General for a renewable term of four years.[2] The Registrar is assisted by a Deputy Registrar. The Registrar assists the judges, the chambers, the plenary and the Prosecutor in the performance of their functions and serves as their general channel of communication. The Registrar maintains the records of the tribunal.[3]

Under rule 34 of the Rules of Procedure and Evidence an additional organ, the Victims and Witnesses Unit, has been set up under the authority of the Registrar.

1 ICTY Statute, art 17(1).
2 Ibid, art 17(3).
3 Rules of Procedure, r 33.

Jurisdiction

Ratione personae

23.12 The tribunal has jurisdiction over *natural* persons accused of serious violations of international humanitarian law committed in the territory of the former Yugoslavia since 1991.[1] The tribunal has no jurisdiction over states, legal persons and organisations.

1 ICTY Statute, art 6.

Ratione materiae

23.13 The tribunal's competence is limited to the following group of crimes:[1]
(a) grave breaches of the Geneva Conventions of 12 August 1949;[2]
(b) violations of the laws or customs of war;[3]
(c) genocide;[4]
(d) crimes against humanity.[5]

1 It must be noted that some of the crimes (eg genocide) may entail individual criminal liability as well as the responsibility of a state. As the individual criminal liability does not exclude state responsibility and vice versa, the same act of genocide could be the subject of parallel and simultaneous legal proceedings before the International Court of Justice and the tribunal. Application of the Convention on the Prevention and Punishment of the Crime of Genocide (*Bosnia and Herzegovina v Yugoslavia*) <www.icj-cij/icjwww/idocket/ibhy/ibhyframe.htm>.
2 ICTY Statute, art 2, under the following grave breaches of the Geneva Conventions of 12 August 1949 may be prosecuted before the ICTY:
  (a) wilful killing;
  (b) torture or inhuman treatment, including biological experiments;
  (c) wilfully causing great suffering or serious injury to body or health;
  (d) extensive destruction and appropriation of property, not justified by military necessity and carried out unlawfully and wantonly;
  (e) compelling a prisoner of war or a civilian to serve in the forces of a hostile power;

(f) wilfully depriving a prisoner of war or a civilian of rights of fair and regular trial;
(g) unlawful deportation or transfer or unlawful confinement of a civilian;
(h) taking civilians as hostages.
The conventions referred to in the Statute are: Geneva Convention for the Amelioration of the Condition of the Wounded and Sick in Armed Forces in the Field, 12 August 1949, 75 UNTS 31; Geneva Convention for the Amelioration of the Condition of the Wounded, Sick and Shipwrecked Members of Armed Forces at Sea, 12 August 1949, 75 UNTS 85; Geneva Convention Relative to the Treatment of Prisoners of War, 12 August 1949, 75 UNTS 135; Geneva Convention Relative to the Protection of Civilian Persons in Time of War, 12 August 1949, 75 UNTS 287.
3   ICTY Statute, art 3.
4   Ibid, art 4.
5   Ibid, art 5.

Ratione temporis

23.14   The temporal jurisdiction of the tribunal extends from a period beginning on 1 January 1991[1] and is limited to crimes that have been committed following that date in the territory of the former Socialist Federal Republic of Yugoslavia.

1   ICTY Statute, art 8.

RELATIONSHIP WITH NATIONAL COURTS

23.15   The power of the tribunal to prosecute crimes punishable under national laws has created a potential conflict between the jurisdiction of the tribunal and that of the national courts. Although the Statute recognises the concurrent jurisdiction of national courts, it is subject to the primacy of the tribunal.[1] The tribunal is empowered to intervene at any stage of the proceedings and request the national court to defer to the competence of the tribunal.[2] Request for deferral may be initiated by the Prosecutor if :
(a)   the act in question is characterised as an ordinary crime in the national proceedings;
(b)   there is a lack of impartiality and independence, or the proceedings are designed to shield the accused from international criminal liability, or the case is not diligently prosecuted; or
(c)   the matter involves factual or legal questions which may have implications for proceedings before the tribunal.[3]
The state concerned is obliged to comply with a request for deferral issued by a Trial Chamber.

The Statute declares that no person can be tried before a national court for acts in respect of which he or she has already been tried before the tribunal (*non bis in idem*).[4] This, however, does not apply to the tribunal in so far as it does not prevent the subsequent prosecution of a person before the tribunal if:
(a)   the act in question was characterised as an ordinary crime in the national proceedings; or
(b)   there was a lack of impartiality and independence, or the proceedings were designed to shield the accused from international criminal liability, or the case was not diligently prosecuted.[5]

1   ICTY Statute, art 9(1).
2   Ibid, art 9(2).
3   Rules of Procedure, r 9.
4   ICTY Statute, art 10(1).
5   Ibid, art 10(2).

Advisory jurisdiction

23.16   The tribunal does not exercise advisory jurisdiction.

PROCEDURAL ASPECTS

Languages

23.17   The working languages of the tribunal are English and French.[1] The accused, however, and other persons appearing before the tribunal (including counsel for an accused, subject to leave by a chamber) have a right to use their own language through the entire procedure.[2] The accused must be informed of all charges and the details of the proceedings in a language which he or she understands. The accused and other persons involved in the proceedings are entitled to the free assistance of an interpreter if they cannot understand the language of the tribunal.[3]

A copy of the judgment and of the judges' opinions must be served on the accused in a language that he or she understands.[4]

1   ICTY Statute, art 33, in general see Rules of Procedure, r 3.
2   Rules of Procedure, r 3(B)–(D).
3   ICTY Statute, art 21(4)(a),(f) also see Rules of Procedure, rr 42(A)(ii) and 43(i).
4   Rules of Procedure, r 98*ter*(C).

Instituting proceedings

23.18   The investigation of crimes is initiated and carried out by the Prosecutor ex officio on the basis of information from any source, in particular governments, UN organs, intergovernmental and non-governmental organisations.[1] The Prosecutor has broad powers of investigation, such as the power to question suspects, witnesses and victims, to collect evidence and conduct on-site investigations. The Prosecutor may seek the assistance of the authorities of any state. States are under a general obligation to co-operate for the fulfilment of the request.[2]

Upon a determination that a prima facie case exists the Prosecutor prepares an indictment and transmits it to the duty judge for confirmation.[3] If the judge is satisfied that a prima facie case has been established he or she confirms the indictment. If not so satisfied the judge may request additional material, adjourn the review or dismiss the indictment.[4]

The Prosecutor may amend the indictment –
   (i)   at any time before its confirmation;
  (ii)   thereafter with leave of the judge who has confirmed the indictment; or
 (iii)   after the commencement of the presentation of the evidence only with the leave of the Trial Chamber hearing the case.[5]
The indictment may be withdrawn under similar conditions.[6]

1   ICTY Statute, art 18(1).
2   Ibid, art 18(2), Rules of Procedure, r 39.
3   ICTY Statute, arts 18(4) and 19(1).
4   Ibid, art 19(1), Rules of Procedure 47(B).
5   Rules of Procedure, r 50(A).
6   Ibid, r 51(A).

Financial assistance

23.19 A person subject to investigation or prosecution has a right to legal assistance without payment, provided that he or she cannot pay for it, as well as to free assistance of an interpreter or other translation services.[1]

1 Rules of Procedure, r 42(A)(i),(ii).

Preliminary objections and proceedings

23.20 As mentioned above, the commencement of proceedings before the tribunal is subject to confirmation of indictment by a judge. Once the indictment is confirmed the judge may, at the request of the prosecutor, issue such orders and warrants as may be necessary for the conduct of the trial.[1] Once the accused has been detained and transferred to the seat of the tribunal the President assigns the case to a Trial Chamber. The accused must be brought before that Trial Chamber without delay and must be formally charged.[2]

The defence can file preliminary motions, no later than 30 days after the delivery to the defence of the indictment and all supporting documents. Such motions may:

(a) challenge jurisdiction;
(b) allege defects in the form of indictment;
(c) seek the severance of counts joined in one indictment or seek separate trials; or
(d) raise objections based on the refusal of a request for assignment of counsel.[3]

The motions must be disposed of before the commencement of the opening statements of the trial.[4] A decision on motions challenging jurisdiction can be generally appealed as a matter of right, whereas other decisions only at the discretion of the Appeals Chamber.[5]

At the initial pre-trial hearing, after the reading of the indictment, the accused is called upon to enter a plea of guilty or not guilty. In case of a plea of not guilty the chamber instructs the Registrar to set a date for trial.[6] The Trial Chamber may enter a finding of guilt and instruct the Registrar to set a date for the sentencing hearing[7] if an accused pleads guilty and the Trial Chamber is satisfied that:

(a) the guilty plea has been made voluntarily;
(b) the guilty plea is not equivocal; and
(c) there is a sufficient factual basis for the crime and the accused's participation in it.

During the pre-trial proceedings the prosecutor must disclose evidence in support of each charge. Prior to the commencement of the trial, subject to certain restrictions, both the prosecutor and the defence must reciprocally disclose any further evidence, names of witnesses etc.[8] In order to ensure an expeditious trial the Trial Chamber holds a pre-trial conference and may hold a pre-defence conference whereby the parties are to clarify and finalise their trial positions (eg disputed matters of fact and law, list of witnesses etc).[9]

1 ICTY Statute, art 19(2).
2 Rules of Procedure, r 62.
3 Ibid, r 72(A).
4 Id.
5 Rules of Procedure, r 72(B), also see para 23.31 infra.

6 Ibid, r 62.
7 Ibid, r 62*bis*.
8 Ibid, rr 66–68.
9 Ibid, rr 73*bis* and 73*ter*.

Provisional measures

Urgent measures

23.21 During the investigations, in case of urgency, the prosecutor may request any state:
(a) to arrest a suspect provisionally;
(b) to seize physical evidence; and
(c) to take all necessary measures to prevent the escape of the suspect or an accused, injury to or intimidation of a victim or a witness, or the destruction of evidence.
The state concerned must comply with the request.[1] Any other provisional measures are valid only if ordered by a judge or a chamber.

1 Rules of Procedure, r 40.

Transfer and provisional detention of suspects

23.22 A judge may order the provisional detention and the transfer to the detention units of the tribunal of a person already detained or subject to a request for provisional arrest under the following conditions:
(a) after the hearing of the prosecutor the judge considers that there is a reliable and consistent body of material which tends to show that the suspect may have committed the crime in question; and
(b) the judge considers provisional detention to be a necessary measure to prevent the escape of the suspect or an accused, injury to or intimidation of a victim or a witness, or the destruction of evidence, or to be otherwise necessary for the conduct of investigation.[1]
The provisional detention may not exceed 30 days, but may be renewed twice at the request of the Prosecutor. After a maximum of 90 days if the indictment is not confirmed (and an arrest warrant issued) the suspect must be released.[2]

1 Ibid, r 40*bis*(B).
2 Ibid, r 40*bis*(D).

Warrant of arrest

23.23 A warrant of arrest and any other orders, summons, subpoenas, warrants and transfer orders as may be necessary for the purposes of the investigation or for the preparation of the trial are issued by a judge or Trial Chamber at the request of either the prosecutor or the defence, or proprio motu.[1] A state to which the warrant is transmitted must promptly comply therewith.[2] Once detained by the state concerned, the accused must be transferred to the seat of the tribunal (see para 23.22, supra).[3] The obligation of the state to transfer or surrender the accused prevails over restrictions of national extradition laws.[4] If, within a reasonable time after the warrant of arrest or transfer no action has been taken by the state concerned, the tribunal may notify the Security Council.[5]
Once detained, an accused may be released by the Trial Chamber only in

exceptional circumstances and if the Trial Chamber is satisfied that the accused will appear for trial and, if released, will not pose a danger to any victim, witness or any other person. To that end the Trial Chamber may impose conditions on release, including the execution of a bail bond.[6]

Other provisional measures include protection of victims and witnesses[7] and transfer of detained witnesses.[8]

1 Rules of Procedure, r 54.
2 Ibid, r 56.
3 Ibid, r 57.
4 Ibid, r 58.
5 Ibid, r 59(B).
6 Ibid, r 65(A)–(C).
7 Ibid, rr 69 and 75.
8 Ibid, r 90.

Written pleadings

23.24 The charges raised by the prosecutor must be presented to the tribunal and to the accused in written form.[1] The indictment sets forth the name and particulars of the suspect, and must contain a concise statement of the facts of the case and of the crime with which the suspect is charged.[2] The defence is entitled to submit to the tribunal a written statement in reply to the indictment.

Preliminary motions must be submitted in writing.[3]

1 Rules of Procedure, r 47.
2 Ibid, r 47(C).
3 Ibid, r 72(A).

Oral arguments

23.25 As mentioned above, the reading of the charges and the plea of guilty or not guilty by the accused take place during the preliminary proceedings. A trial is conducted only if the accused pleads not guilty.

At the beginning of the trial each party may make an opening statement.[1] This is followed by the presentation of evidence and the hearing of witnesses.[2] Examination-in-chief, cross-examination and re-examination are allowed in each case. A judge may, at any stage, put any questions to the witness.[3] The Trial Chamber may order either party to produce additional evidence and may summon witnesses *proprio motu*.[4]

After the presentation of all evidence both the prosecutor and the defence may present a closing argument. The prosecutor may thereafter present a rebuttal and the defence a rejoinder.[5] When both parties have completed their presentation the presiding judge closes the hearing and the Trial Chamber retires for deliberation.[6]

All proceedings before the Trial Chamber, except for the deliberations, are held in public.[7] The Trial Chamber may exclude the press and the public only for reasons of public order or morality; safety, security or non-disclosure of the identity of a victim or a witness; or protection of the interests of justice.[8]

1 Rules of Procedure, r 84.
2 Ibid, r 85(A).
3 Ibid, r 85(A),(B).

4   Ibid, r 98.
5   Ibid, r 86(A).
6   Ibid, r 87(A).
7   Ibid, r 78.
8   Ibid, r 79(A),(B).

Third party intervention/multiple proceedings

23.26   The Rules of Procedure and Evidence envisage only a very limited role for third parties in the proceedings.

As the tribunal has primacy over national courts, no state has a right to intervene for the purpose of asserting its interest of prosecuting a crime concurrently tried before the tribunal (the Trial Chamber may, however, suspend the indictment pending the proceedings before national courts, if it considers it appropriate).[1]

A state directly affected by an interlocutory decision of the Trial Chamber may seek review of that decision if that decision concerns issues of general importance relating to the powers of the tribunal.[2] If the Appeals Chamber considers that request admissible it may suspend the execution of that decision.[3]

In proceedings concerning restitution of property, third parties with a lawful interest in that property must be given an opportunity to justify their claim before the Trial Chamber.[4] Claims for compensation of victims, on the other hand, may only be adjudicated by competent national courts. In respect of such claims victims or other persons on behalf of them have no right to be heard by the tribunal.[5]

Persons accused of crimes committed in the course of the same transaction may be jointly charged and tried.[6] Two or more crimes may be joined in one indictment if the series of acts were committed in the same transaction and by the same person.[7]

1   Rules of Procedure, r 11*bis*(A).
2   Ibid, r 108*bis*(A).
3   Ibid, r 108*bis*(C).
4   Ibid, r 105(B),(C).
5   Ibid, r 106(A),(B).
6   Ibid, r 48.
7   Ibid, r 49.

Amicus curiae

23.27   The Trial and Appeal Chambers may, if it is considered desirable for the proper determination of the case, invite or grant leave to a state, organisation or person to appear before it and make submissions on any issue specified by the chambers.[1]

1   Rules of Procedure, r 74.

Representation of the parties

23.28   An accused is entitled to be tried in his or her presence and to defend himself or herself in person or through legal assistance of his or her choosing or to have legal assistance assigned without payment if he or she does not have sufficient means.[1] When questioned, a suspect has the right to be assisted by counsel of his or her choice or to be assigned legal assistance without payment if he or she does not have sufficient means.[2]

1 ICTY Statute, art 21(4)(d).
2 Rules of Procedure, r 42.

Decision

23.29 The decision of the Trial or Appeals Chamber is reached by the majority of the judges. The judgment must be delivered in public and be accompanied by a reasoned opinion in writing to which separate and dissenting opinions may be appended.[1]

A finding of guilt can be reached only if the majority of the judges of the chamber is satisfied that the guilt has been proved beyond reasonable doubt.[2] At the same time the chamber must determine the penalty to be imposed on the convicted person.[3]

The only available penalty is imprisonment, for a maximum term up to the convicted person's life.[4] In determining the terms of imprisonment the Trial Chamber must take into consideration factors such as the gravity of the offence, any aggravating circumstances, any mitigating circumstances, including co-operation of the convicted person, the general practice regarding prison sentences in the former Yugoslavia, and the extent to which any penalty imposed by a court of any state for the same act has been served.[5]

In addition to imprisonment the Trial Chamber may order the return to the rightful owner of any property and its proceeds acquired by criminal conduct.[6] As noted above (para 23.26) compensation to victims, based on the finding of guilt by the tribunal, may only be rendered by national courts.

1 ICTY Statute, art 23(2).
2 Rules of Procedure, r 87(A).
3 Ibid, r 87(C).
4 ICTY Statute, art 24(1); Rules of Procedure, r 101(A).
5 ICTY Statute, art 24(2); Rules of Procedure, r 101(B).
6 ICTY Statute, art 24(3).

Revision of judgments

23.30 The convicted person or the prosecutor may submit an application for review of the judgment where a new fact has been discovered which was not known at the time of the proceedings before the Trial Chamber or the Appeals Chamber, provided that such a fact would have been a decisive factor in reaching the decision.[1] The time limit for such a motion by the prosecutor is one year from the date of judgment.[2] If the majority of judges of the chamber agree that the new fact could have been such a decisive factor, the chamber reviews the decision and after the hearing of the parties delivers a further judgment.[3] An appeal as of right lies against the judgment on review.[4]

1 ICTY Statute, art 26.
2 Rules of Procedure, r 119.
3 Ibid, r 120.
4 Ibid, r 121.

Appeal

23.31 A Trial Chamber decision on guilt or non-guilt or the terms of sentence can be appealed before the Appeals Chamber by the convicted person or the

prosecutor. The grounds of appeal are as follows:
(a) an error of a question of law invalidating the decision, or
(b) an error of fact which has occasioned a miscarriage of justice.[1]
In addition, the following interlocutory decisions can be appealed, subject to the restrictions below:
(a) provisional release of the accused where leave is granted by a bench of three judges of the Appeals Chamber;[2]
(b) a decision on preliminary motions: in case of challenge to jurisdiction generally; in case of any other motions where a leave is granted by a bench of three judges of the Appeals Chamber upon demonstration of a good cause;[3]
(c) decision on any other motion if the decision would cause such a prejudice to the case of the party that it could not be cured by the final disposal of the trial, or if the issue is of general importance to the proceedings before the tribunal or in international law generally;[4]
(d) decision concerning a contempt of tribunal, where a good cause is shown;[5]
(e) decision concerning false testimony under solemn declaration.[6]
On appeal the Appellate Chamber holds a hearing, based on the record of appeal and the briefs of the appellant and the respondent.[7] A party may apply to present additional evidence that was not available at the trial. Such new evidence may only be admitted, however, if the Appeals Chamber considers that the interests of justice so require.[8]

The Appeals Chamber reaches its judgment by majority. It may affirm, reverse or revise the decision of the Trial Chamber.[9] In appropriate circumstances the Appeals Chamber may order that the accused be retried.[10]

1 ICTY Statute, art 25(1).
2 Rules of Procedure, r 65(D).
3 Ibid, r 72(B).
4 Ibid, r 73(B).
5 Ibid, r 77(D).
6 Ibid, rr 91, 116*bis*(A).
7 Ibid, rr 109 and 111–113.
8 Ibid, r 115(A),(B).
9 ICTY Statute, art 25(2).
10 Rules of Procedure, r 117(C).

Costs

23.32 The costs of the criminal proceedings are borne by the tribunal. The expenses of the tribunal are covered by the regular budget of the United Nations in accordance with Article 17 of the UN Charter.[1]

1 ICTY Statute, art 32.

Enforcement of sentences

23.33 The imprisonment is served in a state designated by the tribunal from a list of states which have indicated to the Security Council their willingness to accept convicted persons. The imprisonment must be in accordance with the applicable law of the state concerned.[1] Transfer of the convicted person must take place as soon as possible.[2] All sentences of imprisonment are supervised by the tribunal.[3]

Restitution of property ordered by the tribunal is to be effected with the co-operation of the national courts.[4]

1   ICTY Statute, art 27.
2   Rules of Procedure, r 103(B).
3   Ibid, r 104.
4   Ibid, r 105(G).

REFERENCE

Sources of case law, including case reports

Reports of judgments of the ICTY can also be found on the tribunal's website.

ICTY Judicial Reports/Recueils Judiciaires (Kluwer Law International).

Selected bibliography

Books

M Cherif Bassiouni *The Law of the International Criminal Tribunal for the Former Yugoslavia*, Transnational Publishers (1996).

John R W D Jones *The Practice of the International Criminal Tribunals for the Former Yugoslavia and Rwanda*, Transnational Publishers (1998).

Virginia Morris, Michael Scharf *An Insider's Guide to the International Criminal Tribunal for the former Yugoslavia*, Transnational Publishers (1995).

Articles

Seean D Murphy 'Progress and Jurisprudence of the International Criminal Tribunal for the former Yugoslavia' (1999) 93(1) American Journal of International Law 57.

Alain Pellet 'Le Tribunal Criminel International Pour l'ex-Yougoslavie: Poudre aux Yeux ou Avance Décisive?' (1994) Revue Général de Droit International Public 7.

Daphna Shraga and Ralph Zacklin 'The International Criminal Tribunal for the former Yugoslavia' (1994) 5 European Journal of International Law 360.

Philippe Weckel 'L'Institution d'un tribunal international pour répression des crimes de droit humanitaire en Yougoslavie (1993) 39 Annuaire Français de Droit International 232.

CHAPTER 24

International Criminal Tribunal for Rwanda

INTRODUCTORY

Name and seat of the body

24.1 The International Criminal Tribunal for the Prosecution of Persons Responsible for Genocide and Other Serious Violations of International Humanitarian Law Committed in the Territory of Rwanda and Rwandan Citizens Responsible for Genocide and Other Such Violations Committed in the Territory of Neighbouring States, between 1 January 1994 and 31 December 1994 (International Criminal Tribunal for Rwanda, hereinafter 'the tribunal' or 'ICTR') has its seat in Arusha, Tanzania. The address of the tribunal is:

> International Criminal Tribunal for Rwanda
> PO Box 6016
> Arusha
> Tanzania
>
> Tel: 212-963-2850, 255-57-4369/72
> Fax: 212-963-2848, 255-57-4000
> website: http://www.ictr.org

The Office of the Prosecutor – which is shared with the International Criminal Tribunal for the former Yugoslavia (hereinafter 'the Yugoslavia Tribunal') – is located in The Hague, The Netherlands; the Deputy Prosecutor of the ICTR is based in Kigali, Rwanda.

A chamber or a judge may exercise their functions away from the seat of the tribunal if it is so authorised by the President of the tribunal in the interests of justice.[1]

---

1 Rules of Procedure and Evidence, *The International Criminal Tribunal for the Prosecution of Persons Responsible for Genocide and Other Serious Violations of International Humanitarian Law Committed in the Territory of Rwanda and Rwandan Citizens Responsible for Genocide and Other Such Violations Committed in the Territory of Neighbouring States, between 1 January 1994 and 31 December 1994* ('Rules of Procedure'), r 4. Available on ICTR website.

Introductory description

24.2 The ICTR is an ad hoc international criminal tribunal with a specific mandate to prosecute persons responsible for genocide and other serious violations of international humanitarian law committed in the course of or in relation to the 1994 Rwandan genocide. The tribunal was established by a UN Security Council resolution under Chapter VII of the UN Charter.[1]

The tribunal and the competent national courts exercise concurrent jurisdiction over the crimes enumerated in the ICTR Statute.[2] The jurisdiction of the national courts, however, is subject to the primacy of the tribunal: at the request of the ICTR, national courts must defer to the competence of the tribunal.[3] Similarly, as provided for in the Statute, other national authorities must comply with the orders and requests of the organs of the tribunal.[4] As the authority of the tribunal is based on a Security Council resolution binding on all states, the President of the tribunal may refer cases of non-compliance to the Security Council.[5]

In many respects the ICTR was modelled on the Yugoslavia Tribunal with which it maintains significant institutional links.

The ex officio investigation and prosecution of matters falling within the jurisdiction of the ICTR is the responsibility of the Prosecutor,[6] who is assisted by a Deputy Prosecutor.[7] The cases are heard by the Trial Chambers, whose decisions – subject to restrictions – may be challenged before the Appeals Chamber. The Appeals Chamber serves both the ICTR and ICTY.[8]

By December 1998, the ICTR had handed down four judgments and further public indictments implicating 27 more accused persons have been issued and/or confirmed. The tribunal has made more than 200 decisions on motions. As of April 1999, 34 persons are detained in Arusha and four other suspects are in custody pending extradition to Arusha.

1 SC Res 955 (1994), UN Doc S/RES/955 (1994); Statute of the International Tribunal for Rwanda, *The International Criminal Tribunal for the Prosecution of Persons Responsible for Genocide and Other Serious Violations of International Humanitarian Law Committed in the Territory of Rwanda and Rwandan Citizens Responsible for Genocide and Other Such Violations Committed in the Territory of Neighbouring States, between 1 January 1994 and 31 December 1994*, UN Doc S/RES/955 Annex (1994) ('ICTR Statute or Statute').
2 ICTR Statute, arts 2–4, 8.
3 Ibid, art 8.
4 Ibid, art 28.
5 Rules of Procedure, r 11.
6 ICTR Statute, art 15(1).
7 Ibid, art 15(3).
8 Ibid, art 12(2).

INSTITUTIONAL ASPECTS

Governing texts

Procedural law

24.3 The principal texts governing the activities of the tribunal are the Statute of the International Tribunal ('Statute'), adopted by the Security Council,[1] and the Rules of Procedure and Evidence ('Rules').[2] The Rules, together with any other internal procedural regulation are adopted by the tribunal itself. In accordance with the Statute,[3] the Rules elaborated and used by the Yugoslavia Tribunal[4] have been adapted for use by the ICTR, though the Rules at the Yugoslavia Tribunal have been amended more frequently. Other texts concerning proceedings before the tribunal include the Directive on the Assignment of Defence Counsel ('Defence Counsel Directive')[5] and the Directive for the Registry of the ICTR.[6]

1 See para 24.3 n 1, supra, as amended by SC Res 1165 (UN Doc S/RES/1165/1998).
2 See para 24.2 n 1, supra.
3 ICTR Statute, art 14.

4 Rules of Procedure and Evidence, *International Tribunal for the Prosecution of Persons Responsible for Serious Violations of International Humanitarian Law Committed in the Territory of the Former Yugoslavia since 1991,* UN Doc IT/32 (1993).
5 'Code of Professional Conduct for Defence Counsel'; 'Regulations to Govern the Supervision of Visits to and Communication with Detainees'; 'Rules Covering the Detention of Persons Awaiting Trial or Appeal before the Tribunal or Otherwise Detained on the Authority of the Tribunal': available on ICTR website and from ICTR Registry.
6 Available on ICTR website and from ICTR Registry.

Substantive law

24.4 The substantive law to be applied by the tribunal is set forth in Articles 2–4 of the Statute. This includes genocide, crimes against humanity, violations of the Geneva Convention and the fundamental rules of international humanitarian law, the violation of which entails individual criminal responsibility.[1]

1 ICTR Statute, art 6.

Organisation

24.5 The organisational structure of the ICTR is modelled on that of the Yugoslavia Tribunal. The tribunal consists of three Trial Chambers and an Appeals Chamber, together with the Prosecutor and the Registry. The third chamber was approved by the Security Council on 30 April 1998 (Reg 1165) and three new judges were sworn in on 22 February 1999. For purposes of reducing cost and sharing experience, the Office of the Prosecutor and Appeals Chamber serve both the ICTR and ICTY.[1]

1 ICTR Statute, arts 10, 11, 12(2) and 15(3). Accordingly, at the establishment of the ICTR no judges were elected for Appeals Chamber positions.

Composition

24.6 The tribunal comprises 14 judges, three judges serving in each Trial Chamber and five judges in the Appeals Chamber.[1] The judges are elected for a renewable term of four years by the UN General Assembly from a list of candidates prepared by the Security Council from the nominees of the states.[2] The judges must be persons of high moral character, impartiality and integrity. They must possess qualifications required for the highest judicial offices in their respective countries. The judges must have established competence in criminal law and international law, including international humanitarian and human rights law. In the composition of the judges due account must be taken of the adequate representation of the principal legal systems of the world.[3] No two judges can be nationals of the same state.[4]

The judges of the tribunal elect a President and a Vice-President,[5] both of whom may be re-elected once. The President generally co-ordinates the work of the Chambers, supervises the activity of the Registry and presides at the plenary meetings.[6]

The President, after consultation with the judges, assigns judges to the Trial Chambers.[7] Under the Rules of Procedure and Evidence, however, judges are required to rotate on a regular basis between the Trial Chambers.[8]

1 ICTR Statute, art 11. Currently the judges are:
  President: Laïty Kama (Senegal). **Vice-President:** Yakov Ostrovsky (Russia). **Judges:** William Sekule (Tanzania); Lennart Aspegren (Sweden); Navanethem Pillay (South

> Africa); Tafazzal Hossain Khan (Bangladesh); Pavel Dolenc (Slovenia); Dionysios Kondylis (Greece); and Lloyd George Williams (Jamaica and Saint Kitts). In May 1999 Mehmet Güney (Turkey) replaces Judge Aspegren and Erik Møse (Norway) replaces Judge Khan.
> The Appeals Chamber includes:
> **President:** Gabrielle Kirk MacDonald (USA). **Vice-President:** Mohamed Shahabuddeen (Guyana). **Judges:** Lal Chand Vohrah (Malaysia); Rafael Nieto Navia (Colombia) and Tieya Wang (China).
2 ICTR Statute, art 12(3).
3 Ibid, art 12(1).
4 Ibid, art 11.
5 Ibid, art 13(1), Rules of Procedure, r 20.
6 Rules of Procedure, r 19.
7 ICTR Statute, art 13(3).
8 Rules of Procedure, r 27(A). This, however, has not taken place in the practice of the ICTR.

DISQUALIFICATION OF JUDGES

24.7 A judge may not sit on a trial or appeal in a case in which he or she has a personal interest or where his or her impartiality can be otherwise questioned. In any such circumstance the judge must withdraw or may be disqualified by the Bureau[1] (the internal consulting organ of the tribunal) at the motion of the Prosecutor or the defendant.[2] No judge can sit on a trial for which he or she has reviewed the indictment or on an appeal in a case in which a judge of the same nationality has already participated.[3]

1 Rules of Procedure, r 23.
2 Ibid, r 15(A),(B).
3 Ibid, r 15(C),(D).

Plenary/chambers

24.8 The tribunal deals with cases in chambers. The judges meet in plenary only to elect the President and the Vice-President; to adopt and amend the Rules of Procedure and Evidence; to adopt the Annual Report of the tribunal; to determine or supervise the conditions of detention; or to decide upon matters relating to the internal functioning of the tribunal.[1]

The pre-trial proceedings are conducted by a duty judge (eg review of indictment, handling applications for warrant) designated by the President,[2] or by a Trial Chamber. Some of the responsibilities of the Trial Chamber can be exercised by a designated member of that Chamber, such as handling motions, conducting status conferences.[3]

The trials are dealt with by three-judge Trial Chambers and appeals are heard by the five-judge Appeals Chamber.

1 Rules of Procedure, r 24.
2 Ibid, r 28.
3 Ibid, r 65*bis*.

Appeals structure

24.9 A Trial Chamber decision of acquittal or conviction, or a decision on the sentence can be challenged before the Appeals Chamber by the Prosecutor or the accused person. The grounds of challenge have been narrowly formulated: an appeal lies against the decision where an error of law invalidates the decision or an error of fact that has resulted in a miscarriage of justice.[1] Some interlocutory decisions can also be challenged (see para 24.31, infra). The Appeals Chamber may affirm, reverse or revise the decision of the Trial Chambers.[2]

1   ICTR Statute, art 24(1).
2   Ibid, art 24(2).

Technical/scientific experts

24.10   The Rules of Procedure and Evidence envisage the broad use of experts. Moreover, the parties are free to present expert statements as evidence.[1] Linguistic, forensic, historical and other experts have testified to date at ICTR.

1   Rules of Procedure, r 94*bis*.

Secretariat

24.11   The Registry of the tribunal is responsible for administering and servicing the tribunal.[1] The Registry is headed by the Registrar appointed by the Secretary-General for a renewable term of four years.[2] The Registrar is assisted by a Deputy Registrar. The Registrar assists the judges, the chambers, the plenary and the Prosecutor in the performance of their functions; serves as a general channel of communication; and maintains the records of the tribunal.[3]

Under rule 34 of the Rules of Procedure an additional organ, the Victims and Witnesses Support Unit, was set up under the authority of the Registrar.

1   Rules of Procedure, r 74.
2   ICTR Statute, art 16(3).
3   Rules of Procedure, r 33.

Jurisdiction

Ratione personae

24.12   The tribunal has jurisdiction over *natural* persons accused of the crimes listed in Articles 2–4 of the Statute.[1] The tribunal has no jurisdiction over states, legal persons and organisations. The ratione personae jurisdiction of the ICTR covers Rwandan citizens and non-citizens alike. Violations committed in states neighbouring Rwanda, however, may be prosecuted before the tribunal if the perpetrator was a Rwandan citizen.[2]

1   ICTR Statute, art 5.
2   Ibid, art 1.

Ratione materiae

24.13   The tribunal's competence is limited to the prosecution of the following groups of crimes:
(a)   genocide;[1]
(b)   crimes against humanity;[2]
(c)   violations of art 3 common to the Geneva Conventions and of Additional Protocol II.[3]

1   ICTR Statute, art 2.
2   Ibid, art 3.
3   Ibid, art 4.

Ratione temporis

24.14 The temporal scope of the jurisdiction of the tribunal extends to the period between 1 January 1994 and 31 December 1994. The jurisdiction of the ICTR covers the above crimes committed throughout the entire territory of Rwanda as well as the territory of the neighbouring states by Rwandan citizens.[1]

1   ICTR Statute, arts 1, 7.

RELATIONSHIP WITH NATIONAL COURTS

24.15 The ICTR and national courts have concurrent jurisdiction to prosecute persons for the violations of international humanitarian law falling within the jurisdiction of the tribunal.[1] Such concurrence is, however, subject to the primacy of the ICTR: a Trial Chamber at any stage of the procedure may request a national court to defer to its competence.[2] The grounds for intervention in national proceedings include:

(i)   the seriousness of the offence;

(ii) the status of the accused at the time of the alleged offence; and

(iii) the general importance of the legal questions involved in the case.

Moreover, a Trial Chamber may request a national court to discontinue the ongoing proceedings if the crime in question is subject to investigation by the prosecutor or is subject to indictment before the tribunal.[3] The state to which the request is addressed must comply therewith without undue delay. In case of non-compliance the President of the tribunal may report the matter to the Security Council.[4]

The Statute declares that no person can be tried before national courts for acts for which he or she has already been tried before the tribunal (*non bis in idem*).[5] On the other hand a person who has been tried before a national court may be brought before the ICTR if:

(i)   the act for which he or she has been tried was characterised as an ordinary crime; or

(ii) the national court proceedings were not impartial or independent, were designed to shield the accused from international criminal responsibility, or the case was not diligently prosecuted.[6]

1   ICTR Statute, art 8(1).
2   Ibid, art 8(2).
3   Rules of Procedure, r 9.
4   Ibid, rr 10(C), 11.
5   ICTR Statute, art 9(1).
6   Ibid, art 9(2).

Advisory jurisdiction

24.16 The ICTR has no advisory jurisdiction.

PROCEDURAL ASPECTS

Languages

24.17 The working languages of the tribunal are English and French.[1] The accused is, however, entitled to use his or her own language throughout the entire procedure. Other persons, including counsel appearing for the accused, are allowed to use their own language subject to certain restrictions. In each case the expenses of the interpretation and translation are borne by the tribunal.[2] All courtroom proceedings are simultaneously interpreted into English, French and Kinyarwandan.

A copy of the judgment and all communications must be served on the accused in a language that he or she understands.

1   ICTR Statute, art 31; Rules of Procedure, r 3(A).
2   Rules of Procedure, r 3(B)–(D).

Instituting proceedings

24.18   The investigation of crimes is initiated and carried out by the Prosecutor ex officio or on the basis of information from any source, in particular governments, UN organs, intergovernmental and non-governmental organisations.[1] The Prosecutor has broad powers to investigate matters, such as the power to question suspects, victims and witnesses, to collect evidence and to conduct on-site investigations. The Prosecutor may seek the assistance of state authorities[2] as well as any relevant international body, including INTERPOL and request such orders from a Trial Chamber or a judge as may be necessary.[3]

Upon a determination that a prima facie case exists the Prosecutor prepares the indictment and forwards it to the duty or 'confirming' judge for confirmation. The indictment must contain a concise statement of the facts and the crimes with which the accused is charged.[4] If the judge is satisfied that a prima facie case has been established, ie sufficient evidence has been supplied by the Prosecutor to provide reasonable grounds for believing that a suspect has committed a crime, the judge confirms the indictment. If not so satisfied, the reviewing judge may request additional material, adjourn the review or dismiss the entire indictment.[5]

The Prosecutor may amend the indictment –
  (i)   at any time before its confirmation;
  (ii) thereafter with leave of the judge who has confirmed the indictment;
  (iii) after the commencement of the presentation of the evidence only with the leave of the Trial Chamber hearing the case.
The indictment may be withdrawn under similar conditions.[6]

1   ICTR Statute, art 17(1).
2   Ibid, art 17(2).
3   Rules of Procedure, r 39(iii),(iv).
4   ICTR Statute, art 17(4).
5   Ibid, art 18(1); Rules of Procedure, r 47(E),(F).
6   Rules of Procedure, rr 50, 51.

Financial assistance in appointment of counsel and interpreter

24.19   An accused person is entitled to have legal assistance without payment if he or she cannot pay for it and free assistance of an interpreter if he or she cannot understand or speak the language used in the tribunal.[1] All of the accused, to date, have claimed to be indigent, requiring tribunal-appointed defence counsel.

1   ICTR Statute, art 20(4)(d),(f).

Provisional measures

Urgent measures

24.20 During the investigations in case of urgency the Prosecutor may request any state:
(a) to arrest a suspect and place him in custody;
(b) to seize physical evidence; or
(c) to take all necessary measures to prevent the escape of the suspect or an accused, injury to or intimidation of a victim or a witness, or the destruction of evidence.[1]
The state concerned must comply with the request.[2] Any other provisional measures are valid only if ordered by a judge or a chamber.

1   Rules of Procedure, r 40(A).
2   ICTR Statute, art 28; Rules of Procedure, r 40(A).

Transfer and provisional detention of suspects

24.21 In the conduct of investigation the Prosecutor may request an order by a duty judge for the transfer and the provisional detention of a suspect in the detention premises of the tribunal. The judge may fulfil the request only if:
(a) the Prosecutor has already requested a state to arrest the suspect provisionally, or the suspect is otherwise detained by a state;
(b) after hearing the Prosecutor the judge considers that there is a reliable and consistent body of material that tends to show that the suspect may have committed the crime in question; and
(c) the judge considers the provisional detention a necessary measure to prevent the escape of the suspect or an accused, injury to or intimidation of a victim or a witness, or the destruction of evidence.[1]
The provisional detention may not exceed 30 days but, at the request of the Prosecutor, it may be renewed twice up to a total of 90 days. Thereafter, if the indictment has not been confirmed and an arrest warrant signed the suspect must be released (or returned to the place of original detention).[2]

Upon showing that a major impediment does not allow a state to keep a suspect in custody or to prevent his escape, the Prosecutor may apply to a judge for an order to transfer the suspect to the seat of the tribunal and detain him provisionally.[3] Due to urgent necessity to act, the provisional detention can be ordered by a judge without considering whether a prima facie case may be established. Once detained, however, the suspect may immediately apply for review by a Trial Chamber of the decision. The suspect must be released if (i) the chamber so rules or (ii) the Prosecutor fails to prepare an indictment within 20 days after the transfer.[4]

1   Rules of Procedure, r 40*bis*(B).
2   Ibid, r 40*bis*(C),(F),(G),(H).
3   Ibid, r 40(B). Provision for these special powers was necessitated by the inherent weakness of the judicial enforcement mechanisms of the states concerned, especially those of Rwanda. See Preamble to Resolution 955, eight recital.
4   Rules of Procedure, r 40(C),(D).

Warrant of arrest

24.22 A warrant of arrest, or any other orders, summons, subpoenas, warrants and transfer orders as may be necessary for the purposes of the investigation or for the conduct of the trial are issued by a judge or Trial Chamber at the request of the either the Prosecutor or the defence or *proprio motu*.[1]

A state to which the warrant is transmitted must promptly comply therewith.[2] Once detained by the state concerned, the accused must be transferred to the seat of the tribunal.[3] The obligation of the state to transfer or surrender the accused prevails over restrictions of national extradition laws.[4] If within a reasonable time after the warrant of arrest or transfer no action has been taken by the state concerned, the tribunal may notify the Security Council.[5]

Once detained, an accused may be released by the Trial Chamber only in exceptional circumstances and if the Trial Chamber is satisfied that the accused will appear for trial and, if released, will not pose a danger to any victim, witness or any other person. To that end, the Trial Chamber may impose conditions on release, including the execution of a bail bond.[6]

Other provisional measures include protection of victims and witnesses,[7] and transfer of detained witnesses.[8]

1   Rules of Procedure, r 54.
2   ICTR Statute, art 28; Rules of Procedure, r 56.
3   Rules of Procedure, rr 55(C) and 57.
4   Ibid, r 58.
5   Ibid, r 59(B).
6   Ibid, r 65(B),(C).
7   Ibid, r 69, 75.
8   Ibid, r 90*bis*.

Preliminary proceedings and objections

24.23   Once the indictment has been confirmed, the judge, at the request of the Prosecutor, may issue such orders and warrants, including orders for arrest, detention, surrender or transfer of persons as may be required for the fair and expeditious conduct of the trial.[1] Once the accused has been detained and transferred to the seat of the tribunal, he or she must be brought before a Trial Chamber and be formally charged at an initial appearance.[2]

At the initial appearance of the accused, subsequent to the reading of the indictment, the accused is called upon to enter a plea of guilty or not guilty on each count. If the accused fails to plead or pleads not guilty, the Trial Chamber instructs the Registrar to set a date for trial. If the accused pleads guilty and the Trial Chamber is satisfied that the guilty plea –

(i)   was made freely;

(ii)   is unequivocal; and

(iii)   is based on sufficient facts for the crime and the accused's participation, the Trial Chamber may enter a finding of guilt and instruct the Registrar to set a date for sentencing hearing.[3]

During the pre-trial phase both the Prosecutor and the defence must reciprocally disclose evidence.[4] In order to ensure an expeditious trial, the Trial Chamber holds a pre-trial conference and may hold a pre-defence conference whereby the parties are to clarify and finalise their trial positions (eg disputed questions of facts and law, list of witnesses, etc).[5]

Within 60 days following the disclosure by the Prosecutor of all supporting material to the indictment, but in any case before the hearing on the merits of the case, either party may by way of preliminary motions:

(a)   challenge jurisdiction;

(b) allege defects in the form of the indictment;

(c) apply for severance of crimes joined in one indictment or seek separate trials;

(d) raise objections based on the denial of a request for assignment of counsel.[6]

The Trial Chamber must dispose of preliminary motions *in limite litis*. Decisions on preliminary motions are without interlocutory appeal, except for a motion challenging jurisdiction, where an appeal lies as a right.[7]

1 ICTR Statute, art 18(2).
2 Rules of Procedure, r 62.
3 Id.
4 Rules of Procedure, rr 66, 67.
5 Ibid, rr 73*bis*, 73*ter*.
6 Ibid, r 72(B).
7 Ibid, r 72(C),(D).

Written pleadings

24.24 The charges raised by the Prosecutor must be presented to the tribunal and to the accused in written form.[1] The indictment sets forth the name and particulars of the suspect, and must contain a concise statement of the facts of the case and of the crime with which the suspect is charged.[2] The defence is entitled to submit to the tribunal a written statement in reply to the indictment.

1 Rules of Procedure, r 47.
2 Ibid, r 47(C).

Oral arguments

24.25 At the beginning of the trial each party may make an opening statement.[1] This is followed by the presentation of evidence and the hearing of witnesses.[2] Examination-in-chief, cross-examination and re-examination is allowed in each case. The judge may at any stage put any questions to the witness.[3] The Trial Chamber may order either party to produce additional evidence and may summon witnesses *proprio motu*.[4]

After the presentation of all evidence, both the Prosecutor and the defence may present a closing argument. The Prosecutor may thereafter present a rebuttal and the defence a rejoinder.[5] When both parties have completed their presentations the presiding judge closes the hearing and the Trial Chamber retires for deliberation.[6]

All proceedings before the Trial Chamber, except for the deliberations, are held in public.[7] The Trial Chamber may exclude the press and the public only for reasons of public order or morality; safety, security or non-disclosure of the identity of a victim or a witness; or protection of the interest of justice (the Trial Chamber, however, must make public the reasons for a closed session).[8]

1 Rules of Procedure, r 84.
2 Ibid, r 85(A).
3 Ibid, r 85(A),(B).
4 Ibid, r 98.
5 Ibid, r 86(A).
6 Ibid, r 87(A).
7 Ibid, r 78.
8 Ibid, r 79(A),(B).

Third-party intervention/multiple proceedings

24.26 The Rules of Procedure allow almost no role for third parties in any proceedings before the tribunal.

One specific exception to the above rule is that in proceedings concerning restitution of property, third parties with a lawful interest in that property must be given an opportunity to justify their claims before the Trial Chamber.[1] On the other hand, claims for compensation of victims are handled exclusively by national courts; victims and other persons on behalf of them have no right to be heard by the tribunal.[2]

Persons accused of crimes committed in the course of the same transaction may be jointly charged and tried.[3] Two or more crimes may be joined in one indictment if the series of acts were committed in the same transaction and by the same person.[4]

1 Rules of Procedure, r 105(B),(C).
2 Ibid, r 106(A),(B).
3 Ibid, r 48.
4 Ibid, r 49.

Amicus curiae

24.27 The Trial and Appeal Chambers may, if it is considered desirable for the proper determination of the case, invite or grant leave to a state, organisation or person to appear before it and make submissions on any issue specified by the Chamber.[1] Amicus curiae briefs were submitted, for example, in the *Bagosora*, *Akayesu* and *Ntuyahaga* cases.

1 Rules of Procedure, r 74.

Representation of the parties

24.28 An accused has the right to defend himself or herself in person or through legal assistance of his or her choosing, or to have legal assistance assigned to him or her in any case where the interests of justice so require, and without payment where he or she lacks sufficient means.[1]

When questioned, a suspect has the right to be assisted by counsel of his or her choice or to have legal assistance assigned to him or her without payment if he or she does not have sufficient means to pay for it.[2]

The ICTR has adopted a policy, in the appointment of defence counsel, of attempting to achieve a geographic balance and representation of the principal legal systems of the world.[3]

1 ICTR Statute, art 20.
2 ICTR Rules of Procedure, r 42(A)(i).
3 ICTR/INFO Press Release, 22 February 1999.

Decision

24.29 The decision of the Trial or Appeals Chamber is reached by the majority of the judges. The judgment must be delivered in public and be accompanied by a reasoned opinion in writing to which separate and dissenting opinions may be appended.[1]

A finding of guilt can be reached only if the majority of the judges of the chamber is satisfied that the guilt has been proved beyond reasonable doubt.[2] The chamber also must determine the penalty to be imposed on each count for the convicted person.[3]

The only available penalty is imprisonment, for a maximum term up to the convicted person's life.[4] In determining the terms of imprisonment the Trial Chamber must take into consideration factors such as the gravity of the offence, any aggravating circumstances, any mitigating circumstances, including co-operation of the convicted person, the general practice regarding prison sentences in the courts of Rwanda, and the extent to which any penalty imposed by any state on the convicted person for the same act has been served.[5]

In addition to imprisonment the Trial Chamber may order the return to the rightful owner of any property and its proceeds acquired by criminal conduct.[6] As noted at para 24.26 supra, compensation to victims, based on a finding of guilt by the tribunal, may only be rendered by national courts.

1   ICTR Statute, art 22(2).
2   Rules of Procedure, r 87(A).
3   Ibid, r 87(C).
4   ICTR Statute, art 23(1); Rules of Procedure, r 101(A).
5   ICTR Statute, art 23(2); Rules of Procedure, r 101(B).
6   ICTR Statute, art 23(3).

Revision of judgments

24.30   Where a new fact has been discovered, which was not known to the moving party at the time of the proceedings, and could not have been discovered through the exercise of due diligence, the defence, or within one year of the delivery of the judgment, the prosecutor may apply for revision of the judgment.[1] If the majority of the judges finds that the new fact could have been a decisive factor in reaching the underlying decision, the reviewing chamber pronounces a further judgment.[2] A right to appeal lies against the judgment on review.[3]

1   Rules of Procedure, r 120.
2   Ibid, r 121.
3   Ibid, r 122.

Appeal

24.31   A Trial Chamber decision on guilt or acquittal or on the terms of sentence can be appealed by the prosecutor or the accused person on the grounds that:
(a) an error of law invalidates the decision; or
(b) an error of fact has occasioned a miscarriage of justice.[1]
Interlocutory decisions can be challenged only where the Rules of Procedure specifically allow appeal.[2]

On appeal, the Appeals Chamber holds a hearing on the basis of the record of appeal and the briefs of the appellant and the respondent.[3] A party may apply to present additional evidence which was not available at trial. The Appeals Chamber authorises such evidence only if it considers that the interests of justice so require.[4]

The Appeals Chamber reaches its decision by majority. It may affirm, reverse or revise the judgment of the Trial Chamber.[5] In appropriate circumstances the Appeals Chamber may order that the accused be re-tried before a Trial Chamber.[6]

1 ICTR Statute, art 24(1).
2 See dismissal of jurisdiction (r 77(D)), a decision concerning contempt of tribunal (r 77(D)) or false testimony (r 91).
3 Rules of Procedure, rr 111–113.
4 Ibid, r 115(A),(B).
5 ICTR Statute, art 24(2).
6 Rules of Procedure, r 118(C).

Costs

24.32 The costs of the criminal proceedings are borne by the tribunal. The expenses of the tribunal are covered by the regular budget of the United Nations in accordance with art 17 of the UN Charter.[1]

1 ICTR Statute, art 30.

Enforcement of sentences

24.33 Any sentence of imprisonment is served in Rwanda or any state designated by the ICTR from a list of states which have indicated to the Security Council their willingness to accept convicted persons. The transfer of a convict to the place of imprisonment must take place as soon as possible.[1] The imprisonment must be in accordance with the applicable law of the state concerned, subject to the supervision of the tribunal.[2] The tribunal signed the first agreement regarding enforcement of sentences with the government of Mali. Belgium, Denmark, Norway, Sweden and Switzerland have indicated their willingness to imprison those convicted. The UK has agreed to help fund the imprisonment of convicts in African states.

Restitution of property ordered by the tribunal is to be effected by competent national authorities.[3]

1 Rules of Procedure, r 103(B).
2 ICTR Statute, art 26.
3 Rules of Procedure, r 105(G).

REFERENCE

Sources of case law, including case reports

Decisions of the ICTR can be found on the ICTR website.

Selected bibliography

Books

Virginia Morris and Michael Scharf *The International Criminal Tribunal for Rwanda*, Transnational Publishers (1998).

John R W D Jones *The Practice of the International Criminal Tribunals for the Former Yugoslavia and Rwanda*, Transnational Publishers (1998).

Articles

Roy S Lee 'The Rwanda Tribunal' (1996) 9 Leiden Journal of International Law 37.

Lyal S Sunga 'The Commission of Experts on Rwanda and the Creation of the International Criminal Tribunal for Rwanda' (1995) 16 Human Rights Law Journal 121.

Inspection panels

INTRODUCTION

This Part reviews three 'inspection procedures' which have been established by multilateral or regional development banks: the World Bank, the Asian Development Bank and the Inter-American Development Bank. The purpose of the inspection procedures is to provide a forum within which affected parties may bring complaints alleging that the bank in question has not followed its own internal procedures, such as procedures relating to expropriation, environmental impact assessment, or relocation of communities. The principal interest of the inspection procedures lies in the fact that they offer communities or persons affected by projects financed by the banks an opportunity to hold development banks to account. The principal limitation of the inspection procedures is that the review extends only to considering compliance with the bank's existing policies and procedures. The inspection panels are not entitled to consider the adequacy of the policies and procedures themselves.

The first such mechanism to be established was the Inspection Panel of the World Bank. The Inter-American Development Bank and the Asian Development Bank have since followed suit, adopting similar, but not identical, procedures. The World Bank Inspection Panel was created in 1993. The Panel itself is independent from the Bank in terms of its operation, although it does receive administrative assistance, and is located at the headquarters of the Bank. Where a complaint is submitted, its admissibility is reviewed by the Panel, which decides whether or not to recommend to the Board of Executive Directors inspection of the complaint. If an inspection is initiated, written submissions may be requested. It is for the Board of Executive Directors of the World Bank to decide what follow-up action should be taken with regard to the financing of a project subject of a complaint in order to implement a report of the Panel. Between 1993 and 1997, the Bank received 11 complaints relating to various projects. The merits of five complaints have been subject to inspection. Most recently a first corporate complaint has been filed, alleging non-compliance with the Bank's internal rules relating to expropriation.

The Inter-American Development Bank (IADB) established an investigation mechanism in 1994. It operates in a similar manner to the World Bank's Inspection Panel. However, the IADB has not established a standing inspection panel, but rather a roster of 10 investigators from which panels may be drawn. The Asian Development Bank (ADB), which established an inspection policy in 1995, has set up two bodies, a permanent Inspection

Committee and an ad hoc panel of Independent Experts. The permanent Committee is made up of members of the ADB's Board; it is the ad hoc panel which is responsible for investigating any complaint.

While the mechanisms in this section differ greatly from the courts and tribunals considered elsewhere in this manual, they nevertheless represent important developments in institutional arrangements for administrative review of the multilateral development banks, and present a significant opportunity for non-governmental actors to hold intergovernmental institutions to account.

CHAPTER 25

Inspection Panel of the World Bank

INTRODUCTORY

Contact information

25.1   The Inspection Panel of the World Bank is an independent administrative body authorised to investigate certain complaints concerning projects financed by the Bank. It is located at:

>   1818 H Street, NW
>   Washington, DC,
>   USA

>   Tel: 1 202 458 5200
>   Fax: 1 202 522 0916
>   email: IPANEL@WorldBank.org
>   website: http://www.worldbank.org/html/ins-panel/

Description

25.2   The Inspection Panel of the World Bank is a permanent body created in 1993 to review projects financed by the World Bank, the International Bank for Reconstruction and Development (IBRD) and the International Development Association, which are the subject of complaints alleging non-compliance by the Bank with its own operational policies and procedures. The Panel may receive requests for review from groups of people who claim to be adversely affected by the execution of a Bank project. The investigation of the complaint may include on-site inspection of the project area, subject to the consent of the borrowing state.

Although the Panel is independent in its operation, it is assisted in its work by the administrative facilities of the World Bank, and is located at the Bank's headquarters. Furthermore, Panel decisions to investigate complaints are subject to the prior approval of the Bank's Executive Directors. The findings and recommendations of the Panel are presented in the form of a report to the President of the Bank and the Executive Directors. The Board of Directors may decide what action to take, if any, to implement the report.

As of June 1999 the Panel has registered 14 complaints against various Bank projects. On five of these cases the Panel has conducted an investigation or a quasi-investigation of the merits, or was asked to keep the project under continuing review.

In April 1999 the Board of Executive Directors of the Bank approved the report of the Inspection Panel Working Group which contains clarifications and recommendations to improve the effectiveness of the Inspection Panel process.[1]

1   See World Bank website at http://www.worldbank.org/html/extdr/ipwg/index.htm.

INSTITUTIONAL ASPECTS

Governing texts

25.3   The principal text governing the operations of the Inspection Panel is the Resolution establishing the World Bank Inspection Panel, adopted on 22 September 1993 ('Panel Resolution').[1] The Resolution provides guidance on the selection of Panel members and powers of the Panel and provides general outlines of the Panel's rules of procedure. Clarifications on the meaning of the text of the Panel Resolution were made by the Executive Directors in a review of the experience of the inspection procedure completed in 1996 ('1996 Clarification').[2] The Conclusions of the Board's Second Review of the Inspection Panel, adopted on 20 April 1999 ('1999 Board Review') complement and in some respects supersede the 1996 Clarifications.

The detailed rules of procedure regulating the operation of the Panel are to be found in the Operating Procedures adopted by the Panel in 1994.[3]

1   IBRD Res No 93-10 and IDA Res No 93-6, 22 September 1993, 34 ILM 520 (1995) ('Panel Resolution').
2   Review of the Resolution establishing the Inspection Panel – Clarification of certain aspects of the Resolution, 17 October 1996, Annual Report of the Inspection Panel 29 (1 August 1996 – 31 July 1997) ('Review decision').
3   Operating Procedures, Inspection Panel for the International Bank for Reconstruction and Development and the International Development Association, 19 August 1994, 34 ILM 510 (1995) ('Operating Procedures').

Substantive law

25.4   The applicable standards to be applied by the Inspection Panel are the World Bank's operational policies and procedures. These include instructions adopted by the management of the Bank under titles such as 'Operational Policies', 'Bank Procedures', 'Operational Directives', which are, generally speaking, binding upon Bank employees. The Panel can not rely upon non-binding policy statements such as 'Guidelines' and 'Best Practices'.[1] The Panel may not review the adequacy of the policies and procedures themselves.

1   Panel Resolution, para 12.

Organisation

Composition

25.5   The Inspection Panel is composed of three members of different nationalities from countries which are members of the Bank.[1] They are appointed by the Bank's Board of Directors, acting upon the recommendation of the President of the World Bank for a non-renewable five-year term.[2] The members of the Panel elect a Chairperson for a renewable one-year term

Panel members are selected on the basis of the following characteristics:
(a) ability to deal with cases thoroughly and fairly;
(b) independence from Bank management;
(c) exposure to developmental issues and living conditions in developing states; and preferably,
(d) knowledge and experience of the operations of the World Bank.[3]

Former officers of the Bank and other members of staff can be selected to serve on the Panel only if certain conditions are fulfilled.[4] Panellists may not be employed by the World Bank group after the end of their service on the Panel.[5]

1 Panel Resolution, para 2. The original members of the Panel were Mr Ernst Gunther Broder (Germany); Mr Alvaro Umana Quesada (Costa Rica); and Mr Richard E Bissell (US). In 1997 Mr Bissell was replaced by Mr Jim MacNeill (Canada) and in 1998 Professor Edward S Ayensu (Ghana) replaced Mr Quesada.
2 Panel Resolution, paras 2, 3. However, the original members of the Panel are replaced in a staggered method after three, four and five years in office, respectively.
3 Panel Resolution, para 4.
4 Ibid, para 5.
5 Ibid, para 10.

INELIGIBILITY OF PANEL MEMBERS

25.6 Panel members may not participate in the review of a case in relation to which they have a personal interest, or have had significant involvement in any prior capacity.[1] The Executive Directors of the Bank may remove a Panel member from office, for this reason.[2]

1 Panel Resolution, para 6.
2 Ibid, para 8.

Plenary/chambers

25.7 All members of the Inspection Panel participate in the review of a request for inspection.

Appellate structure

25.8 There are no appeals over the recommendations of the Inspection Panel.

Technical/scientific experts

25.9 During the conduct of its investigation the Panel may hire independent consultants to research specific issues related to the case.[1] The Panel may also receive written or oral submissions from any independent expert (other than one hired by the Panel).[2] An additional area where expertise is required is knowledge of Bank policies and procedures. Under the Panel Resolution, the Panel will consult, as needed, with officers of the Bank with particular knowledge on the method of execution of the Bank's projects (Director General, Operations Evaluation Department and the Internal Auditor).[3] Similarly, the advice of the Legal Department of the World Bank will be sought by the Panel.[4]

1 Operating Procedures, para 45(e).
2 Ibid, paras 45(d), 50.
3 Panel Resolution, para 21.
4 Ibid, para 15; Operating Procedures, para 62.

Secretariat

25.10 The Inspection Panel is assisted in the conduct of its investigation by an Executive Secretary,[1] who is in turn assisted by an Assistant Executive Secretary and two additional staff members. The Secretariat is responsible for maintaining the Panel's register and for providing administrative support to Panel operations, handling communications with requesters and potential requesters, and disseminating information regarding Panel activities and Panel reports.

1 Panel Resolution, para 11.

Jurisdiction and access

Ratione personae

25.11 The Panel shall receive Requests for inspection presented to it by an affected party from the territory of the borrowing state, if it is directly affected by an act or omission of the Bank committed in relation to a Bank financed project. A Request cannot be made by a single individual (or on his or her behalf), but rather by a community of persons, such as an organisation, association, society or other grouping of individuals.[1] The Executive Director's 1996 Clarification explained that the term 'community of persons' implies any two or more persons who share some common interests or concerns.

The request is to be presented by the affected party, or by its local representative. In exceptional cases, where the requesting party alleges that no appropriate local representative is available, it may proceed with a foreign representative, subject to approval by the Executive Directors at the time the Panel authorises inspection. A request for investigation may be made, in special cases, by any Executive Director and, at any time, by the Executive Directors acting as a body.[2]

1 Panel Resolution, para 12.
2 Ibid.

Ratione materiae

25.12 A request for inspection must allege the following grounds:
(a) the rights or interests of the requesting party have been, or are likely to be seriously affected by an act or omission on the part of the Bank; and
(b) the act or omission resulted from a failure on the part of the Bank to follow operational policies and procedures[1] pertaining to the design, appraisal and/or implementation of a project financed by the Bank (including failure to require the borrower state to comply with its loan-related obligations).[2]

Complaints submitted on the part of an Executive Director need only demonstrate that a serious violation of the Bank's policies and procedures has taken place.[3]

All complaints against acts and omissions not attributable to the Bank (but to other legal actors such as the borrower state) are inadmissible. This is also the case for complaints against decisions on procurement of goods and services financed with Bank loans, whether taken by Bank borrowers or by the Bank.[4] In addition, complaints on matters reviewed by the Panel in the past may not be reintroduced (unless new evidence or circumstances are shown).[5]

The Panel is not charged with reviewing the appropriateness of the policies or procedures of the Bank, but merely with ensuring that the Bank observes them. Furthermore, the current competence of the Panel extends ipso facto only to acts and omissions of the two organisations which adopted the Panel Resolution – the International Bank for Reconstruction and Development (IBRD), and the International Development Association (IDA).

1 These include the following instruments: Bank's Operational Policies; Bank Procedures and Operational Directives and similar documents issued in the past. The scope of review does not encompass Bank Guidelines and Best Practices and similar statements or documents.
2 Panel Resolution, paras 12, 13.
3 Ibid, para 12.
4 Ibid, para 14(a),(b); See 1996 Clarifications.
5 Panel Resolution, para 14(d).

Ratione temporis

25.13 The request must meet two temporal requirements:
(a) it may not be presented before the requesting party has taken measures to bring the issue to the attention of the Bank's management, and the management's response has proved to have been unsatisfactory (exhaustion of remedies);[1] and
(b) the request must not be presented after the loan has been fully or substantially disbursed (at least 95 per cent of the loan sum).[2]

1 Panel Resolution, paras 13, 16.
2 Ibid, para 14(c).

Advisory jurisdiction

25.14 The Inspection Panel does not have jurisdiction beyond review of requests for inspection.

PROCEDURAL ASPECTS

Languages

25.15 The working language of the Inspection Panel is English and requests for inspection should be submitted in that language.[1] However, a party without representation who is unable to obtain a translation may submit a request in its local language (although this might delay the work of the Panel).

1 Operating Procedures, para 8.

Instituting proceedings

25.16 Panel proceedings are initiated by a submission of a request for investigation. The request must be made in writing and submitted together with two additional copies.[1] It should include the name of the requesting party, its contact address, its signature, the date of the request and proof of authorisation to represent, in the case of requests submitted by a representative.[2] In requests brought by non-local representatives, there must also be proof that no appropriate local representation is available.[3]

As to content, the request should include the underlying facts (including the harm suffered or expected to be suffered); discussion of steps already taken to deal with the problem; nature of alleged acts or omissions of the Bank; the actions taken to bring the matter to the attention of management; and management's response to such actions.[4] No specific form is required and the request may be made by way of a letter.[5] Parties are, however, encouraged to make use of the model request form appended to the Operating Procedures. Under the model form, the requesting party should elaborate specifically on the following points:

(a) nature and importance of damage caused to the requesting party by the project;
(b) establishment of the responsibility of the Bank to the injurious aspects of the project;
(c) the applicable Bank policies and procedures and the manner in which they have been violated;
(d) previous contacts with Bank staff on the issue of the complaint;
(e) other means sought to resolve the problem, if any; and
(f) existence of previous Panel proceedings on the same issue; and – if there were previous proceedings – the new facts or circumstances that justify new proceedings.

The request should be accompanied by supporting documents including:

(a) all correspondence with the World Bank staff;
(b) notes of meetings with Bank staff;
(c) map or diagram indicating the location of the area affected by the project; and
(d) any other evidence in support of the complaint.[6]

If the Chairperson of the Panel finds that additional information is required in order to enable the Panel to consider the request, he or she may ask the requesting party to provide such information.[7]

The request must be delivered by registered, certified, or hand delivered mail to the Inspection Panel or the resident representative of the Bank in the country in which the project is executed.[8]

The commencement of Panel investigation, even of an admissible complaint, is not automatic. The Panel may recommend not to start an investigation on the basis of information provided to it by the Bank's management which shows that the Bank has dealt appropriately with the subject matter of the dispute, that it has clearly followed Bank policies and procedures or that it has undertaken to adequately correct its past failures.[9] In the alternative, the Panel may recommend that investigation shall commence, but the Executive Directors are entitled to reject such a recommendation.[10]

1 Operating Procedures, para 59.
2 Ibid, paras 9, 10, 11.
3 Ibid, para 11.
4 Panel Resolution, para 16.
5 Operating Procedures, para 7.
6 Ibid, para 12.
7 Ibid, paras 19, 20.
8 Ibid, para 14.
9 Ibid, para 33.
10 Inspection Panel Resolution, para 19.

Financial assistance

25.17 The office of the Inspection Panel offers advice on how to prepare and submit a request for inspection, and provides other necessary information required for participation in Panel proceedings.[1] The Bank does not provide additional technical assistance or funding.[2]

1 Operating Procedures, para 15.
2 See Review decision.

Provisional measures

25.18 The Inspection Panel is not authorised to render provisional measures.

Preliminary objections/proceedings

25.19 Before a decision is taken by the Executive Directors on whether to initiate investigation, the Panel conducts a preliminary investigation of the admissibility of the request for inspection. The Chairperson is authorised to instruct the Panel's registrar not to register requests which fall manifestly outside the scope of the Panel's mandate. These are, inter alia, complaints directed against acts or omissions of entities other than the World Bank; complaints on procurement issues; requests submitted after the last permissible date (ie when over 95 per cent of the loan has been disbursed); requests on issues previously dealt with by the Panel; not providing reason for revision; requests that fail to indicate prior contact with the Bank on the issue of the complaint; requests submitted by individuals or by unauthorised representatives; correspondence not constituting a request; or frivolous, absurd or anonymous requests.[1]

In other cases, where the request is likely to be admissible, the Bank management should be notified of the request, and is allowed 21 days to state whether it has complied or intends to comply with the applicable policies and procedures of the Bank.[2] The Panel may subsequently request further clarifications from management and/or the requester.[3]

If the Panel is not satisfied that management is in compliance (or intends to bring itself into compliance) with Bank policies and procedures,[4] it will decide whether to recommend inspection, after establishing prima facie the following facts:

(a) the failure on the part of management to comply has caused, or threatens to cause, a material adverse effect;
(b) the alleged violations are of a serious character; and
(c) the remedial action proposed by management is inadequate.[5]

If the facts are not clear, the Chairperson may appoint a member of the Panel to conduct a preliminary study of the request (including possibly an on-site inspection).[6]

On the basis of its review of the request and the position of management, the Panel will submit its recommendation to the Board of Executive Directors as to whether to carry out an inspection. The Board will then decide whether to accept or reject the recommendation. The recommendation should normally be submitted within 21 days from the date in which the Panel received management's initial response.[7] The 1999 Board Review stated that the original time limit, set forth in the Resolution for both management's response to the request and the Panel's recommendation, will be strictly observed except for reasons of force majeure, ie reasons that are clearly beyond management's or the Panel's control respectively, as may be approved by the Board on a no objection basis.

1 Operating Procedures, paras 2, 22
2 Ibid, para 27.

3 Ibid, para 29.
4 Ibid, para 34.
5 Ibid, para 35.
6 Ibid, paras 24, 36.
7 Panel Resolution, para 19; Operating Procedures, paras 29(a), 30.

Written pleadings

25.20 After a decision to initiate inspection has been adopted, the Panel may request written submissions on specific issues from the requesting party, Bank staff, and a variety of other persons and entities (other affected people, experts, government or project officials or NGOs).[1] In addition, the requesting party and the Bank may present to the Panel or the Inspector (ie the Panel member responsible for the inspection) any supplementary information or evidence considered to be relevant to the request.[2]

1 Operating Procedures, para 45(d).
2 Ibid, preamble, para 47.

Oral arguments

25.21 After a decision to initiate proceedings has been taken, the Panel may arrange to meet or to receive oral submissions from the requesting party, Bank Staff and other interested persons and entities.[1] In addition, the Panel can decide to conduct public hearings in the project area.[2] The panel may also discuss its preliminary findings of fact with the requester (though not necessarily through oral submissions).[3]

1 Operating Procedures, para 45(a),(d). The additional persons and entities specified in the Operating Procedures are other affected people, government and project officials of the borrowing state, and NGO representatives.
2 Operating Procedures, para 45(b).
3 Ibid, para 49.

Third-party intervention

25.22 There is no provision for third-party intervention in the investigation.

Amicus curiae

25.23 Persons who provide the Panel or Inspector with sufficient evidence indicating that they have an interest in the results of the inspection, other than members of the general public, may submit information and evidence to the investigation.[1] The Panel can also request such persons (eg affected persons, government officials, representatives of NGOs) to attend meetings and submit written or oral submissions on specific issues.[2] Furthermore, any member of the public (without having to establish direct interest) may provide the Panel or Inspector (via the Executive Secretary) with a written document not exceeding ten pages (including a one-page summary and appended supporting documents), containing information relevant to the investigation.[3]

The borrowing state, the Executive Director representing this state (or the guaranteeing state), the legal department of the Bank and certain officials of the Bank will also be consulted by the Panel during the inspection proceedings.[4]

1 Operating Procedures, preamble.
2 Ibid, para 45(a),(d).

3 Ibid, para 50.
4 Panel Resolution, paras 15, 21; Operating Procedures, paras 60–62.

Representation of parties

25.24 As noted above, a duly appointed local representative acting on explicit instruction as the agent of adversely affected people may present the Request to the Inspection Panel.[1] In exceptional circumstances, where there is clear evidence that there is no adequate or appropriate local representation, a foreign representative acting as agent of the adversely affected people may submit a Request.[2]

Proof of authority to represent the affected party must be provided.[3]

1 Operating Procedures, para 4(b).
2 Ibid, paras 4(c), 11.
3 Ibid, para 10.

Decision

25.25 The final conclusion of the Panel's inspection is prepared in the form of a report, which is to contain the following information:

(a) summary discussion of relevant facts and steps taken to conduct the investigation;
(b) conclusions on the degree of compliance on the part of the Bank with its policies and procedures; and
(c) a list of supporting documents, available on request from the office of the Inspection Panel.[1]

If a Panel report was adopted by a majority vote, the minority view shall also be stated.[2]

The decision is then submitted to the Executive Directors, together with a written response to the report by the Bank's management (prepared within six weeks from the date of the receipt of the Panel's report).[3] The Executive Directors then decide what action to take, if any, to give effect to the Panel's recommendations.

1 Operating Procedures, para 52.
2 Panel Resolution, para 24
3 Ibid, paras 22, 23; Operating Procedures, paras 53, 54.

Revision of report

25.26 A request may be re-submitted to the Panel if new evidence or circumstances not known at the time of the initial request so justify.[1]

1 Panel Resolution, para 14(d); Operating Procedures, para 25.

Appeal

25.27 There is no right of appeal over Panel reports.

Costs

25.28 Proceedings before the Inspection Panel are free of charge, but the requesting party will incur its own legal or other costs.

Enforcement of reports

25.29   The decision whether to adopt the report of the Inspection Panel is taken by the Executive Directors of the World Bank. The Board of Directors also decides what follow-up action to take in regard to the financing of the project, if any, in order to enforce the Panel's report.[1] The Directors will notify the requesting party of any decision taken on the matter, within two weeks from the date of the decision.[2]

1   Panel Resolution, para 23.
2   Operating Procedures, para 55.

REFERENCE

Case reports

Copies of panel reports, and other documents related to Panel proceedings are available from the World Bank Public Information Centres – at Washington DC, Paris, London or Tokyo, or in the Bank's Resident Mission or Field Office in the state in which the challenged project was contemplated, or in the relevant regional office of the Bank. Relevant materials are also available on the Inspection Panel's website.

Selected bibliography

Book

Ibrahim F I Shihata *The World Bank Inspection Panel*, Oxford University Press (1994).

Articles

Richard E Bissel 'Recent Practice of the Inspection Panel of the World Bank' (1997) 91 AJIL 741.

Laurence Boisson 'Policy Guidance and Compliance Issues in Financial Activities: the World Bank Operational Standards' in D Shelton (ed) *Commitment and Compliance? The Role of Non-Binding Norms in the International Legal System* Oxford University Press (1999).

Daniel D Bradlow 'International Organisations and Private Complaints: The Case of the World Bank Inspection Panel' (1994) 34 Va J Int'l L 553.

Louis Forget 'Le "Panel d'Inspection" de la Banque Mondiale' (1996) XLII Annuaire Français de Droit International, 656.

Ellen Hey 'The World Bank Inspection Panel: Towards Recognition of a New Legally Relevant Relationship in International Law' (1997) 2 Hofstra Law and Policy Symposium 61.

CHAPTER 26
Independent investigation mechanism of the Inter-American Development Bank

GENERAL INFORMATION

26.1 The Inter-American Development Bank ('IDB' or 'the Bank')[1] established an independent investigation mechanism in 1994.[2] The procedure and jurisdiction of the IDB mechanism are closely modelled after that of the World Bank Inspection Panel. In both cases, complaints can be presented against the management of the Bank for alleged failure to follow Bank operational policies or procedures formally adopted for the execution of the policies.[3] Furthermore, investigation of complaints is assigned to an independent panel of experts that prepares its findings of fact and law and its recommendations in the form of a report. Finally, the IDB Board of Executive Directors (like its World Bank counterpart) may determine what action, if any, to take in order to give effect to the Panel's report.[4]

The main difference between the World Bank and IDB investigation procedures is to be found in the method of composition of the investigation panel. In contrast with the World Bank Inspection Panel, which is a permanent body, the IDB mechanism only provides for the establishment of a permanent roster of 10 investigators of different nationalities (coming from the Bank's member states), from which investigators may be drawn in specific cases.[5] Members of the roster are required to be individuals of integrity, with recognised competence in areas related to socio-economic development, who are familiar with Latin America and the Caribbean. They are nominated by the President of the Bank, in consultation with the Executive Directors, and confirmed by the Board of Executive Directors for a non-renewable five-year term.[6] In each case where the Executive Directors decide to initiate an investigation on a complaint filed with the Bank, the Board, consulting with the President of the Bank, will select members of the roster to comprise an ad hoc investigation panel.[7] The panel will include three or more investigators with particular aptitude to deal with the dispute on hand.[8] Once established, the panel receives administrative service from the Secretariat Department of the IDB.[9]

Since the establishment of the mechanism, the IDB Investigation Mechanism has received one formal request for investigation.[10] At present, the IDB is considering the introduction of modifications in the Mechanism.

1 The IDB was established in 1959, and includes 46 member states (of which 27 are American states).
2 IDB Board of Executive Directors Decision on Independent Investigation Mechanism, 10 August 1994, Minutes DEA/94/34, sec 142 ('Investigation Decision').
3 Investigation Decision, para 1.1.
4 Ibid, para 7.1.
5 Ibid, paras 2.1, 2.2.

6 Ibid, paras 2.3, 2.5.
7 Ibid, para 5.1.
8 Ibid, para 5.2.
9 Ibid, para 5.4.
10 The Yacyretó Hydroelectric Project, Report of the Review Panel, 25 September 1997, IDB Doc GN-1947-8.

JURISDICTION AND ADMISSIBILITY

26.2 The President of the Bank can receive requests for investigation from affected parties located in the territory of a borrowing state.[1] A requesting party must show that its rights or interests have been, or are likely to be, directly or materially affected due to an act or omission of the IDB resulting from a failure to follow operational policies or procedures in relation to an IDB financed project.[2] A request cannot be made by a single individual (or on his or her behalf), but rather must be submitted by a community of persons (such as an organisation, association, society or other grouping of individuals).[3] The request is to be presented by the affected party, or by its local representative. In exceptional cases, where allegedly there is no appropriate local representation, the complaint may be presented by another representative, subject to approval by the Executive Directors.[4] Any Executive Director can also make a request for investigation in special cases where serious violation of the IDB's policies and norms has allegedly taken place.[5]

Complaints against acts and omissions not attributable to the IDB (but to other legal actors such as the borrower state), or not involving IDB financed operations, are inadmissible.[6] This is also the case with complaints against decisions on procurement of goods and services; complaints involving projects where more than 95 per cent of the loan proceeds have already been disbursed; and complaints reviewed by a panel in the past (unless substantial new evidence or circumstances are introduced).[7] Like its World Bank counterpart, an IDB panel is not authorised to review the adequacy of the IDB's policies or procedures, but should only verify that the IDB complies with them. A request may not be presented before the requesting party has brought the subject matter of the complaint to the attention of the Bank's management, and the management's response has failed to dispose of the issue.[8]

1 Investigation Decision, para 3.1.
2 Ibid, para 3.2.
3 Ibid, para 3.3.
4 Ibid, para 3.3.
5 Ibid, para 4.7.
6 Ibid, para 1.5(a).
7 Ibid, para 1.5(b)–(d).
8 Ibid, para 4.1.

CONTACT INFORMATION

26.3 The Public Information Centre of the IDB is located at:

1300 New York Avenue, NW
Washington, DC 20577
USA

Tel: 202-623-1000
Fax: 202-623-1400
website: http://www.iadb.org/

REFERENCE

Further information can be obtained on the Bank's website.

CHAPTER 27

Inspection policy of the Asian Development Bank

GENERAL INFORMATION

27.1   In December 1995 the Asian Development Bank ('ADB' or 'the Bank')[1] established a mechanism for inspection of complaints brought against Bank-financed projects. The procedure and jurisdiction of the ADB mechanism (which were adopted in October 1996)[2] are modelled on the Inter-American Development Bank ('IDB') and World Bank investigation procedures. A complaint can be made against the management of the Bank for its alleged failure to follow the Bank's operational policies or procedures in relation to a Bank-financed project; and an independent inspection panel may review each complaint and prepare a report. As with the parallel IDB and World Bank procedures, the ADB Board of Directors will decide whether or not to take action in pursuance of the panel's report.

Unlike the World Bank inspection procedure, the ADB Inspection Policy is executed by two bodies – a permanent Inspection Committee (composed of six members of the Bank's Board appointed for a two-year term),[3] and an ad hoc panel of independent experts. The Committee receives complaints[4] after they have previously been submitted to the Bank's management and the latter has failed to produce a prompt satisfactory response,[5] and recommends to the full Board whether investigation is necessary.[6] At the end of the proceedings, the Committee recommends to the Board what action, if any, to take in light of the panel's report.[7]

In the event that the Board decides to initiate investigation, an ad hoc panel is established from a permanent roster of experts, which is nominated by the President of the Bank and approved by the Board.[8] The experts must be nationals of ADB member states, selected for their judgment, expertise and experience in areas relating to the Bank's developmental activities. The roster as a whole should reflect diversity of backgrounds and disciplines. The experts are appointed to serve on the roster for a non-renewable five-year term.[9] Members of each ad hoc panel are selected by the Committee, which will also prepare terms of reference for the inspection.[10] Panels normally comprise three roster members with aptitude to deal with the case on hand, and who do not have the nationality of any of the states involved in the inspection proceedings.[11] Once established, the panel receives secretarial assistance from the Bank's Office of the Secretary.[12]

Since the establishment of the mechanism, the ADB has received one request for investigation, which was, however, declared inadmissible.

1   The ADB was established in 1966, and includes 57 member states or non-state political entities (of which 40 are Asian states or political entities).

2 Inspection Procedures, Decision of Inspection Committee of the Board of Directors, 9 October 1996, ADB's Inspection Policy: A Guidebook 11 (1996) ('Inspection Procedures').
3 Inspection Procedures, paras 7, 8. Of the six Committee members, four persons should be from regional states and the two other persons from non-regional countries. Of the four regional committee members, at least three must come from borrowing states.
4 Inspection Procedures, para 29.
5 Ibid, paras 15(c), 19, 20, 26.
6 Ibid, paras 41, 42.
7 Ibid, paras 61, 62.
8 Ibid, para 9.
9 The first roster includes 17 experts.
10 Inspection Procedures, paras 45, 47.
11 Ibid, para 46.
12 Ibid, para 67.

JURISDICTION AND ADMISSIBILITY

27.2 The Inspection Committee can receive requests for investigation from affected parties located in the territory of a borrowing state, or in the territory of an adjacent country likely to be affected by the project.[1] The requesting party must show that its rights or interests have been, or are likely to be, directly or materially affected by the project and that this was caused by an act or omission of the Bank resulting from a failure to follow operational policies or procedures.[2] A Request cannot be made by a single individual (or on his or her behalf), but rather by a community of persons (such as an organisation or other grouping of individuals). The request is to be presented by the affected party, or by its local representative.[3] In exceptional cases, where there is no appropriate local representation, non-local representatives (with approval of the Board) may present the complaint. In cases where particularly serious violations of the ADB's policies and procedures have taken place, any member (or members) of the Board of Directors may request an investigation (following a similar procedure to that used in ordinary complaints).[4]

Acts and omissions not attributable to the ADB (but to other legal actors such as the borrower state) cannot be reviewed by a panel. A panel cannot investigate complaints relating to issues of procurement of goods and services (including consulting services); complaints involving completed or substantially completed projects; complaints alleging the inadequacy or unsuitability of the policies and procedures of the ADB, complaints inspected by a panel in the past (unless new evidence is shown); and complaints against ADB personnel or other non-operational matters.

As indicated above, a request must first be presented before the ADB's management (by way of prior submission of the complaint to the President of the ADB). Only if the management has failed to produce a satisfactory response within 45 days from receipt of the initial complaint (unless the Inspection Committee has authorised an extension), can the complaint be brought before the Committee.

1   Inspection Procedures, para 12.
2   Ibid, paras 12, 15.
3   Ibid, para 13.
4   Ibid, para 14.

CONTACT INFORMATION

27.3   The Secretariat of the ADB is located at:

> Office of the Secretary
> Asian Development Bank
> PO Box 789
> 0980 Manila
> Philippines

> Tel: 632 632-4444
> Fax: 632 636-2481 or (632) 636-2444
> email: adbsec@mail.asiandevbank.org
> website: http://www.asiandevbank.org/policy/

REFERENCE

Further information can be obtained on the Bank's website.

Non-compliance procedure

INTRODUCTION

This Part considers what is to date the only example of a treaty-specific non-compliance procedure adopted under a multilateral environmental agreement. Compliance with the provisions on environmental agreements has been the subject of much concern among states and other international actors involved in this growing area of international law. Although multilateral environmental agreements generally contain provisions relating to the settlement of disputes on the interpretation and application of the agreements, these tend to be optional and have not been used in practice. Without prejudice to existing dispute settlement provisions in the treaty, the 1987 Montreal Protocol's Non-Compliance Procedure represents a new approach, which is being taken up in other global agreements, as well as certain regional arrangements (see below).

The Montreal Protocol on Substances that Deplete the Ozone Layer was adopted in 1987 and its governing body, the Meeting of the Parties, adopted the non-compliance procedure in 1990. Although aimed at addressing non-compliance by parties with their obligations under the Protocol, the procedure is intended to be non-confrontational and to facilitate and encourage compliance rather than primarily to 'punish' non-compliance. A standing Implementation Committee has been established to examine possible cases of non-compliance. Review by the Implementation Committee may be promoted by another party to the Montreal Protocol, by the Protocol Secretariat, or by the defaulting party itself.

While the Montreal Protocol non-compliance procedure remains the only such procedure in operation, as mentioned above the development of similar mechanisms for other environmental agreements is envisaged. Thus, for example, the UN Framework Convention on Climate Change provides that the Conference of the Parties is to consider the establishment of a multilateral consultative process for the resolution of questions regarding implementation of the Convention.[1] Work to develop such a process has taken place under the Climate Change Convention, and the issue has now been taken up in relation to the 1997 Kyoto Protocol to the Convention on Climate Change which explicitly requires the governing body of the Protocol, at its first session after entry into force, to approve mechanisms and procedures to determine and address cases of non-compliance with the provisions of the Kyoto Protocol.[2]

1 United Nations Framework Convention on Climate Change, art 13, 31 ILM (1992) 822.
2 Kyoto Protocol to the U N Framework Convention on Climate Change, art 18, 37 ILM (1998) 22.

Non-compliance procedure

In addition the development of similar mechanisms is envisaged in Protocols adopted under the 1979 Convention on Long-Range Transboundary Air Pollution[3] and the 1994 UN Convention to Combat Desertification.[4]

3 1991 Protocol to the 1979 Convention on Long-range Transboundary Air Pollution on Control of Emissions of Volatile Organic Compounds and their Transboundary Fluxes, 31 ILM (1992) 568; 1994 Protocol to the 1979 Convention on Long-range Transboundary Air Pollution on Further Reduction of Sulphur Emissions, 33 ILM (1994) 1540.
4 UN Convention to Combat Desertification in those Countries experiencing Serious Drought and/or Desertification, particularly in Africa, art 27, 33 ILM (1994) 1328.

CHAPTER 28

Non-compliance procedure under the Montreal Protocol on Substances that Deplete the Ozone Layer

GENERAL INFORMATION

28.1 The 1985 Vienna Convention for the Protection of the Ozone Layer ('Vienna Convention')[1] and the 1987 Protocol thereto – the Montreal Protocol on Substances that Deplete the Ozone Layer ('Montreal Protocol')[2] require states to take various measures in order to protect the ozone layer. The primary obligation found in the Montreal Protocol is the introduction of significant restrictions and prohibitions on the production and consumption of ozone-depleting substances.[3] To date, 170 states have ratified the Vienna Convention and 169 states have ratified the Montreal Protocol.[4]

In accordance with Article 8 of the Montreal Protocol, the Meeting of the Parties decided in 1990 to establish a non-compliance procedure[5] to complement the more traditional mechanism for dispute settlement found in the Vienna Convention (eg ICJ adjudication, arbitration, conciliation).[6] The principal component of the procedure is an Implementation Committee comprising 10 state representatives elected by the Meeting of the Parties for two consecutive two-year terms (on the basis of equitable geographic distribution).[7] The Committee is entrusted with monitoring compliance of the states parties with their obligations under the Protocol and is assisted by a Secretariat. The non-compliance procedure is largely non-confrontational and aimed at securing an amicable settlement and facilitating compliance. To this end, its meetings involve not only representatives of the party or parties concerned, but also relevant sources of financial and technical assistance, including the Multilateral Fund of the Montreal Protocol and the Global Environment Facility.

1 Convention for the Protection of the Ozone Layer, 22 March 1985, 26 ILM 1529 (1987).
2 Protocol on Substances that Deplete the Ozone Layer, 16 September 1987, 26 ILM 154 (1987) ('Montreal Protocol').
3 Montreal Protocol, arts 2–2G. Other restrictions found in the Montreal Protocol are on trade in controlled substances: arts 4–4A.
4 There have been three subsequent amendments of the Montreal Protocol – the London (1990), Copenhagen (1993) and Montreal (1997) amendments, which, by April 1999, have been ratified by 131, 92 and 15 states, respectively. For amendments and adjustments to the 1987 Montreal Protocol, see 30 ILM (1991) 537; 32 ILM (1993) 874; UNEP/Oz L Pro 7/12, December 1995; and NEP/Oz L Pro 9/12, 25 September 1997.
5 Non-Compliance Procedure, Decision II/5, Report of Second Meeting of the Parties to the Montreal Protocol on Substances that Deplete the Ozone Layer, Annex IV, UN Doc UNEP/Oz L Pro 2/3, 29 June 1990, revised by UN Doc UNEP/Oz L Pro 2/3, 25 November 1992, 32 ILM 874 (1993) ('Non-Compliance Procedure'), and revised again by Decision X/10 of the Tenth Meeting of the Parties to the Montreal Protocol, UNEP/Oz L Pro 10/9, 3 December 1998.

6   Vienna Convention, art 11.
7   Non-Compliance Procedure, para 5. Originally, there were five members in the committee. A member of the committee who has completed two consecutive terms may run again after a one year hiatus (Decision X/10).

JURISDICTION AND PROCEDURE

28.2   Any party to the Protocol may submit to the Secretariat its reservations regarding the implementation of the Protocol by another state party.[1] The Secretariat will then invite the party concerned to reply (within three months). The complaint and the reply, and supporting information, are then to be referred to the Implementation Committee.[2] A case can also be referred to the Committee by the Secretariat, acting on its own initiative (after giving an opportunity to the state concerned to respond to the allegation),[3] or by a party itself.[4]

The Implementation Committee considers information brought before it alleging failure on the part of states parties to comply with the Protocol.[5] It may request further information and undertake, with the consent of the state concerned, on-site information gathering.[6] The procedure before the Implementation Committee is governed by the Rules of Procedure for the Meeting of the Parties, which apply mutatis mutandis to the Committee.[7] The states parties to the dispute are entitled to participate in the proceedings before the Committee;[8] and the official languages of the proceedings are Arabic, Chinese, English, French, Russian and Spanish.[9]

The Implementation Committee is to try to find an amicable solution of the matter, on the basis of respect for the provisions of the Protocol.[10] The Committee submits its recommendations, which may include the identification of the facts and causes relating to individual cases of non-compliance and steps that the party concerned should take in order to bring itself into compliance on the matter in the form of a report presented to the Meeting of the Parties.[11] The reports of the Implementation Committee are to be made public (except parts containing confidential information).[12] The Meeting of the Parties may decide after receiving the report of the Committee to take steps to ensure compliance with the Protocol.[13] Such steps can include provision of special assistance to the non-complying state, issuing of cautions and suspension of rights and privileges under the Protocol.[14]

All of the cases the Implementation Committee has dealt with thus far have focused on finding pragmatic solutions to the problems of parties having difficulty in complying with their commitments. All cases have been brought before the Implementation Committee at the initiative of the party concerned, or by the Ozone Secretariat, acting in response to information provided by that party. The closest the non-compliance procedure has come to a 'contentious case' involved the potential non-compliance of the Russian Federation. Here the Meeting of the Parties used a combination of financial assistance, financial conditionality and trade restrictions, to help strengthen Russia's political resolve to carry out its obligations. Funding from the Global Environment Facility (GEF), released in tranches conditional on demonstrable progress, was particularly influential, both in assisting compliance and in creating a process for monitoring and enforcement.

The Implementation Committee's ability to recommend trade-related measures is tied directly to the Montreal Protocol's general ban on trade in regulated substances between parties and non-parties. This allows the non-compliance procedure to treat the ability to trade in regulated substances as a privilege granted by the Protocol, and to incrementally suspend that privilege in order to encourage compliance. Efforts to pre-define categories of non-compliance and to associate these with specific non-compliance responses, have thus far failed under the Montreal Protocol. A list of 'possible situations of non-compliance with the Protocol' was developed by an ad hoc group of legal experts, but was rejected by the Meeting of the Parties. Although efforts to clarify these issues under the non-compliance procedure were raised again recently, the parties seem minded to continue to allow the non-compliance procedure to develop its responses as needed, on a case-by-case basis.[15]

The Implementation Committee's mandate was, however, recently clarified and strengthened to tailor its recommendations to the Montreal Protocol's Meeting of the Parties on the basis of the cause and frequency of a particular party's non-compliance. It is now expressly authorised to make a determination of the 'facts and possible causes of non-compliance',[16] ie whether non-compliance was the result of a 'wilful breach or a result of factors beyond the control of the party concerned'.[17] Furthermore, the Meeting of the Parties recognised that 'in situations in which there has been a persistent pattern of non-compliance by a Party, the Implementation Committee should report and make appropriate recommendations to the Meeting of the Parties, taking into account the circumstances surrounding the Party's persistent pattern of non-compliance', including any progress made by the party and any measures taken to assist the party to comply.[18] A critical issue that has yet to be confronted under the Montreal Protocol, is the question of whether the consequences developed by the non-compliance procedure, and adopted by the Meeting of the Parties are binding on the party concerned, and enforceable as distinct legal obligations. The largely facilitative and non-confrontational aspects of the procedure have thus far prevented the issue from being raised formally.

1 Non-Compliance Procedure, para 1.
2 Ibid, para 2.
3 Ibid, para 3.
4 Ibid, para 4.
5 Ibid, para 7(a),(b).
6 Ibid, para 7(c)–(e).
7 Rules of Procedure for Meeting of the Parties to the Montreal Protocol on Substances that Deplete the Ozone Layer, Report of the Parties to the Montreal Protocol on the Work of their First Meeting, Annex I, r 26(6), UN Doc UNEP/Oz L Pro 1/5, 6 May 1989 ('Rules of Procedure').
8 Non-Compliance Procedure, para 10.
9 Rules of Procedure, r 52.
10 Non-Compliance Procedure, para 8.
11 Ibid, para 9.
12 Ibid, para 16. Reports of the Implementation Committee are available on www.unep.ch/ozone/reports.html.
13 Ibid, para 9.
14 Indicative List of Measures that might be taken by a Meeting of the Parties in respect of Non-Compliance with the Protocol, Decision II/5, Report of Second Meeting of the Parties to the Montreal Protocol on Substances that Deplete the Ozone Layer, Annex V, UN Doc UNEP/Oz L Pro 2/3, 25 November 1992.
15 When an Ad Hoc Working Group of Legal and Technical Experts on the Non-Compliance

was recently tasked with reviewing the operations of the Montreal Protocol non-compliance procedure, revision of existing indicative list of measures was specifically excluded from its mandate. Report on the Work of the Ad Hoc Working Group of Legal and Technical Experts on the Non-Compliance with the Montreal Protocol, UNEP/Oz L Pro/WG 4/1/3, 18 November 1998, para 39.

16 Report of the Tenth Meeting of the Parties to the Montreal Protocol on Substances that Deplete the Ozone Layer UNEP/Oz L Pro/10/9, 3 December 1998 ('Report of MOP-X') Decision X/10.

17 Report on the Work of the Ad Hoc Working Group of Legal and Technical Experts on the Non-Compliance with the Montreal Protocol, UNEP/Oz L Pro/WG4/1/3, 18 November 1998, para 27.

18 Report of MOP-X, Decision X/l0.

CONTACT INFORMATION

28.3 The Secretariat of the Vienna Convention and Montreal Protocol is located at:

> The Secretariat for the Vienna Convention and the Montreal Protocol
> PO Box 30552
> Nairobi
> Kenya
>
> Tel: 254 2 62-1234/62-3851
> Fax: 254 2 52-1930/62-3913
> website: http://www.unep.ch/ozone/

REFERENCE

Sources of case law, including case reports

Reports of the Implementation Committee are available on the Ozone Secretariat website at:

> www.unep.ch/ozone/reports.html

Selected bibliography

M Koskenniemi 'Breach of Treaty or Non-Compliance? Reflections on the Enforcement of the Montreal Protocol' in G Handl (ed) 3 *Yearbook of International Environmental Law* (1992).

P Szell 'The Development of Multilateral Mechanisms for Monitoring Compliance' in W Lang (ed) *Sustainable Development and International Law* (1995).

D Victor 'The Operation and Effectiveness of the Montreal Protocol Implementation Committee' in D Victor, K Raustiala and E B Skolnikoff (eds) *The Implementation and Effectiveness of International Environmental Commitments* (1998).

J Werksman 'Compliance and Transition: Russia's Non-compliance Tests the Ozone Regime' (1996) 56/3 Zeitschrift für ausländisches öffentliches Recht und Völkerrecht 750.3.

ANNEX

List of states parties to the Vienna Convention and Montreal Protocol

Algeria, Antigua & Barbuda, Argentina, Australia, Austria, Azerbaïjan, Bahamas, Bahrain, Bangladesh, Barbados, Belarus, Belgium, Belize, Benin, Bolivia, Bosnia and Herzegovina, Botswana, Brazil, Brunei Darussalam, Bulgaria, Burkina Faso, Burundi, Cameroon, Canada, Central African Republic, Chad, Chile, China, Colombia, Comoros, Congo, Democratic Republic of Congo, Costa Rica, Côte d'Ivoire, Croatia, Cuba, Cyprus, Czech Republic, Denmark, Dominica, Dominican Republic, Ecuador, Egypt, El Salvador, Equatorial Guinea,[1] Estonia, Ethiopia, European Community, Fiji, Finland, France, Gabon, Gambia, Georgia, Germany, Ghana, Greece, Grenada, Guatemala, Guinea, Guyana, Honduras, Hungary, Iceland, India, Indonesia, Iran, Ireland, Israel, Italy, Jamaica, Japan, Jordan, Kazakhstan, Kenya, Kiribati, Korea, Democratic People's Republic of Korea, Kuwait, Laos, Latvia, Lebanon, Lesotho, Liberia, Libya, Liechtenstein, Lithuania, Luxembourg, former Yugoslav Republic of Macedonia, Madagascar, Malawi, Malaysia, Maldives, Mali, Malta, Marshall Islands, Mauritania, Mauritius, Mexico, Micronesia, Moldova, Monaco, Mongolia, Morocco, Mozambique, Myanmar, Namibia, Nepal, Netherlands, New Zealand, Nicaragua, Niger, Nigeria, Norway, Oman, Pakistan, Panama, Papua New Guinea, Paraguay, Peru, Philippines, Poland, Portugal, Qatar, Romania, Russia, Saint Kitts & Nevis, Saint Lucia, Saint Vincent and the Grenadines, Samoa, Saudi Arabia, Senegal, Seychelles, Singapore, Slovakia, Slovenia, Solomon Islands, South Africa, Spain, Sri Lanka, Sudan, Suriname, Swaziland, Sweden, Switzerland, Syria, Tajikistan, Tanzania, Thailand, Togo, Tonga, Trinidad and Tobago, Tunisia, Turkey, Turkmenistan, Tuvalu, Uganda, Ukraine, United Arab Emirates, United Kingdom, United States of America, Uruguay, Uzbekistan, Vanuatu, Venezuela, Vietnam, Yemen, Yugoslavia, Zambia, Zimbabwe.

1 Party only to the Vienna Convention.

Index

References in this index are to paragraph numbers, except where the text is not so divided, when they are to page numbers.

Index

Index